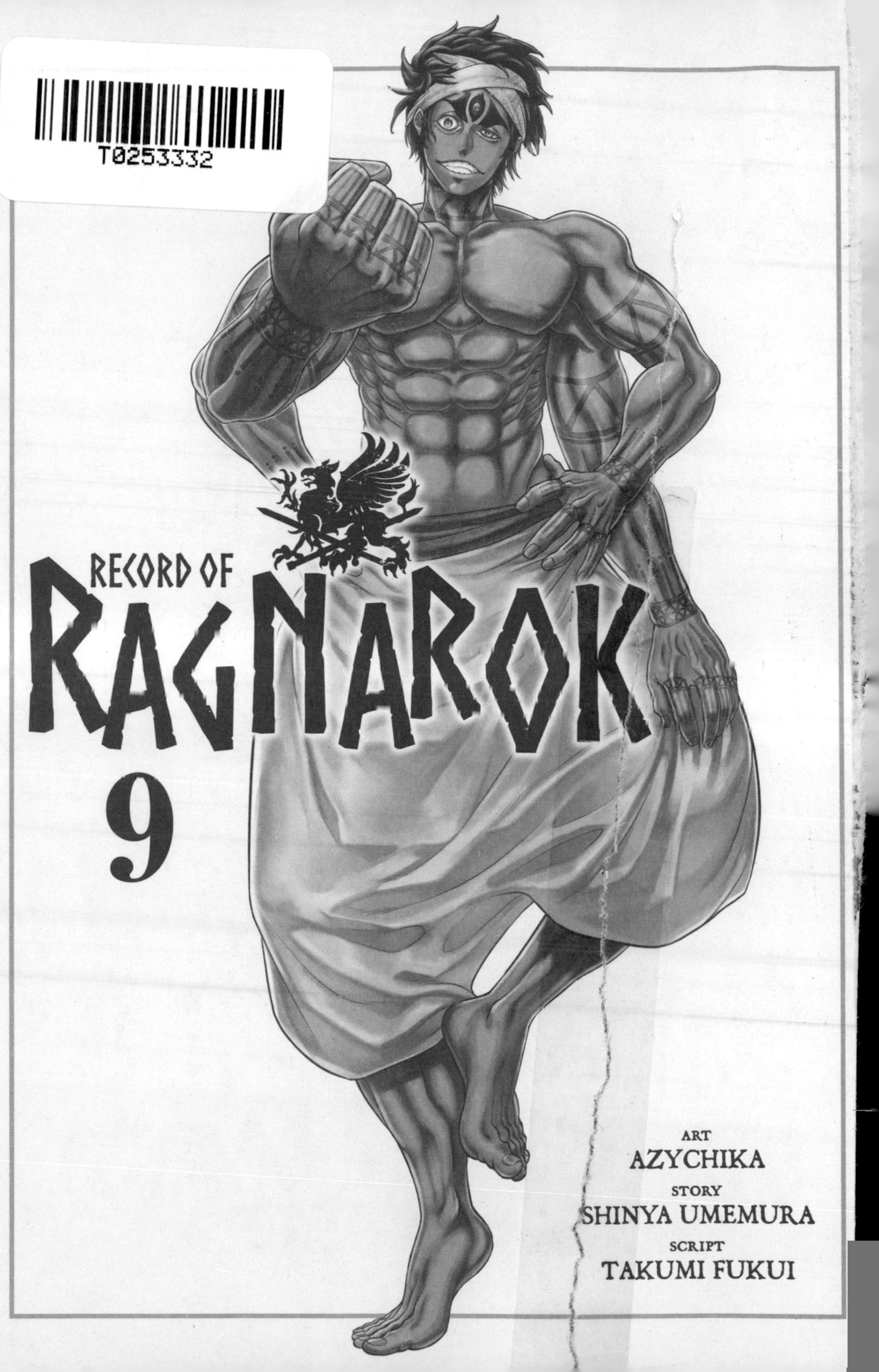

RECORD OF RAGNAROK

9

ART
AZYCHIKA

STORY
SHINYA UMEMURA

SCRIPT
TAKUMI FUKUI

9

RECORD OF RAGNAROK

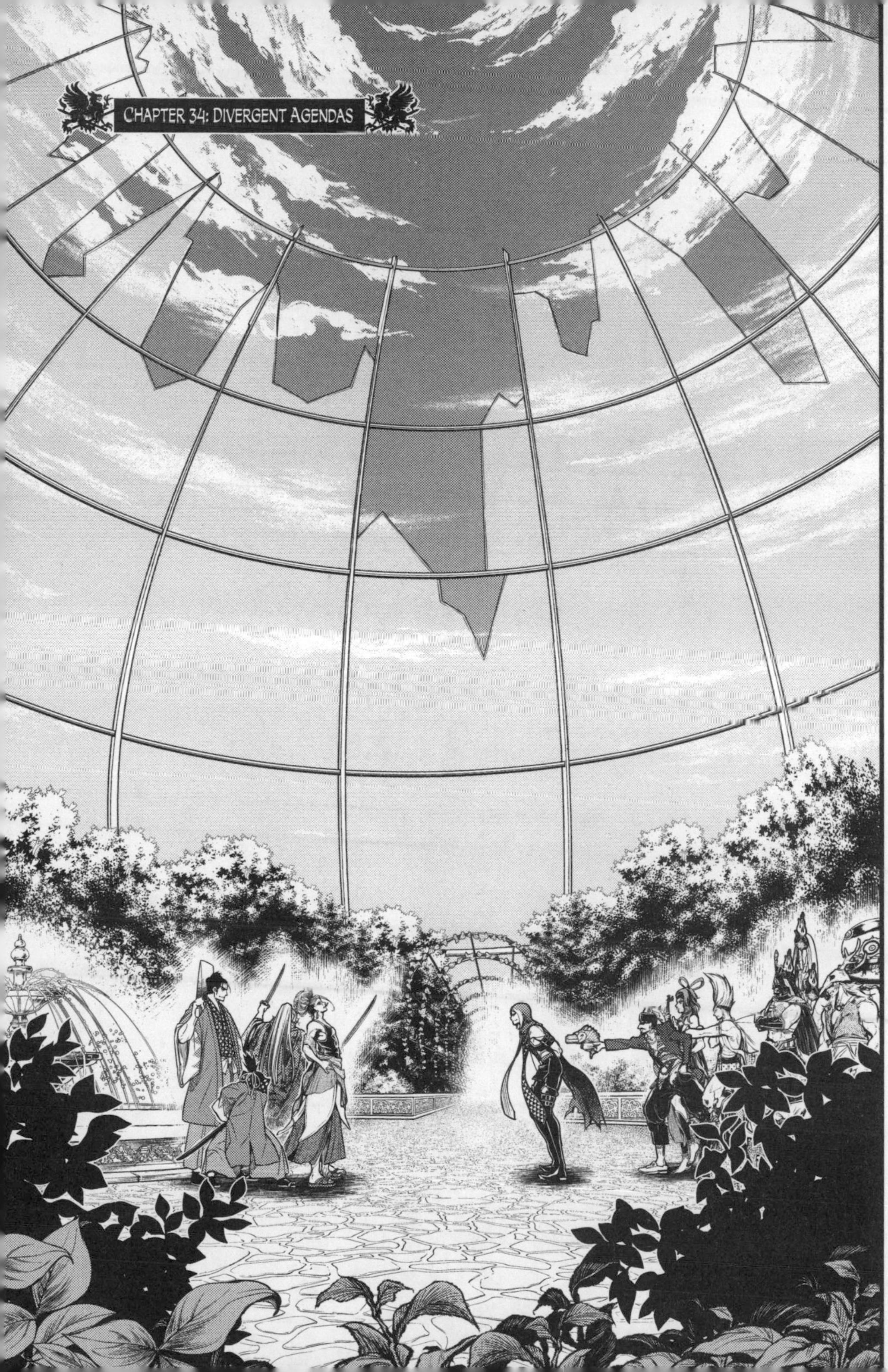
Chapter 34: Divergent Agendas

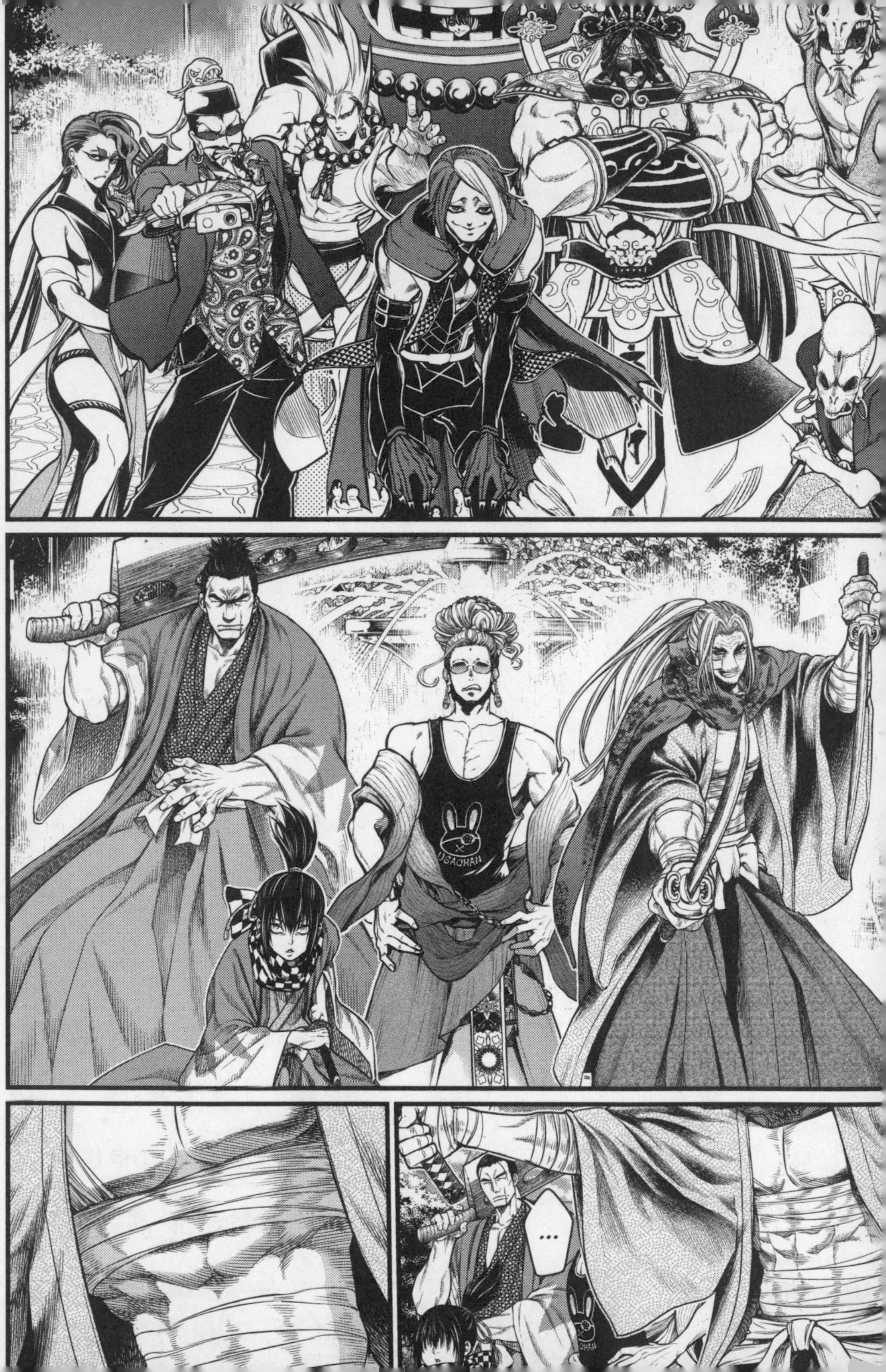
USAOHAN
...

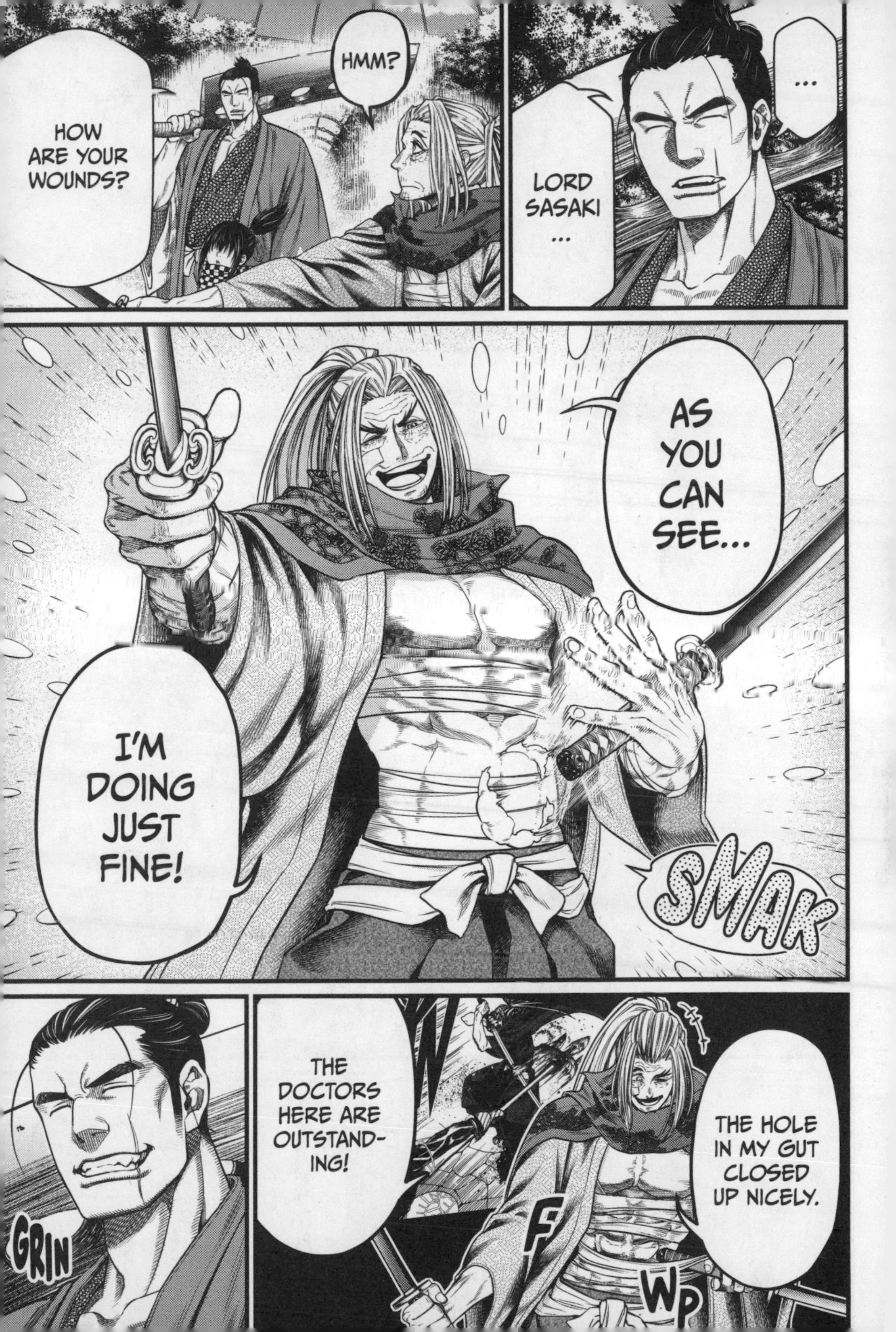
...
LORD SASAKI ...
HOW ARE YOUR WOUNDS?
HMM?
AS YOU CAN SEE...
I'M DOING JUST FINE!
SMAK
THE HOLE IN MY GUT CLOSED UP NICELY.
THE DOCTORS HERE ARE OUTSTAND-ING!
F
WP
GRIN

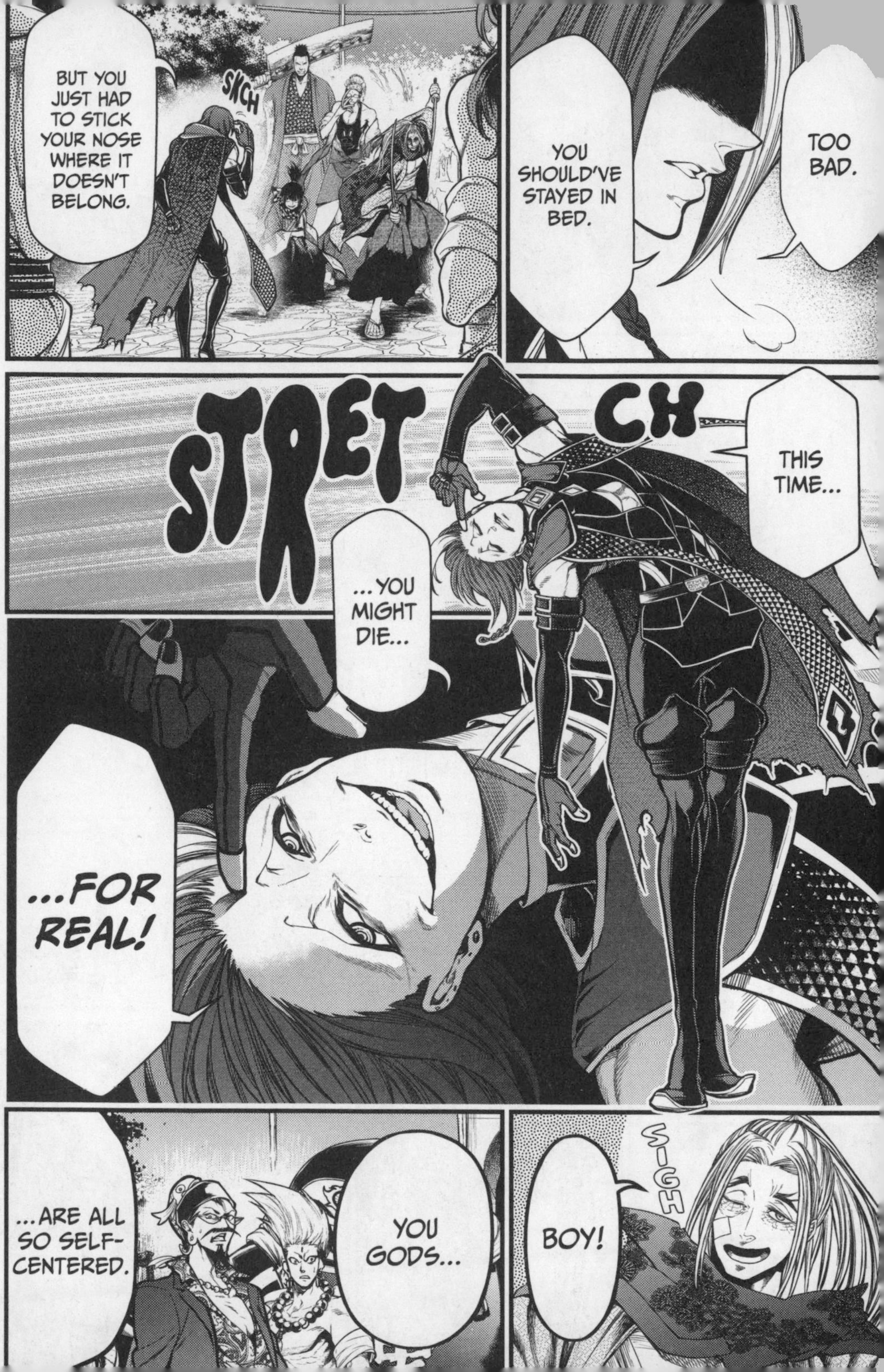
TOO BAD.
YOU SHOULD'VE STAYED IN BED.
SKCH
BUT YOU JUST HAD TO STICK YOUR NOSE WHERE IT DOESN'T BELONG.
THIS TIME...
STRETCH
...YOU MIGHT DIE...
...FOR REAL!
SIGH
BOY!
YOU GODS...
...ARE ALL SO SELF-CENTERED.

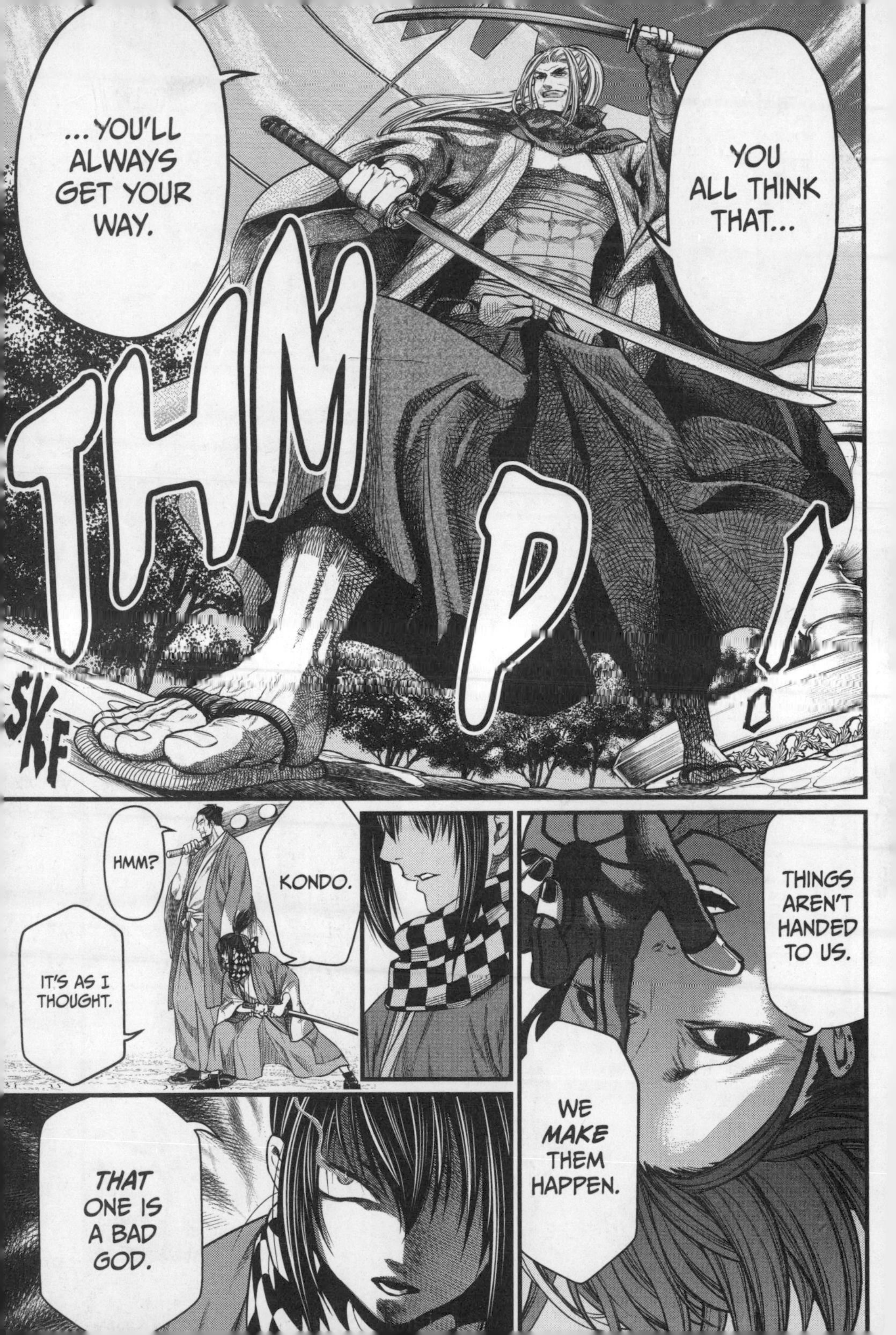
YOU ALL THINK THAT...
...YOU'LL ALWAYS GET YOUR WAY.
THMP!
SKF
THINGS AREN'T HANDED TO US.
WE *MAKE* THEM HAPPEN.
KONDO.
HMM?
IT'S AS I THOUGHT.
THAT ONE IS A BAD GOD.

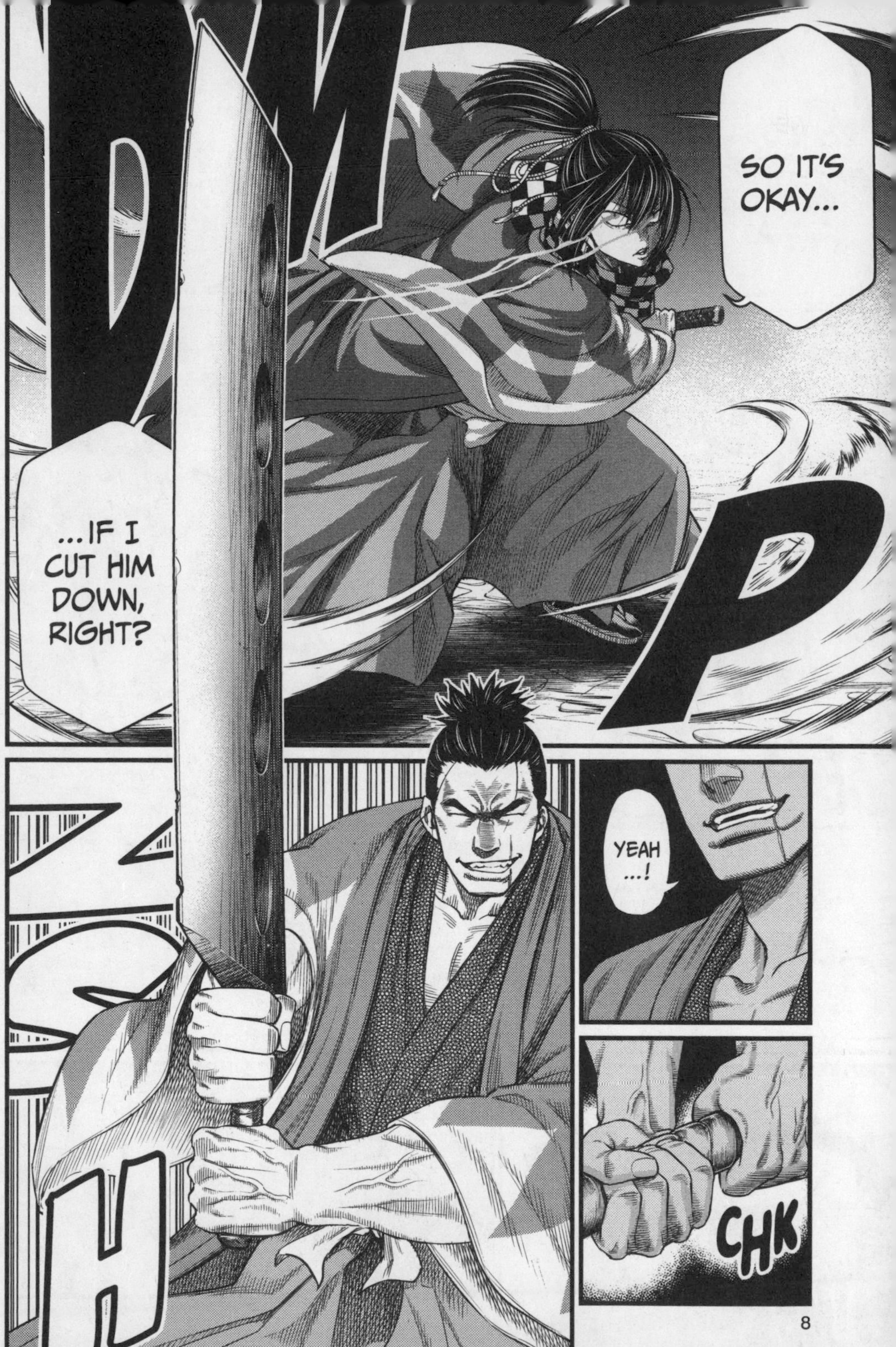
SO IT'S OKAY...
...IF I CUT HIM DOWN, RIGHT?
YEAH ...!
CHK

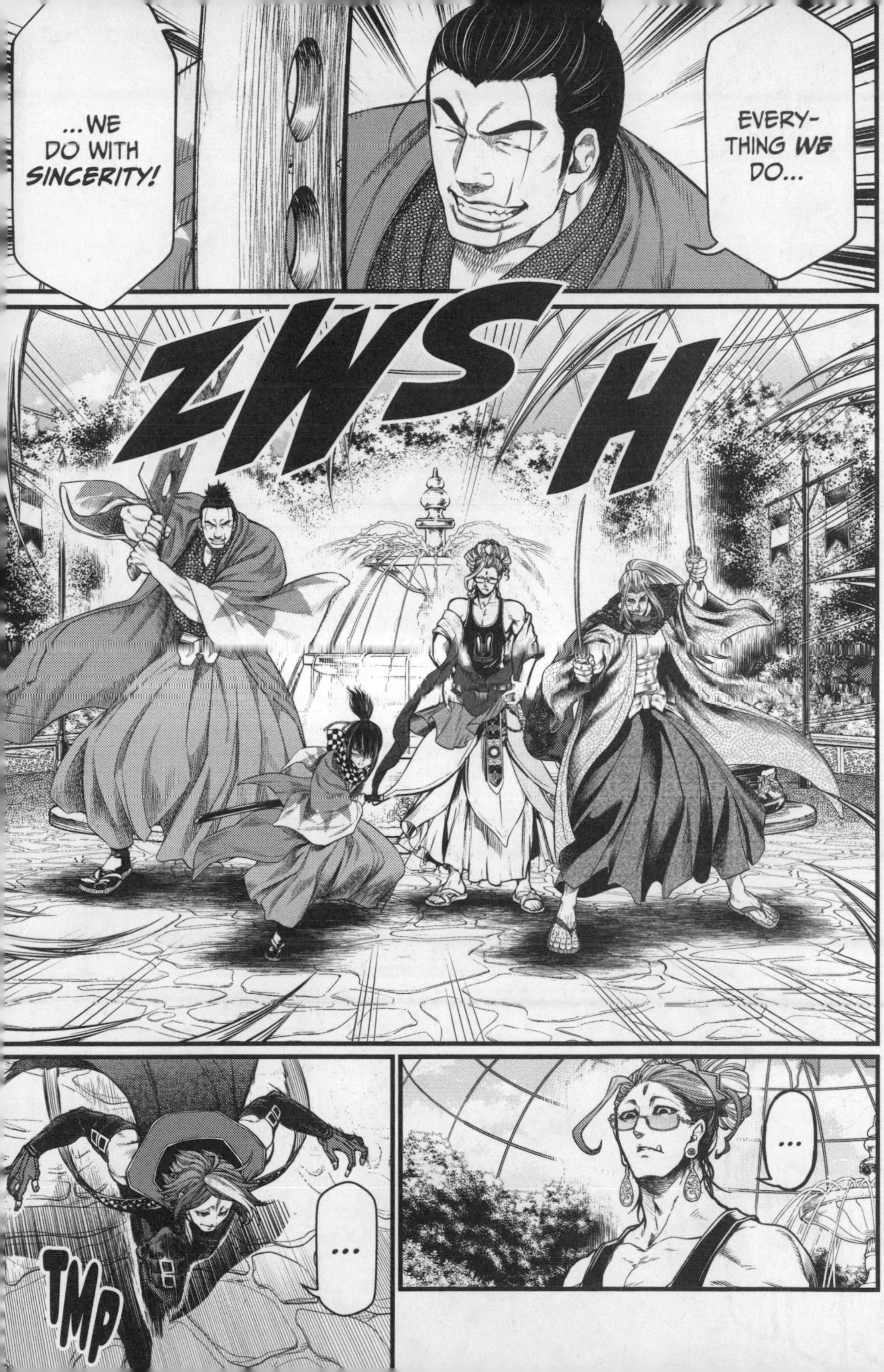
EVERY-THING WE DO...
...WE DO WITH SINCERITY!
ZWSH
...
...
TMP

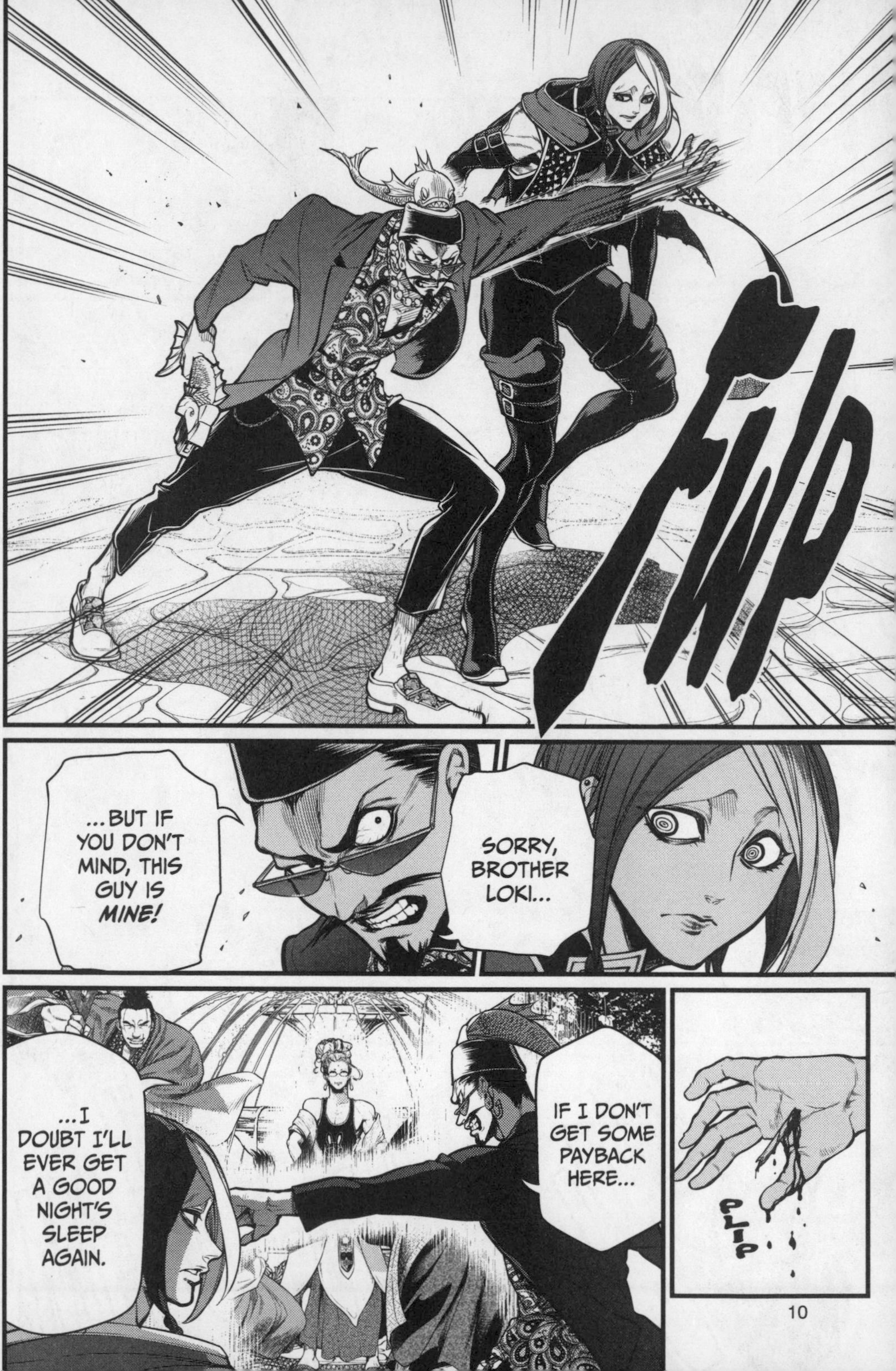
FWIP
SORRY, BROTHER LOKI...
...BUT IF YOU DON'T MIND, THIS GUY IS *MINE!*
PLIP
IF I DON'T GET SOME PAYBACK HERE...
...I DOUBT I'LL EVER GET A GOOD NIGHT'S SLEEP AGAIN.

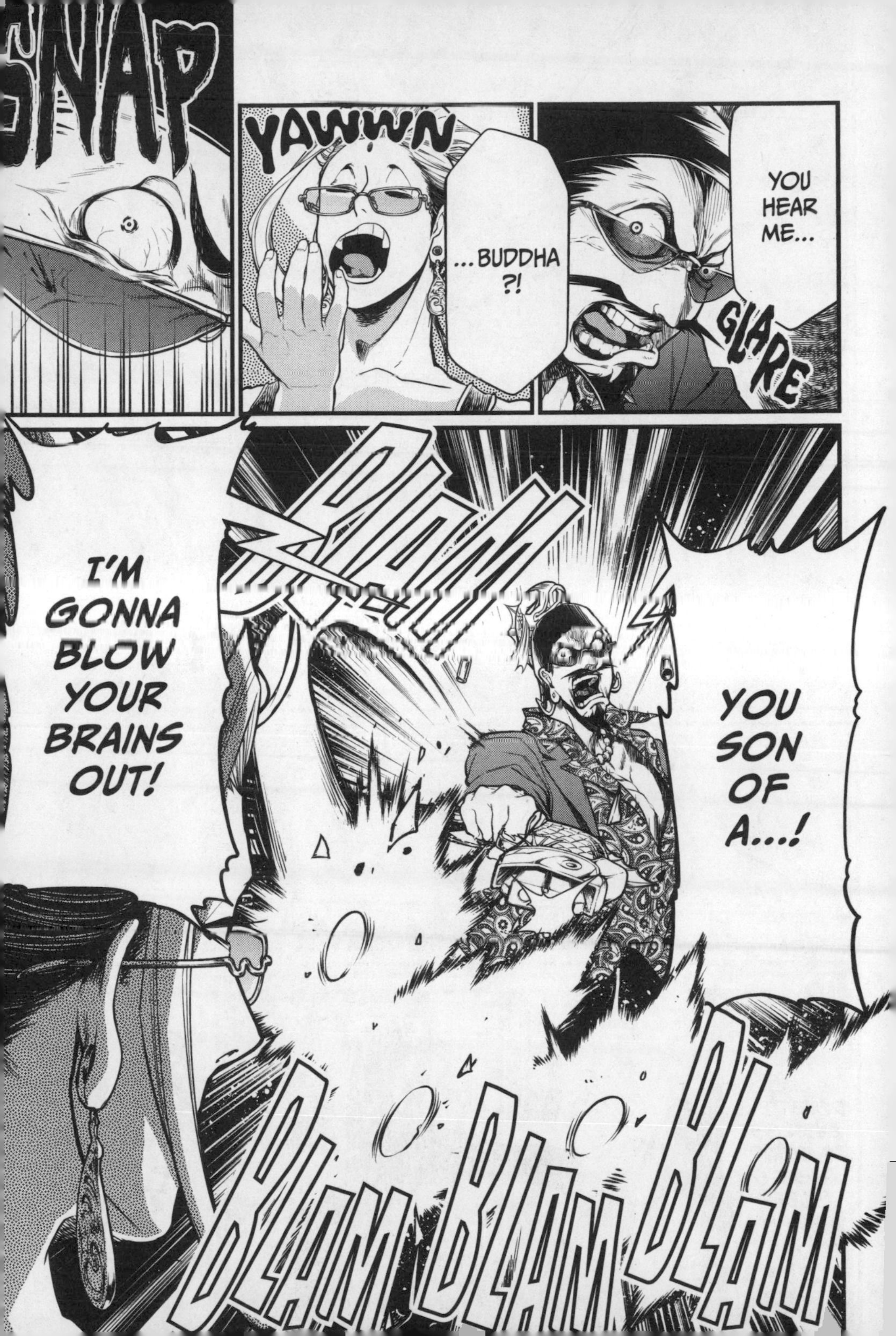
YOU HEAR ME...
GLARE
...BUDDHA ?!
YAWWN
SNAP
YOU SON OF A...!
I'M GONNA BLOW YOUR BRAINS OUT!
BLAM BLAM BLAM

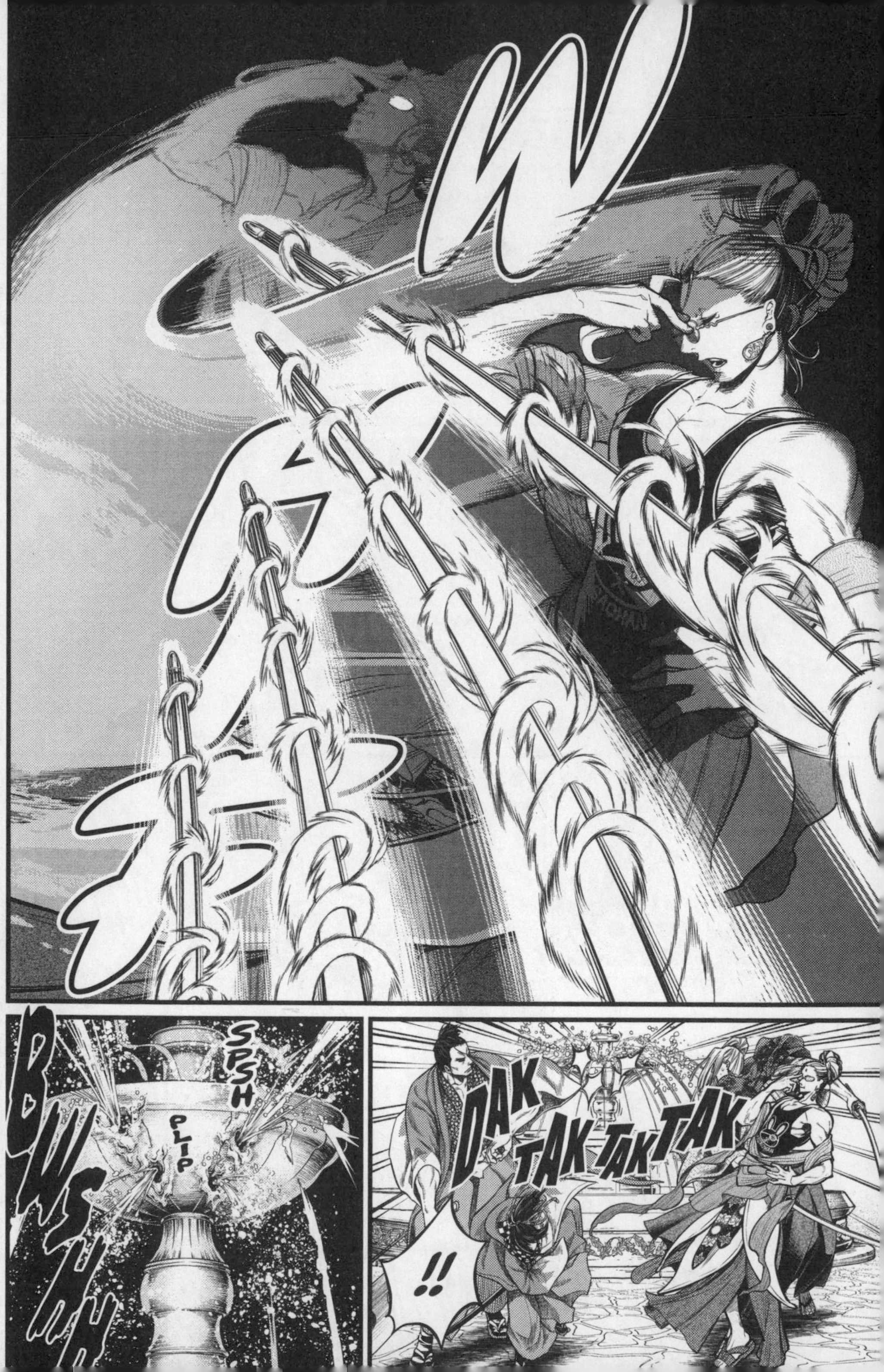
DAK TAK TAK TAK
!!
BWSHHH
SPSH
PLIP

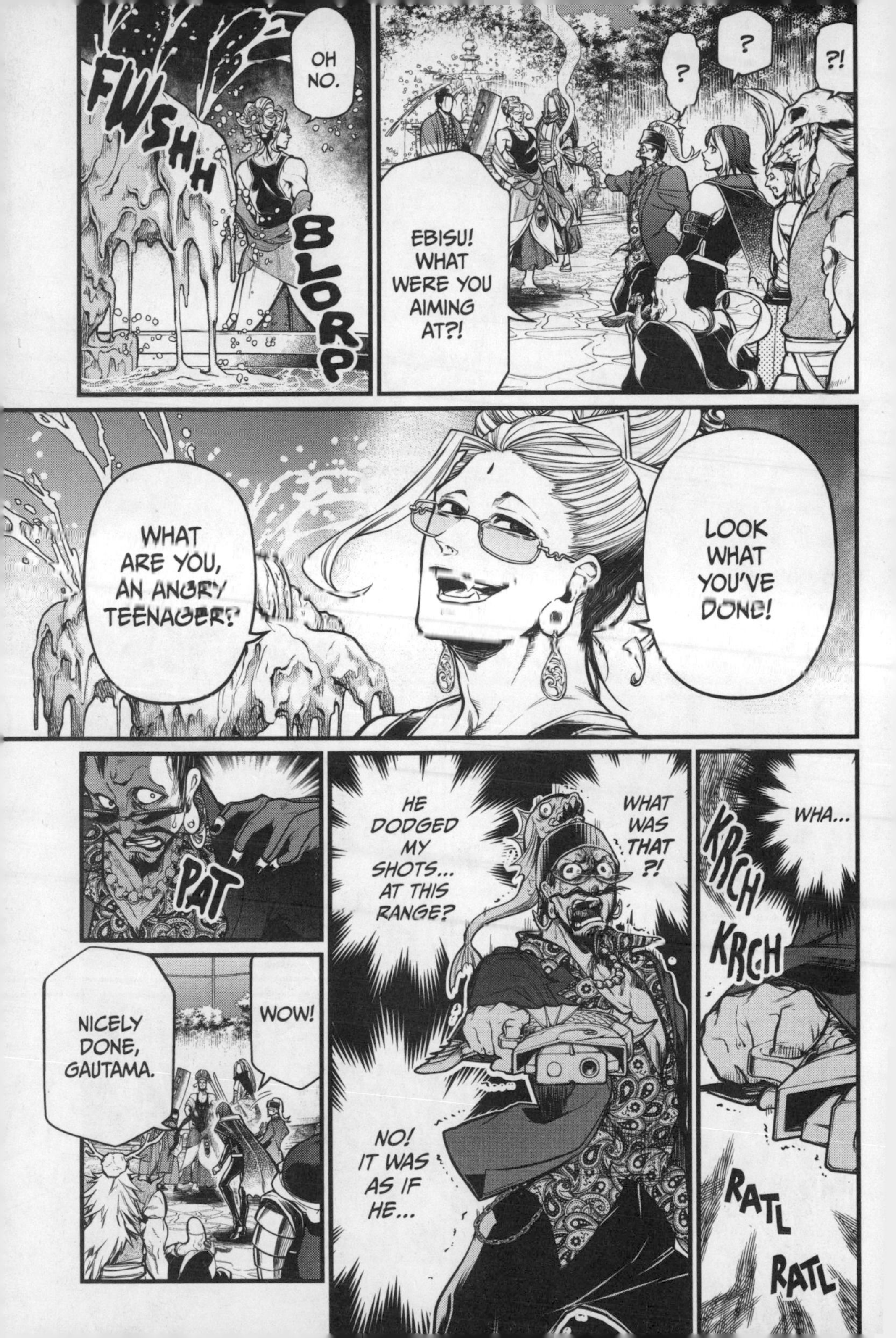
?!
?
?
EBISU! WHAT WERE YOU AIMING AT?!
OH NO.
FWSHH
BLORP
LOOK WHAT YOU'VE DONE!
WHAT ARE YOU, AN ANGRY TEENAGER?!
WHA...
KRCH
KRCH
RATL
RATL
WHAT WAS THAT?!
HE DODGED MY SHOTS... AT THIS RANGE?
NO! IT WAS AS IF HE...
PAT
WOW!
NICELY DONE, GAUTAMA.

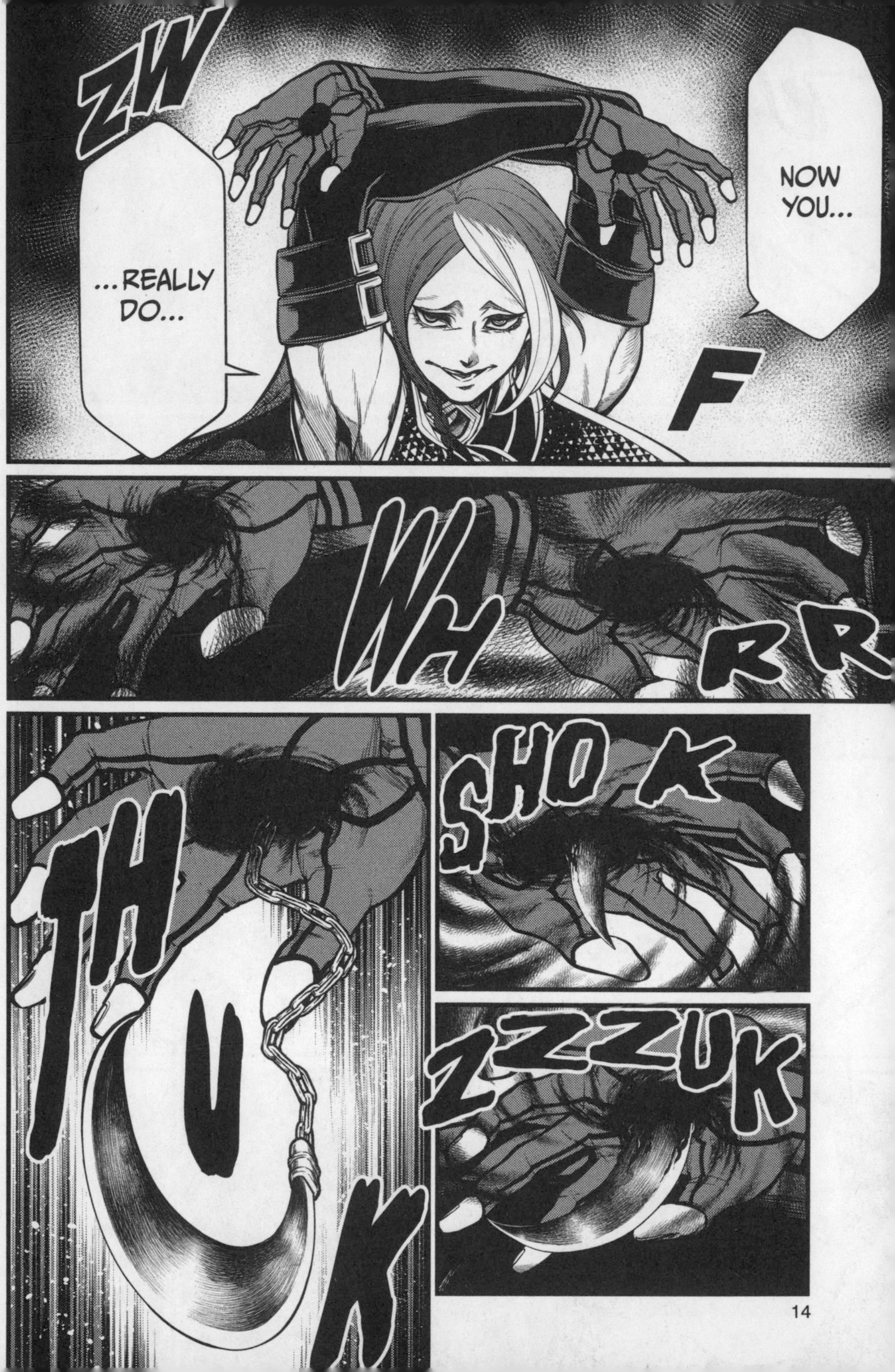
NOW YOU...
...REALLY DO...
ZW
F
WH
RR
SHO K
ZZZZUK
TH U K

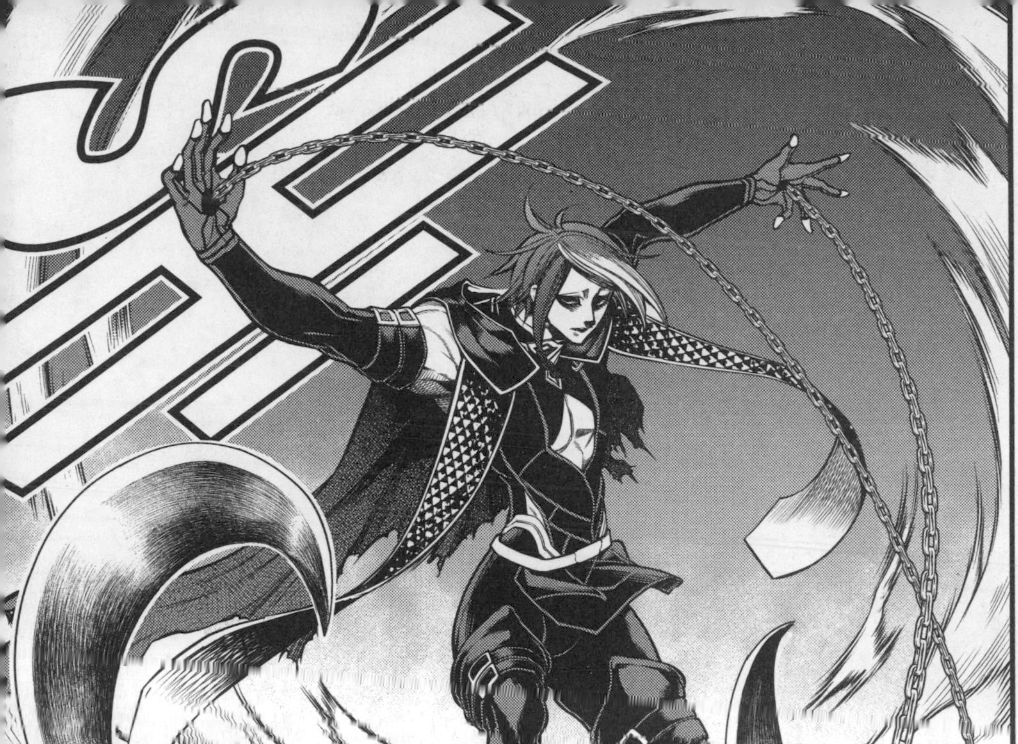

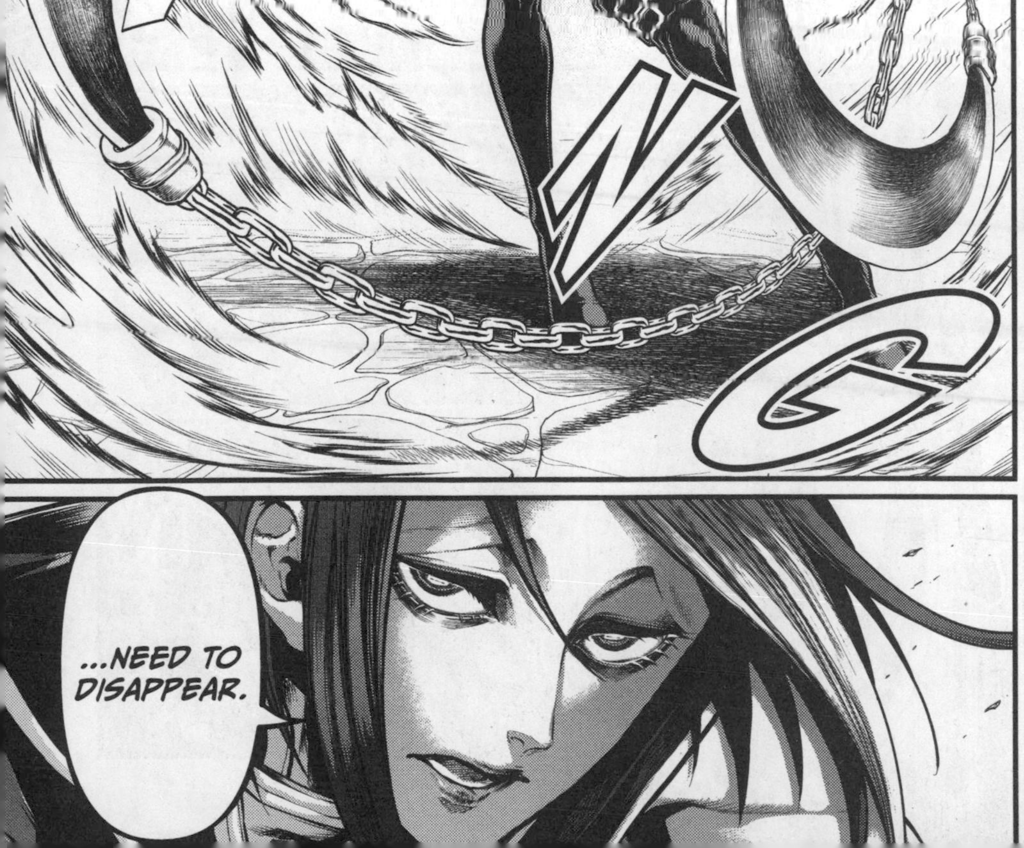
...NEED TO DISAPPEAR.

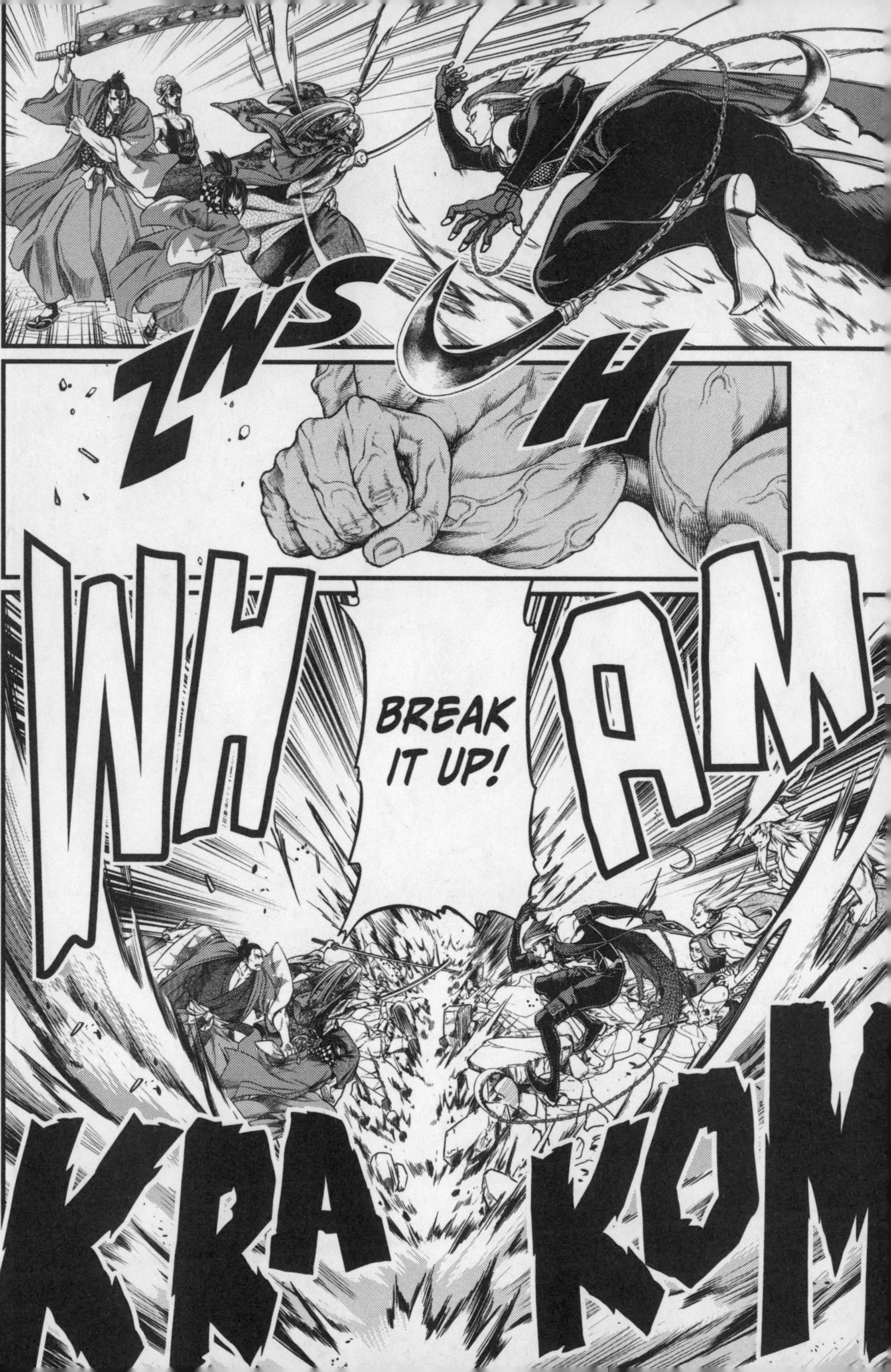
ZWSH
WHAM
BREAK IT UP!
KRA KOM

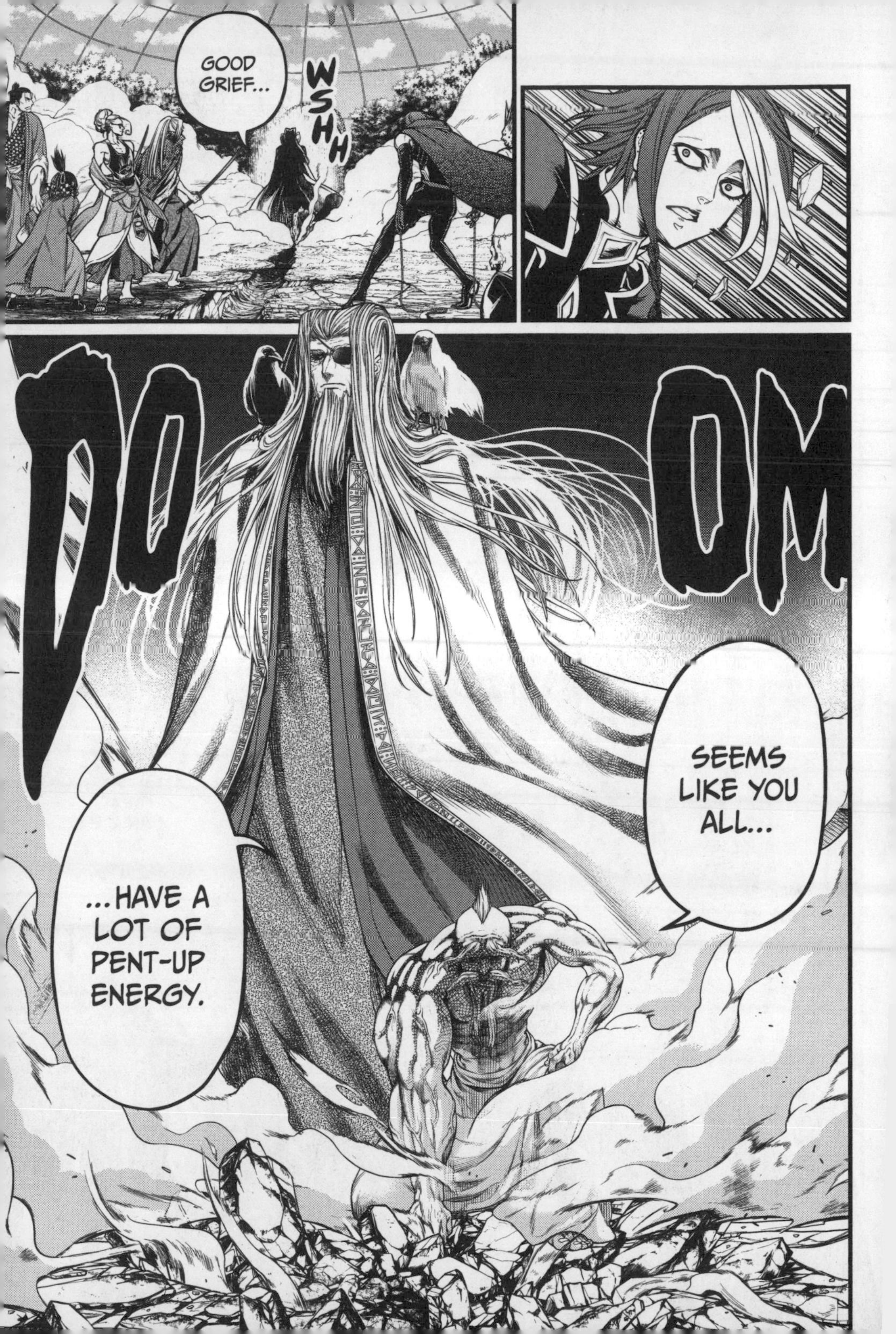
GOOD GRIEF...
WSHH
DOOM
SEEMS LIKE YOU ALL...
...HAVE A LOT OF PENT-UP ENERGY.

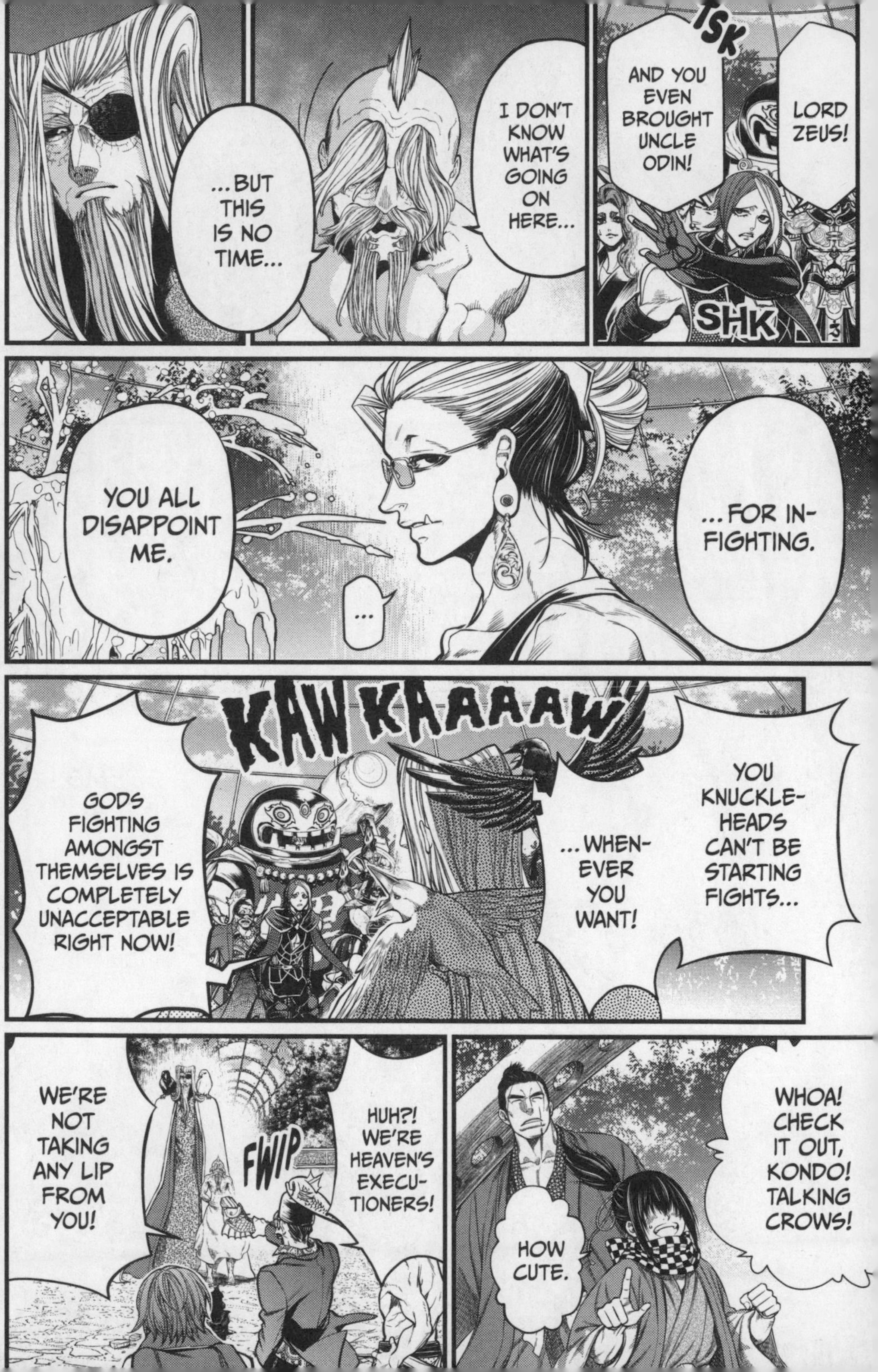
TSK
LORD ZEUS!
AND YOU EVEN BROUGHT UNCLE ODIN!
SHK
I DON'T KNOW WHAT'S GOING ON HERE...
...BUT THIS IS NO TIME...
...FOR IN-FIGHTING.
...
YOU ALL DISAPPOINT ME.
KAW KAAAAW
YOU KNUCKLE-HEADS CAN'T BE STARTING FIGHTS...
...WHEN-EVER YOU WANT!
GODS FIGHTING AMONGST THEMSELVES IS COMPLETELY UNACCEPTABLE RIGHT NOW!
WHOA! CHECK IT OUT, KONDO! TALKING CROWS!
HOW CUTE.
HUH?! WE'RE HEAVEN'S EXECU-TIONERS!
FWIP
WE'RE NOT TAKING ANY LIP FROM YOU!

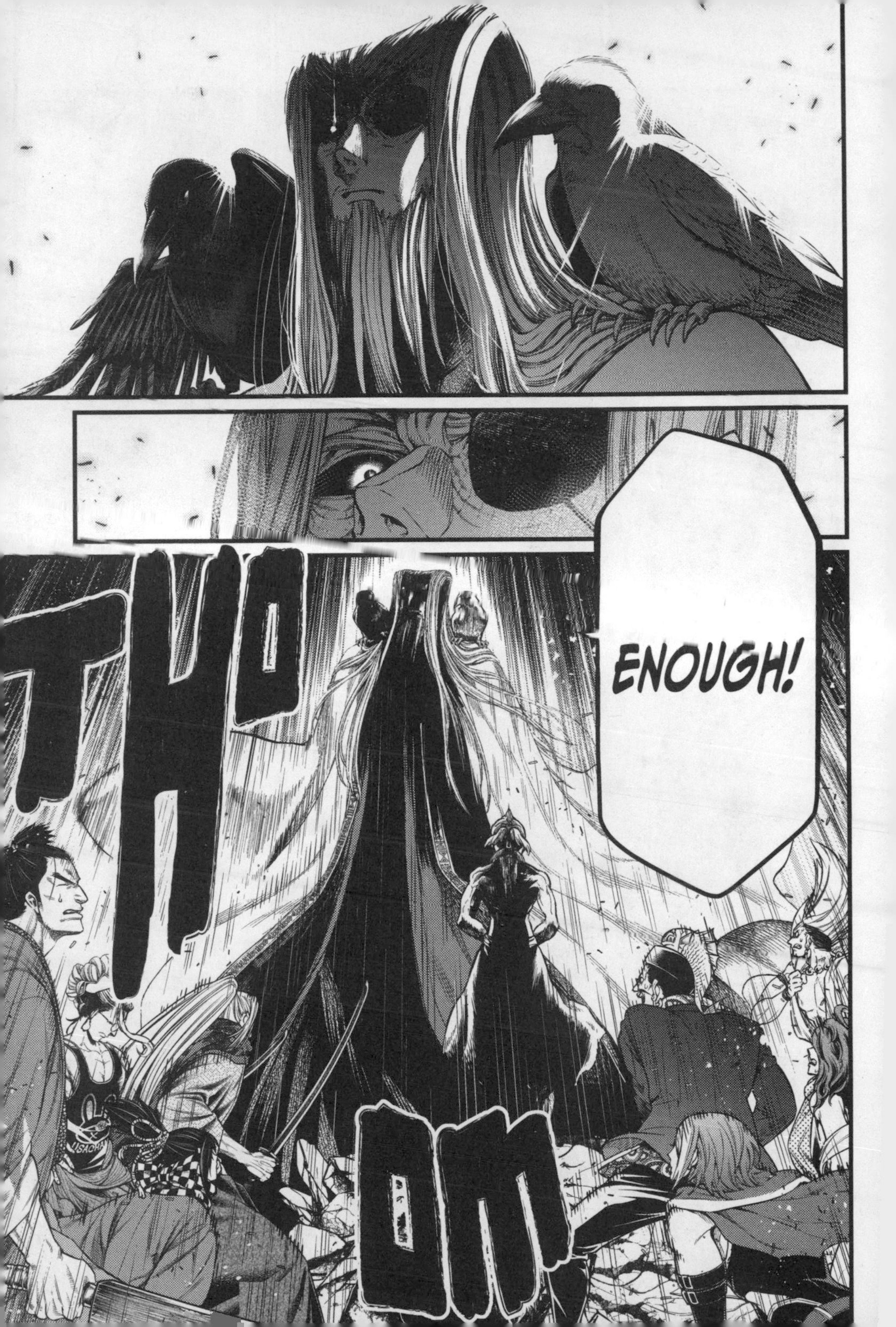
ENOUGH!
THOOM

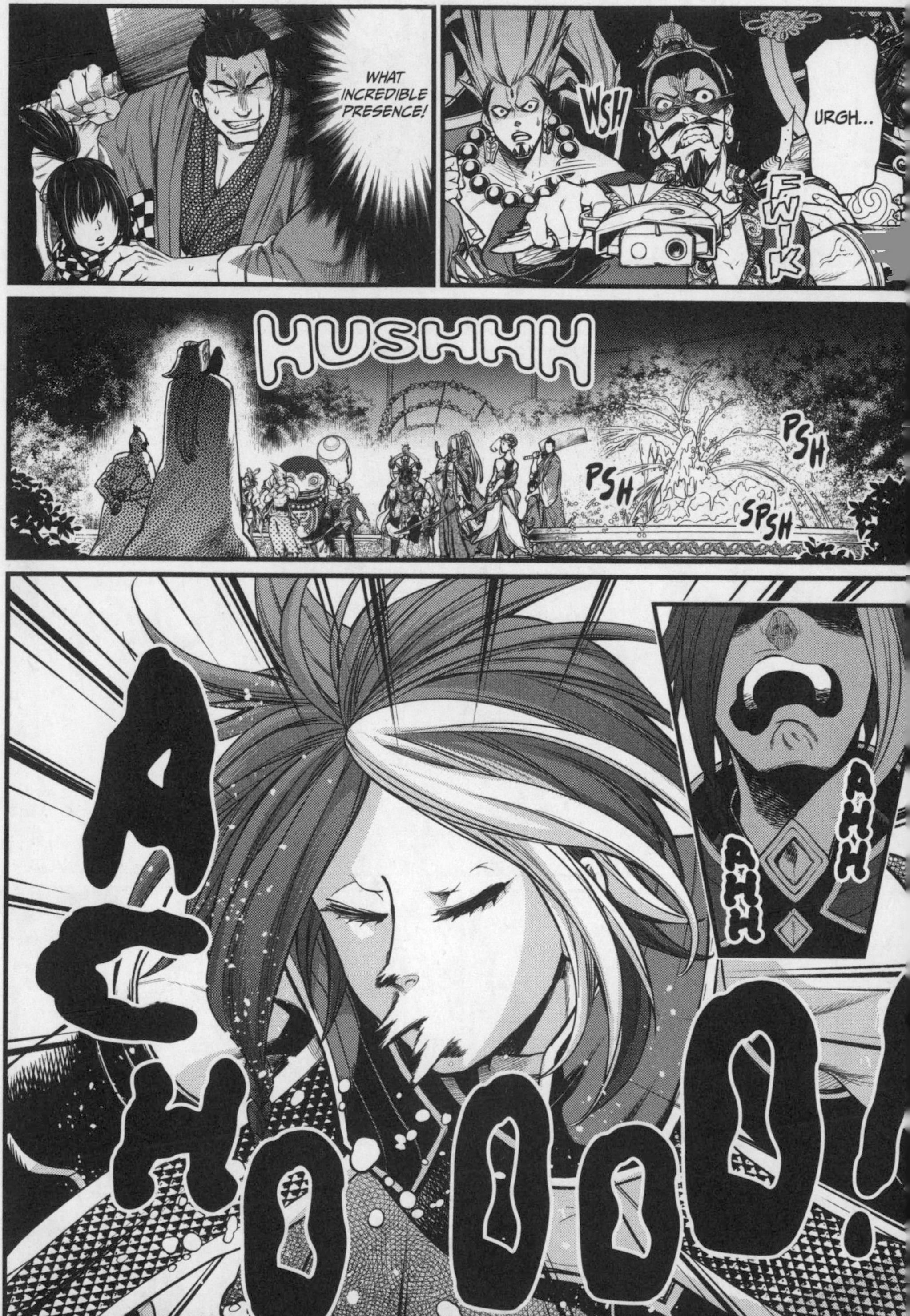
WSH
URGH...
FWIK
WHAT INCREDIBLE PRESENCE!
HUSHHH
PSH
PSH
SPSH
AHHH
AHHH
AHHOOOO!

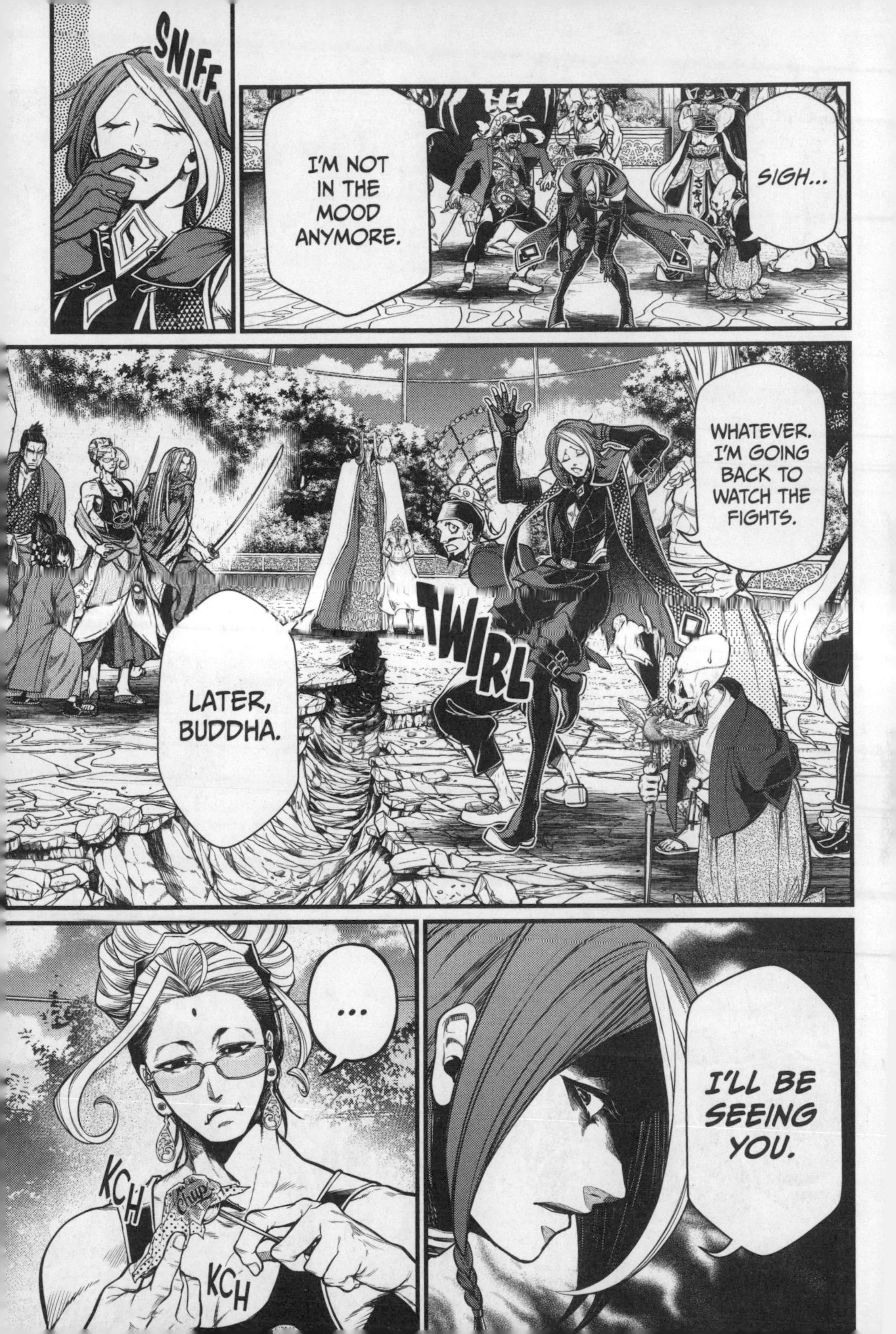
SIGH...
I'M NOT IN THE MOOD ANYMORE.
SNIFF
WHATEVER. I'M GOING BACK TO WATCH THE FIGHTS.
TWIRL
LATER, BUDDHA.
I'LL BE SEEING YOU.
...
KCH
chup
KCH

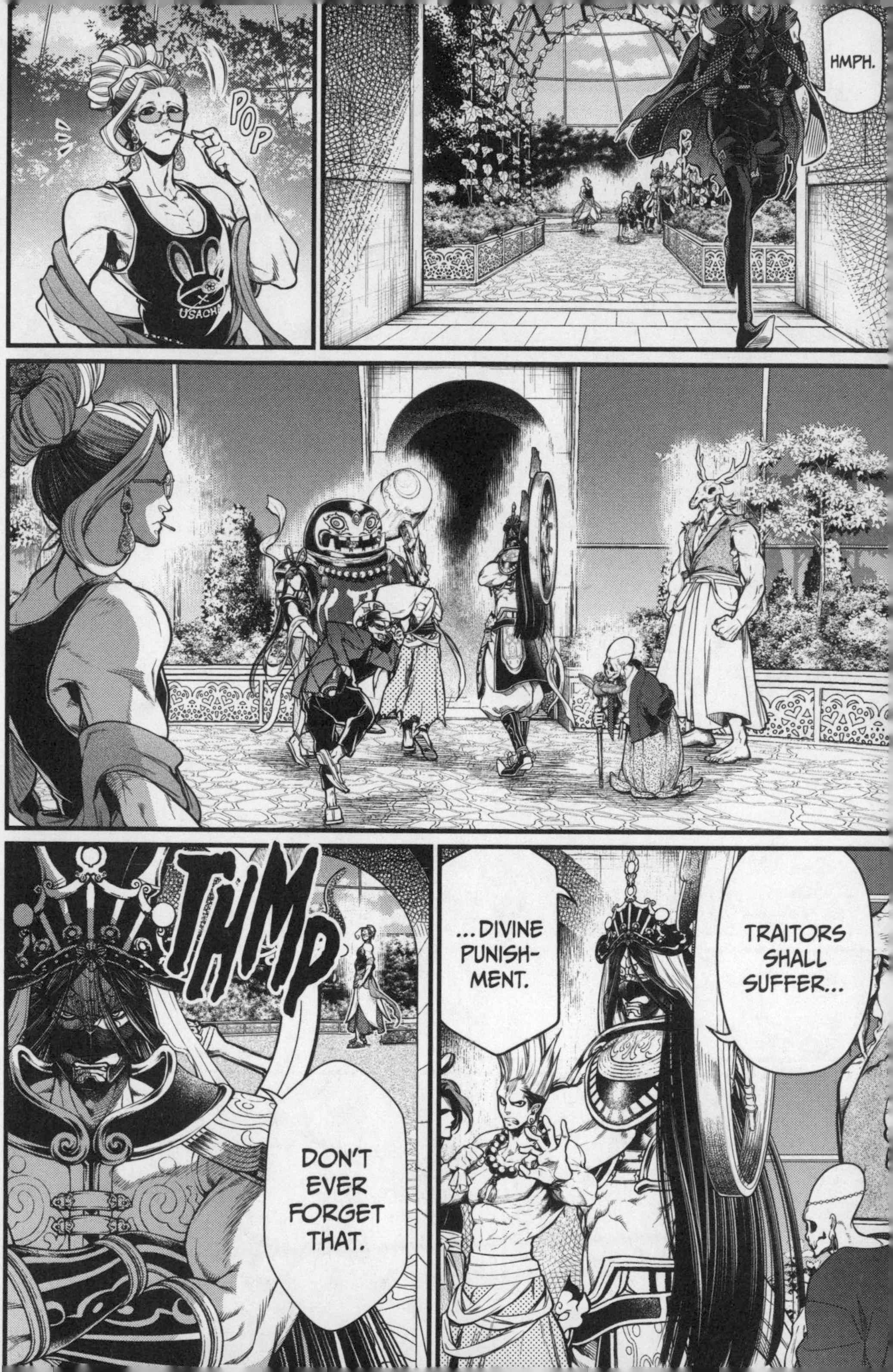
HMPH.
POP
TRAITORS SHALL SUFFER...
...DIVINE PUNISH-MENT.
THMP
DON'T EVER FORGET THAT.

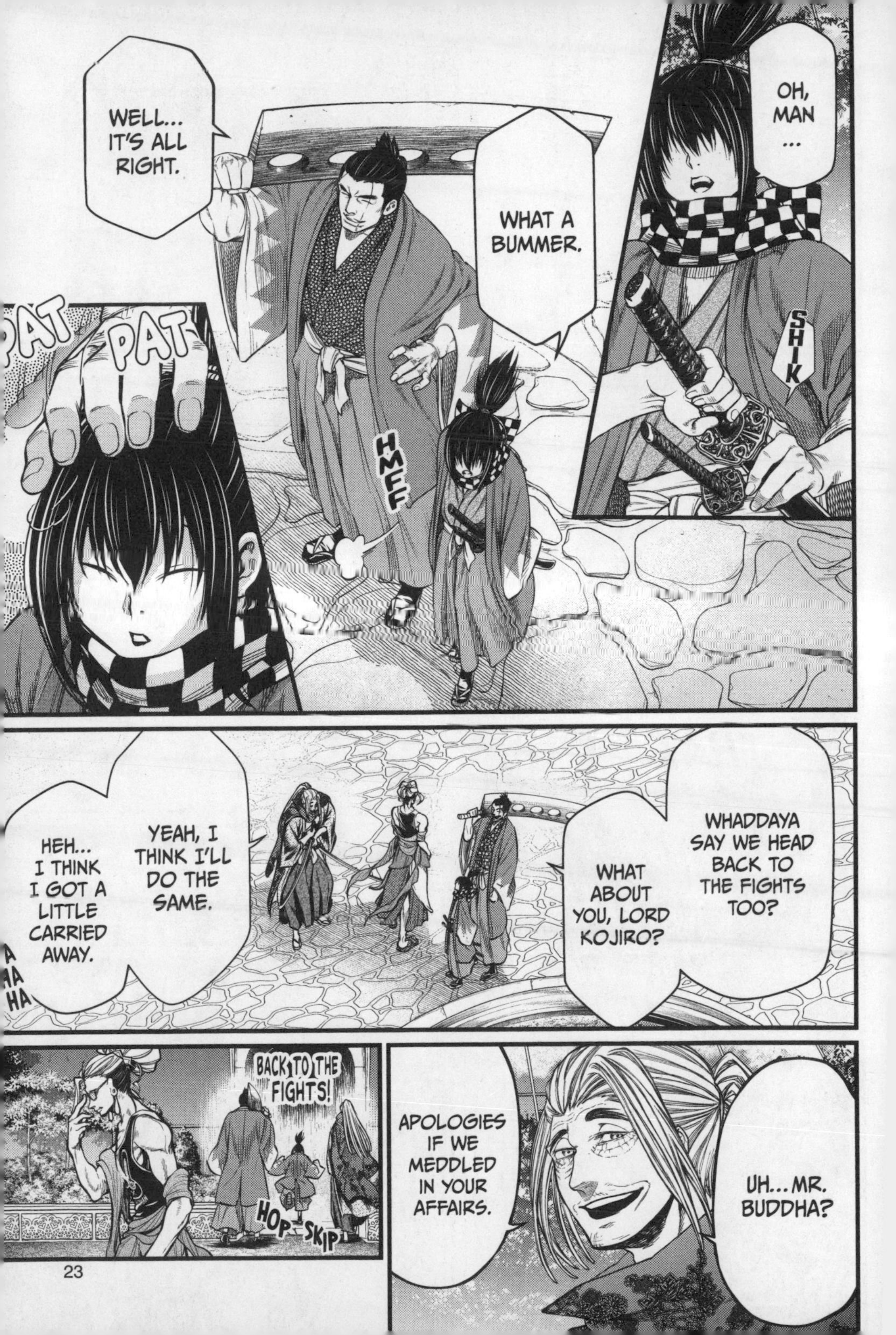
OH, MAN ...
SHIK
WHAT A BUMMER.
WELL... IT'S ALL RIGHT.
HMFF
PAT PAT
WHADDAYA SAY WE HEAD BACK TO THE FIGHTS TOO?
WHAT ABOUT YOU, LORD KOJIRO?
YEAH, I THINK I'LL DO THE SAME.
HEH... I THINK I GOT A LITTLE CARRIED AWAY.
HA HA
UH... MR. BUDDHA?
APOLOGIES IF WE MEDDLED IN YOUR AFFAIRS.
BACK TO THE FIGHTS!
HOP SKIP

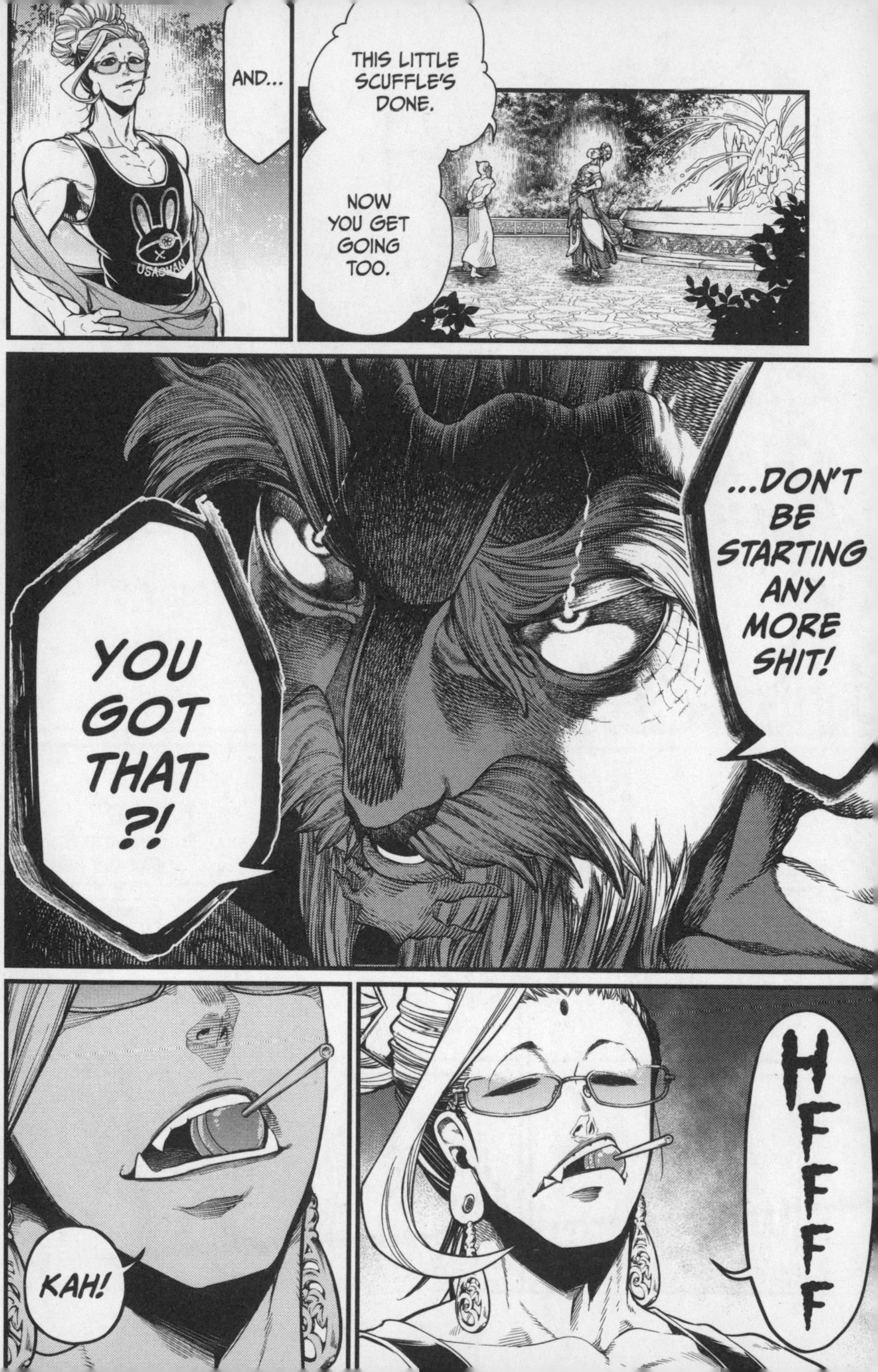
THIS LITTLE SCUFFLE'S DONE.
NOW YOU GET GOING TOO.
AND...
...DON'T BE STARTING ANY MORE SHIT!
YOU GOT THAT?!
HFFFF
KAH!

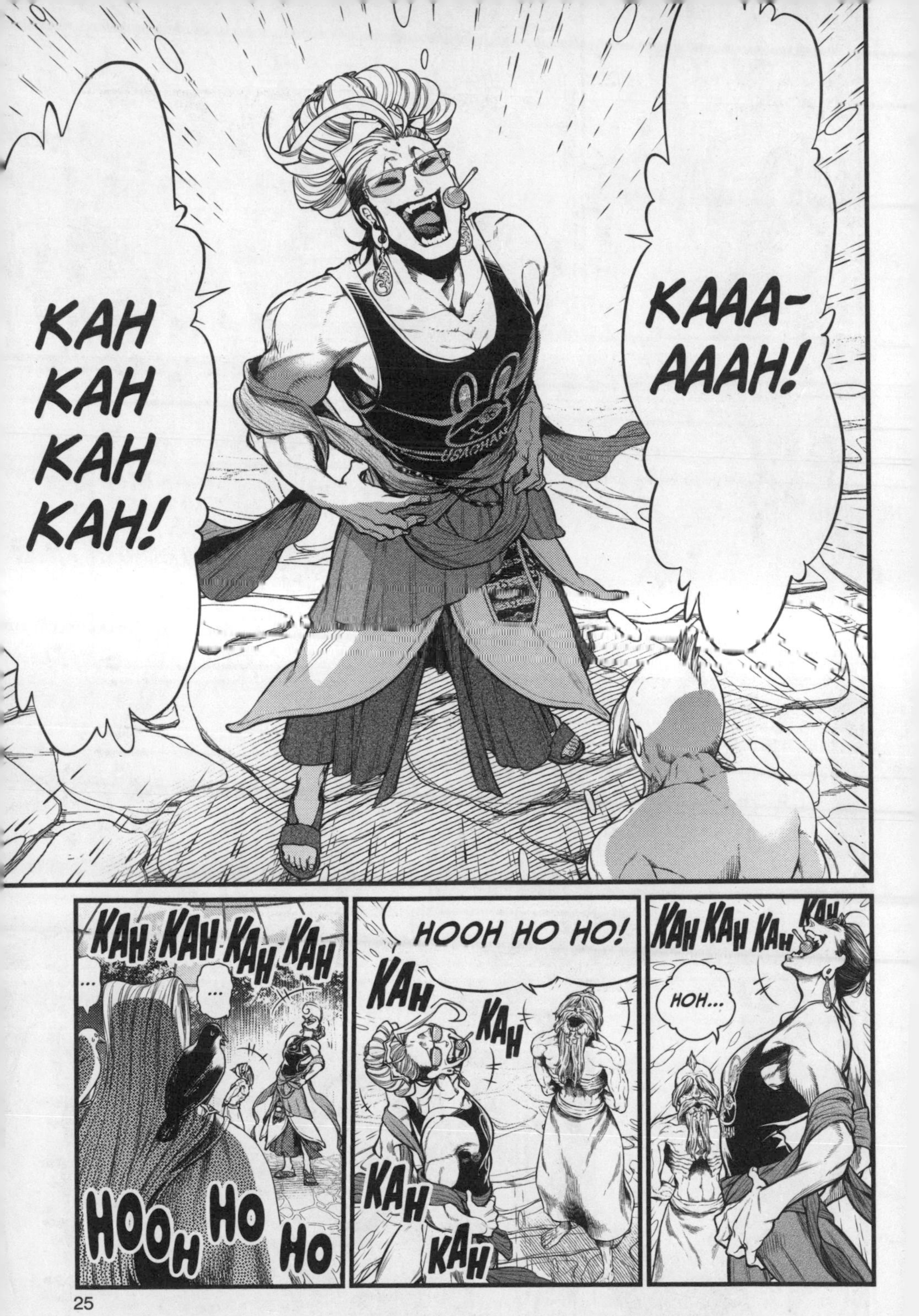
KAAA-AAAH!
KAH KAH KAH KAH!
KAH KAH KAH KAH
HOH...
HOOH HO HO!
KAH KAH
KAH KAH
KAH KAH KAH KAH
...
...
HOOH HO HO

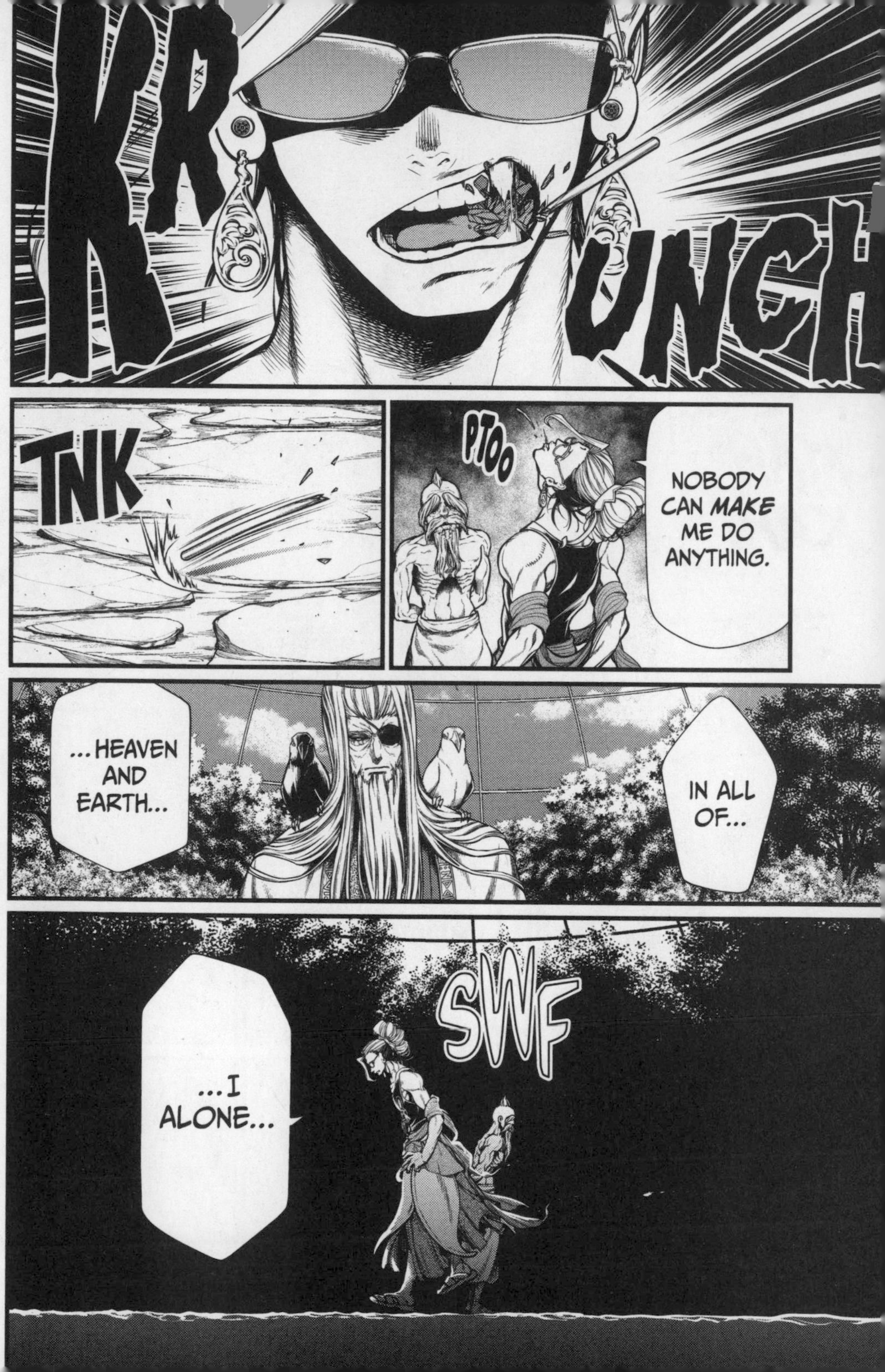
KRUNCH
NOBODY CAN MAKE ME DO ANYTHING.
PTOO
TNK
IN ALL OF...
...HEAVEN AND EARTH...
SWF
...I ALONE...

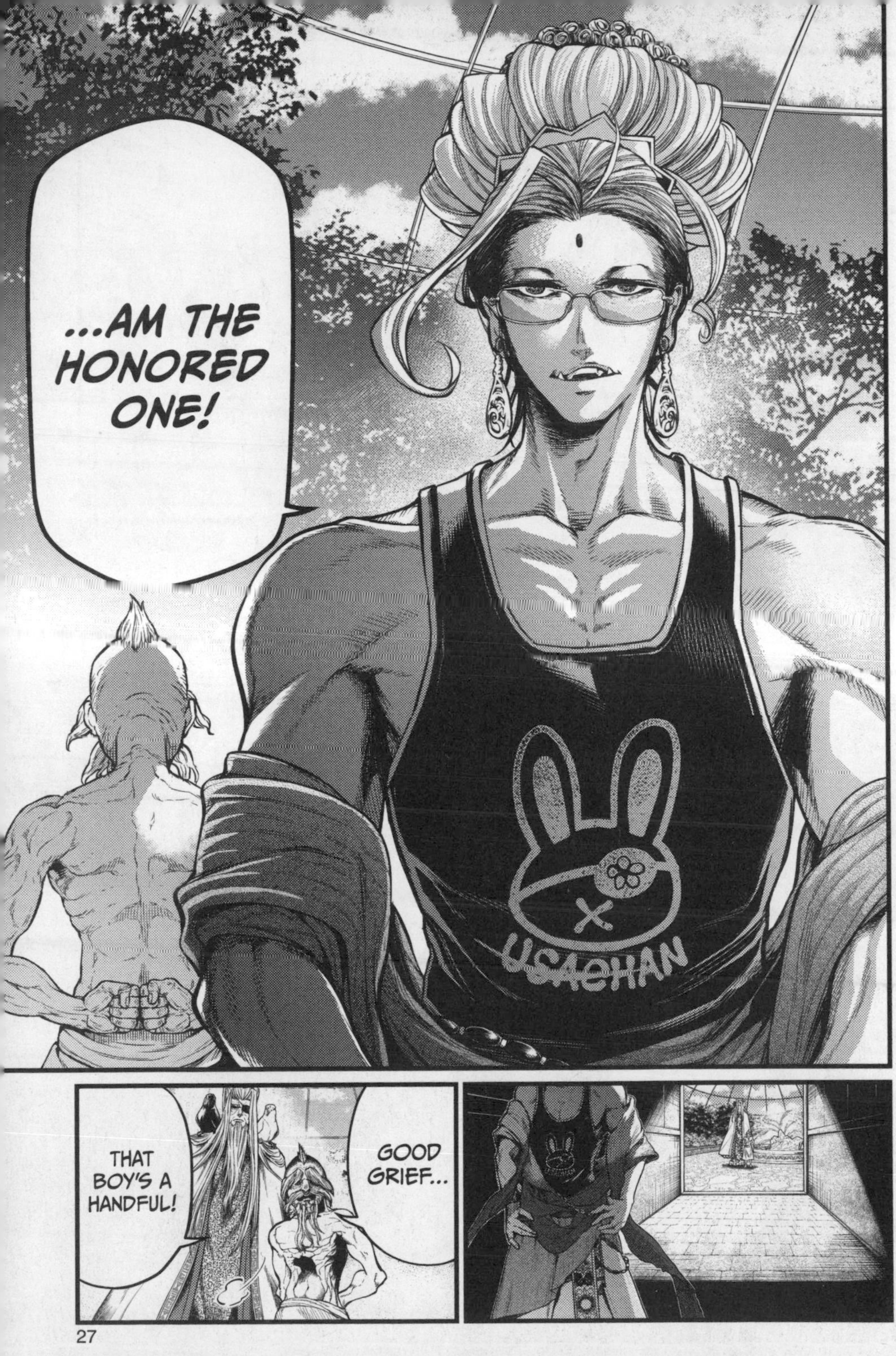
...AM THE HONORED ONE!
USACHAN
GOOD GRIEF...
THAT BOY'S A HANDFUL!

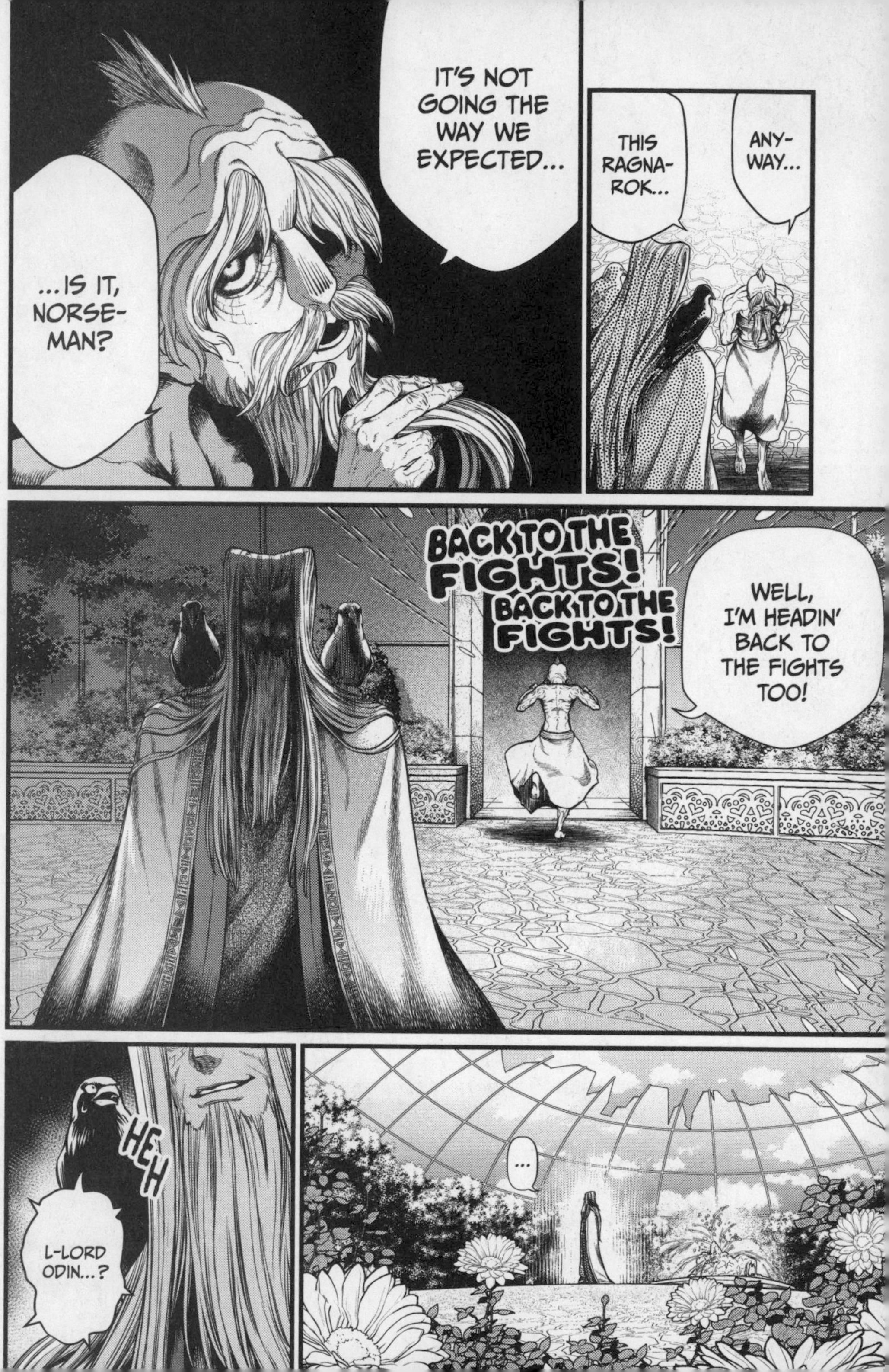
ANY-WAY...
THIS RAGNA-ROK...
IT'S NOT GOING THE WAY WE EXPECTED...
...IS IT, NORSE-MAN?
WELL, I'M HEADIN' BACK TO THE FIGHTS TOO!
BACK TO THE FIGHTS!
BACK TO THE FIGHTS!
...
HEH
L-LORD ODIN...?

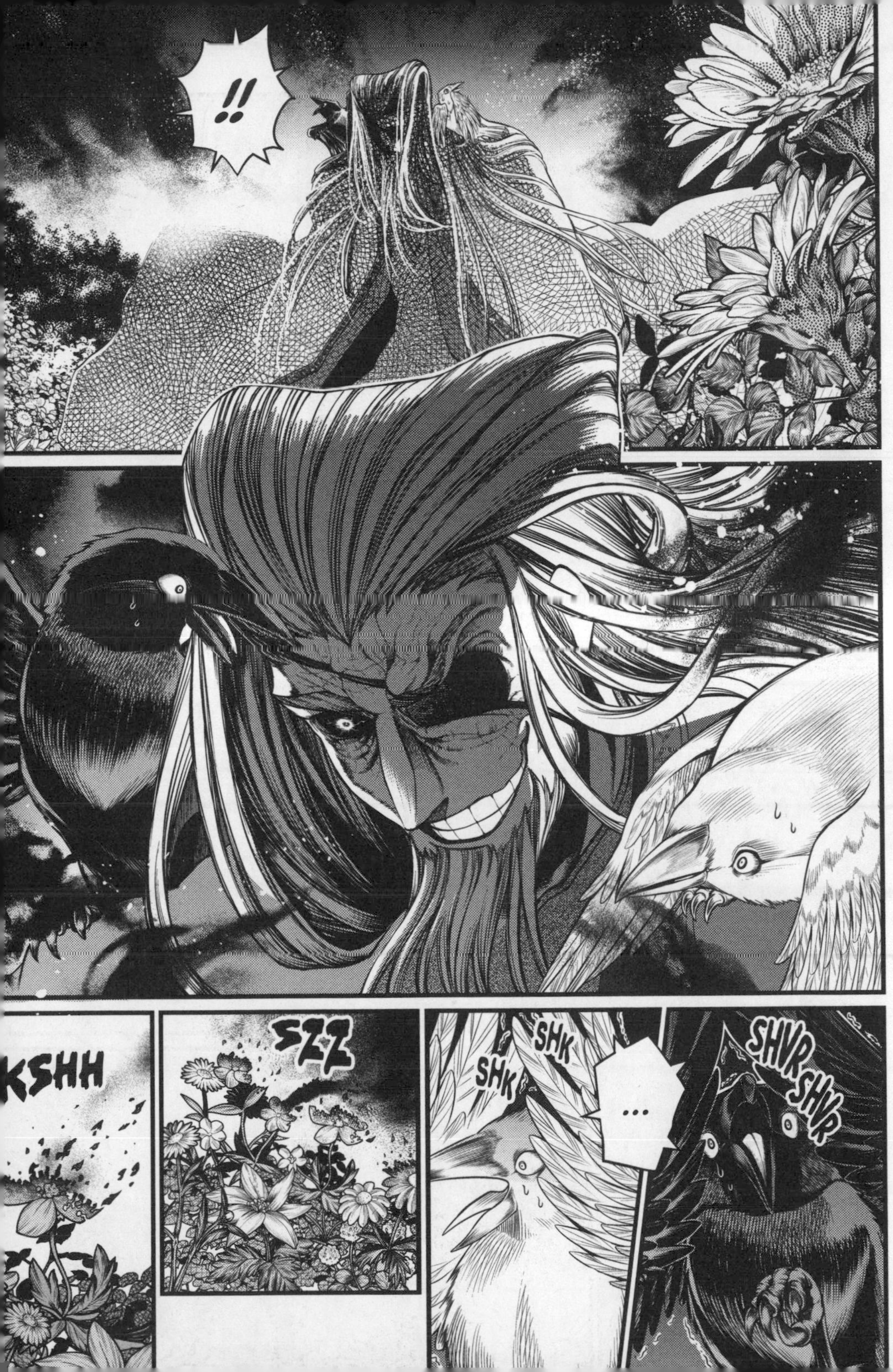
!!
SHVR SHVR
SHK SHK
...
SZZ
KSHH

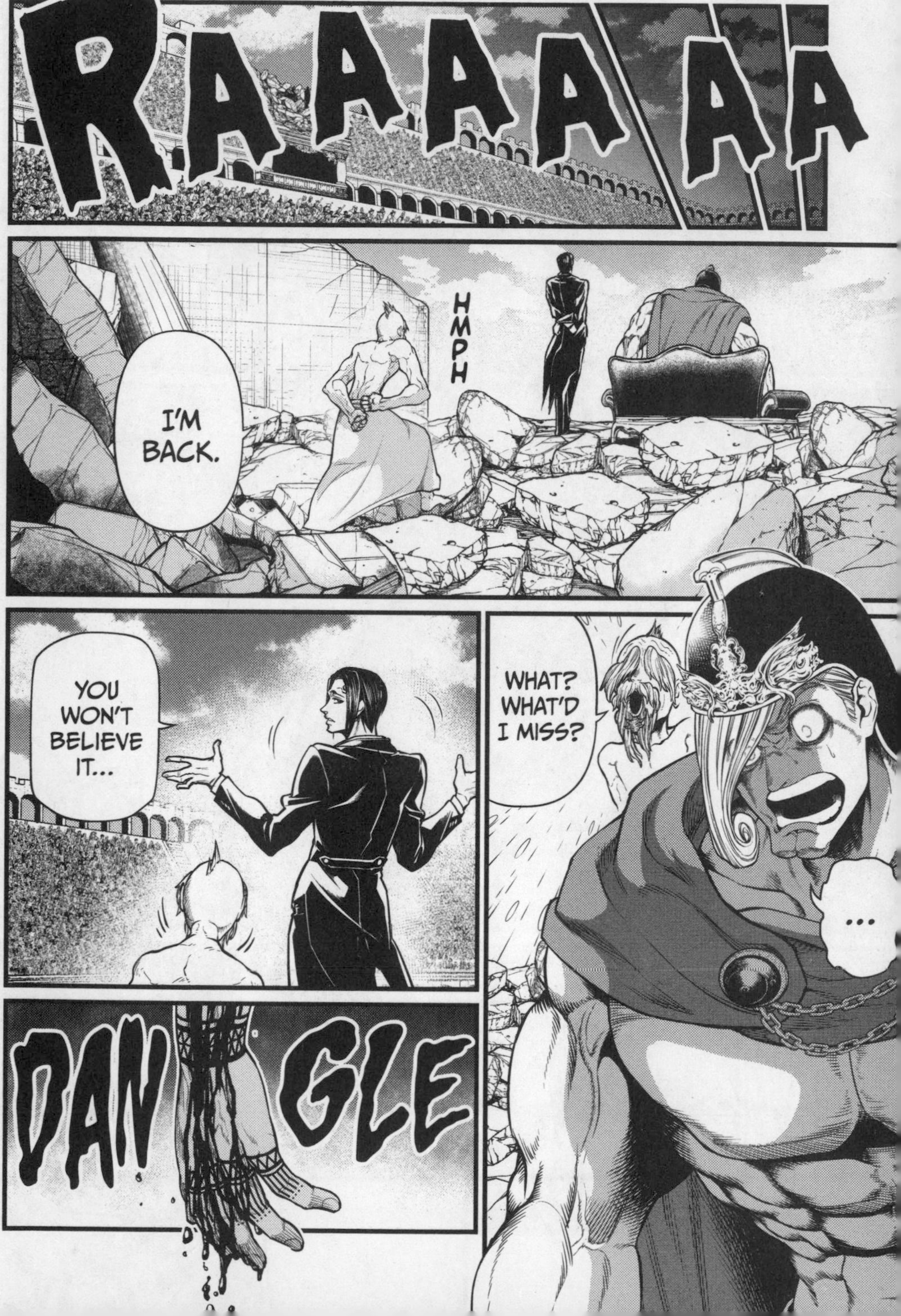
RAAAAAA
HMPH
I'M BACK.
WHAT? WHAT'D I MISS?
...
YOU WON'T BELIEVE IT...
DAN GLE

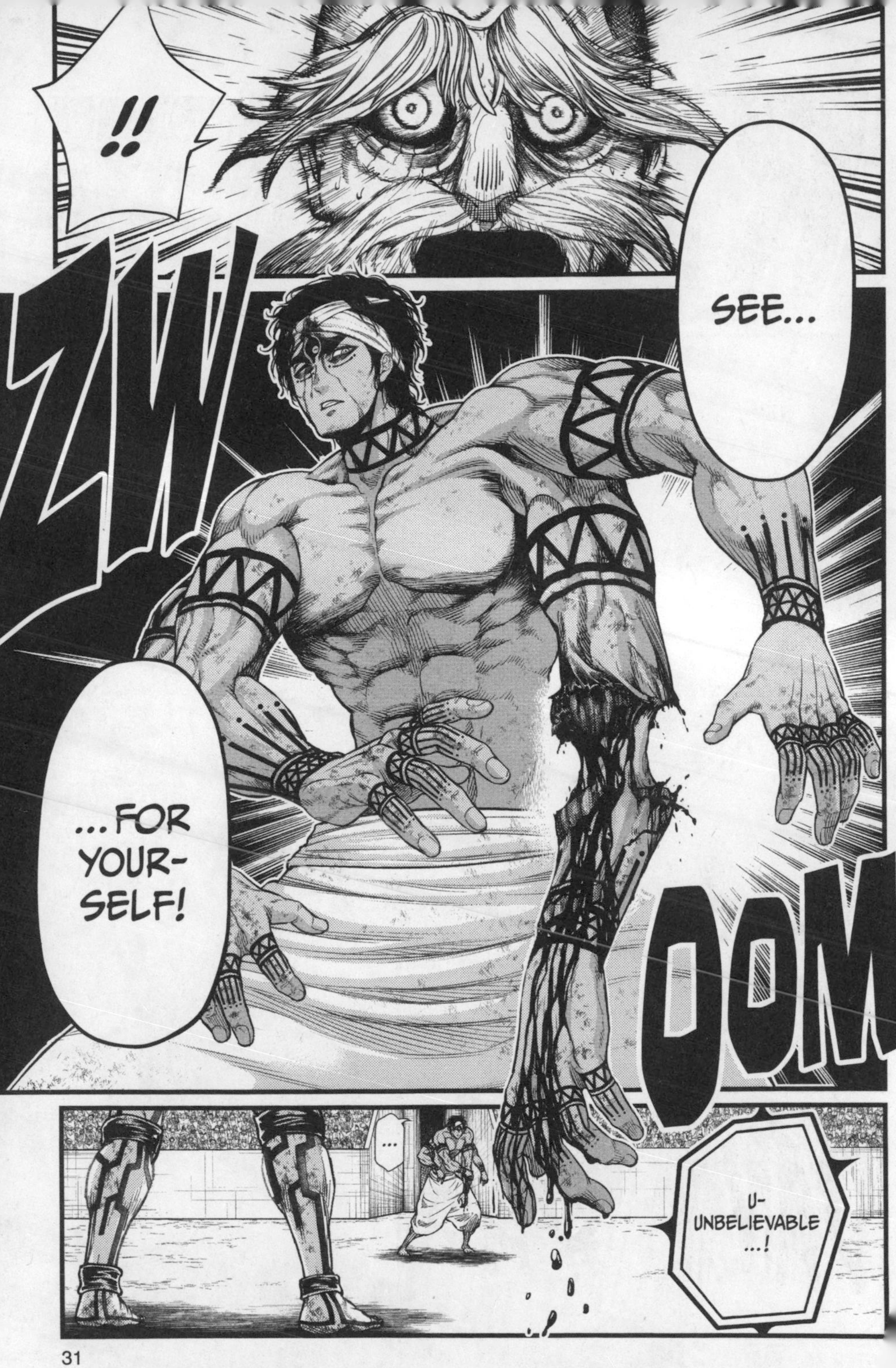
!!
SEE...
...FOR YOUR-SELF!
ZW
OOM
U-UNBELIEVABLE...!
...

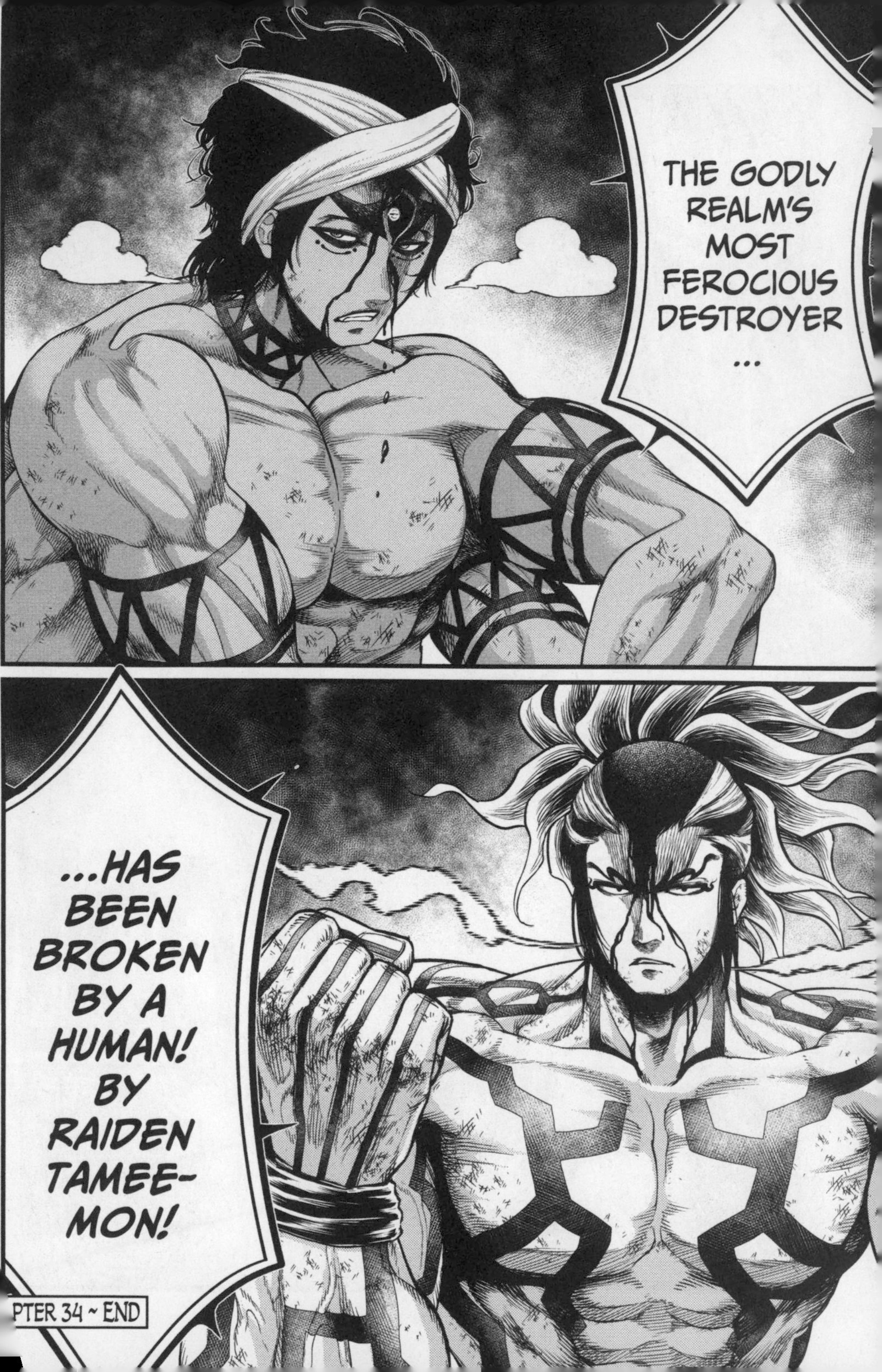
THE GODLY REALM'S MOST FEROCIOUS DESTROYER ...
...HAS BEEN BROKEN BY A HUMAN! BY RAIDEN TAMEE-MON!
PTER 34 ~ END

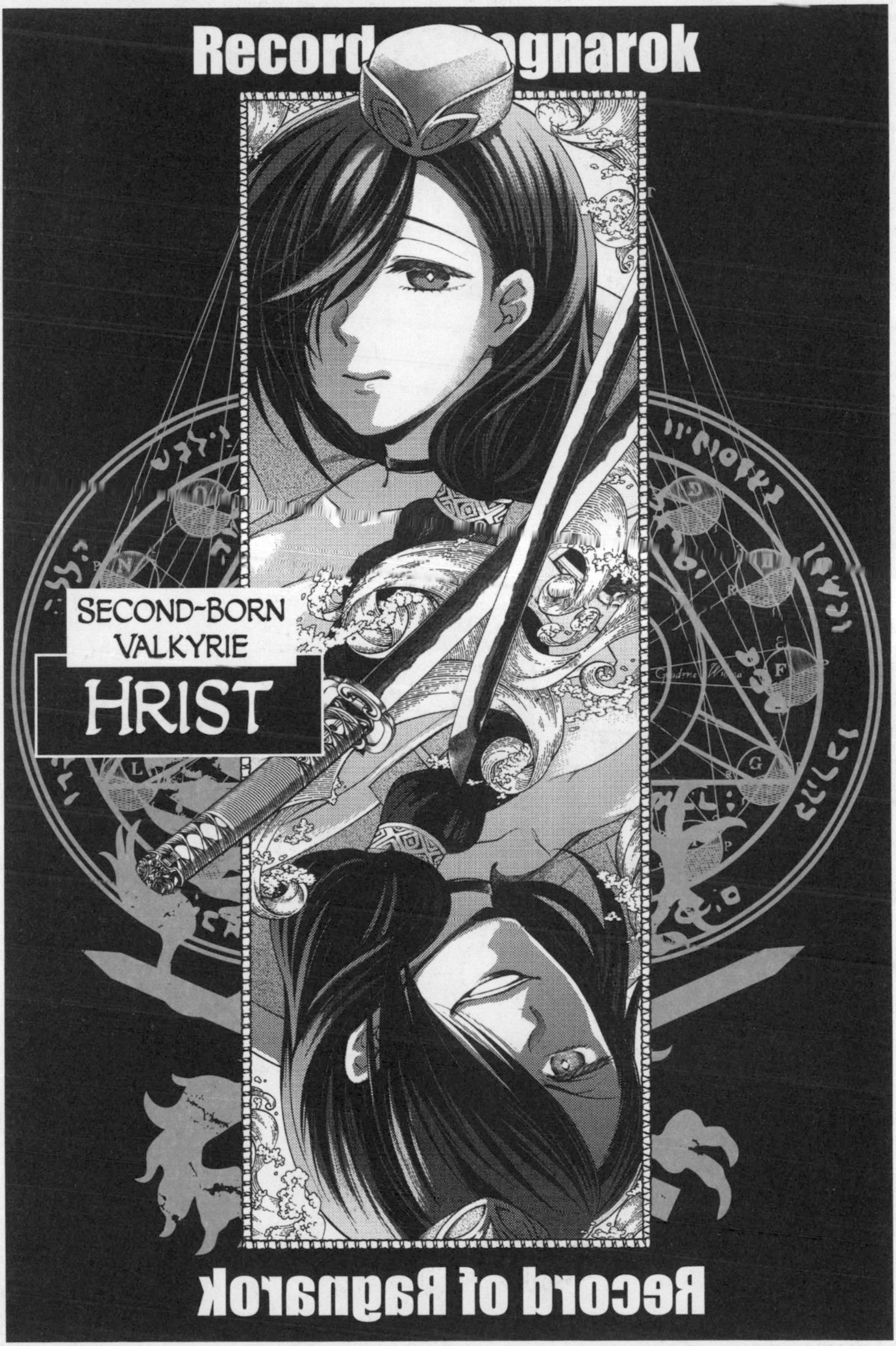
SECOND-BORN VALKYRIE
HRIST
Record of Ragnarok

RECORD OF RAGNAROK

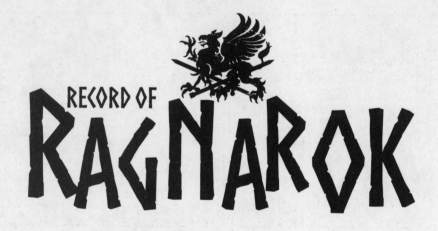

Chapter 35: Unrestrained vs. Unrestrained

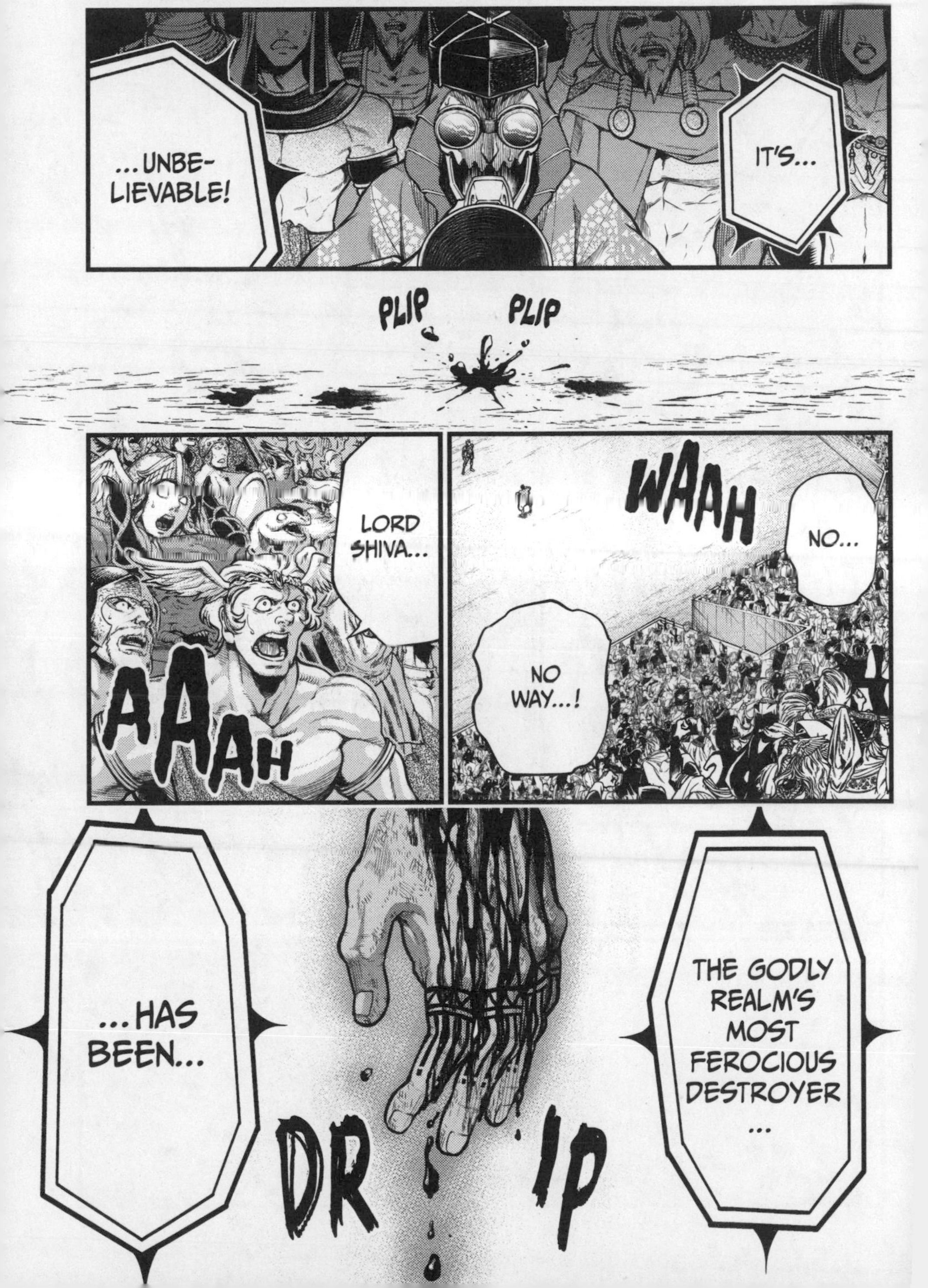
IT'S...
...UNBE-LIEVABLE!
PLIP PLIP
WAAH
NO...
NO WAY...!
LORD SHIVA...
AAAH
THE GODLY REALM'S MOST FEROCIOUS DESTROYER ...
...HAS BEEN...
DR IP

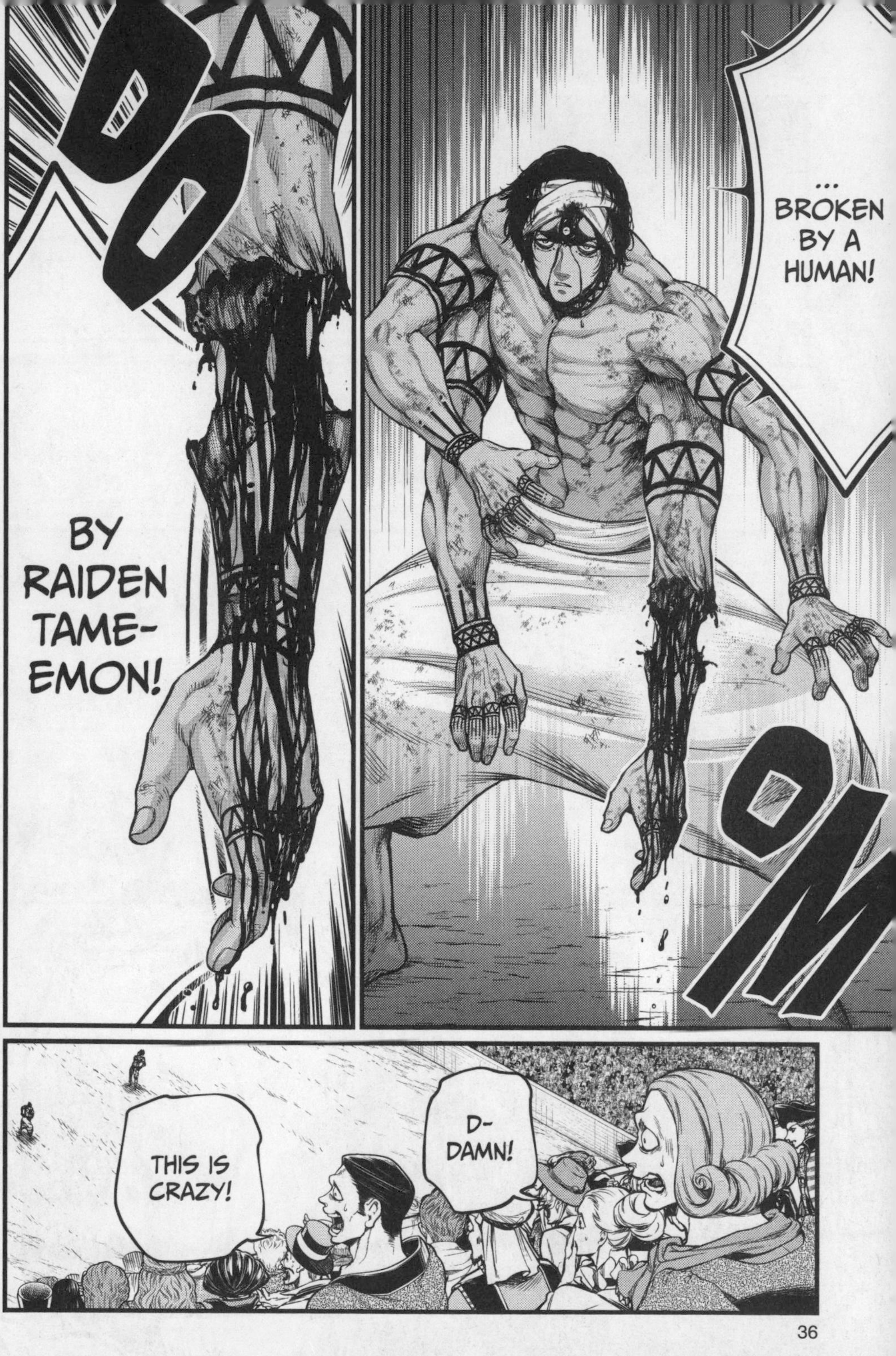
... BROKEN BY A HUMAN!
BY RAIDEN TAME-EMON!
D- DAMN!
THIS IS CRAZY!

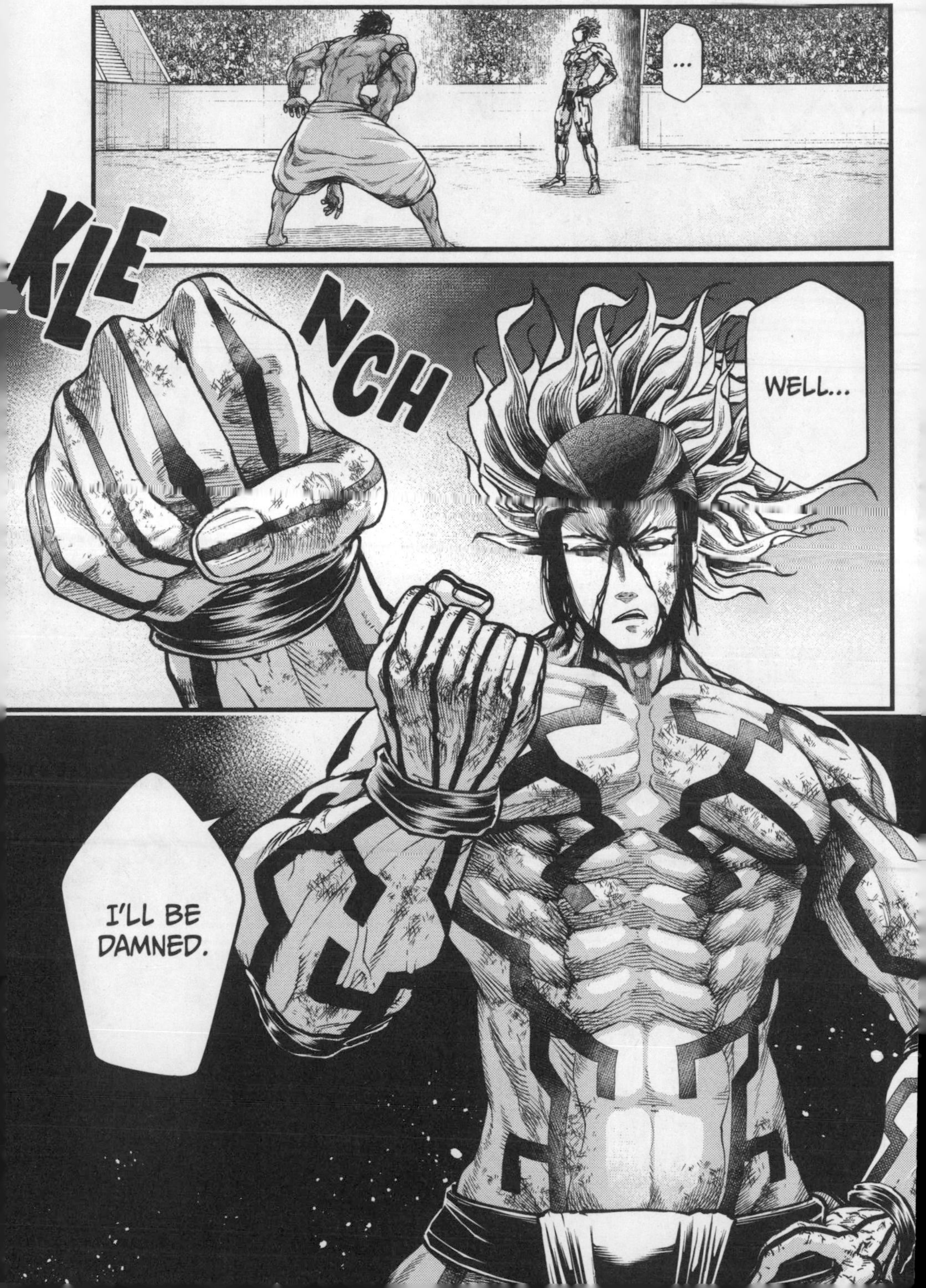
...
WELL...
KLENCH
I'LL BE DAMNED.

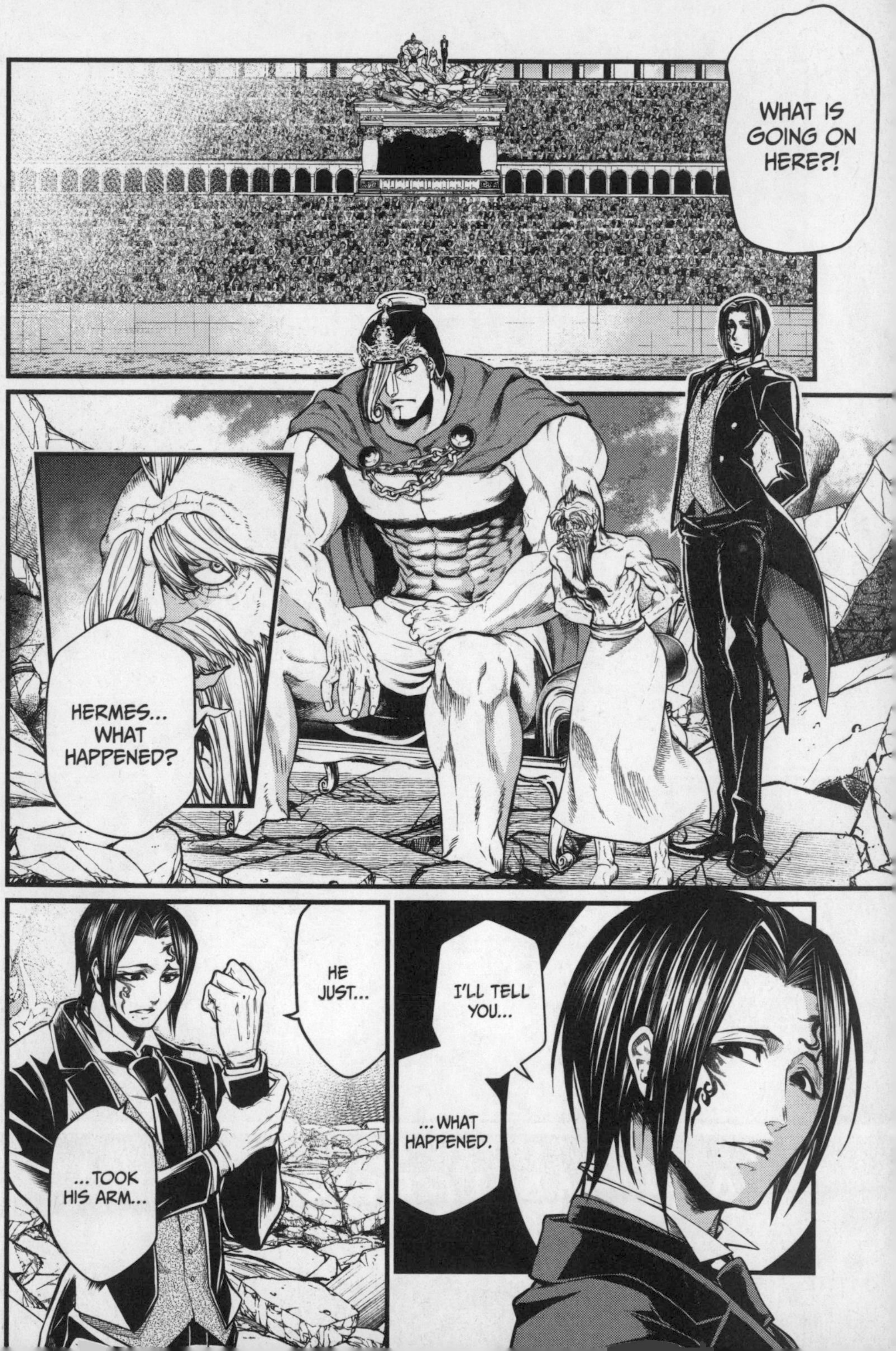
WHAT IS GOING ON HERE?!
HERMES... WHAT HAPPENED?
I'LL TELL YOU...
...WHAT HAPPENED.
HE JUST...
...TOOK HIS ARM...

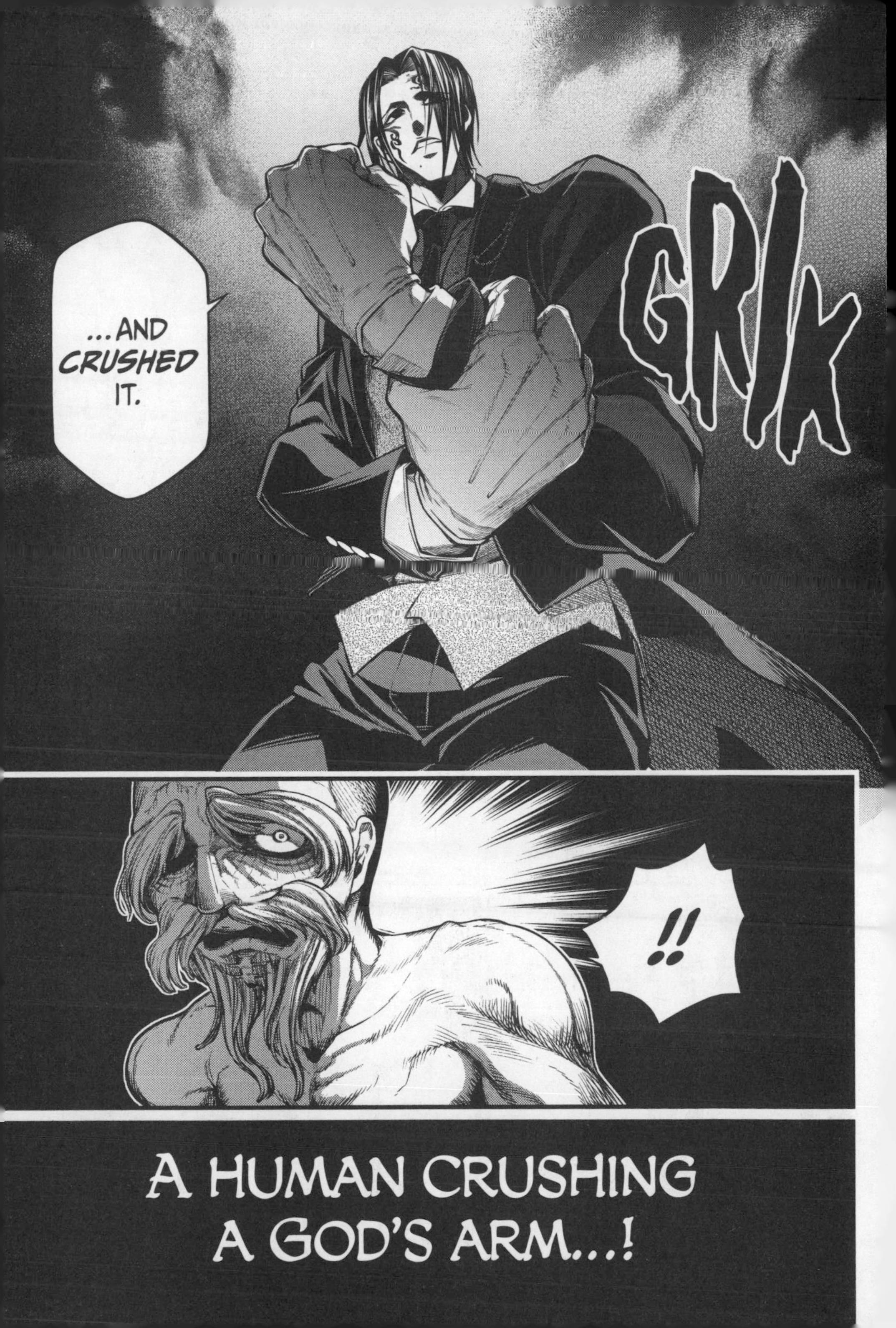
GRIK
...AND CRUSHED IT.
!!
A HUMAN CRUSHING A GOD'S ARM...!

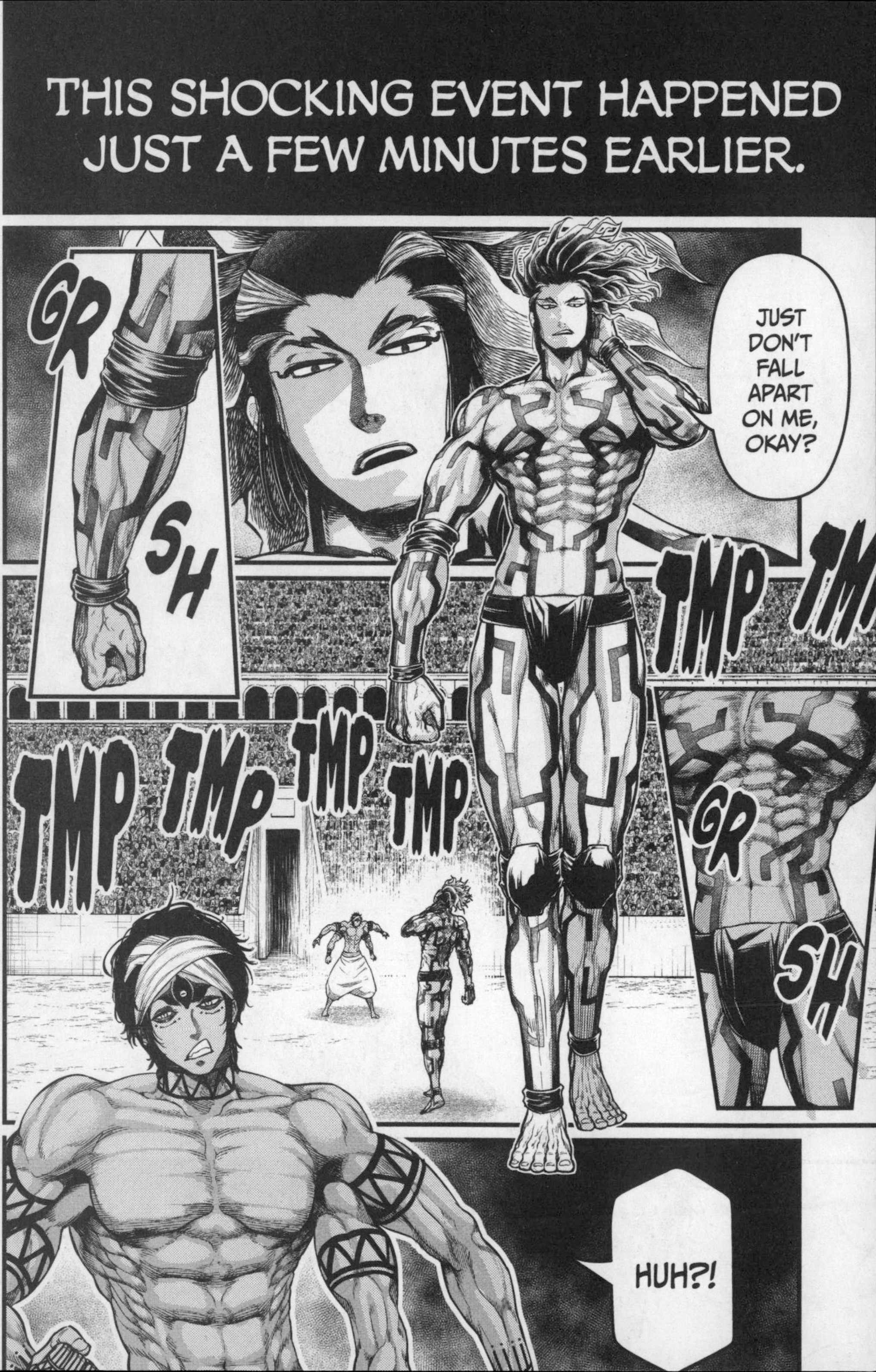
THIS SHOCKING EVENT HAPPENED JUST A FEW MINUTES EARLIER.
JUST DON'T FALL APART ON ME, OKAY?
GRSH
TMP TMP
GRSH
TMP TMP TMP TMP
HUH?!

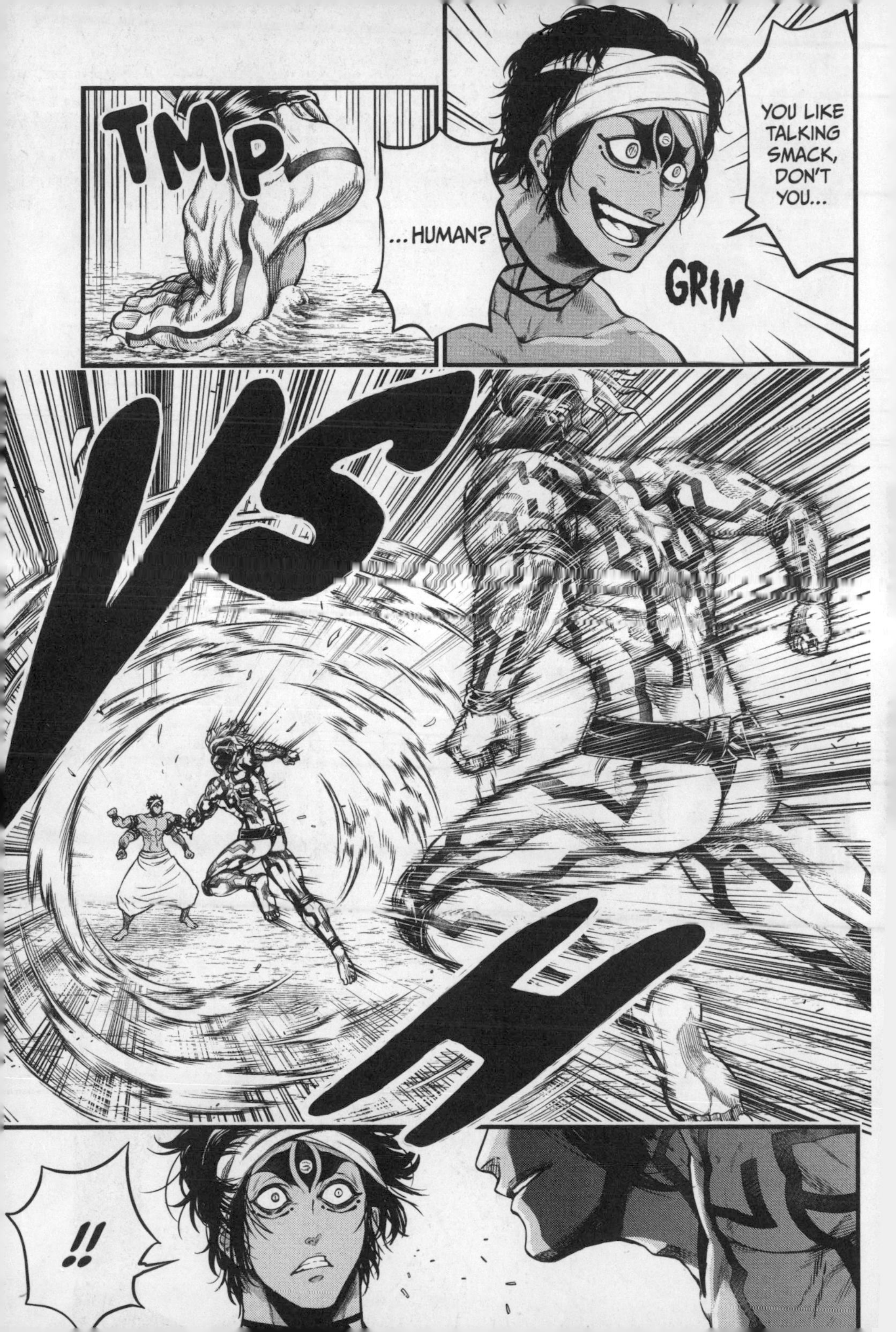
YOU LIKE TALKING SMACK, DON'T YOU...
...HUMAN?
GRIN
TMP
!!

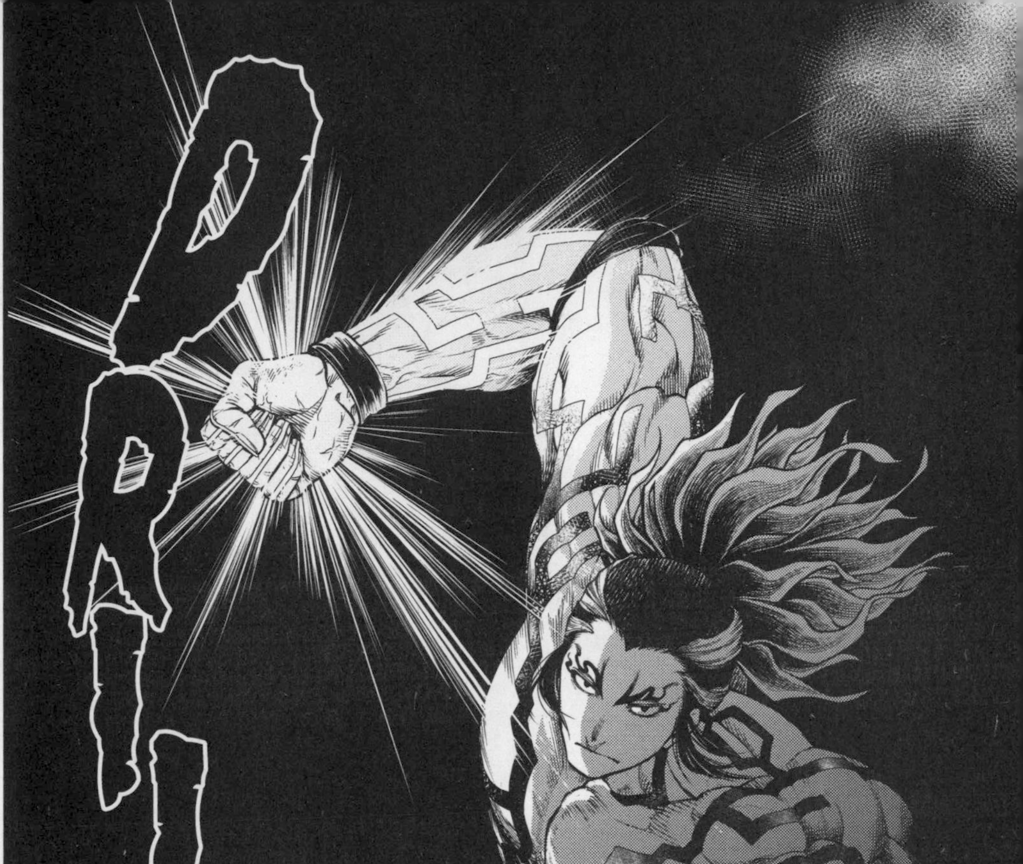
DRIII
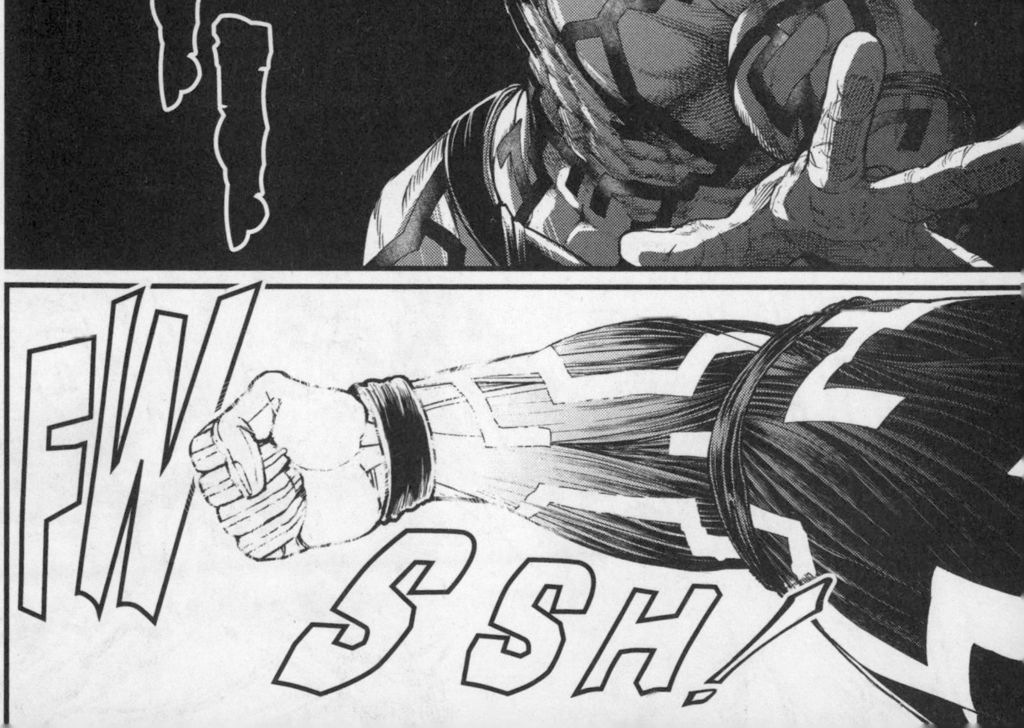
FWSSH!

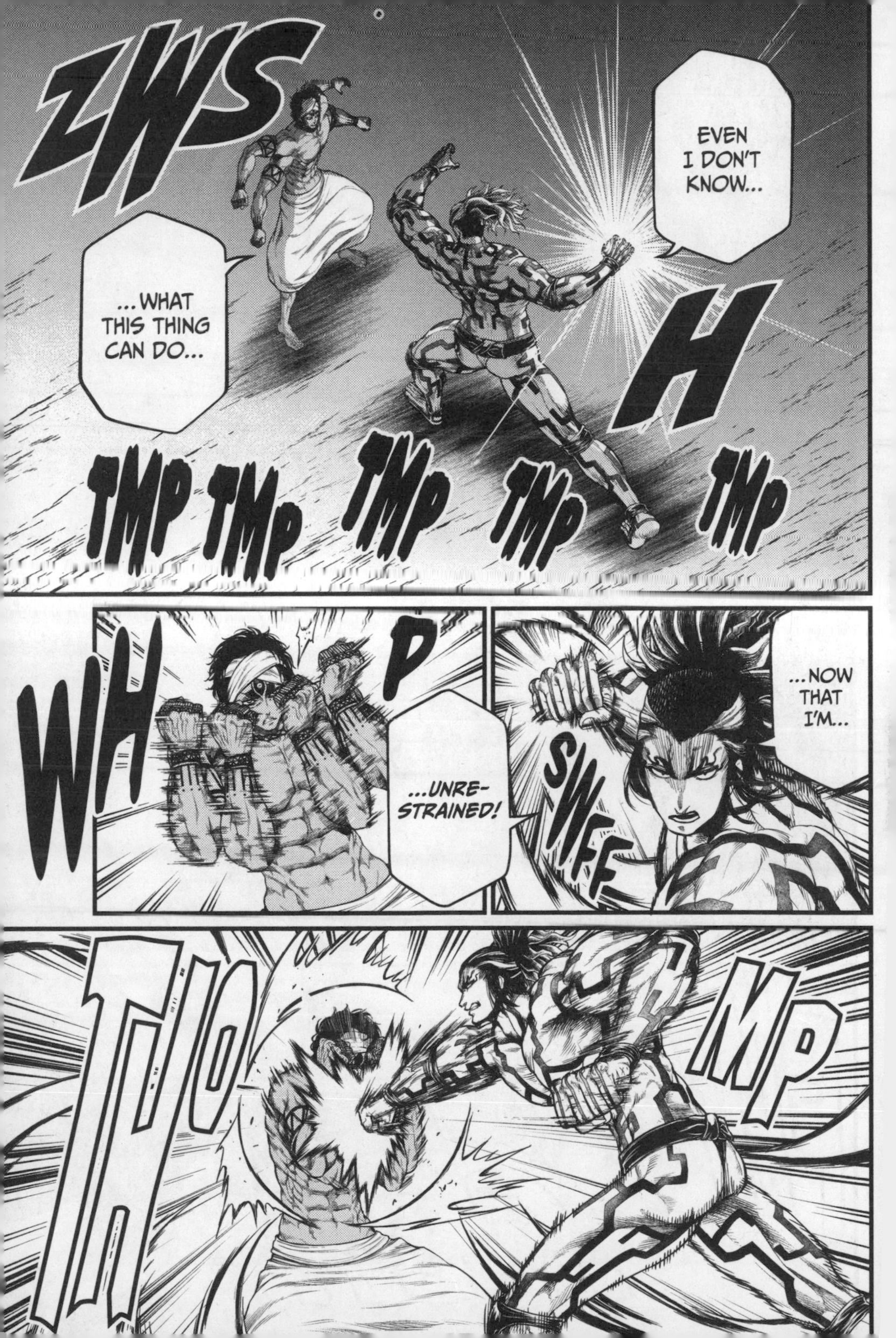
ZWSH
EVEN I DON'T KNOW...
...WHAT THIS THING CAN DO...
TMP TMP TMP TMP TMP
...NOW THAT I'M...
SWFF
WHP
...UNRE-STRAINED!
THOOMP

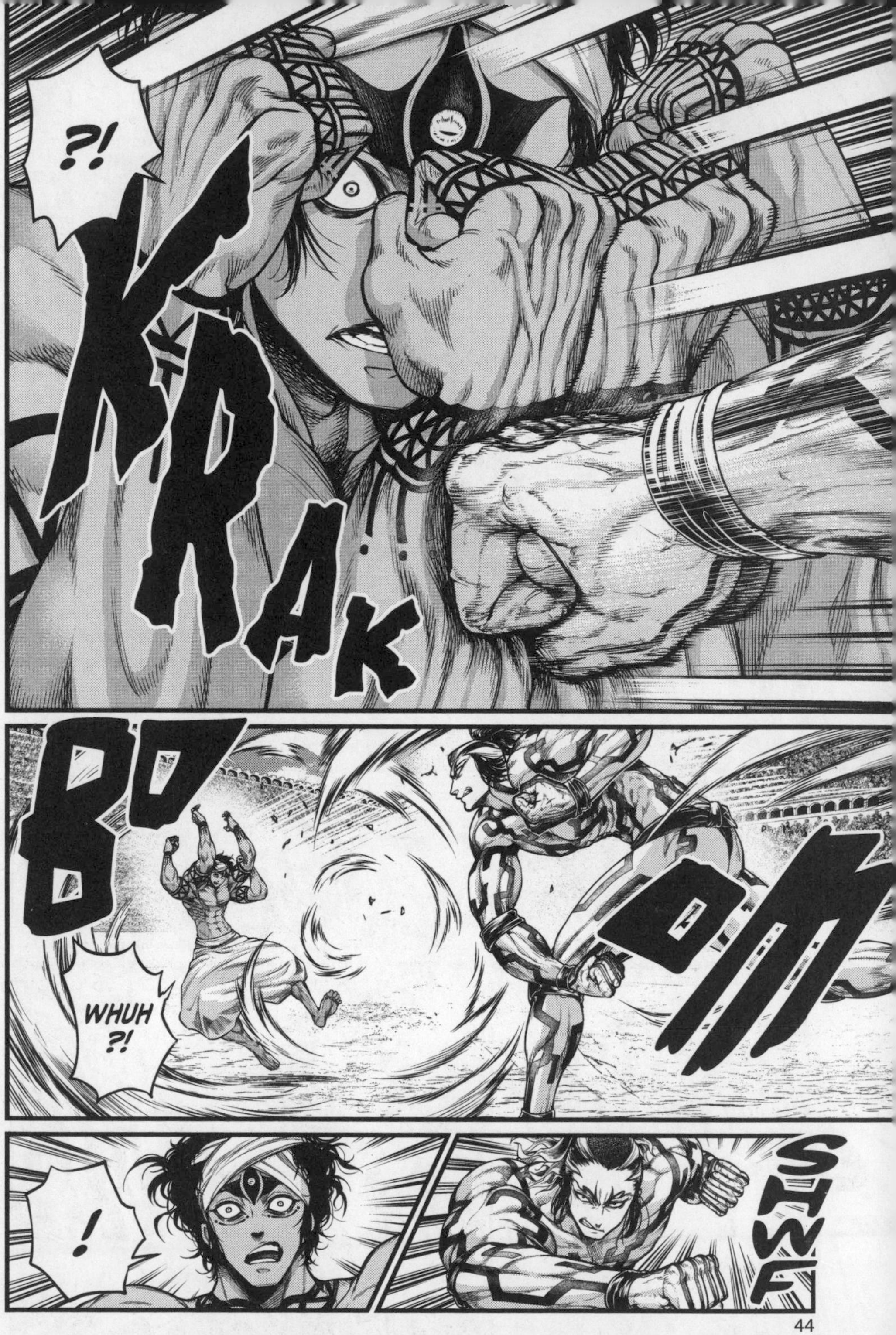
?!
KRRAK
WHUH ?!
SHWF
!

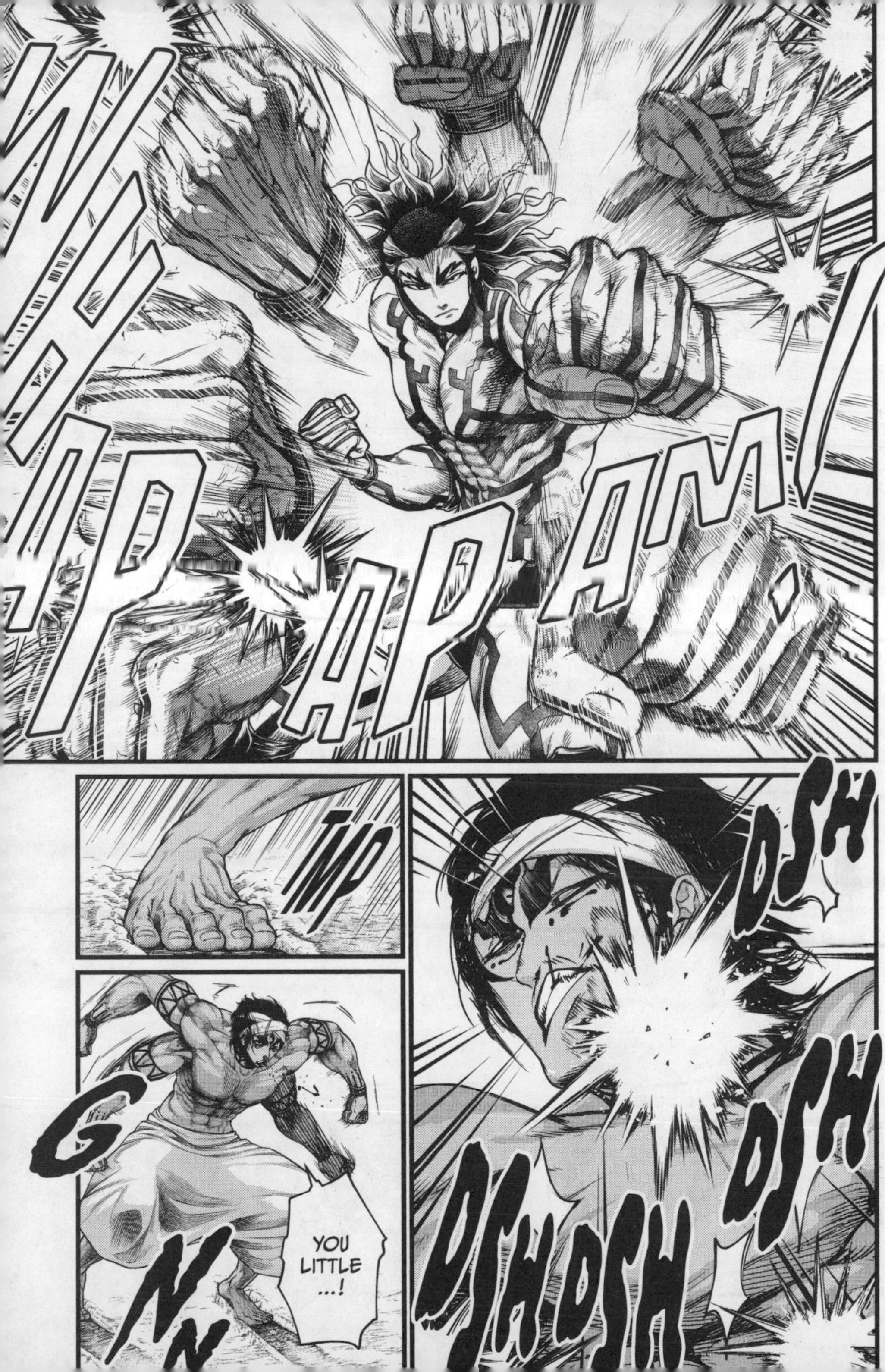
WHAPPAPAM!
DOSH
DOSH DOSH DOSH
TMP
GNN
YOU LITTLE ...!

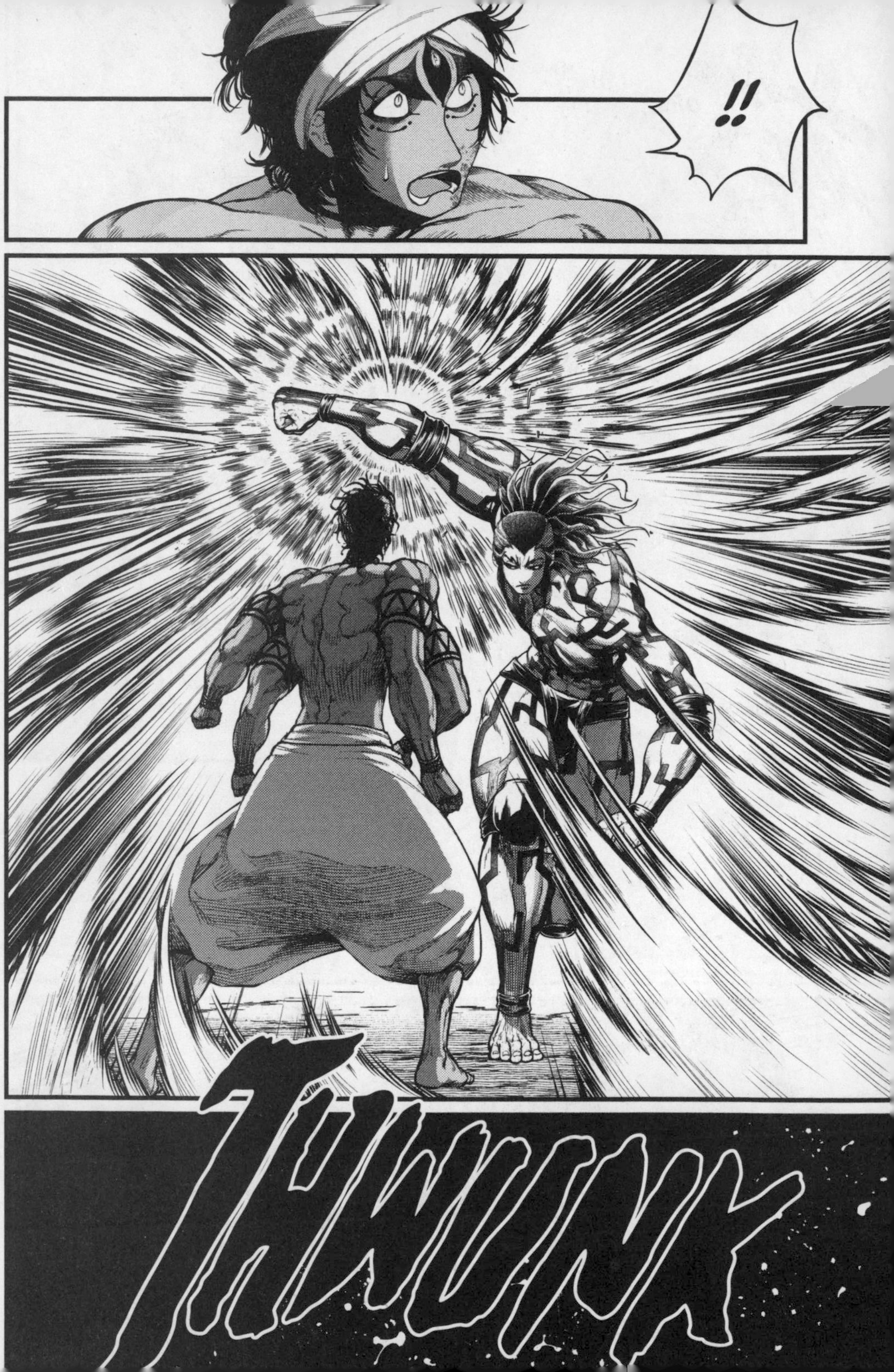
!!
THUNK

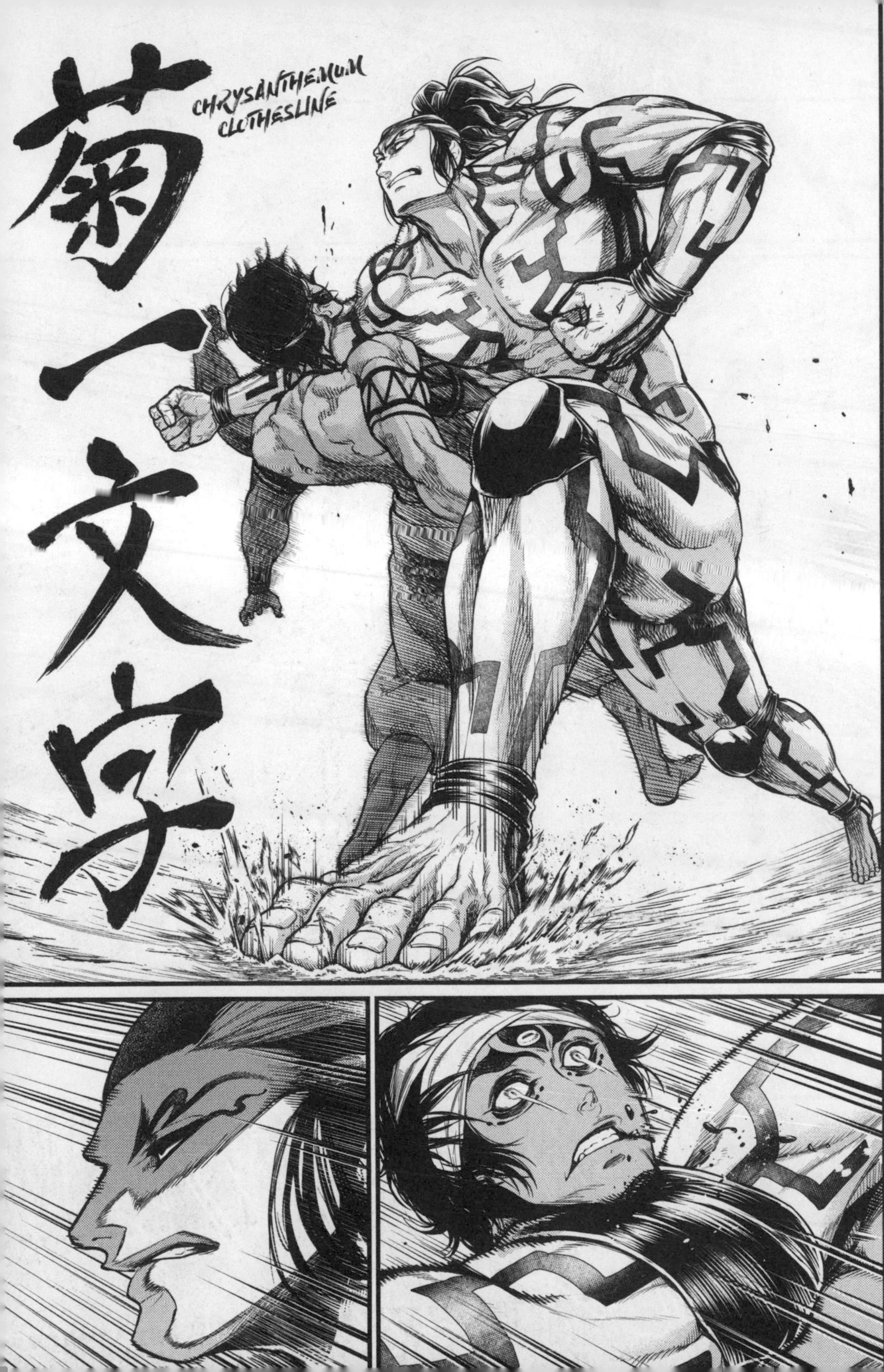
菊一文字
CHRYSANTHEMUM CLOTHESLINE

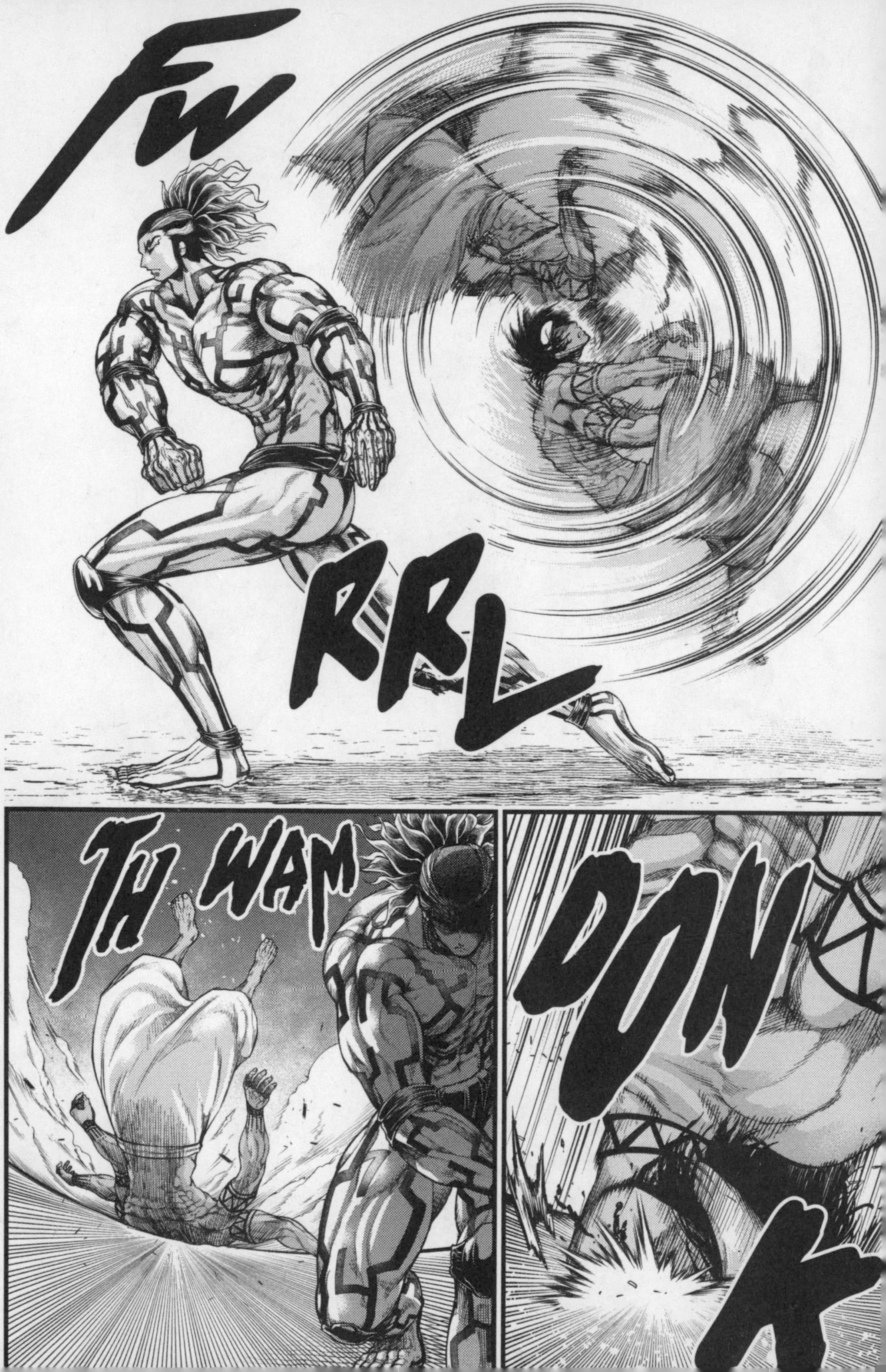
FW
RRL
DON
K
TH
WAM

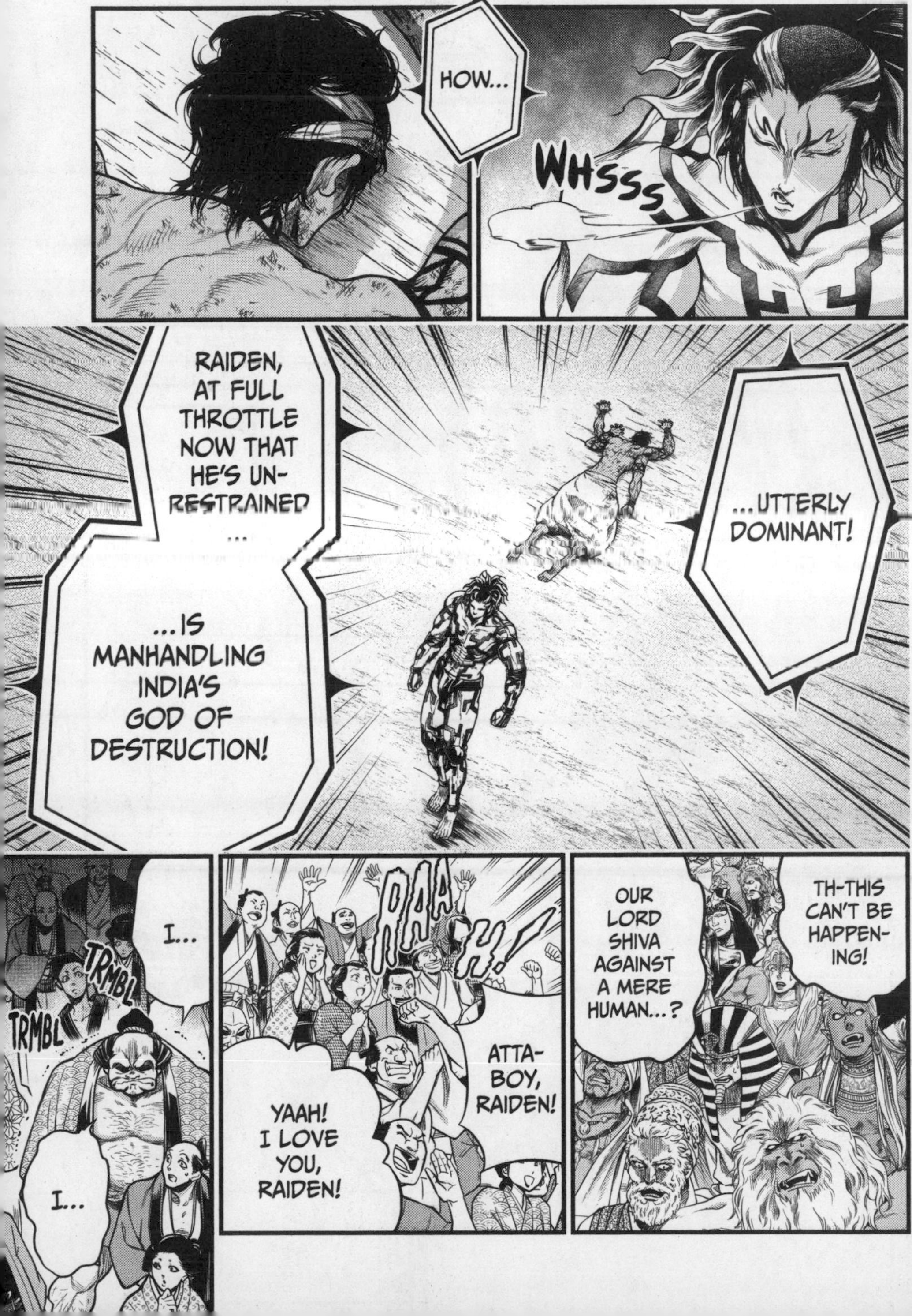
HOW...
WHSSS
RAIDEN, AT FULL THROTTLE NOW THAT HE'S UN-RESTRAINED...
...IS MANHANDLING INDIA'S GOD OF DESTRUCTION!
...UTTERLY DOMINANT!
TH-THIS CAN'T BE HAPPEN-ING!
OUR LORD SHIVA AGAINST A MERE HUMAN...?
RAAAH!!
ATTA-BOY, RAIDEN!
YAAH! I LOVE YOU, RAIDEN!
I...
TRMBL
TRMBL
I...

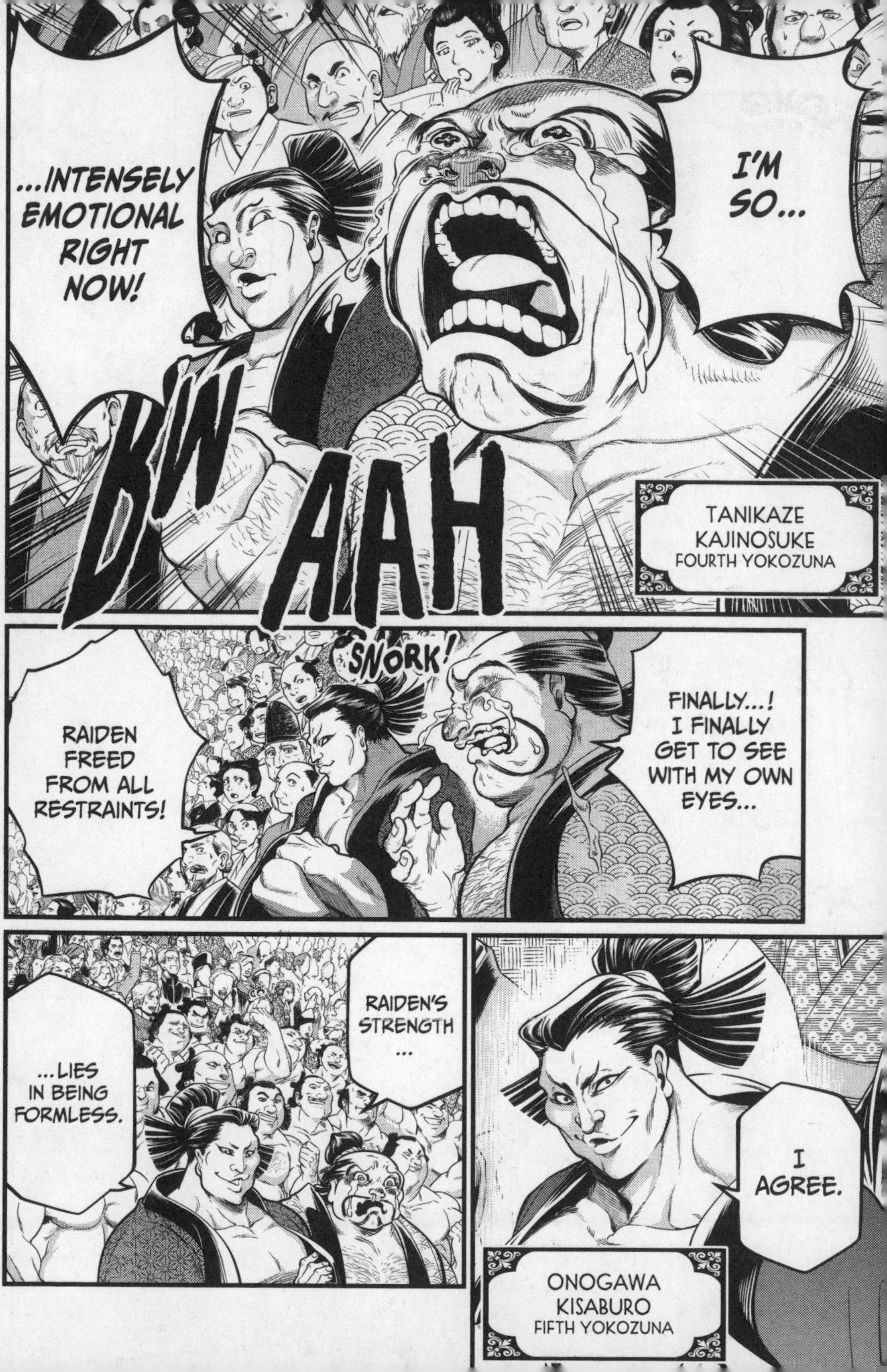
I'M SO...
...INTENSELY EMOTIONAL RIGHT NOW!
BWAAH
TANIKAZE KAJINOSUKE FOURTH YOKOZUNA
SNORK!
FINALLY...! I FINALLY GET TO SEE WITH MY OWN EYES...
RAIDEN FREED FROM ALL RESTRAINTS!
I AGREE.
ONOGAWA KISABURO FIFTH YOKOZUNA
RAIDEN'S STRENGTH ...
...LIES IN BEING FORMLESS.

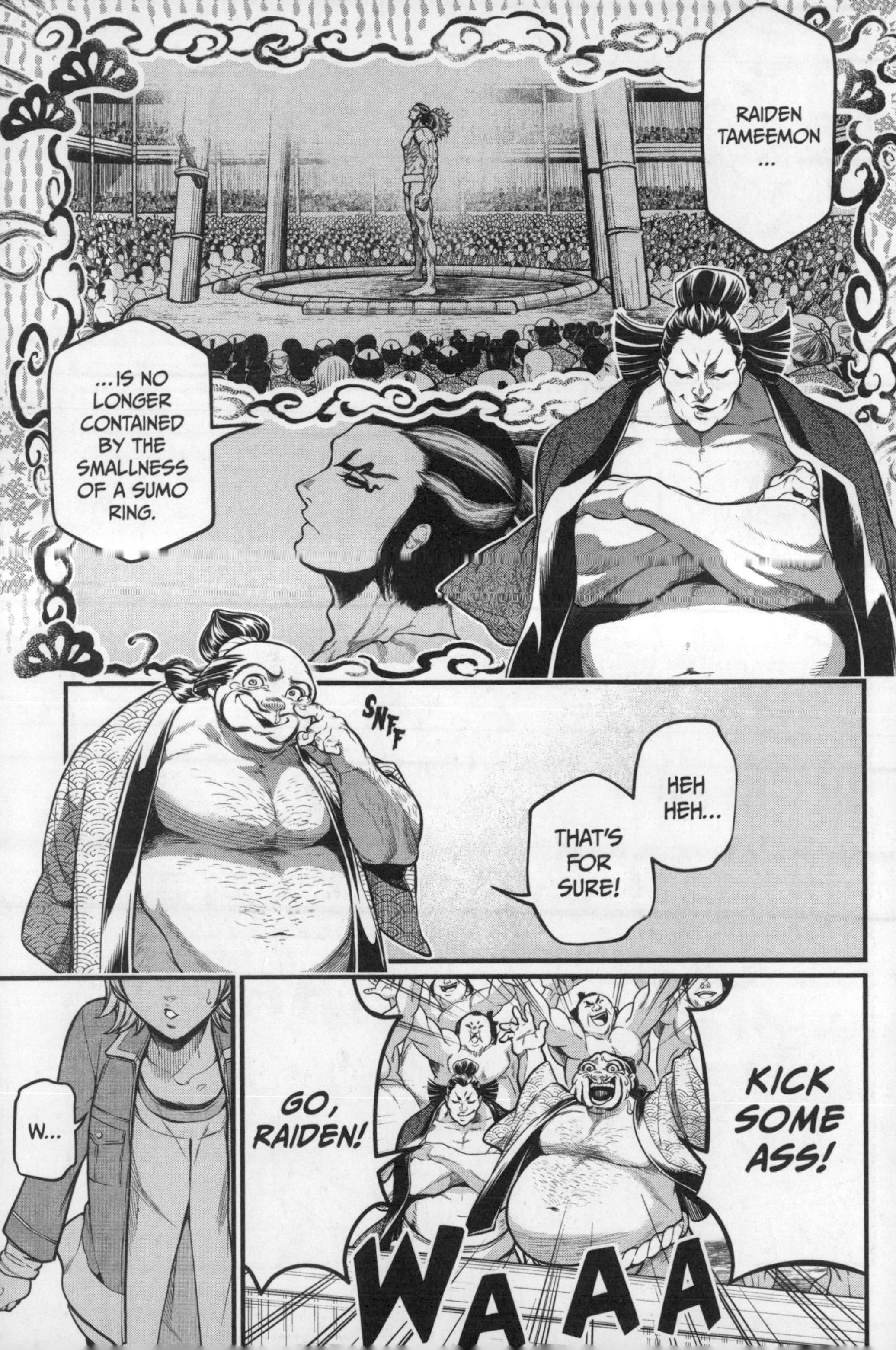
RAIDEN TAMEEMON ...
...IS NO LONGER CONTAINED BY THE SMALLNESS OF A SUMO RING.
SNFF
HEH HEH...
THAT'S FOR SURE!
KICK SOME ASS!
GO, RAIDEN!
WAAA
W...

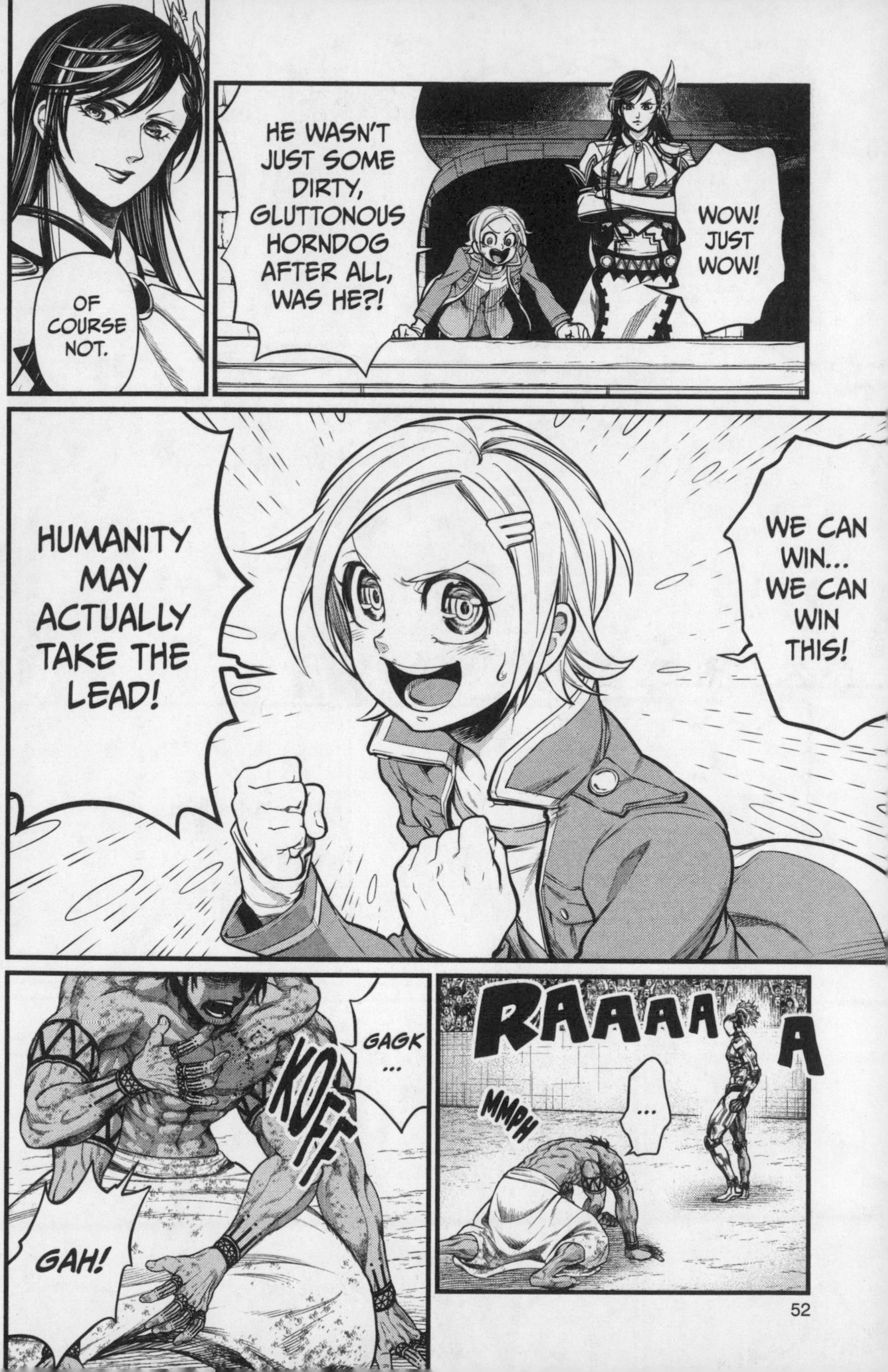
WOW! JUST WOW!
HE WASN'T JUST SOME DIRTY, GLUTTONOUS HORNDOG AFTER ALL, WAS HE?!
OF COURSE NOT.
WE CAN WIN... WE CAN WIN THIS!
HUMANITY MAY ACTUALLY TAKE THE LEAD!
RAAAAA
...
MMPH
GAGK ...
KOFF
GAH!

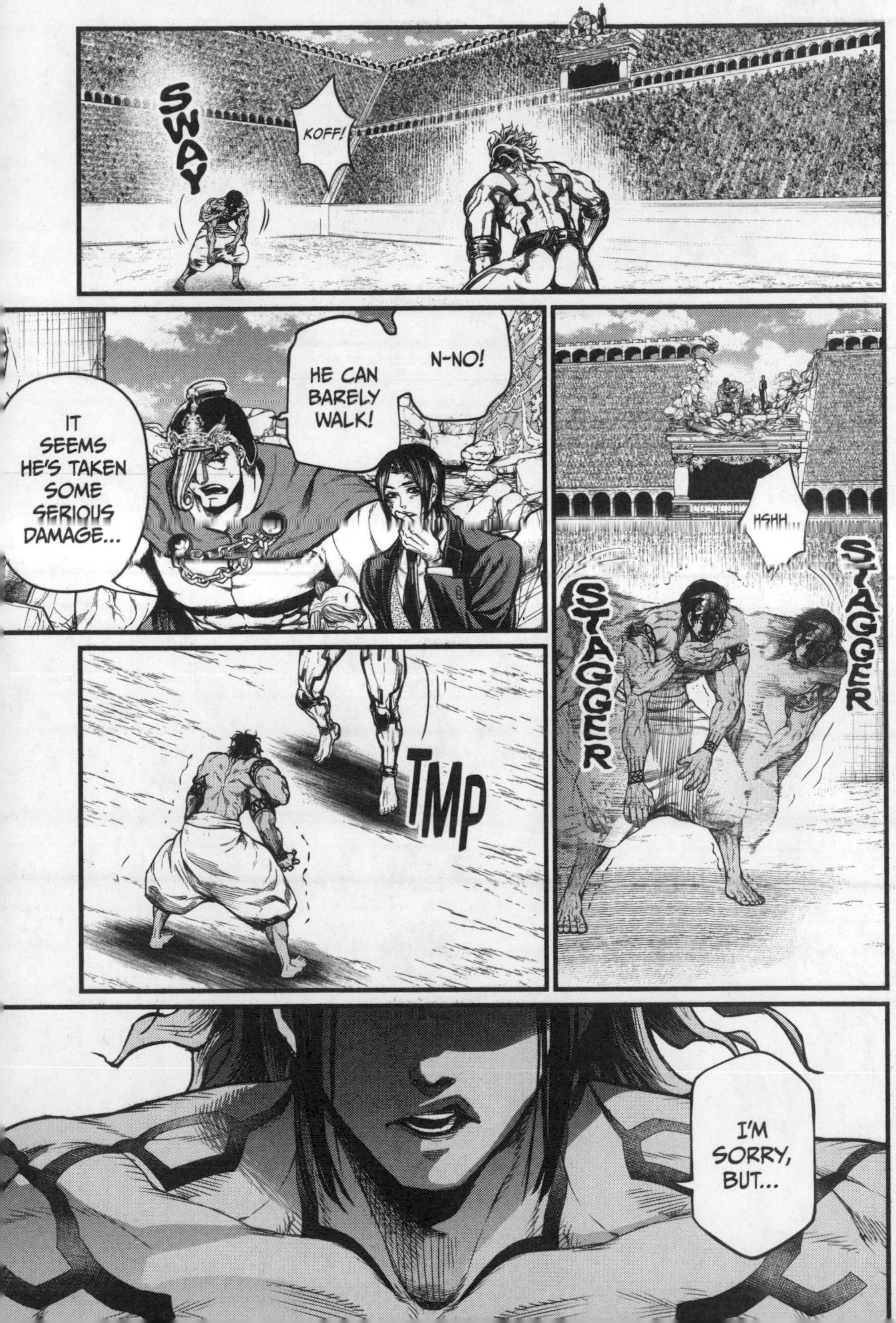
SWAY
KOFF!
HSHH...
STAGGER
STAGGER
N-NO! HE CAN BARELY WALK!
IT SEEMS HE'S TAKEN SOME SERIOUS DAMAGE...
TMP
I'M SORRY, BUT...

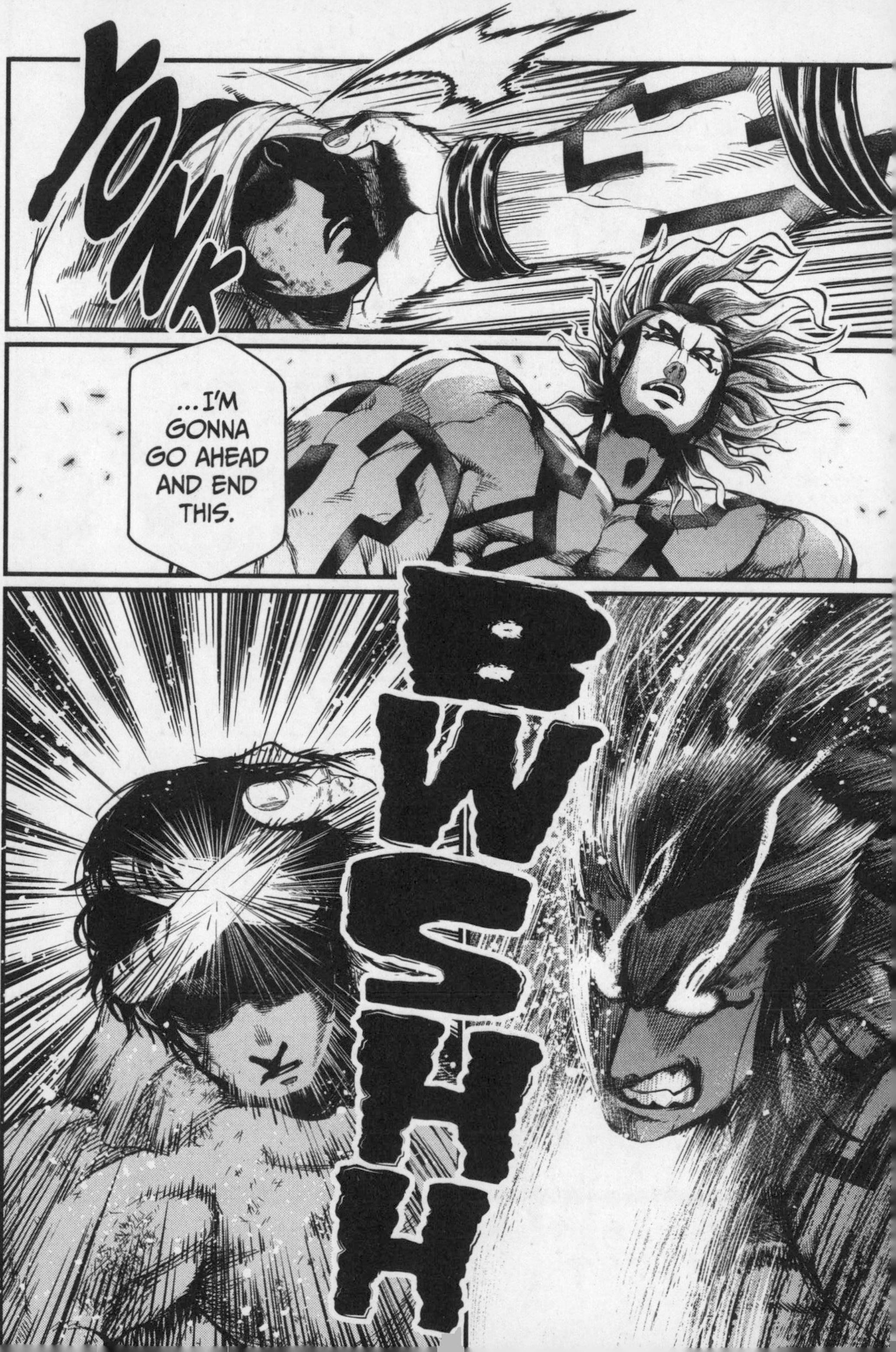
YOINK
...I'M GONNA GO AHEAD AND END THIS.
BWSHH

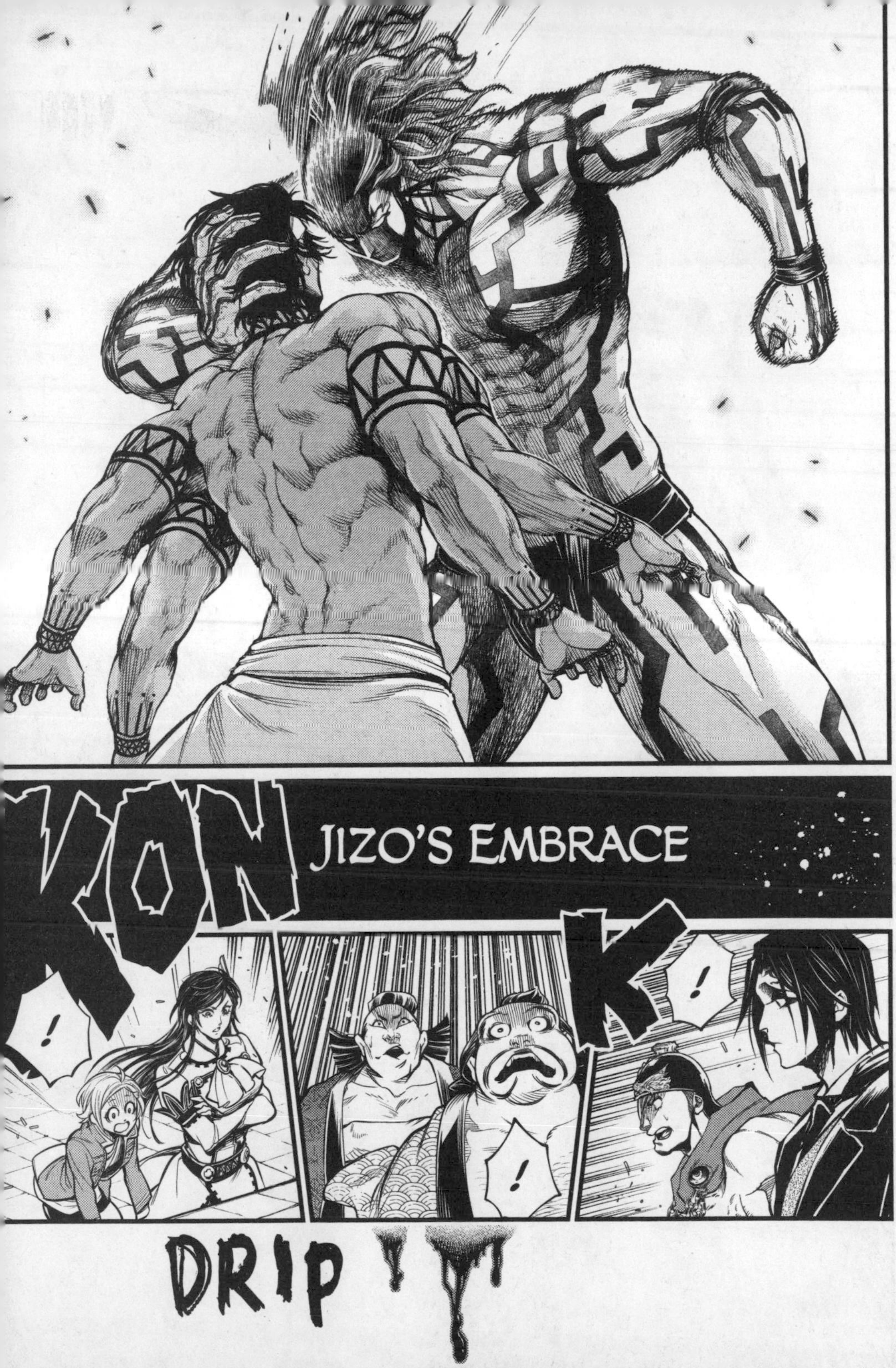
JIZO'S EMBRACE
KON
KO
!
!
!
DRIP

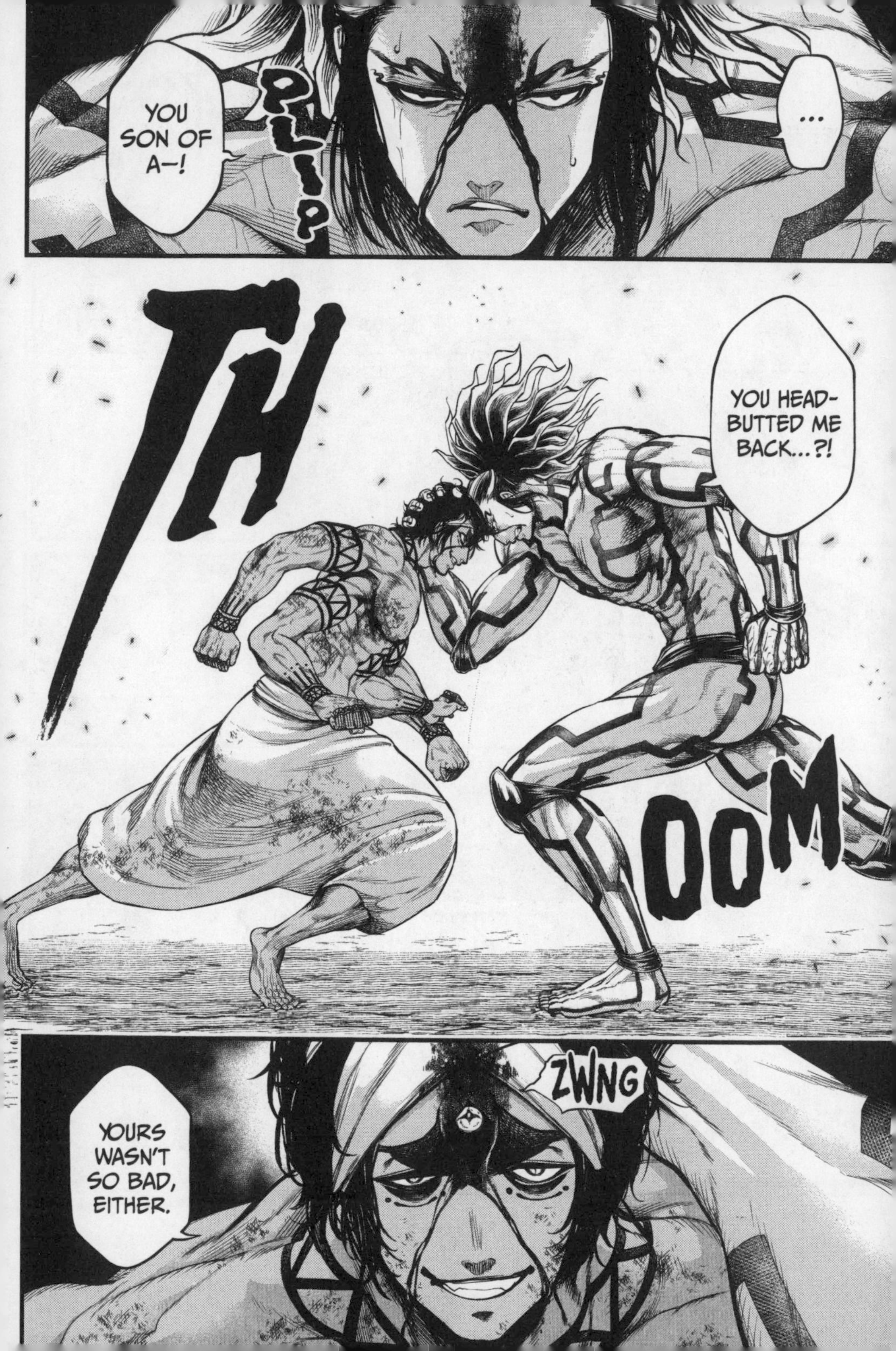
...
PLIP
YOU SON OF A—!
YOU HEAD-BUTTED ME BACK...?!
TH
OOM
ZWNG
YOURS WASN'T SO BAD, EITHER.

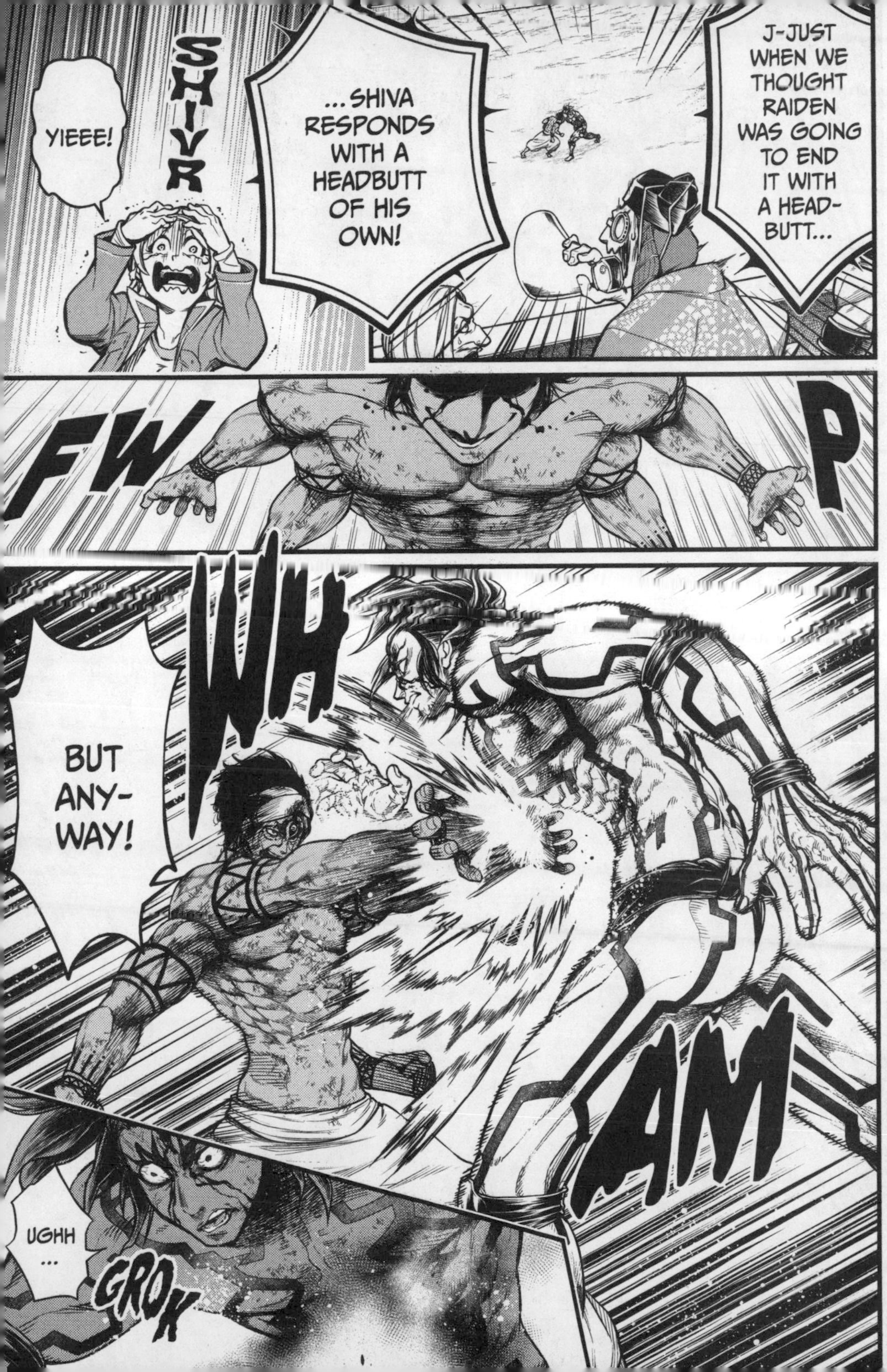
J-JUST WHEN WE THOUGHT RAIDEN WAS GOING TO END IT WITH A HEAD-BUTT...
...SHIVA RESPONDS WITH A HEADBUTT OF HIS OWN!
SHIVR
YIEEE!
FWP
WHAM
BUT ANY-WAY!
UGHH ...
GROK

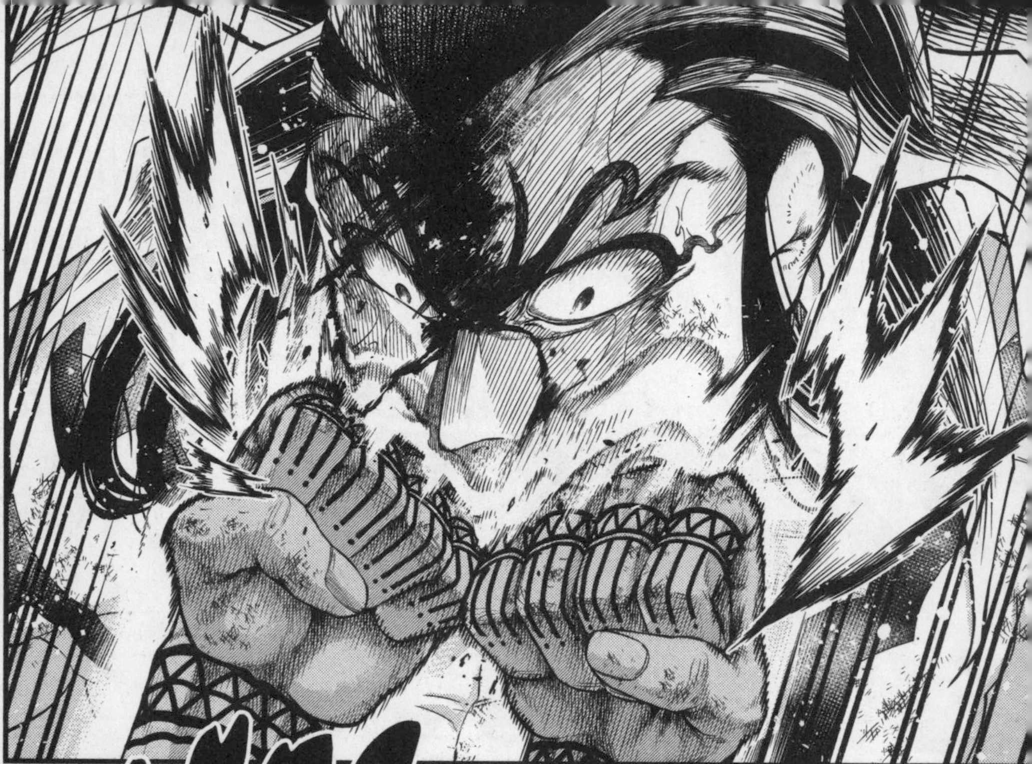

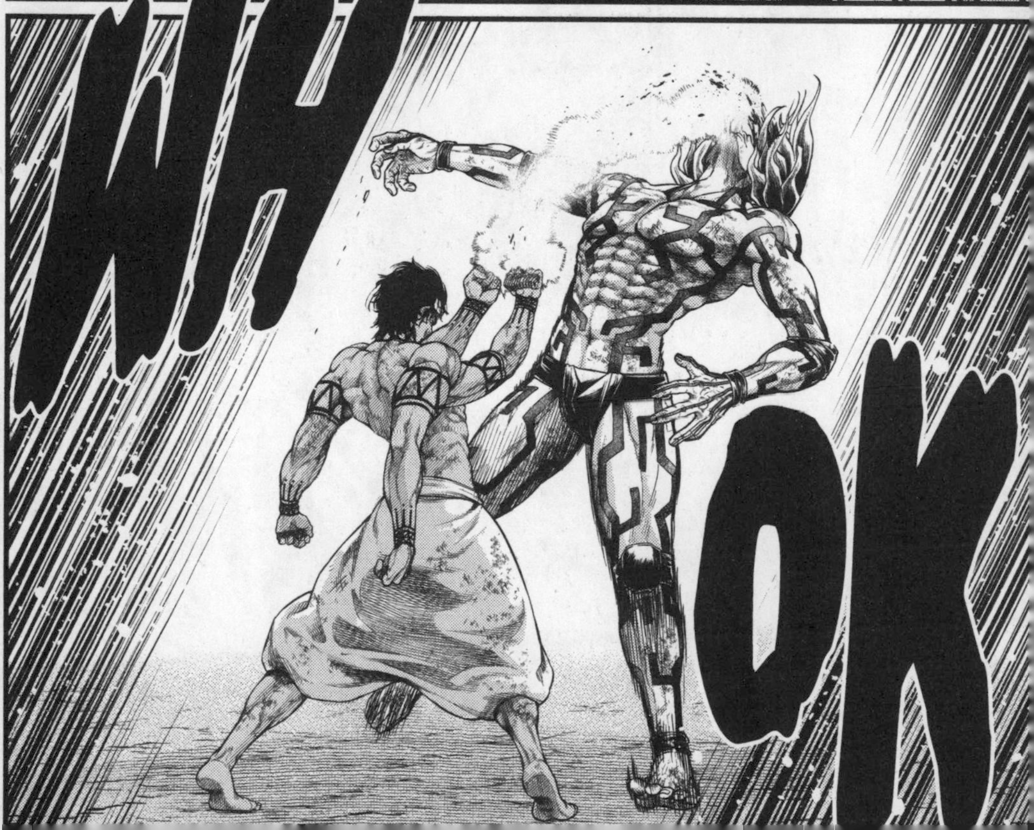
WH
OK

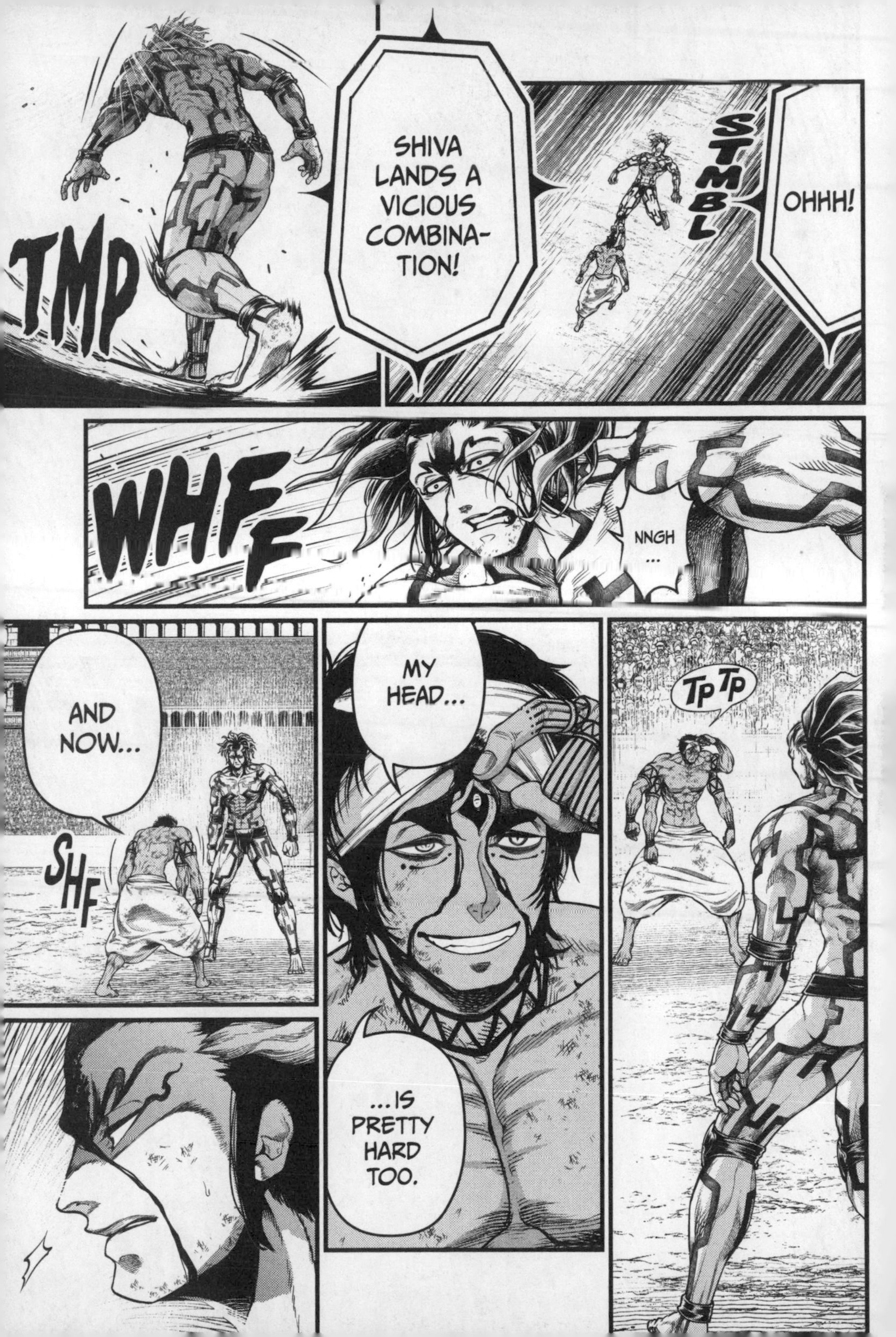
OHHH!
STMBL
SHIVA LANDS A VICIOUS COMBINA-TION!
TMP
NNGH ...
WHFF
TP TP
MY HEAD...
...IS PRETTY HARD TOO.
AND NOW...
SHF

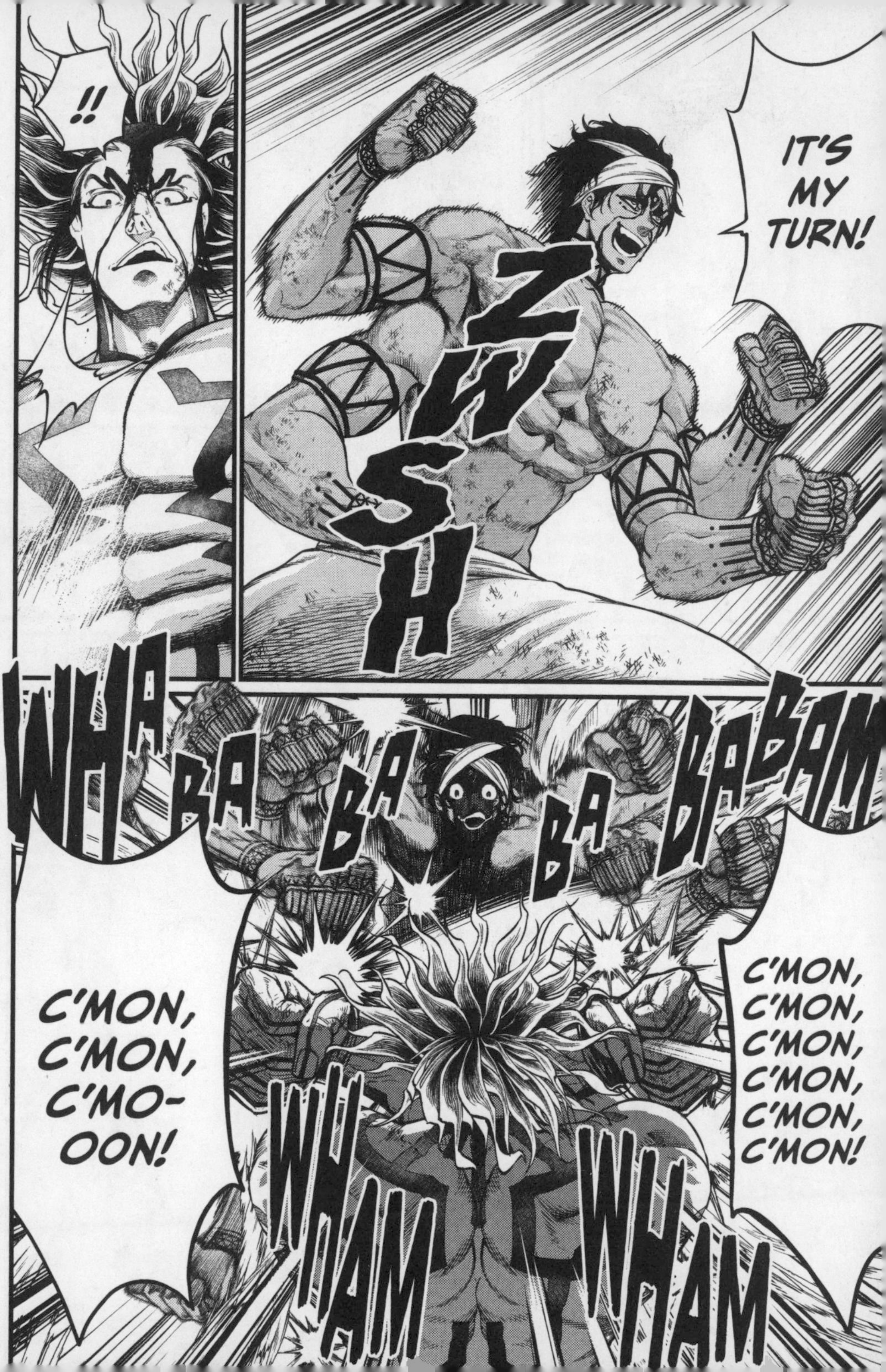
IT'S MY TURN!
ZWSH
!!
WHARABABABABAM
C'MON, C'MON, C'MON, C'MON, C'MON, C'MON!
C'MON, C'MON, C'MO-OON!
WHAM
WHAM

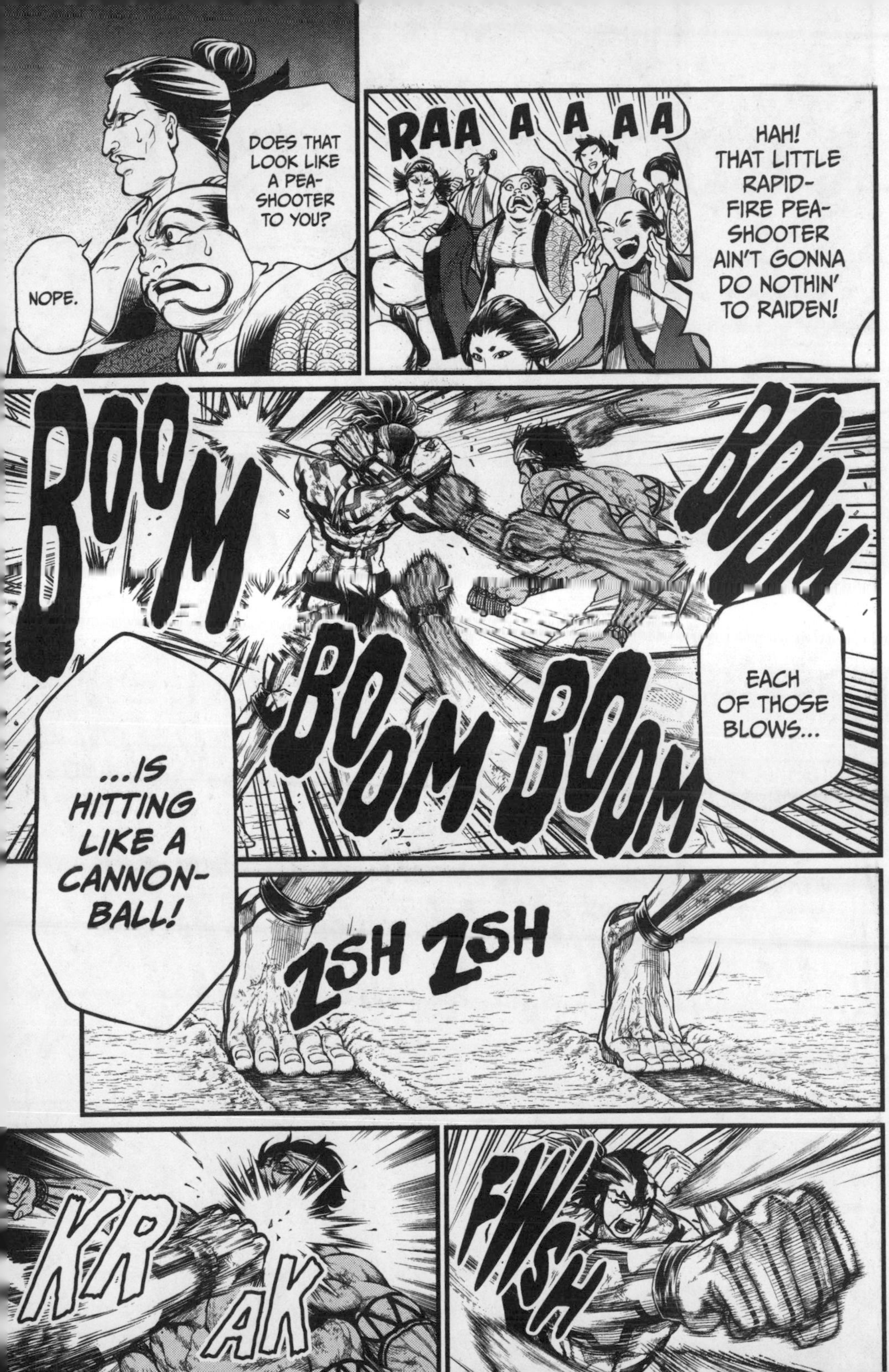
RAA A A A A
HAH! THAT LITTLE RAPID-FIRE PEA-SHOOTER AIN'T GONNA DO NOTHIN' TO RAIDEN!
DOES THAT LOOK LIKE A PEA-SHOOTER TO YOU?
NOPE.
BOOM
EACH OF THOSE BLOWS...
BOOM BOOM
BOOM
...IS HITTING LIKE A CANNON-BALL!
ZSH ZSH
FWSH
KRAK

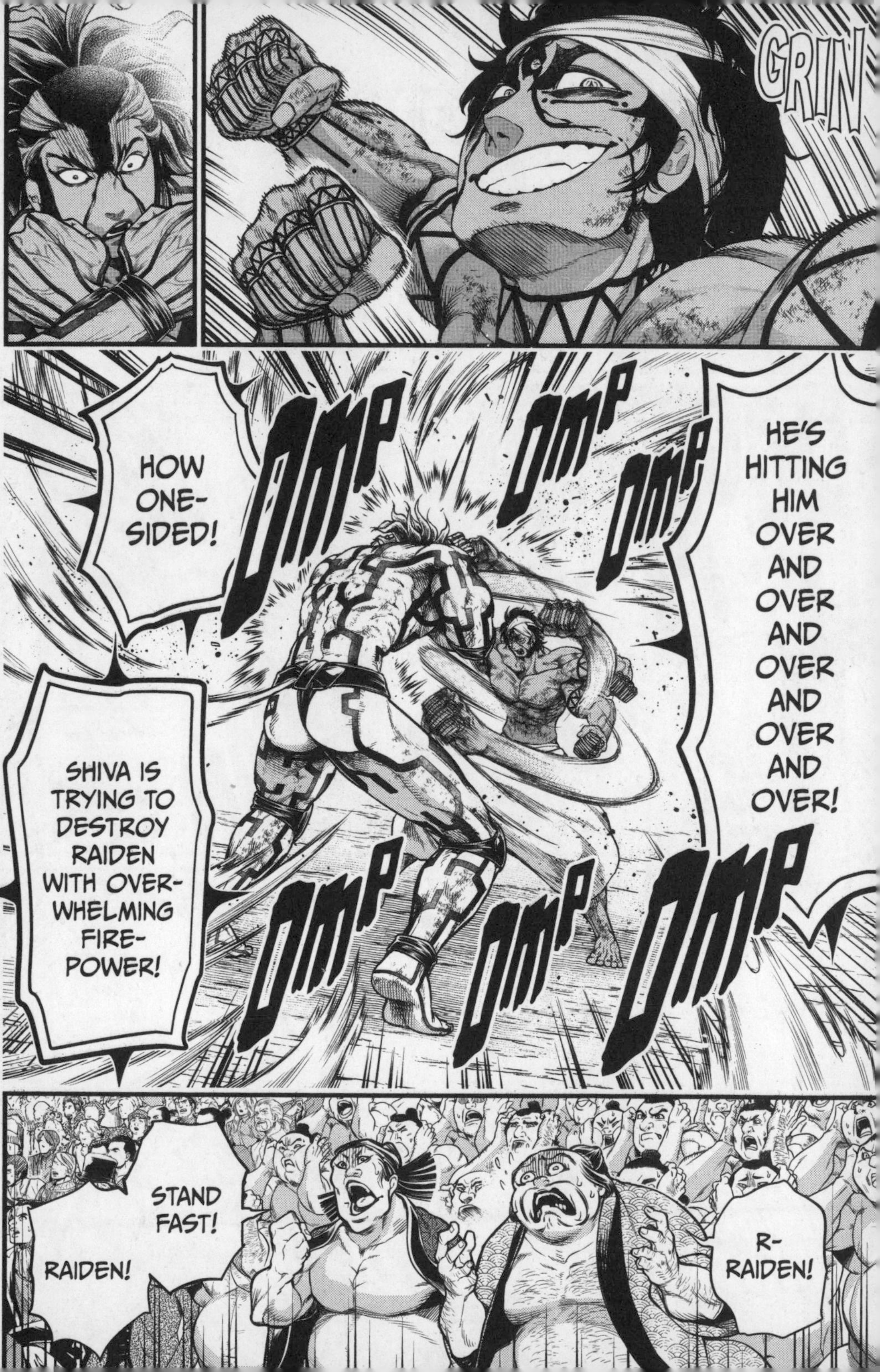
GRIN
HE'S HITTING HIM OVER AND OVER AND OVER AND OVER AND OVER AND OVER!
DMP DMP DMP
DMP
HOW ONE-SIDED!
DMP DMP DMP
SHIVA IS TRYING TO DESTROY RAIDEN WITH OVER-WHELMING FIRE-POWER!
R-RAIDEN!
STAND FAST!
RAIDEN!

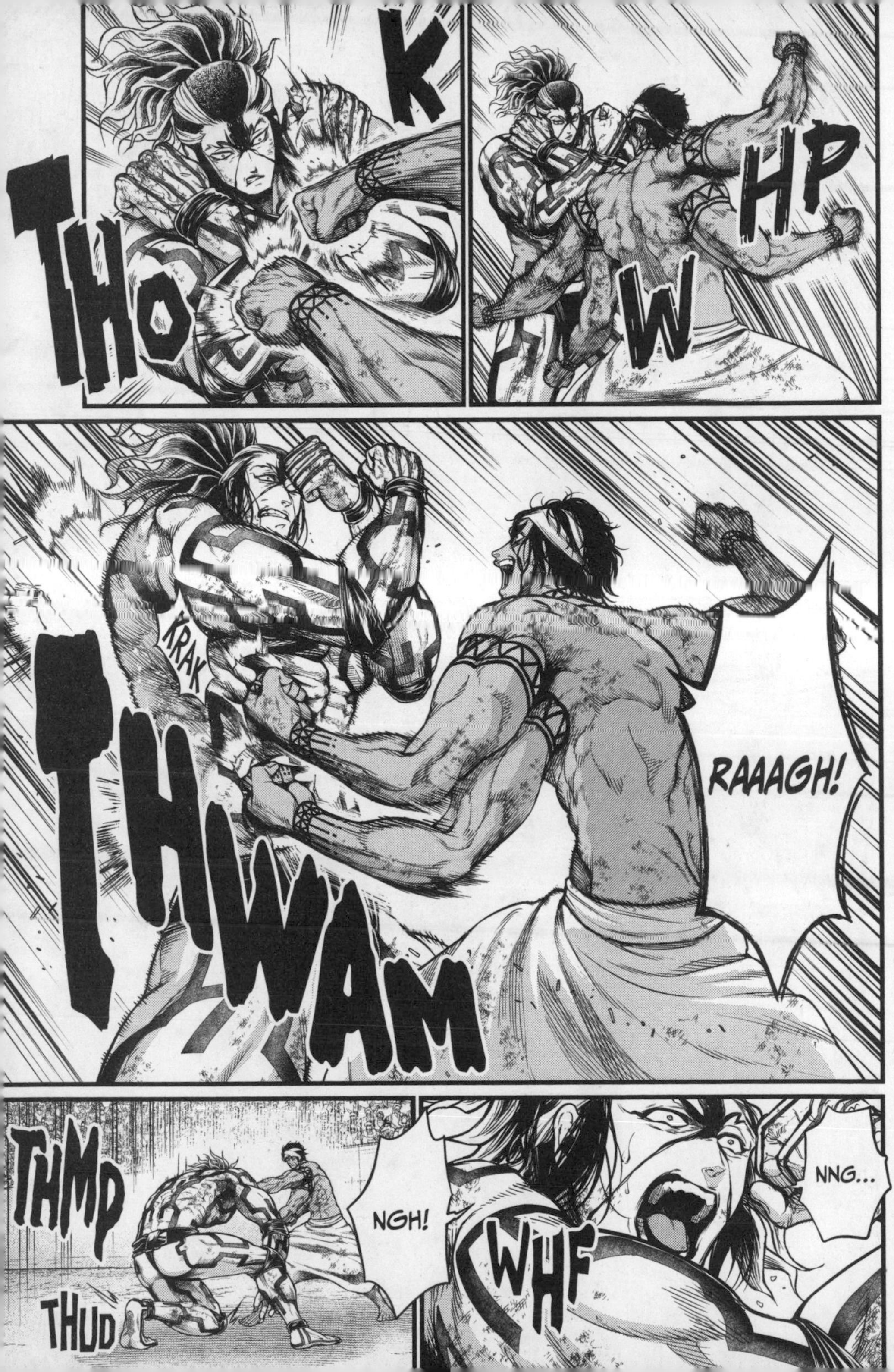
WHP
THOK
RAAAGH!
KRAK
THWAM
NNG...
NGH!
WHF
THMP
THUD

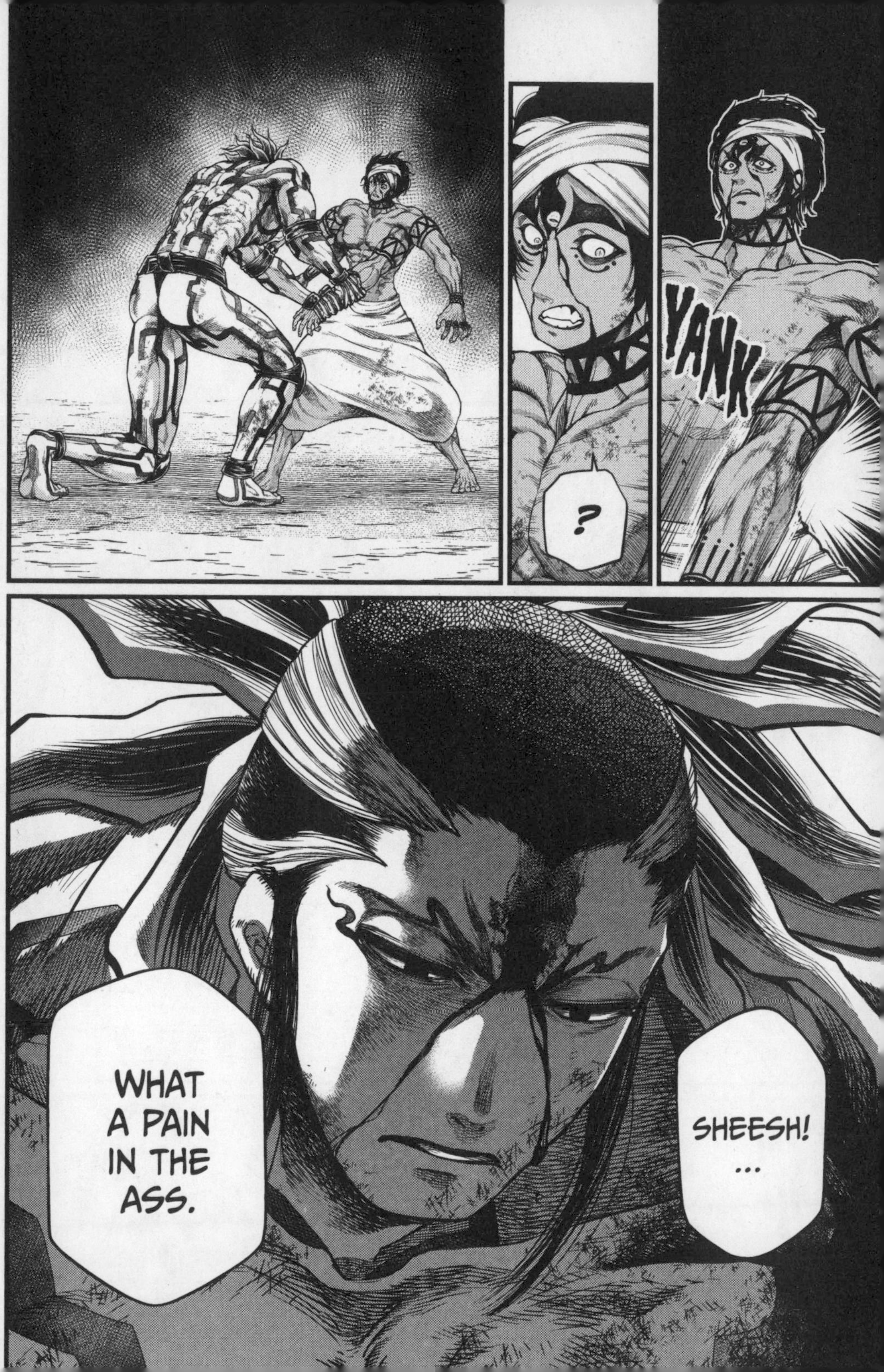
YANK
?
SHEESH! ...
WHAT A PAIN IN THE ASS.

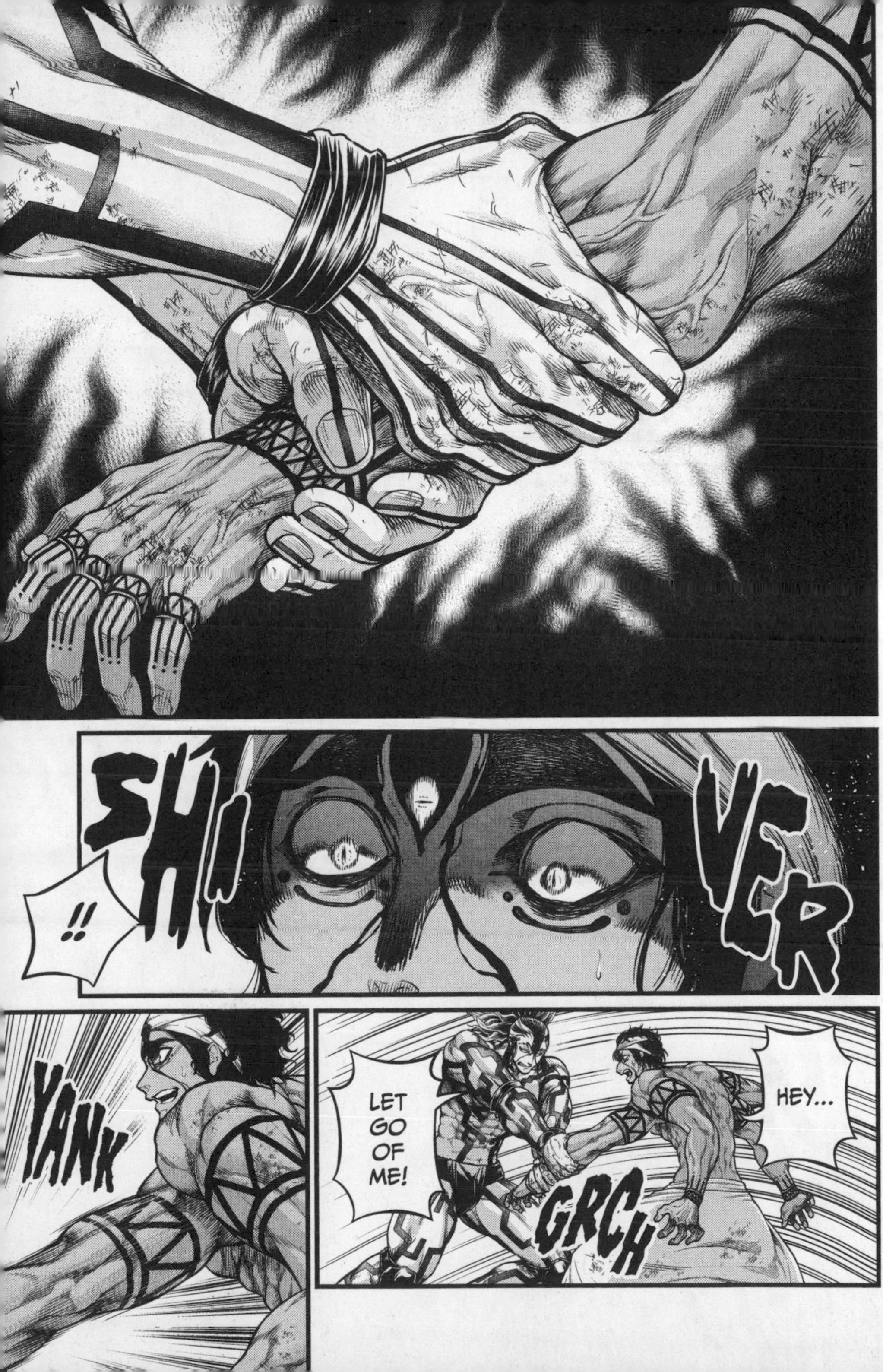
SHIVER
!!
HEY...
LET GO OF ME!
GRCH
YANK

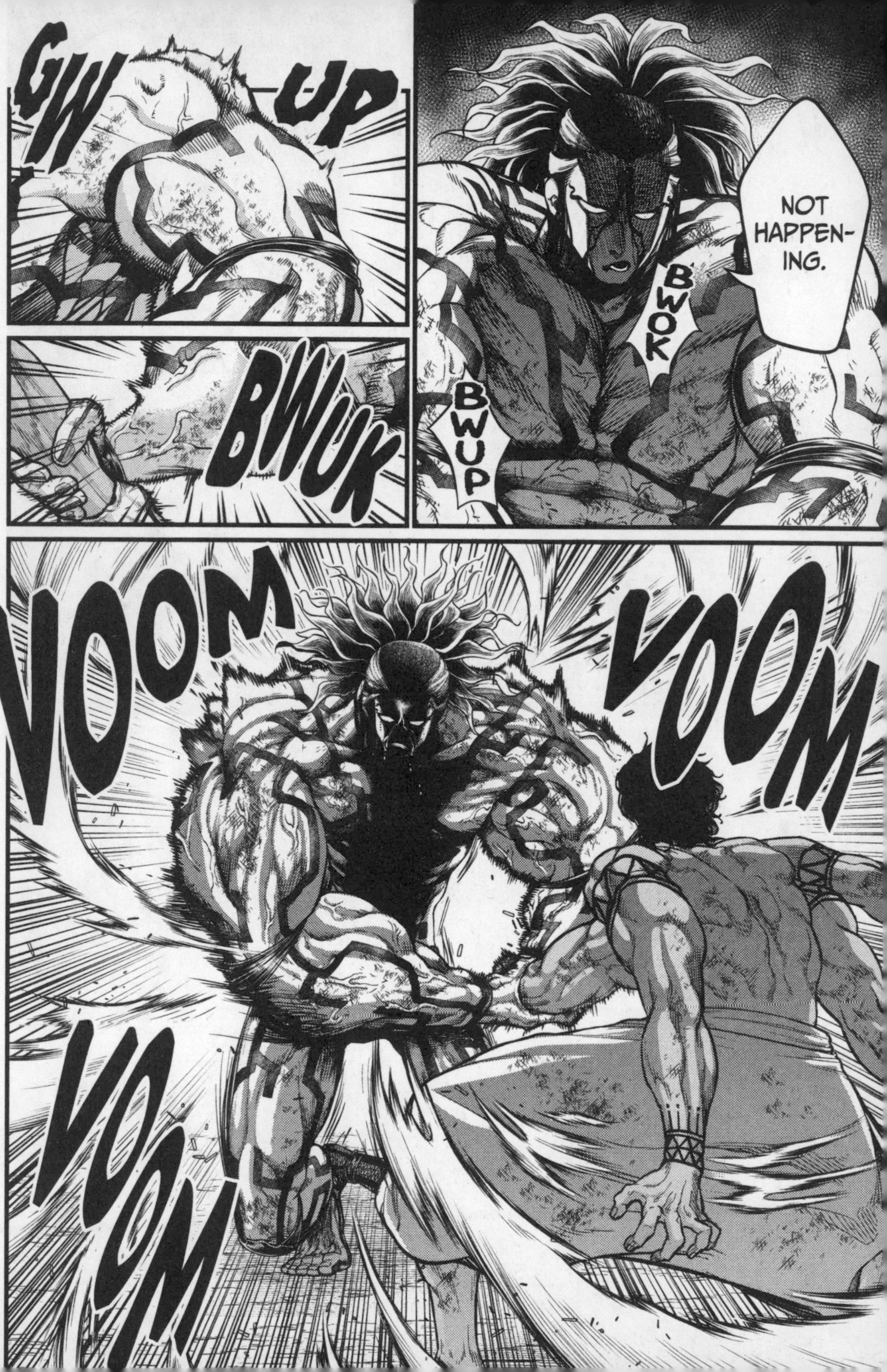
NOT HAPPEN-ING.
BWOK
BWUP
GW-UP
BWUK
VOOM
VOOM
VOOM

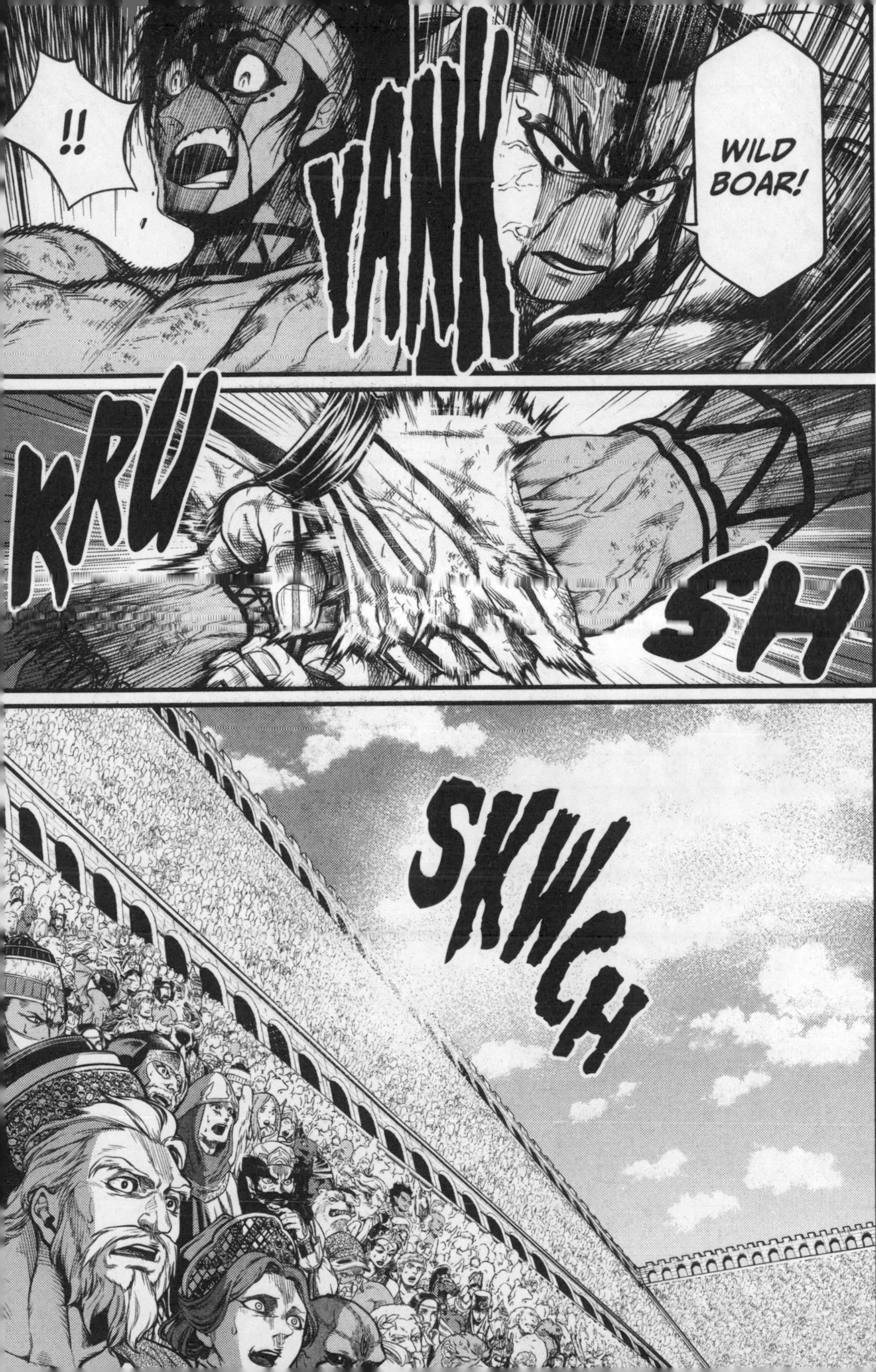
WILD BOAR!
YANK
!!
KRU
SH
SKWCH

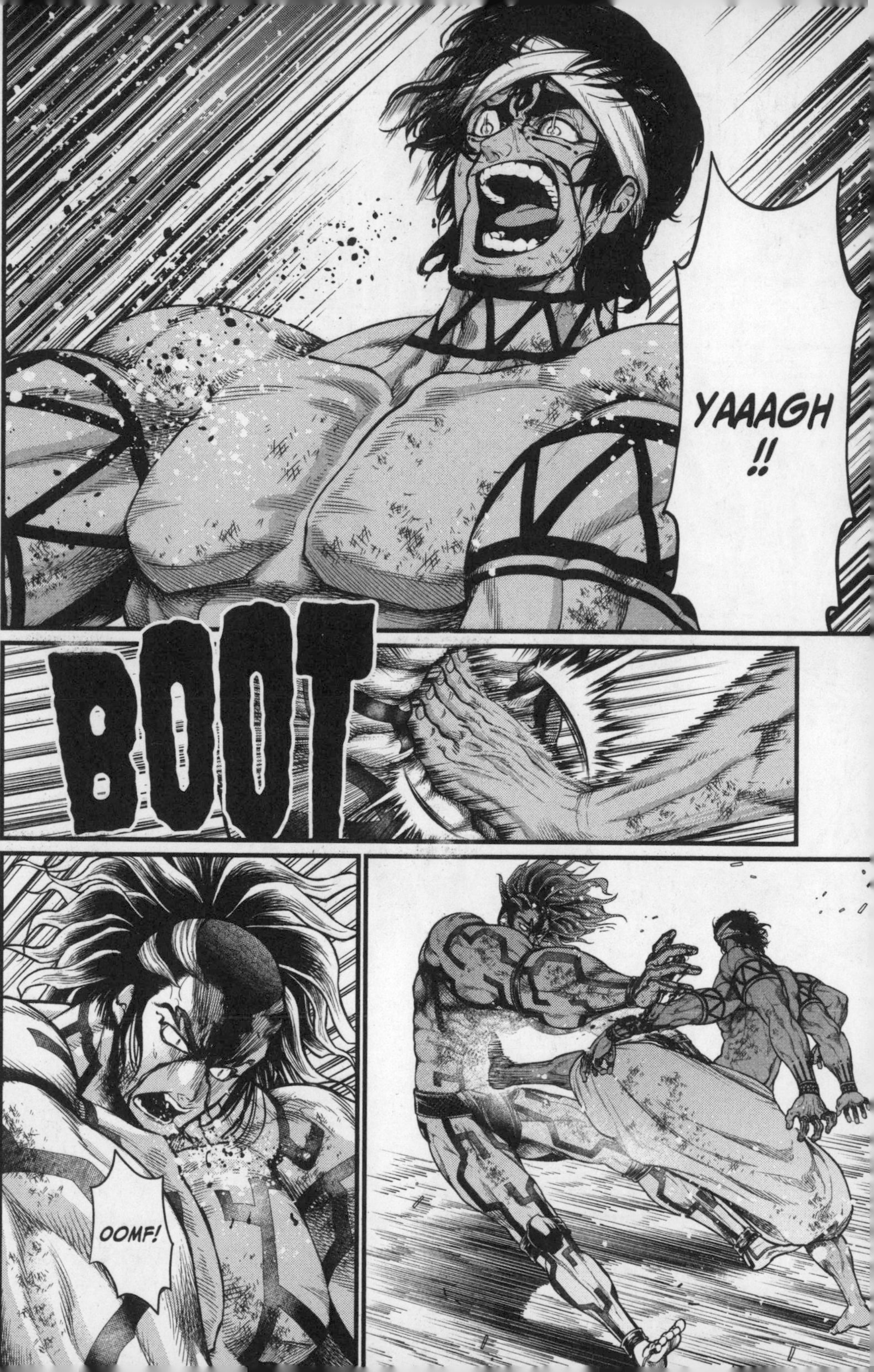
YAAAGH !!
BOOT
OOMF!

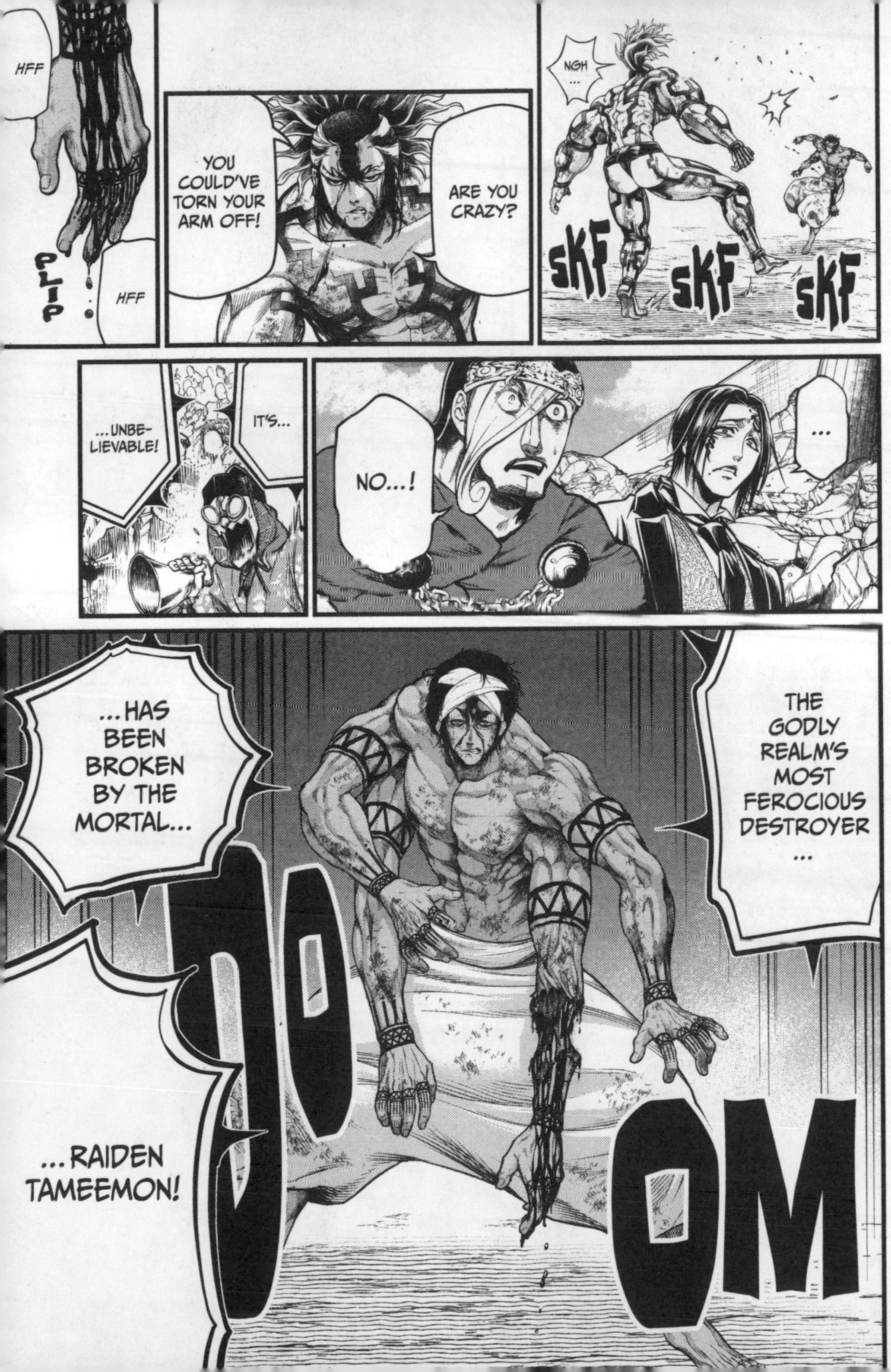
NGH...
SKF
SKF
SKF
ARE YOU CRAZY?
YOU COULD'VE TORN YOUR ARM OFF!
HFF
PLIP
HFF
...
NO...!
IT'S...
...UNBE-LIEVABLE!
THE GODLY REALM'S MOST FEROCIOUS DESTROYER...
...HAS BEEN BROKEN BY THE MORTAL...
...RAIDEN TAMEEMON!
DOOM

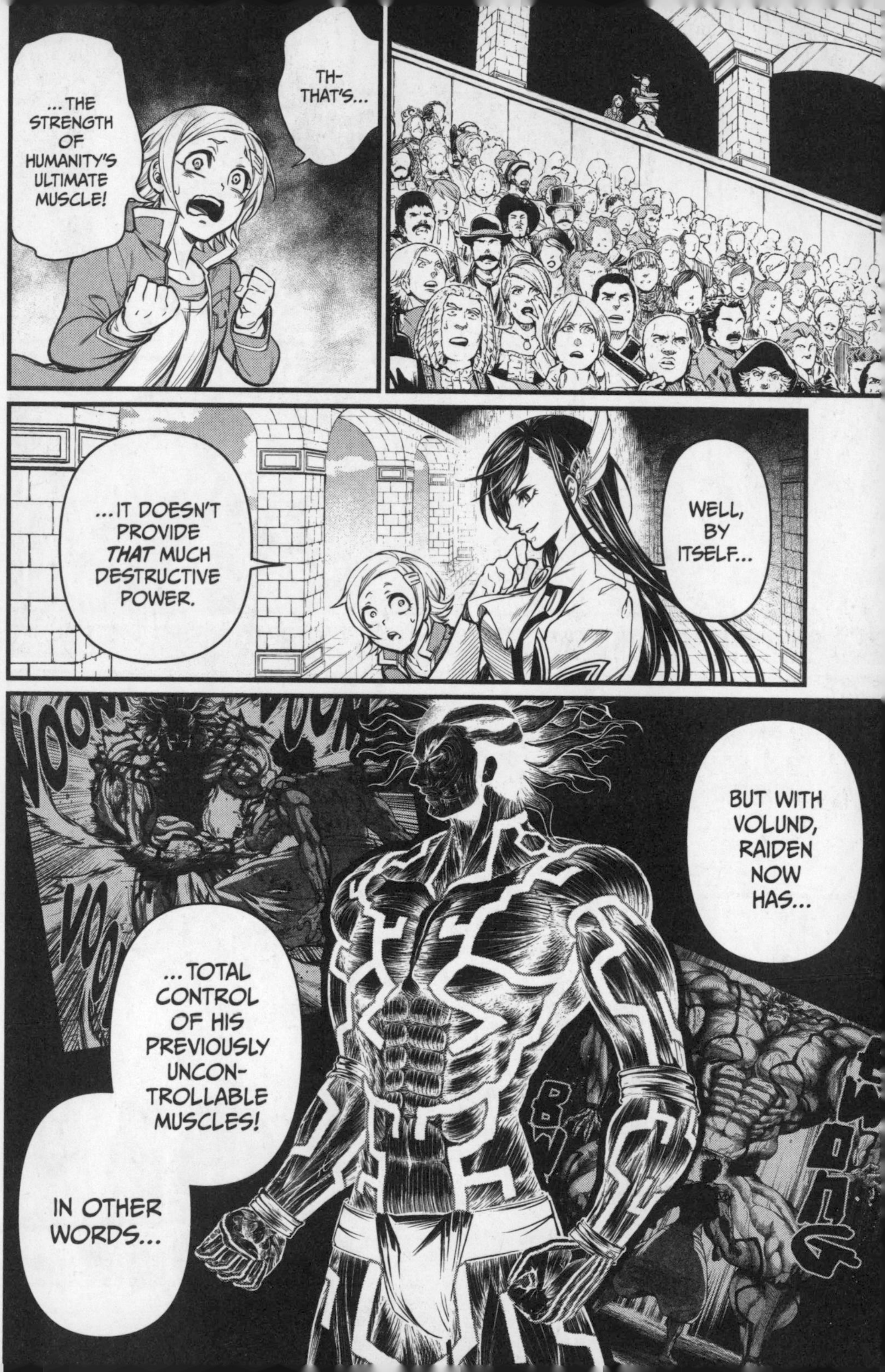
TH- THAT'S...
...THE STRENGTH OF HUMANITY'S ULTIMATE MUSCLE!
WELL, BY ITSELF...
...IT DOESN'T PROVIDE *THAT* MUCH DESTRUCTIVE POWER.
BUT WITH VOLUND, RAIDEN NOW HAS...
...TOTAL CONTROL OF HIS PREVIOUSLY UNCON-TROLLABLE MUSCLES!
IN OTHER WORDS...

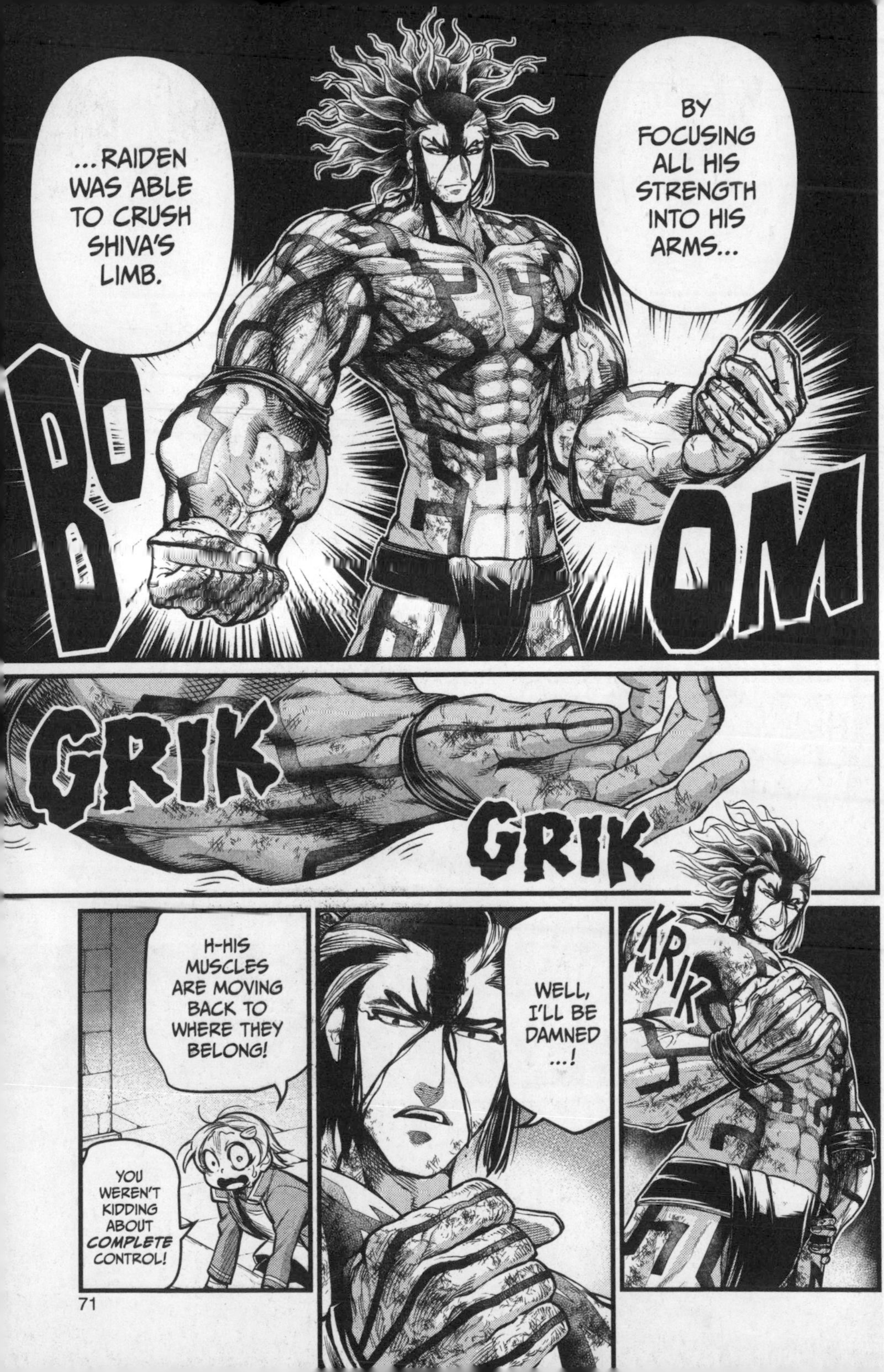
BY FOCUSING ALL HIS STRENGTH INTO HIS ARMS...
...RAIDEN WAS ABLE TO CRUSH SHIVA'S LIMB.
BOOM
GRIK
GRIK
KRIK
KRIK
WELL, I'LL BE DAMNED ...!
H-HIS MUSCLES ARE MOVING BACK TO WHERE THEY BELONG!
YOU WEREN'T KIDDING ABOUT *COMPLETE* CONTROL!

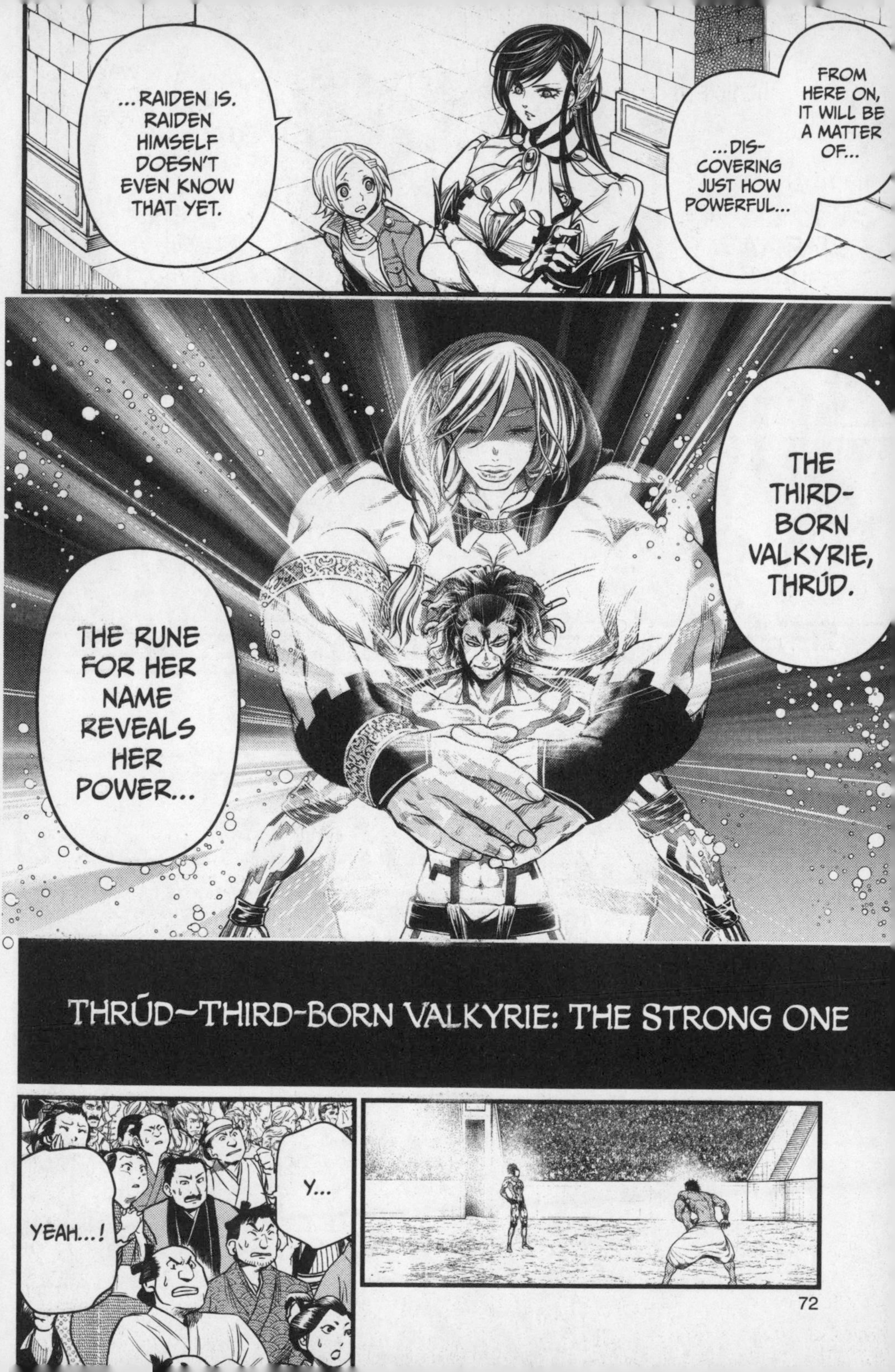
FROM HERE ON, IT WILL BE A MATTER OF...
...DIS-COVERING JUST HOW POWERFUL...
...RAIDEN IS. RAIDEN HIMSELF DOESN'T EVEN KNOW THAT YET.
THE THIRD-BORN VALKYRIE, THRÚD.
THE RUNE FOR HER NAME REVEALS HER POWER...
THRÚD~THIRD-BORN VALKYRIE: THE STRONG ONE
Y...
YEAH...!

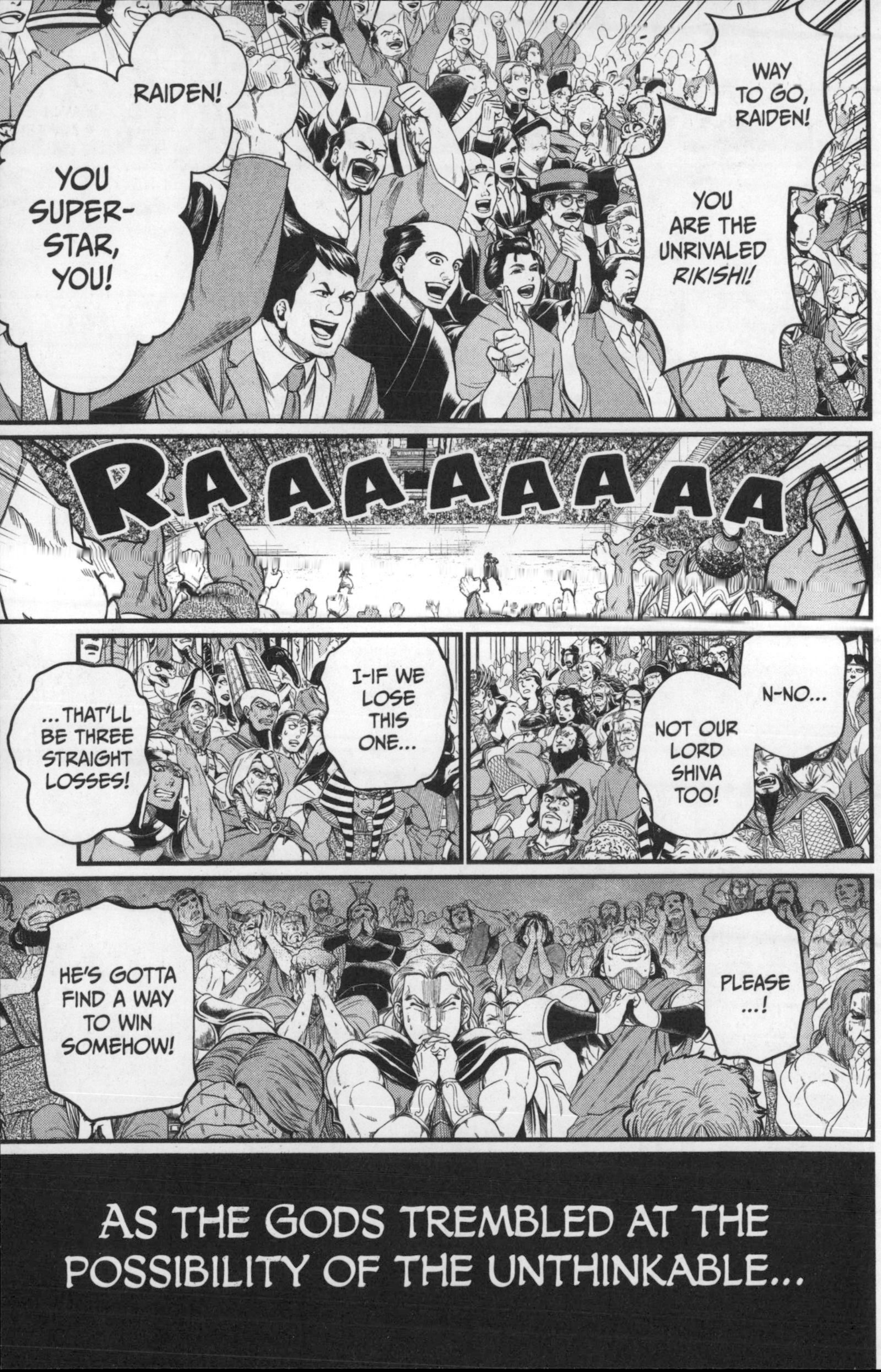
WAY TO GO, RAIDEN!
YOU ARE THE UNRIVALED RIKISHI!
RAIDEN!
YOU SUPER-STAR, YOU!
RAAAAAAAA
N-NO...
NOT OUR LORD SHIVA TOO!
I-IF WE LOSE THIS ONE...
...THAT'LL BE THREE STRAIGHT LOSSES!
PLEASE ...!
HE'S GOTTA FIND A WAY TO WIN SOMEHOW!
AS THE GODS TREMBLED AT THE POSSIBILITY OF THE UNTHINKABLE...

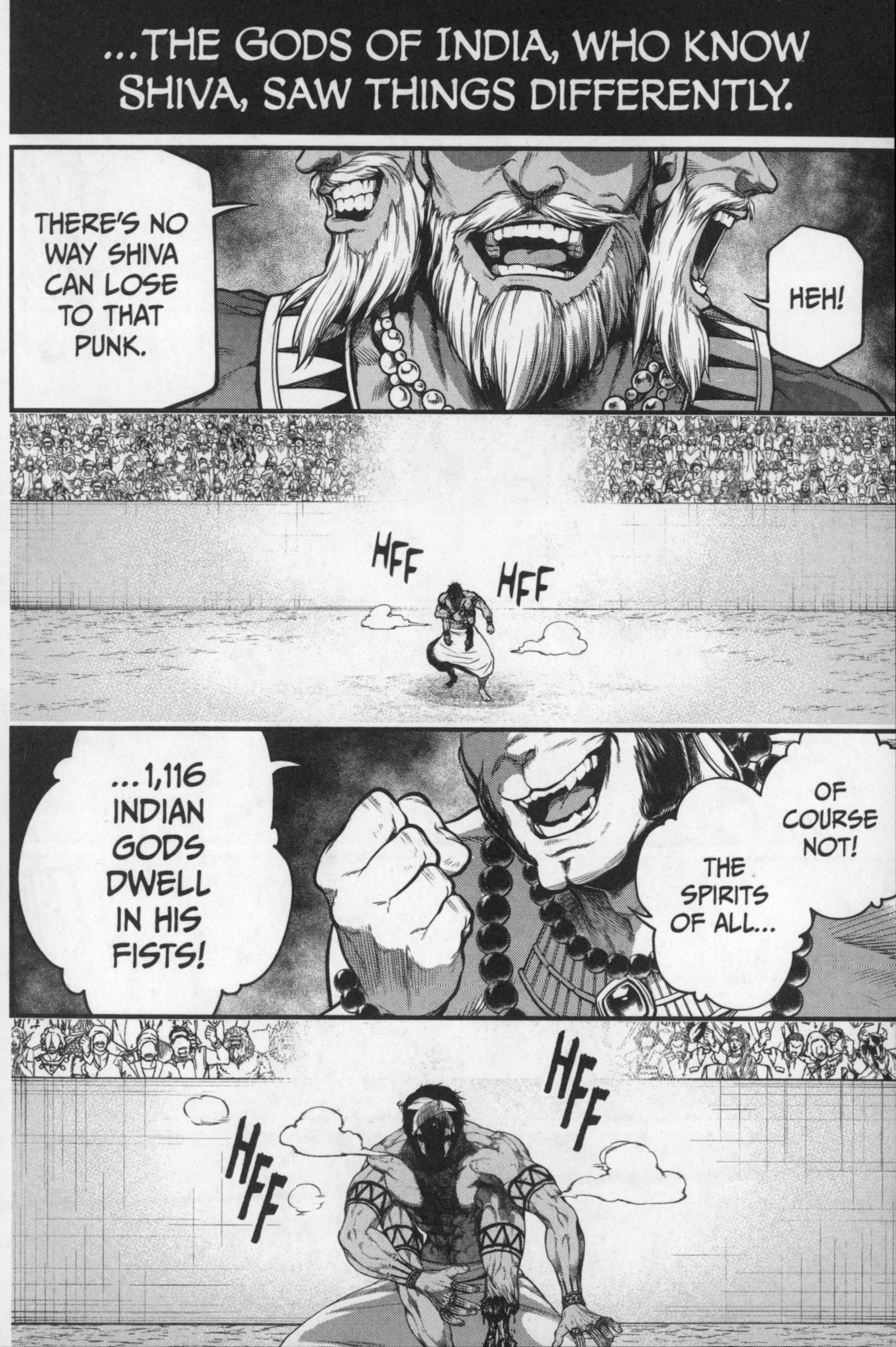
...THE GODS OF INDIA, WHO KNOW SHIVA, SAW THINGS DIFFERENTLY.
HEH!
THERE'S NO WAY SHIVA CAN LOSE TO THAT PUNK.
HFF
HFF
OF COURSE NOT!
THE SPIRITS OF ALL...
...1,116 INDIAN GODS DWELL IN HIS FISTS!
HFF
HFF

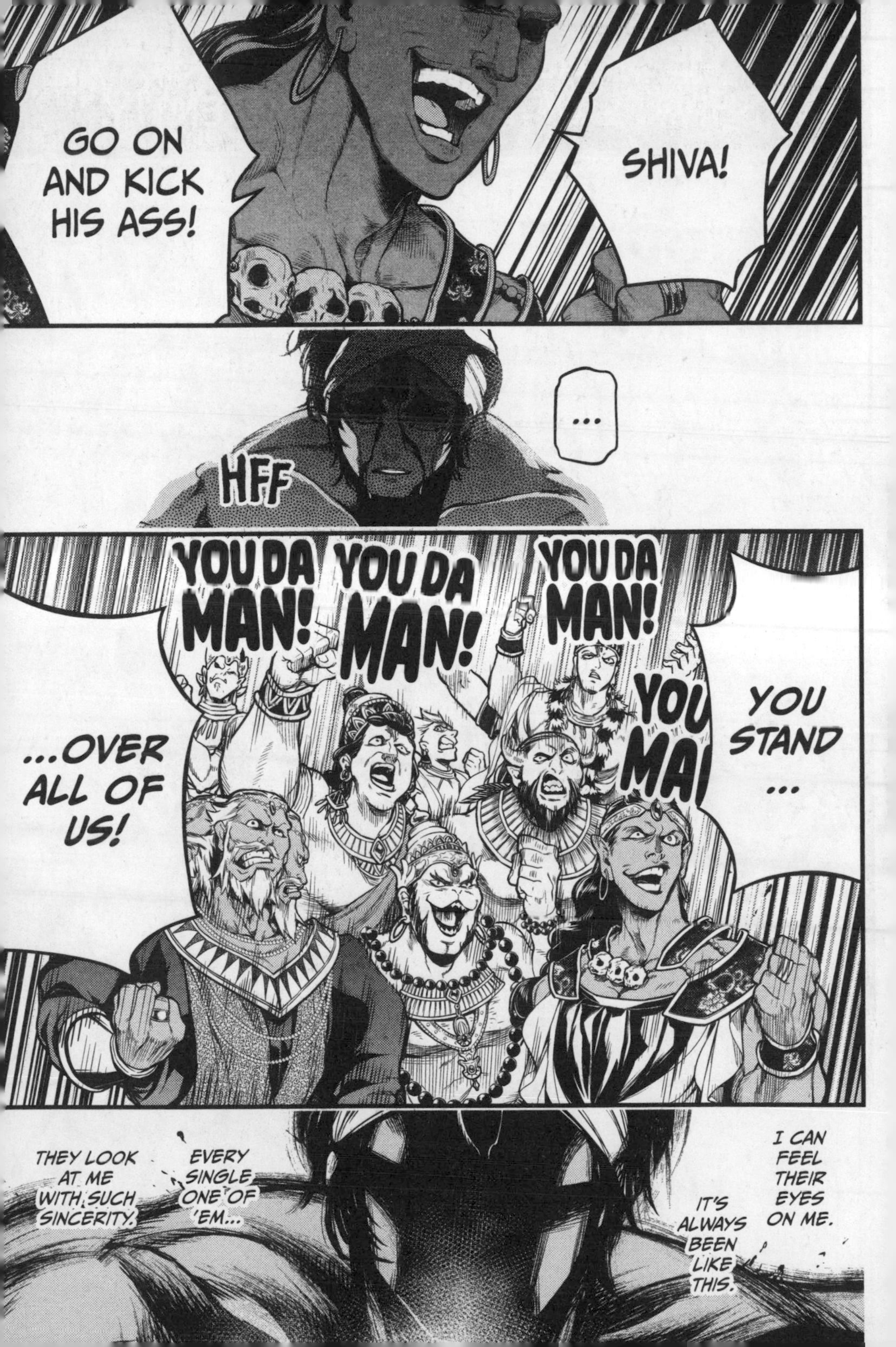
SHIVA!
GO ON AND KICK HIS ASS!
...
HFF
YOU STAND ...
YOU DA MAN!
YOU DA MAN!
YOU DA MAN!
YOU MA
...OVER ALL OF US!
I CAN FEEL THEIR EYES ON ME.
IT'S ALWAYS BEEN LIKE THIS.
EVERY SINGLE ONE OF 'EM...
THEY LOOK AT ME WITH SUCH SINCERITY.

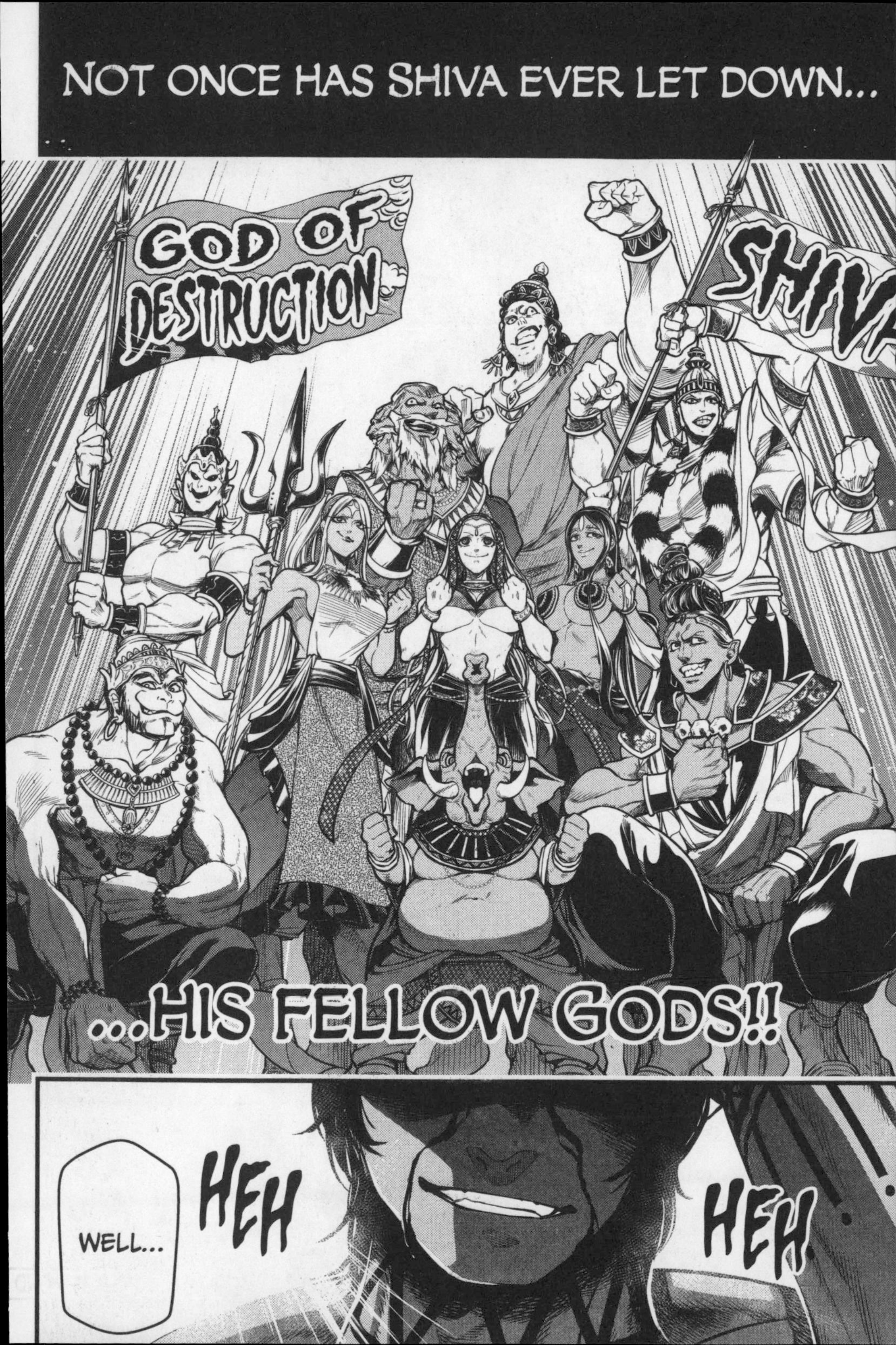
NOT ONCE HAS SHIVA EVER LET DOWN...
SHIV
GOD OF DESTRUCTION
...HIS FELLOW GODS!!
HEH
HEH
WELL...

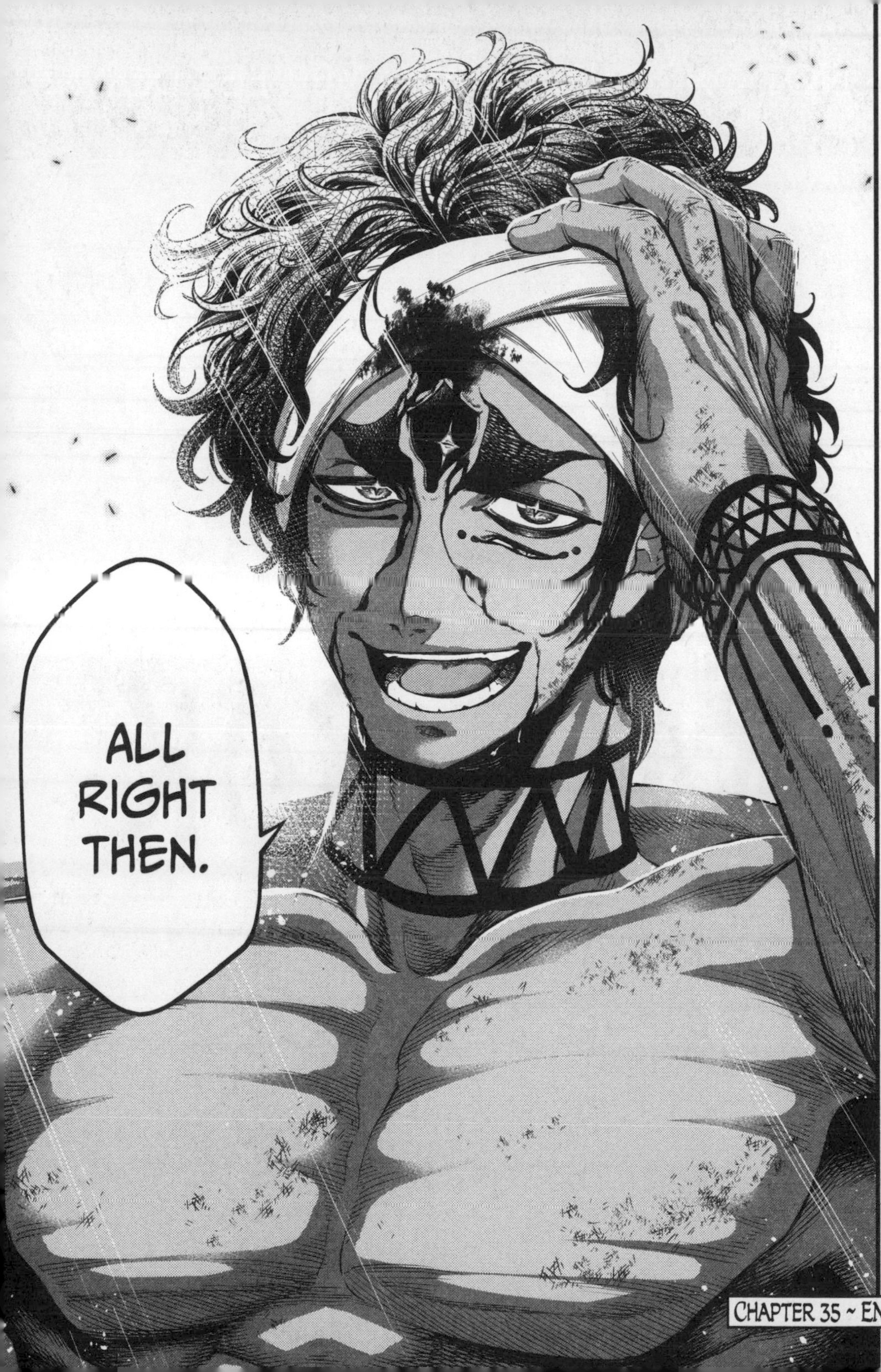
ALL RIGHT THEN.
CHAPTER 35 ~ END

RECORD OF

RAGNAROK

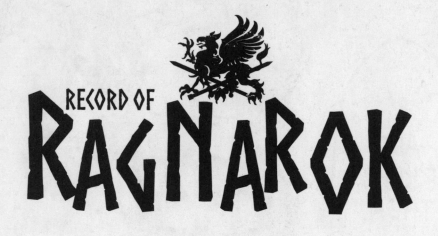

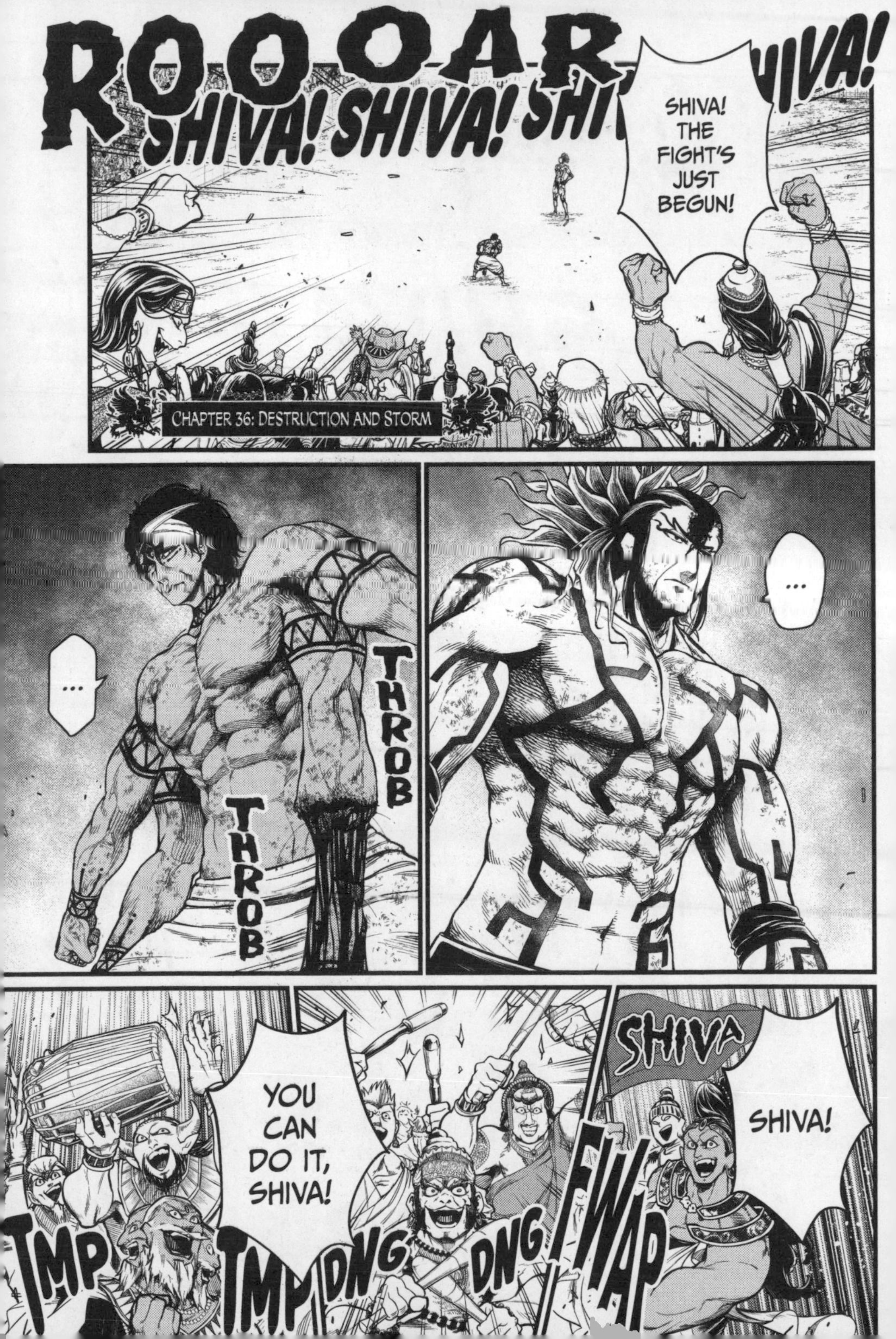
ROOOAR
SHIVA! SHIVA! SHI IVA!
SHIVA! THE FIGHT'S JUST BEGUN!
CHAPTER 36: DESTRUCTION AND STORM
...
...
THROB THROB
SHIVA
SHIVA!
FWAP
DNG DNG
YOU CAN DO IT, SHIVA!
TMP TMP

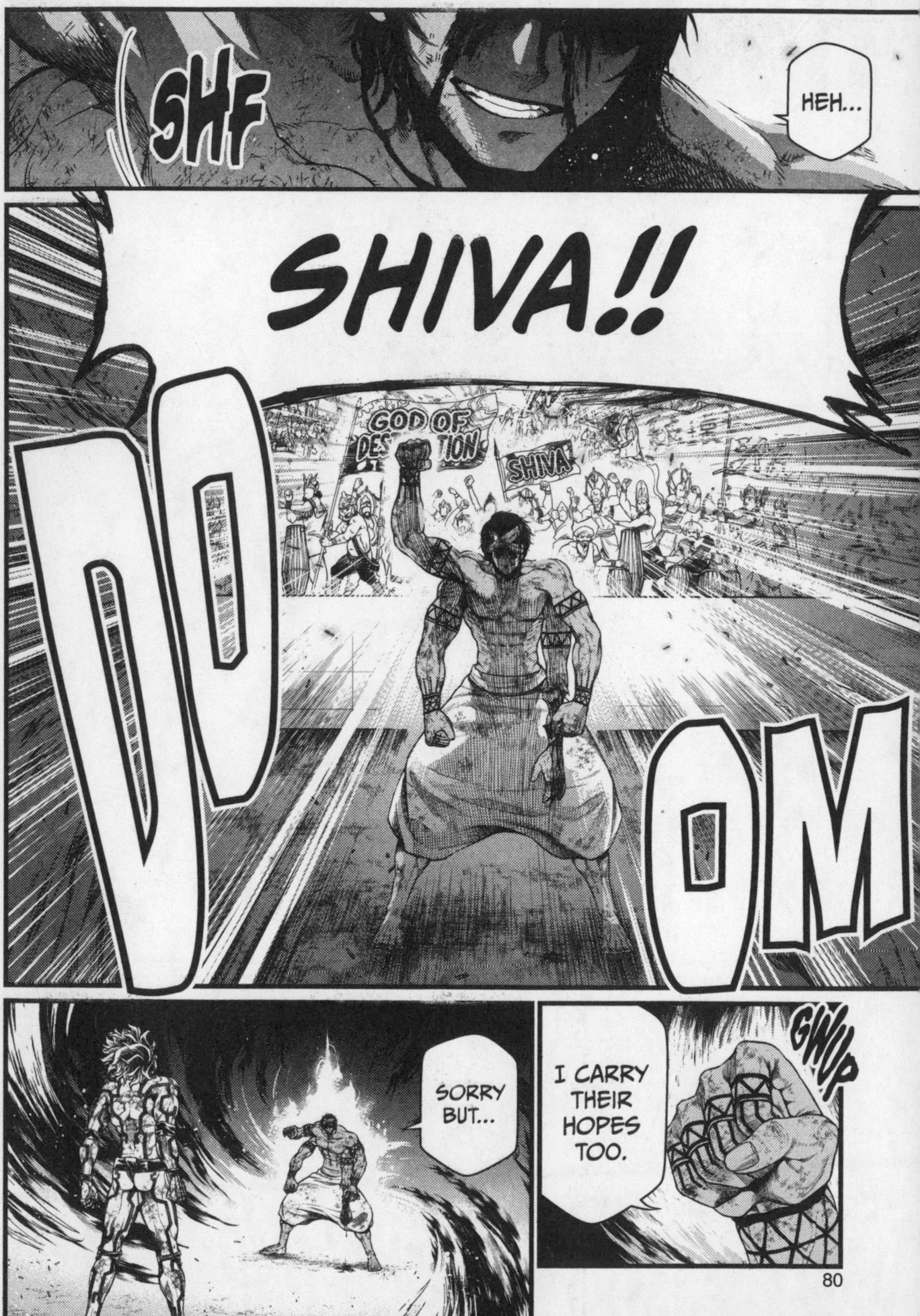
SHF
HEH...
SHIVA!!
GOD OF DES TION
SHIVA
DOOM
SORRY BUT...
I CARRY THEIR HOPES TOO.
GWUP

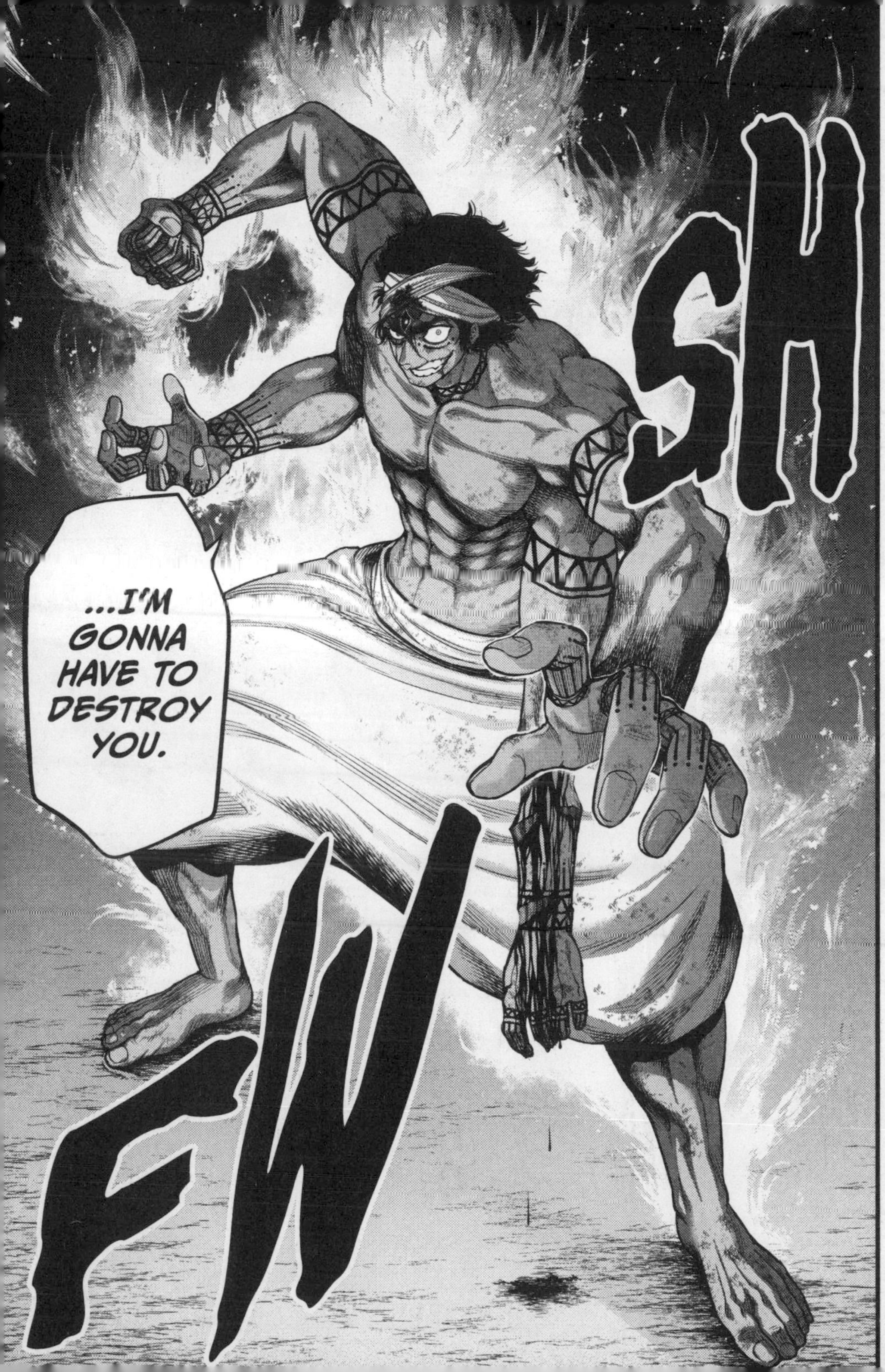
SH
...I'M GONNA HAVE TO DESTROY YOU.
FW

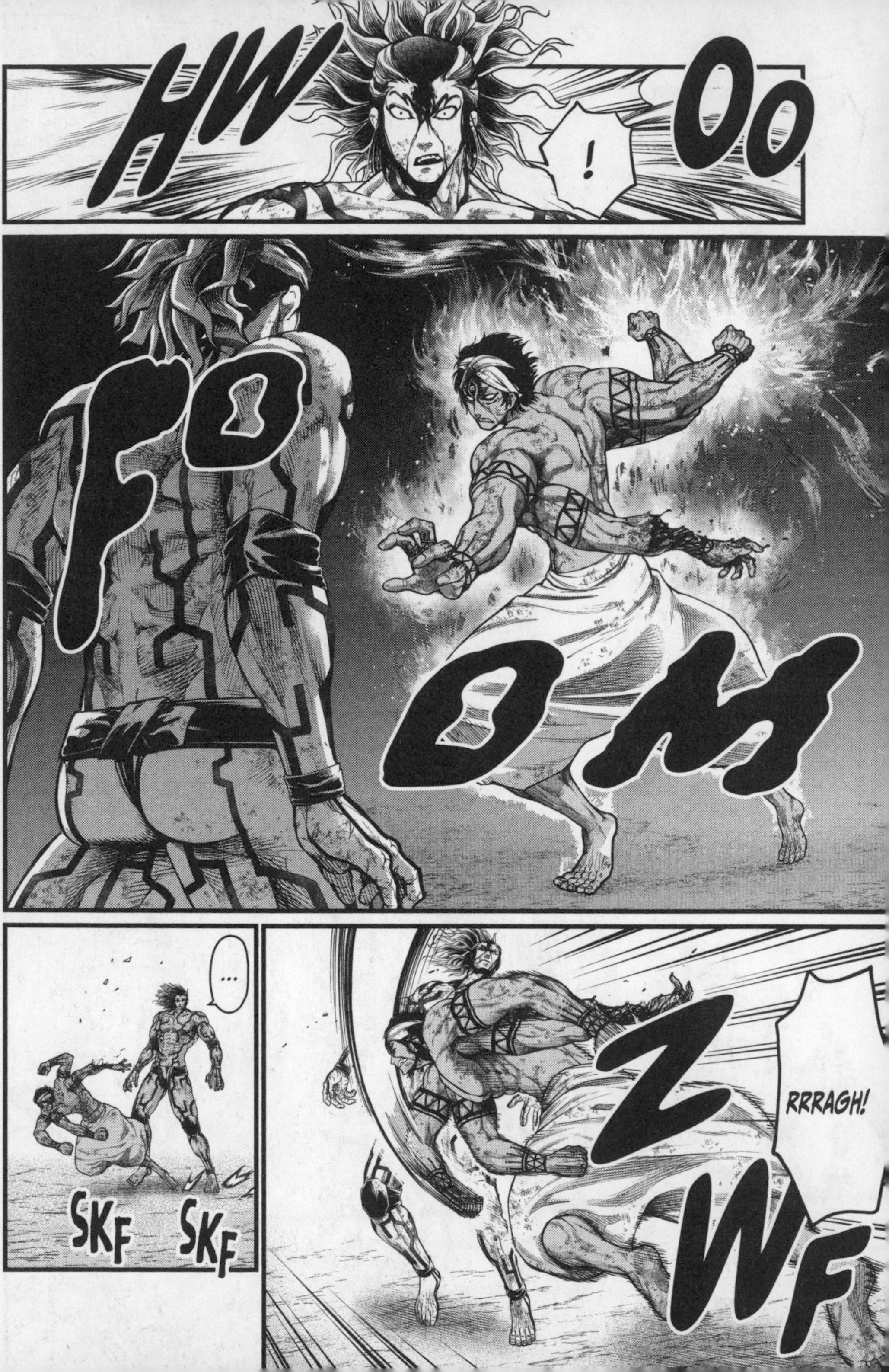
HW OO
!
FO OM
RRRAGH!
Z WF
...
SKF SKF

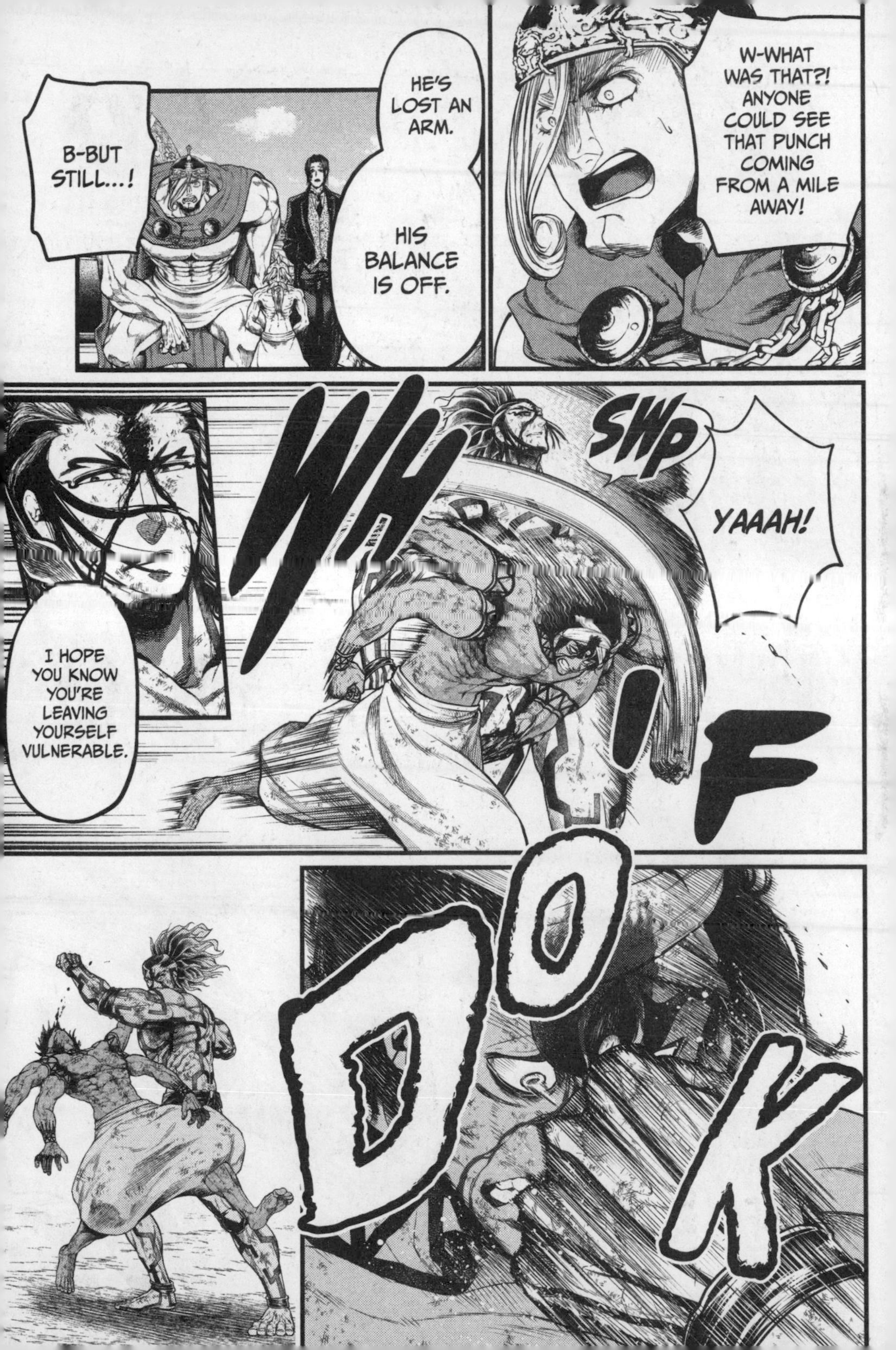
W-WHAT WAS THAT?! ANYONE COULD SEE THAT PUNCH COMING FROM A MILE AWAY!
HE'S LOST AN ARM.
HIS BALANCE IS OFF.
B-BUT STILL...!
SWP
YAAAH!
I HOPE YOU KNOW YOU'RE LEAVING YOURSELF VULNERABLE.

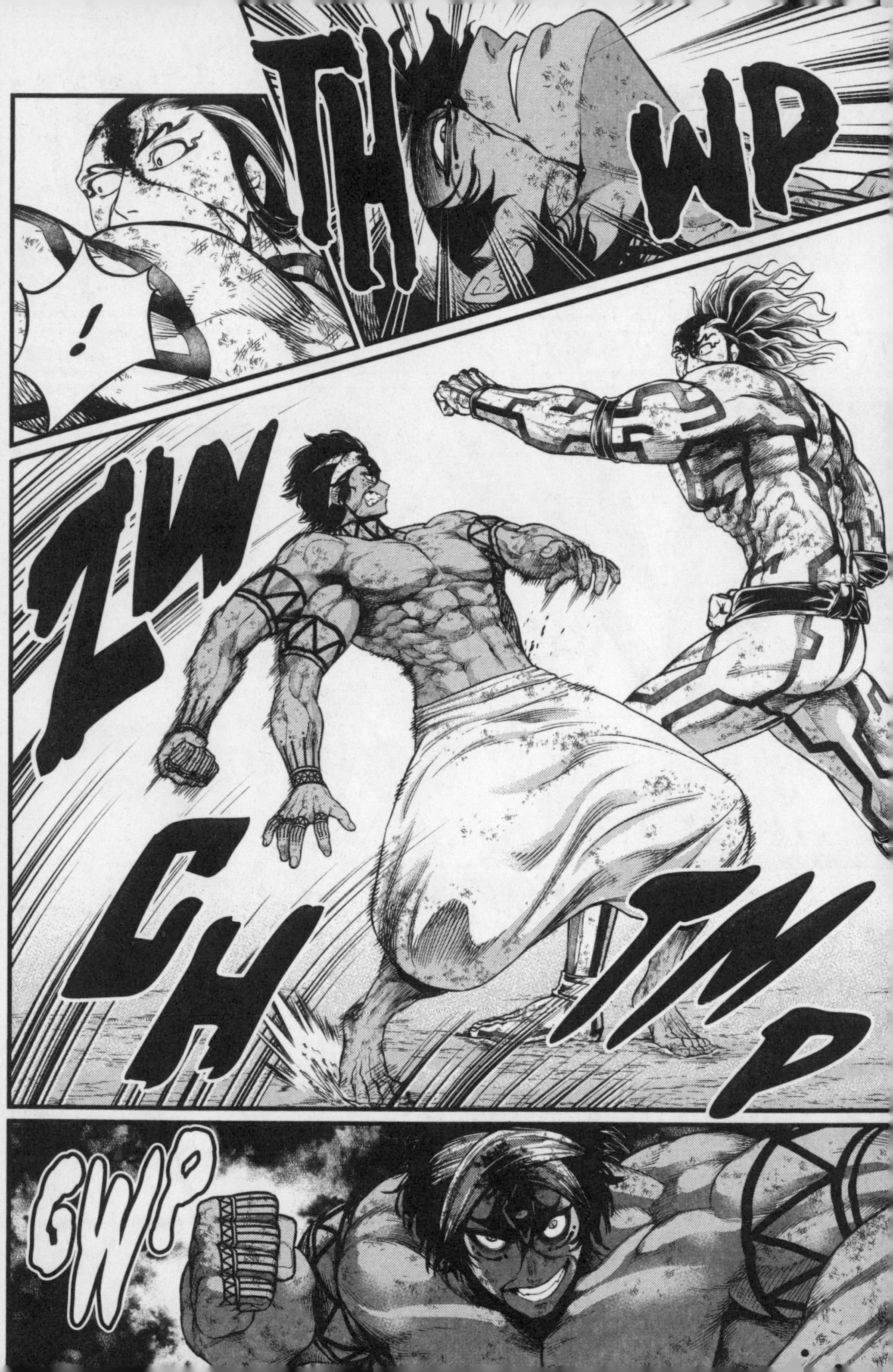

THWP
!
ZW
CH
TMP
GWP

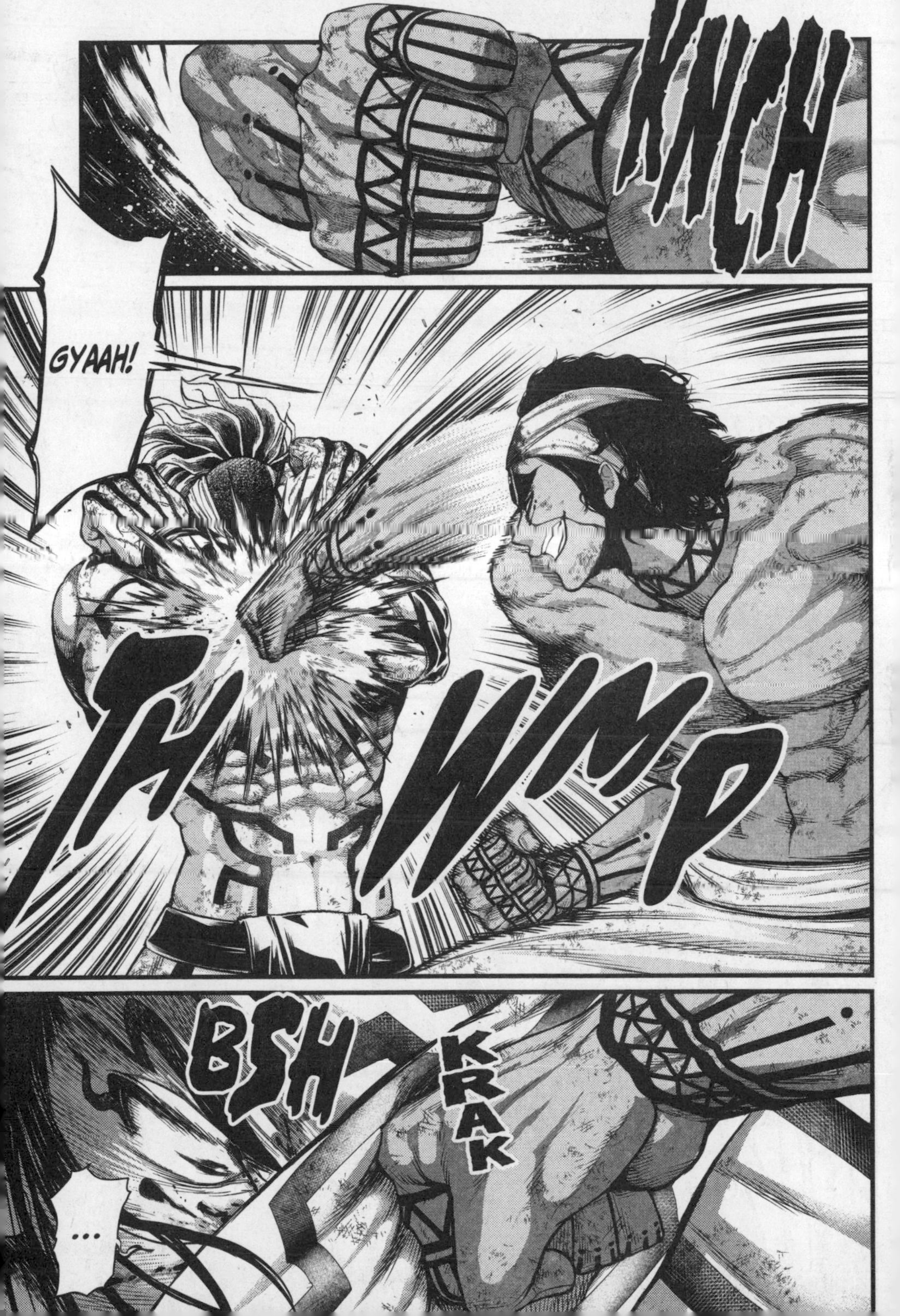
KNCH
GYAAH!
THWMP
KRAK
BSH
...

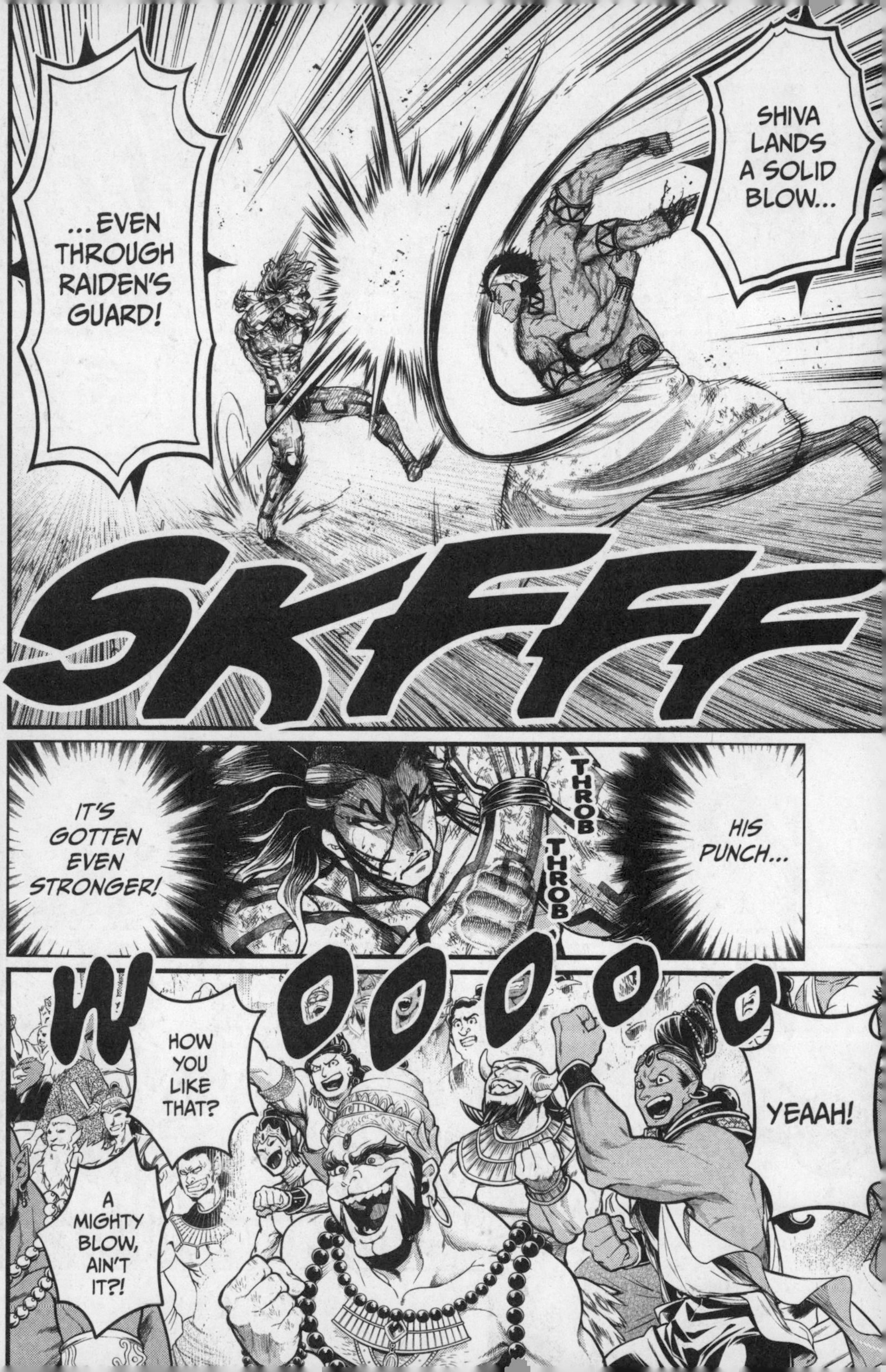
SHIVA LANDS A SOLID BLOW...
...EVEN THROUGH RAIDEN'S GUARD!
SKFFF
HIS PUNCH...
THROB THROB
IT'S GOTTEN EVEN STRONGER!
WOOOOO
YEAAH!
HOW YOU LIKE THAT?
A MIGHTY BLOW, AIN'T IT?!

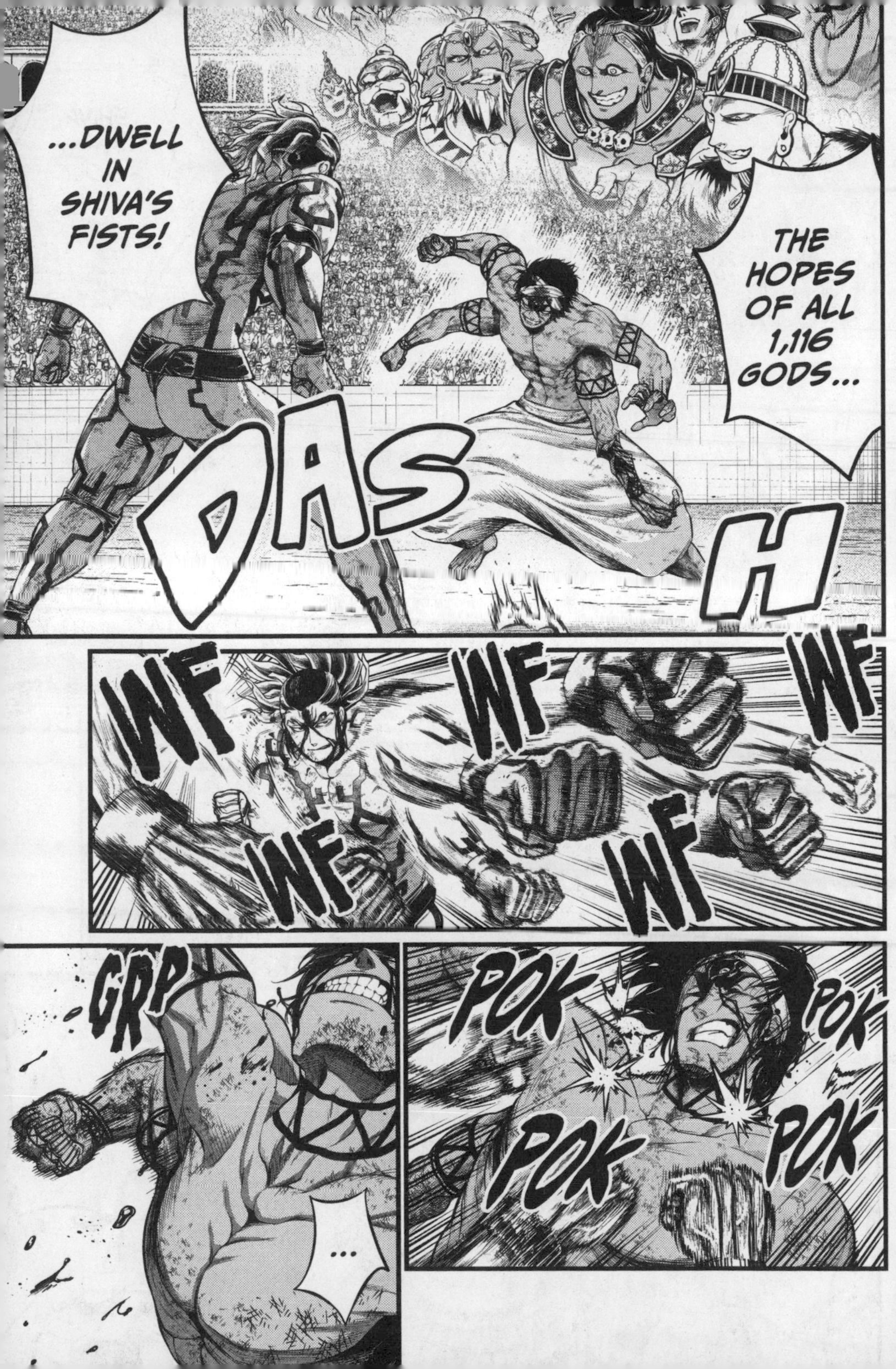
THE HOPES OF ALL 1,116 GODS...
...DWELL IN SHIVA'S FISTS!
DASH
WF
WF
WF
WF
WF
POK
POK
POK
POK
GRP
...

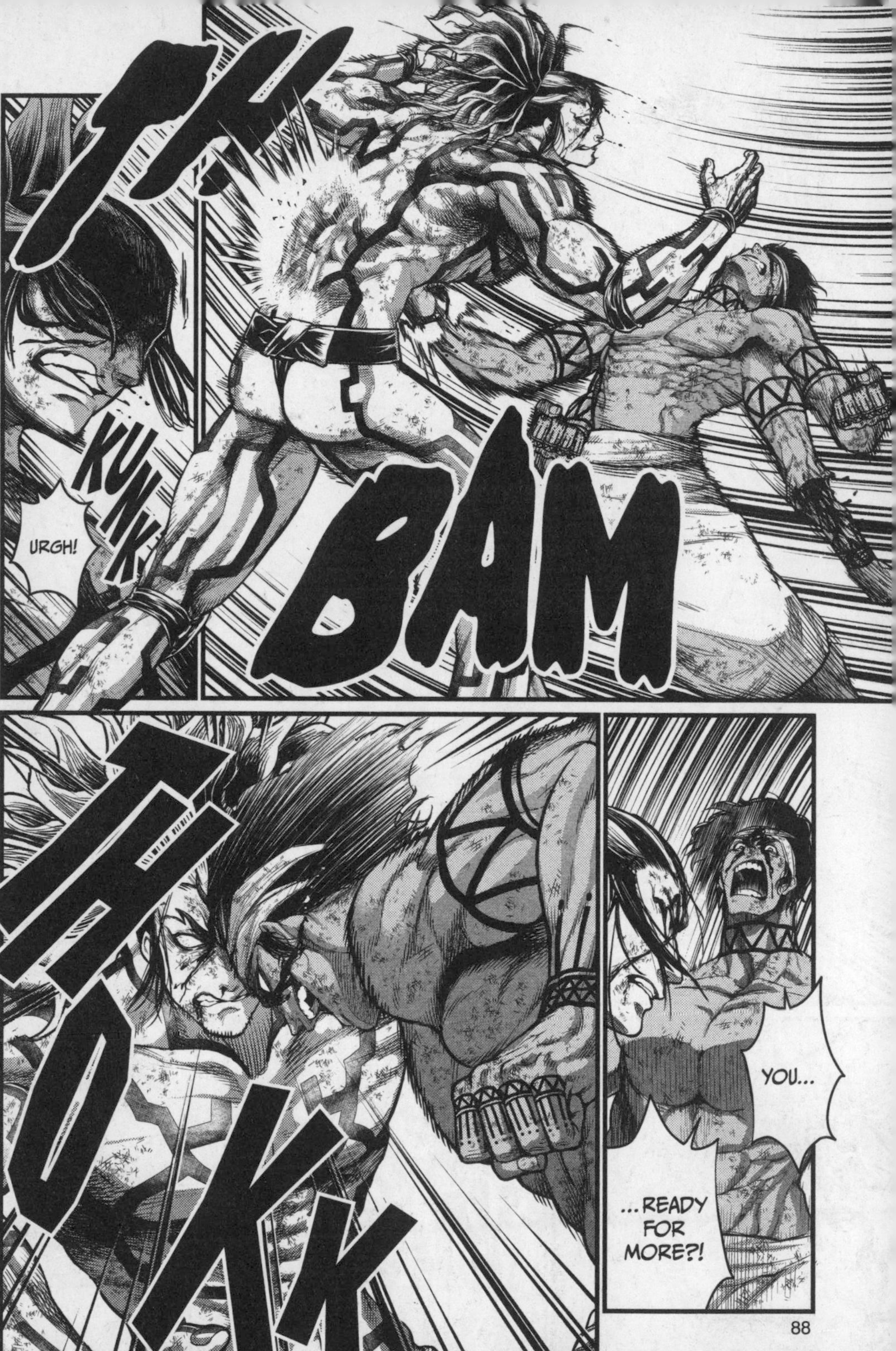
BAM
KUNK
URGH!
YOU...
...READY FOR MORE?!

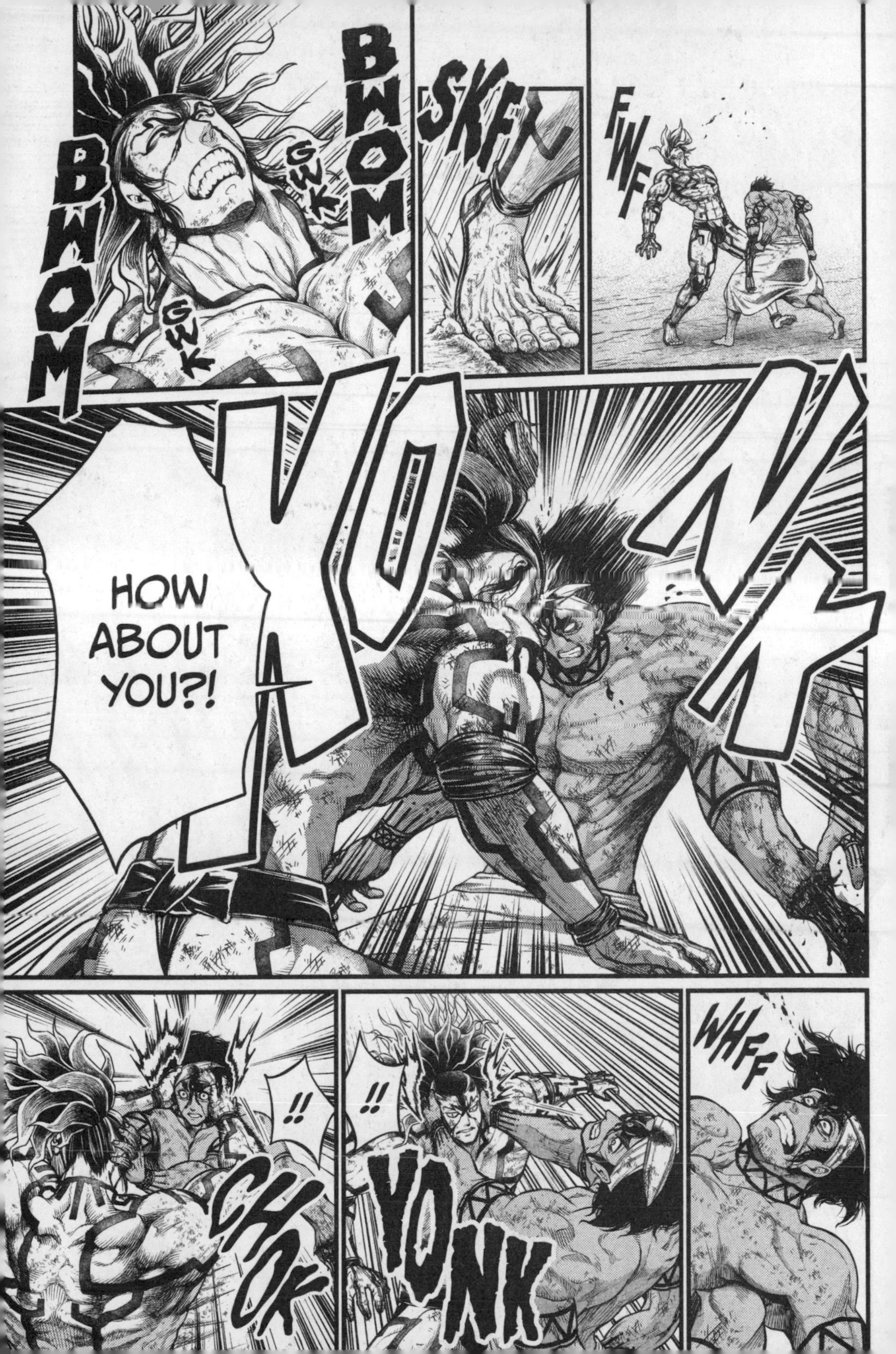
FWF
SKFF
BWOM
GWK
GWK
BWOM
YONK
HOW ABOUT YOU?!
WHFF
!!
YONK
!!
CHOK

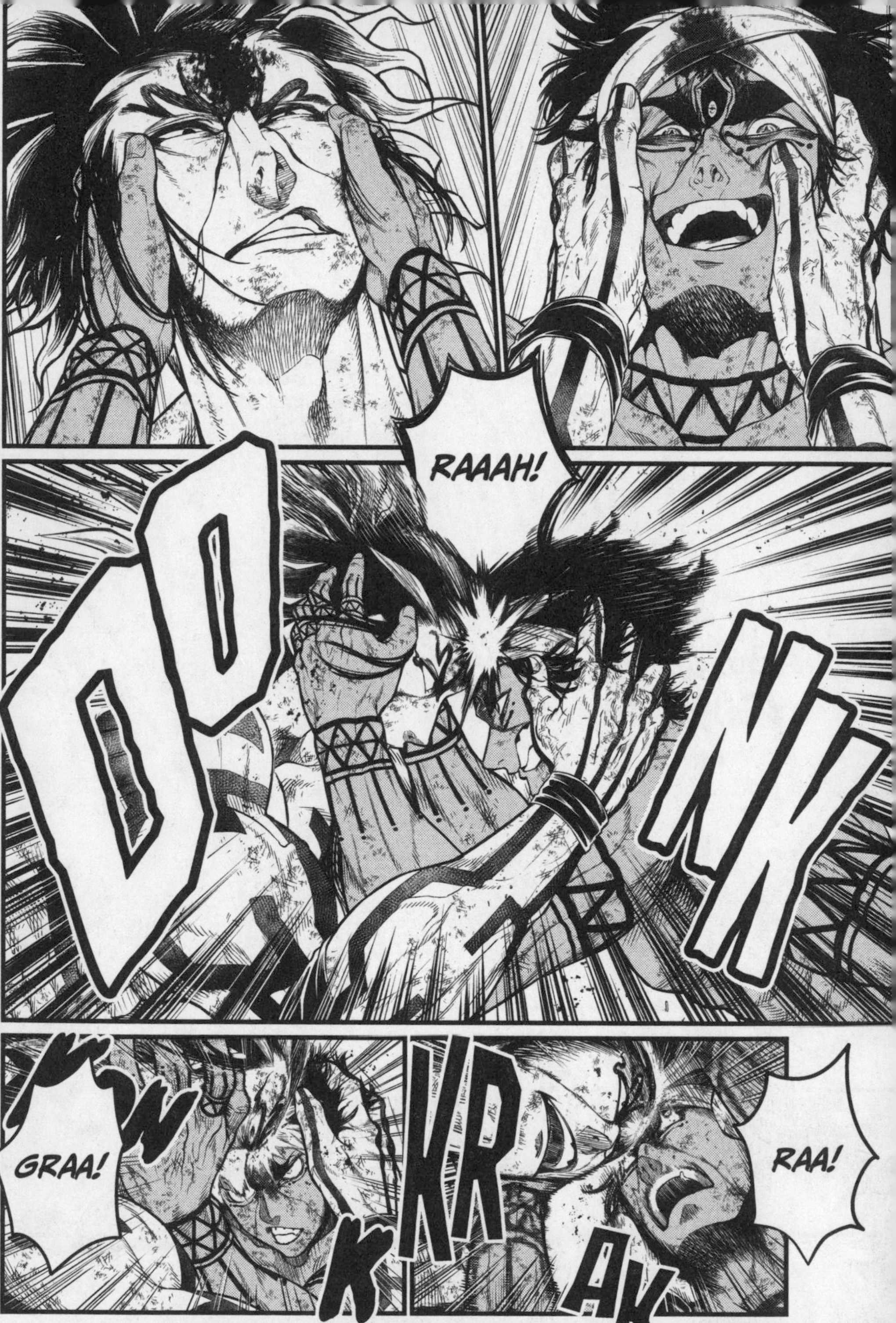
RAAAH!
DONK
RAA!
KR
AK
GRAA!
K

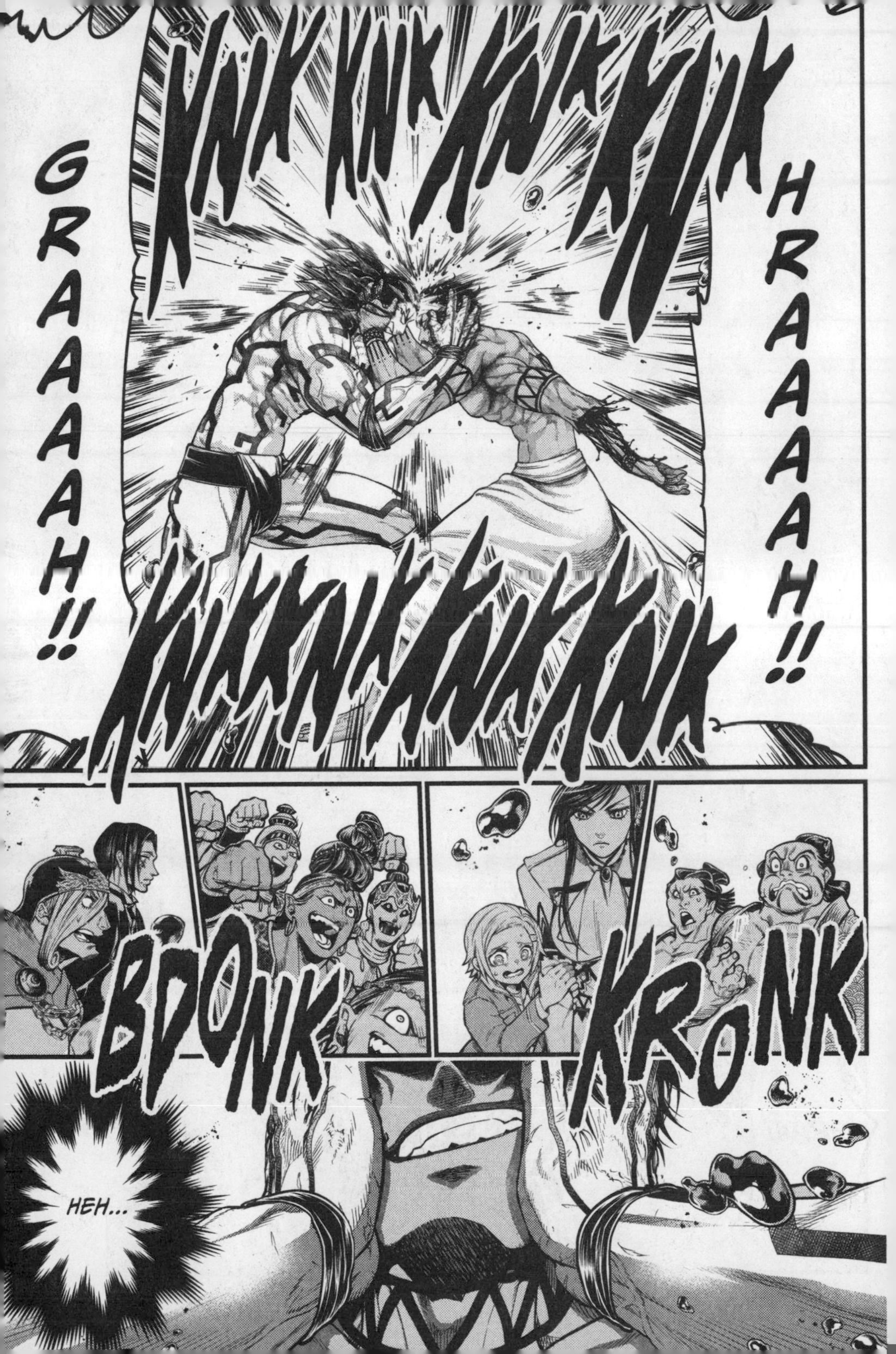
HRAAAAH!!
GRAAAAH!!
KRONK
BDONK
HEH...

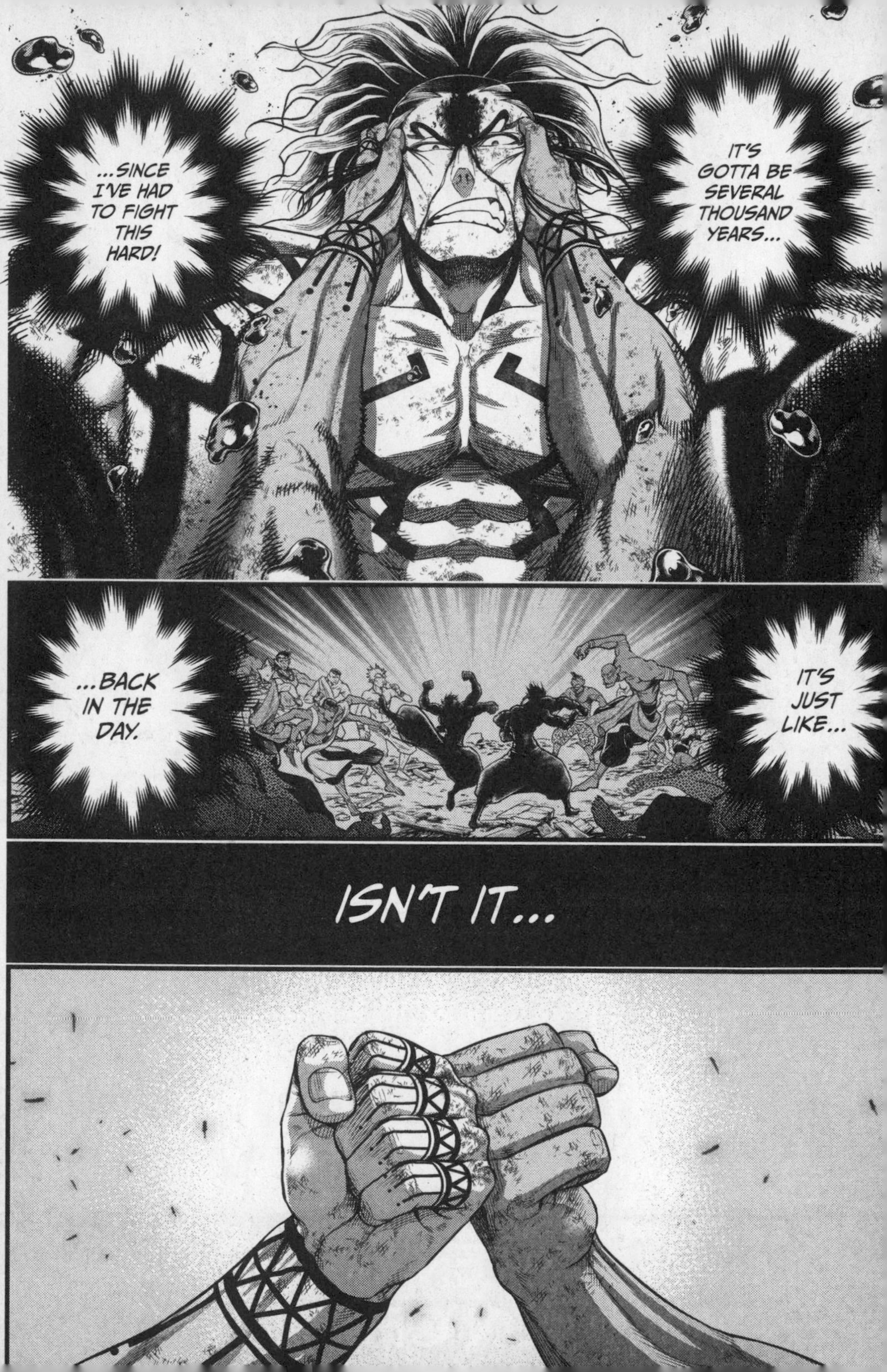
IT'S GOTTA BE SEVERAL THOUSAND YEARS...
...SINCE I'VE HAD TO FIGHT THIS HARD!
IT'S JUST LIKE...
...BACK IN THE DAY.
ISN'T IT...

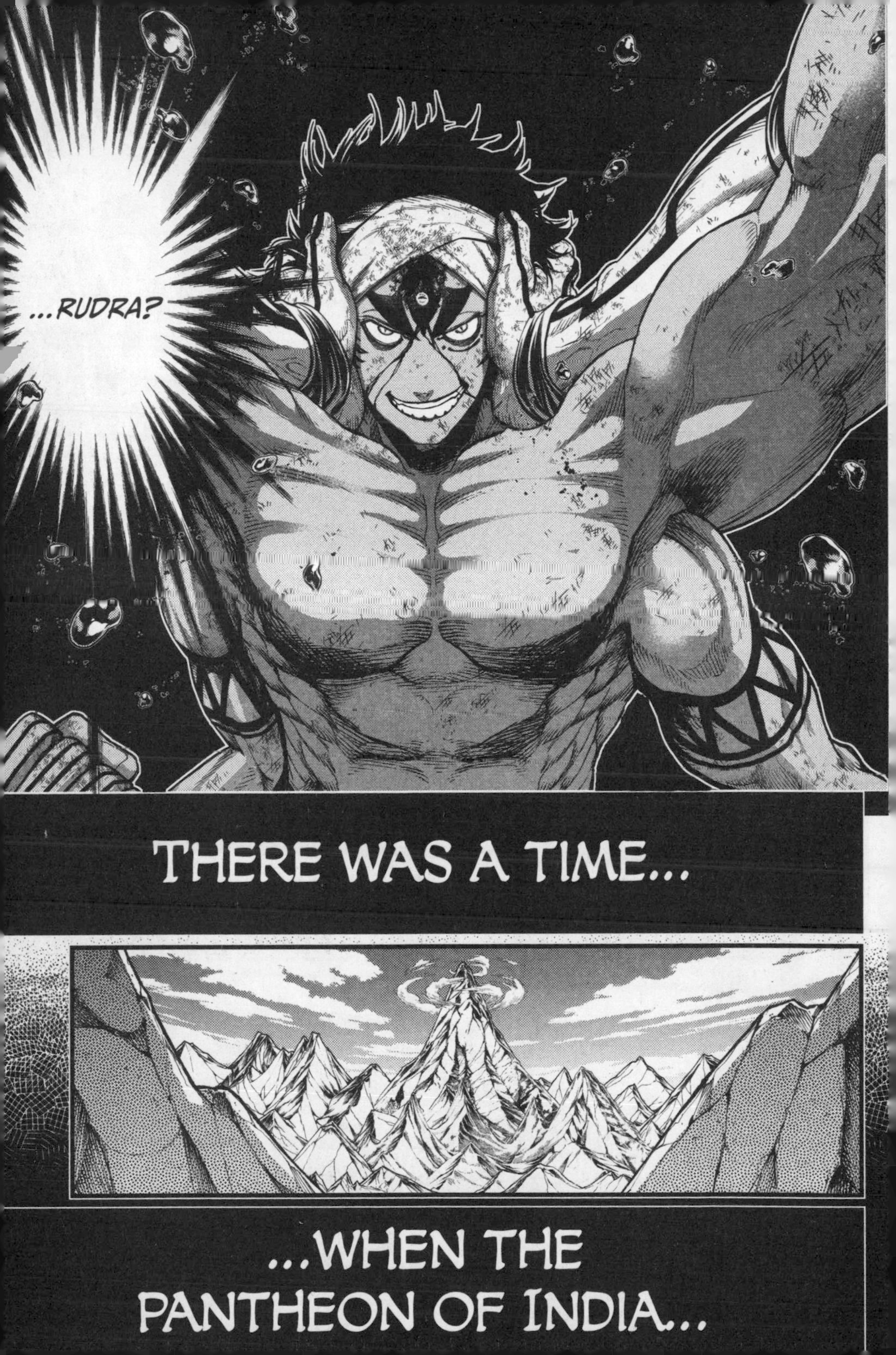
...RUDRA?
THERE WAS A TIME...
...WHEN THE PANTHEON OF INDIA...

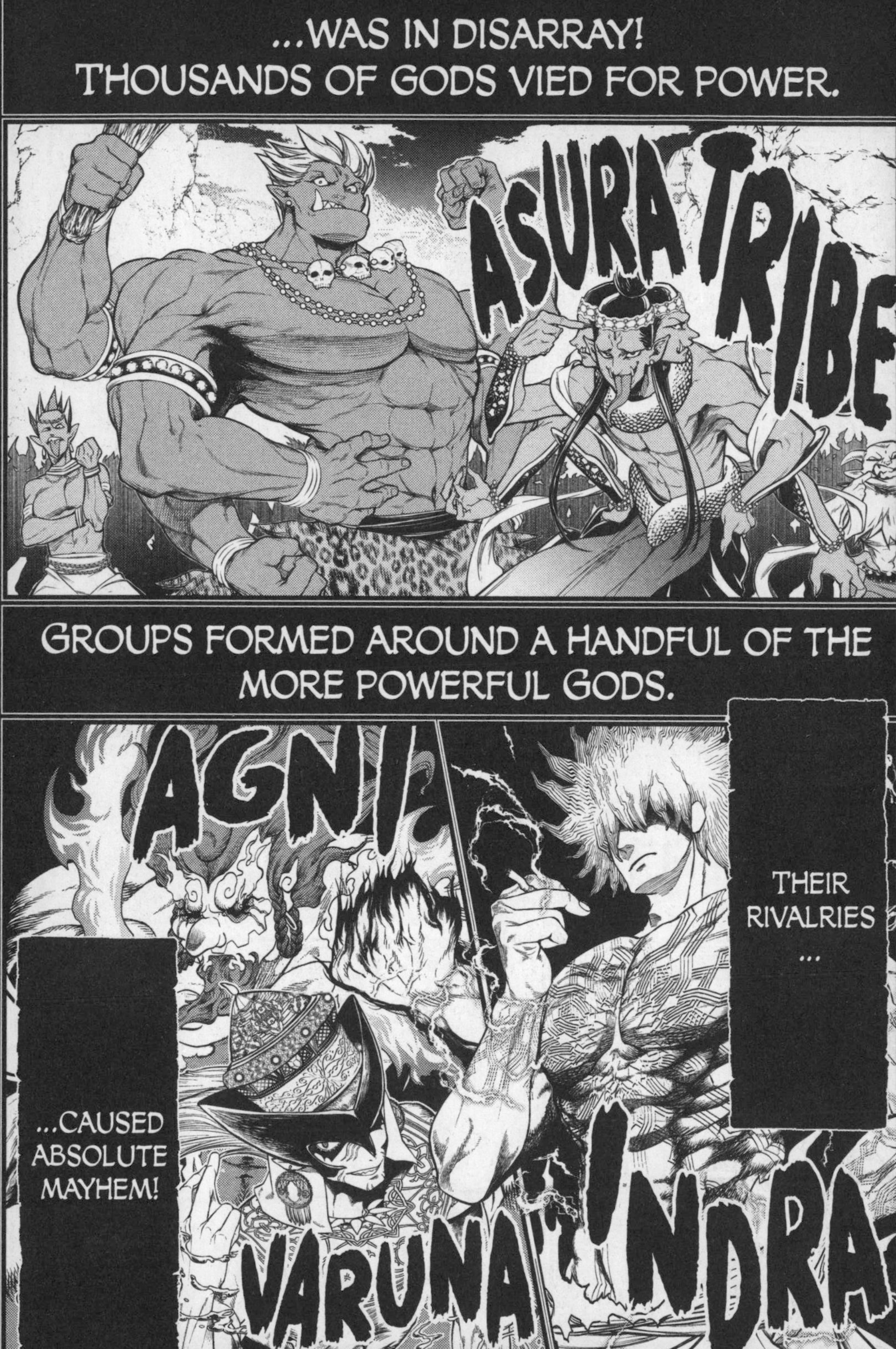
...WAS IN DISARRAY! THOUSANDS OF GODS VIED FOR POWER.
ASURA TRIBE
GROUPS FORMED AROUND A HANDFUL OF THE MORE POWERFUL GODS.
THEIR RIVALRIES ...
AGNI
INDRA
VARUNA
...CAUSED ABSOLUTE MAYHEM!

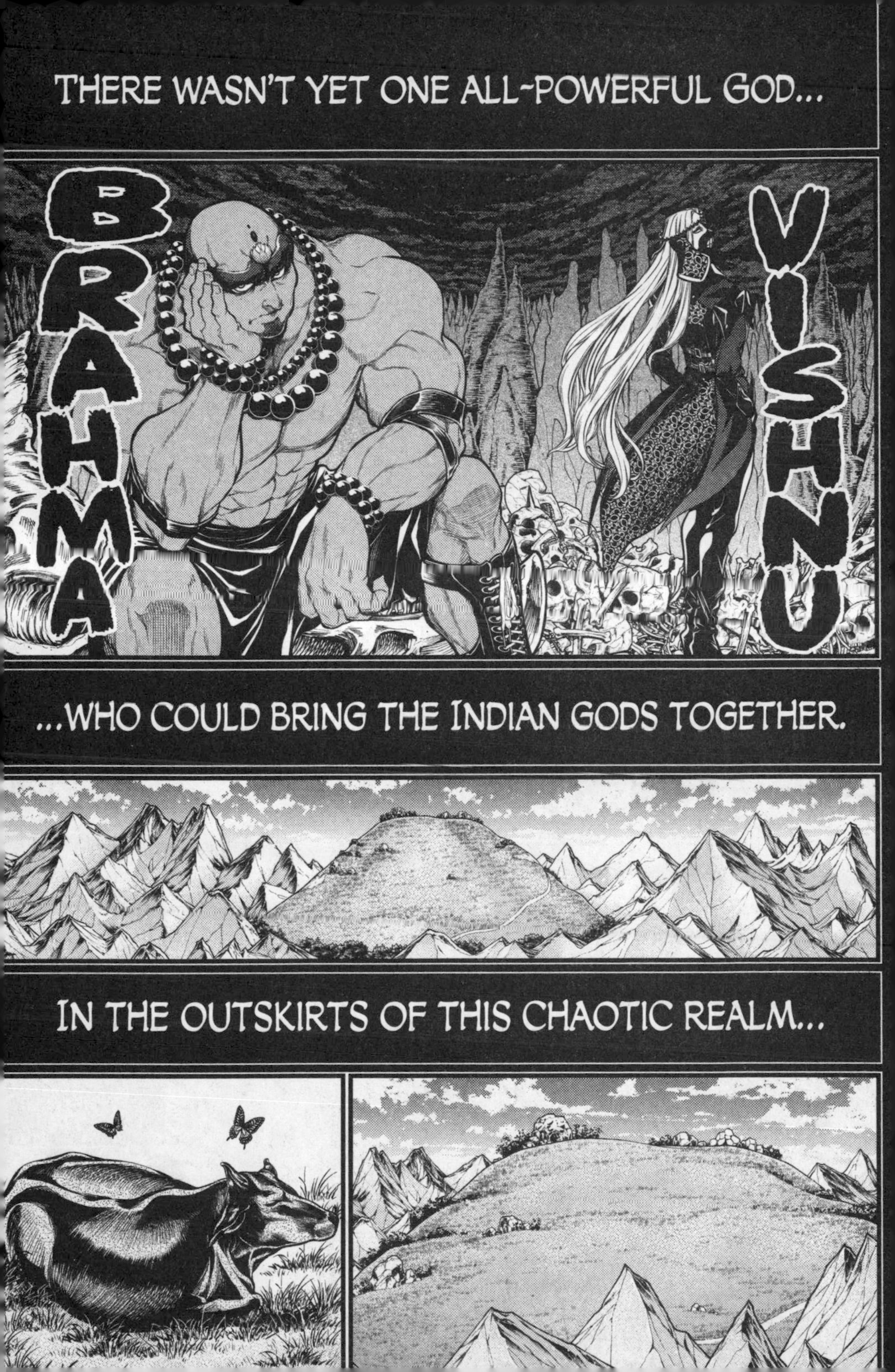
THERE WASN'T YET ONE ALL-POWERFUL GOD...
VISHNU
BRAHMA
...WHO COULD BRING THE INDIAN GODS TOGETHER.
IN THE OUTSKIRTS OF THIS CHAOTIC REALM...

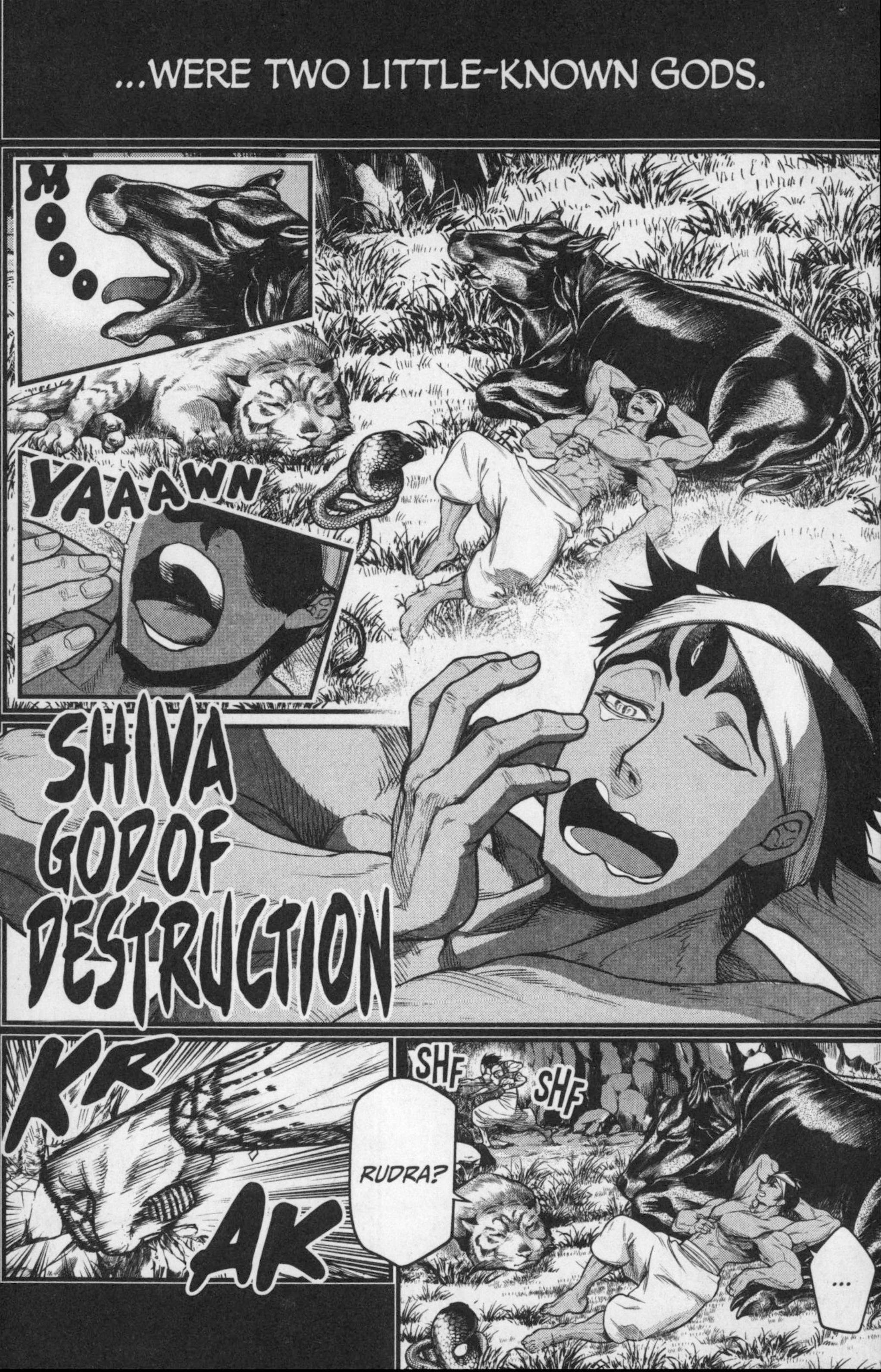
...WERE TWO LITTLE-KNOWN GODS.
MOOO
YAAAWN
SHIVA
GOD OF
DESTRUCTION
SHF
SHF
RUDRA?
...
KR
AK

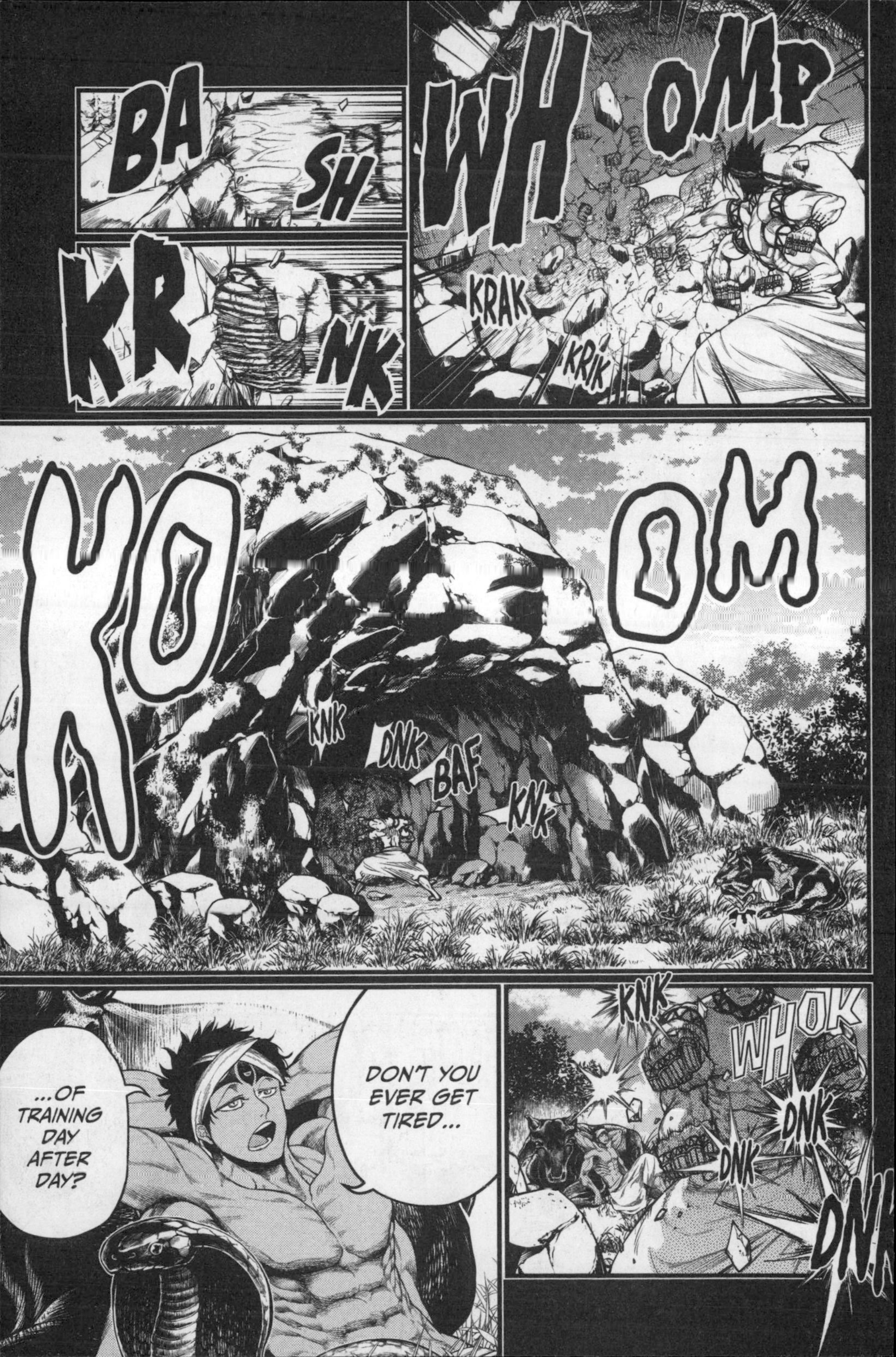
WH OMP
KRAK
KRIK
BA SH
KR NK
KO OM
KNK
DNK
BAF
KNK
KNK
WH OK
DNK
DNK
DN
DON'T YOU EVER GET TIRED...
...OF TRAINING DAY AFTER DAY?

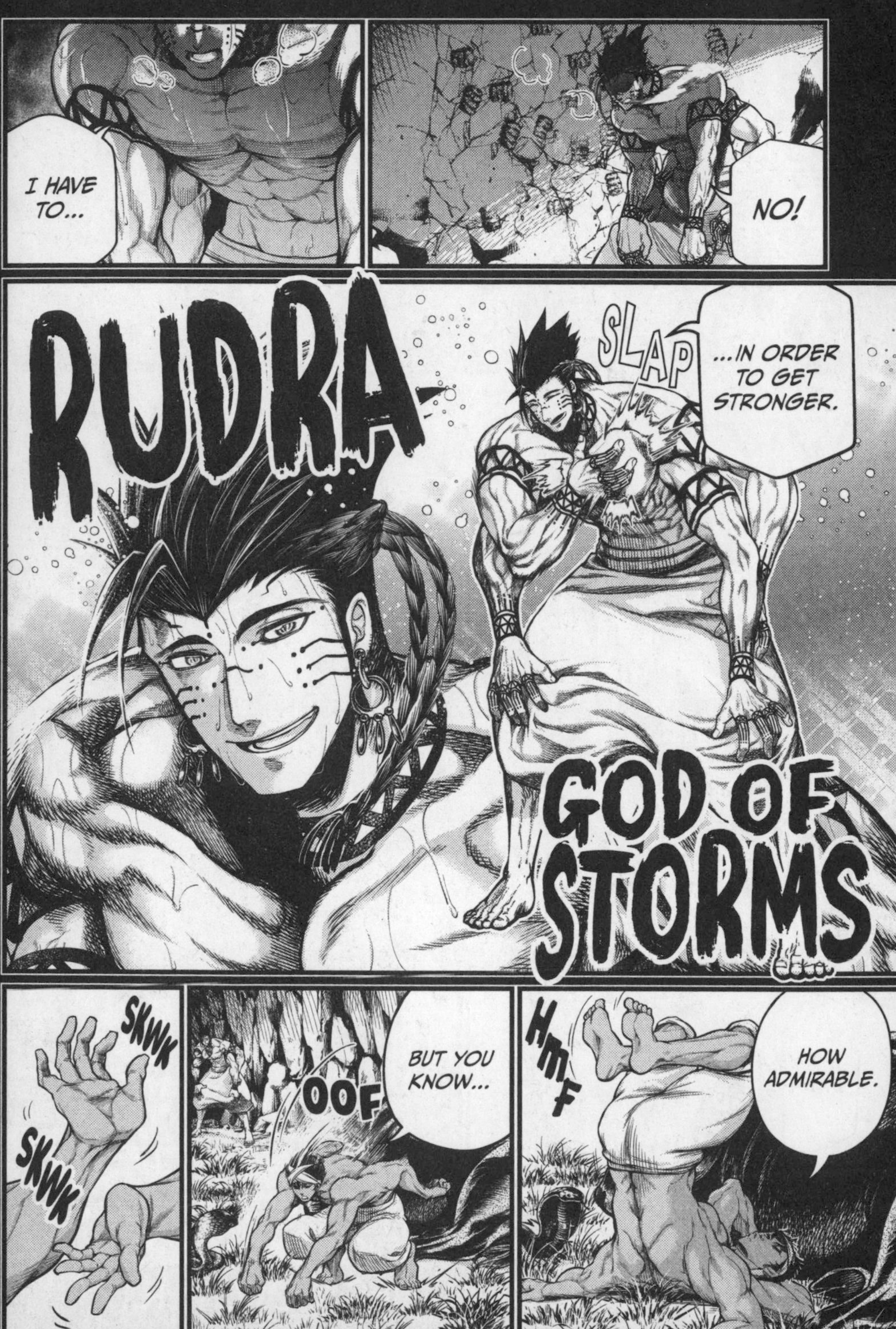
NO!
I HAVE TO...
...IN ORDER TO GET STRONGER.
SLAP
RUDRA
GOD OF STORMS
HOW ADMIRABLE.
HMF
BUT YOU KNOW...
OOF
SKWK
SKWK

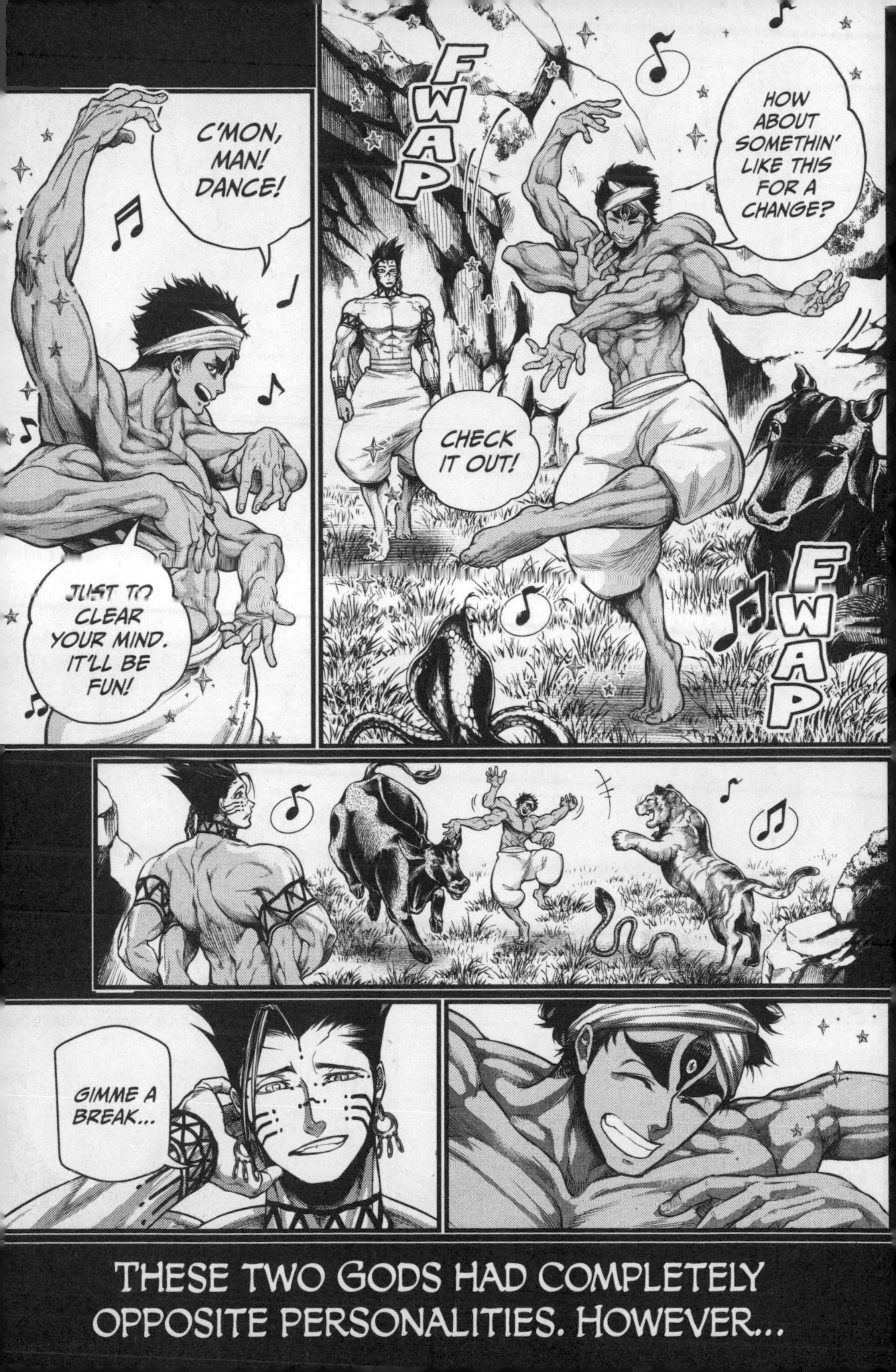
HOW ABOUT SOMETHIN' LIKE THIS FOR A CHANGE?
FWAP
CHECK IT OUT!
FWAP
C'MON, MAN! DANCE!
JUST TO CLEAR YOUR MIND. IT'LL BE FUN!
GIMME A BREAK...
THESE TWO GODS HAD COMPLETELY OPPOSITE PERSONALITIES. HOWEVER...

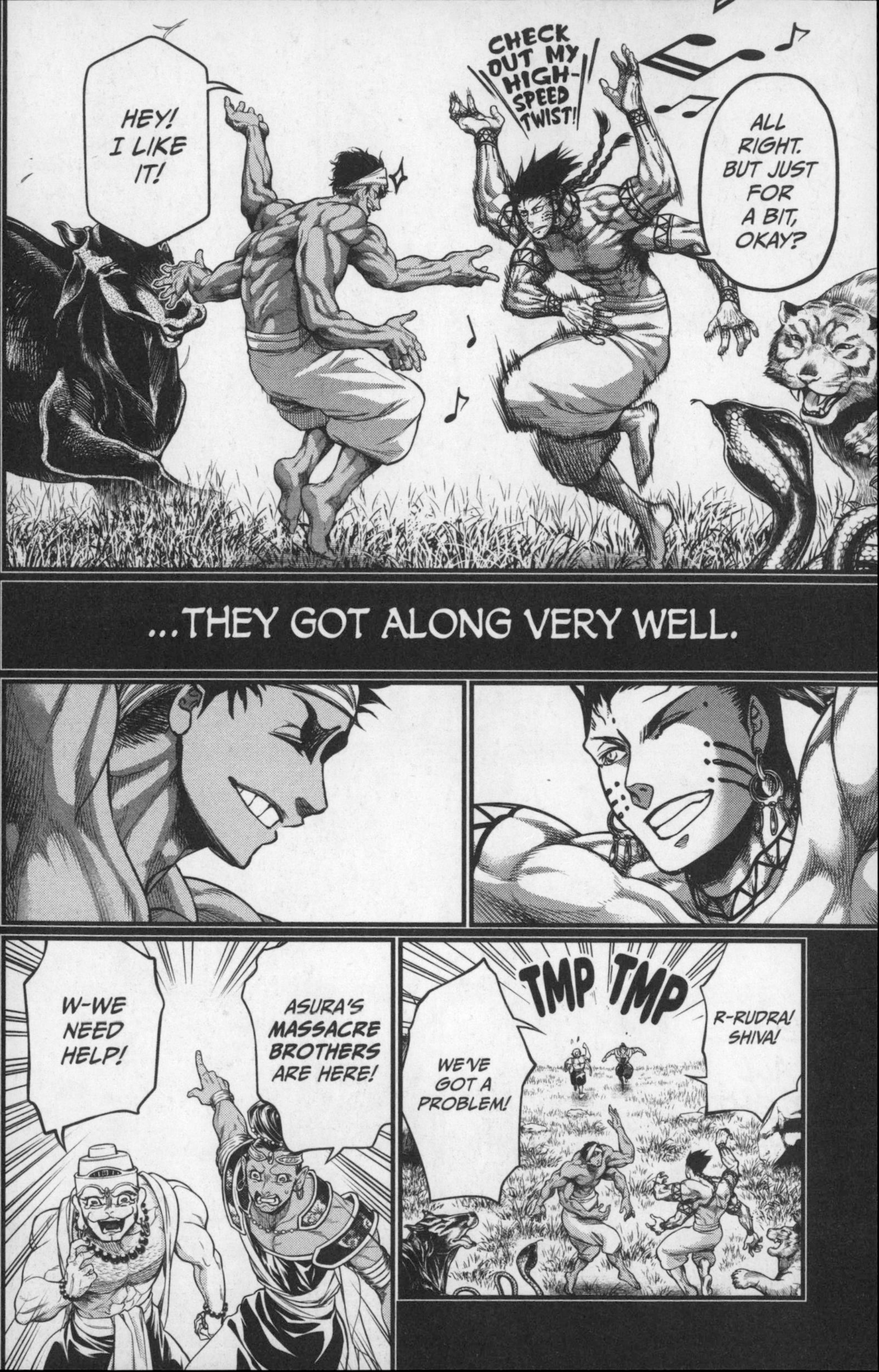
ALL RIGHT. BUT JUST FOR A BIT, OKAY?
CHECK OUT MY HIGH-SPEED TWIST!
HEY! I LIKE IT!
...THEY GOT ALONG VERY WELL.
TMP TMP
R-RUDRA! SHIVA!
WE'VE GOT A PROBLEM!
ASURA'S MASSACRE BROTHERS ARE HERE!
W-WE NEED HELP!

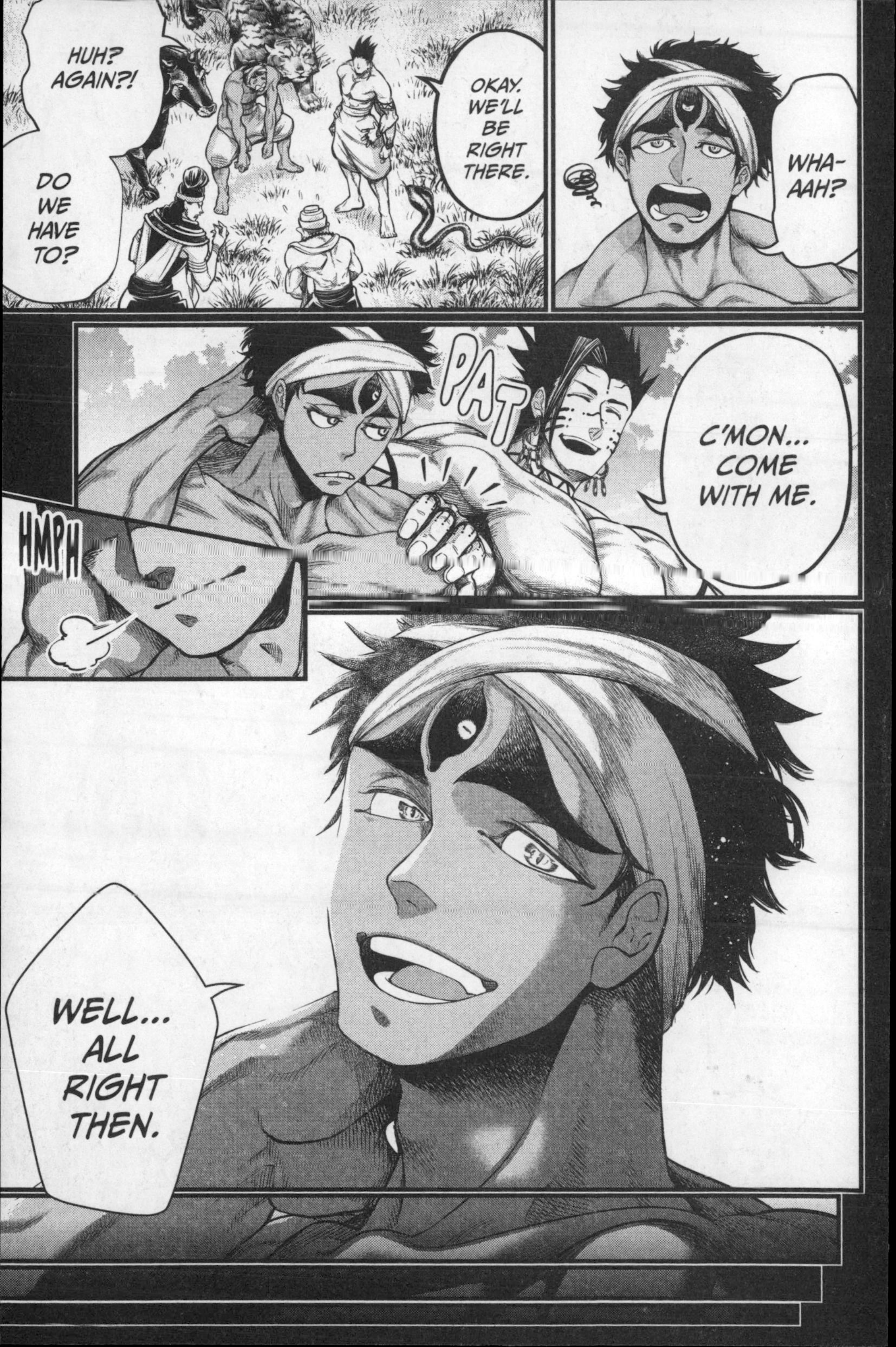
WHA-AAH?
OKAY. WE'LL BE RIGHT THERE.
HUH? AGAIN?!
DO WE HAVE TO?
C'MON... COME WITH ME.
PAT
HMPH
WELL... ALL RIGHT THEN.

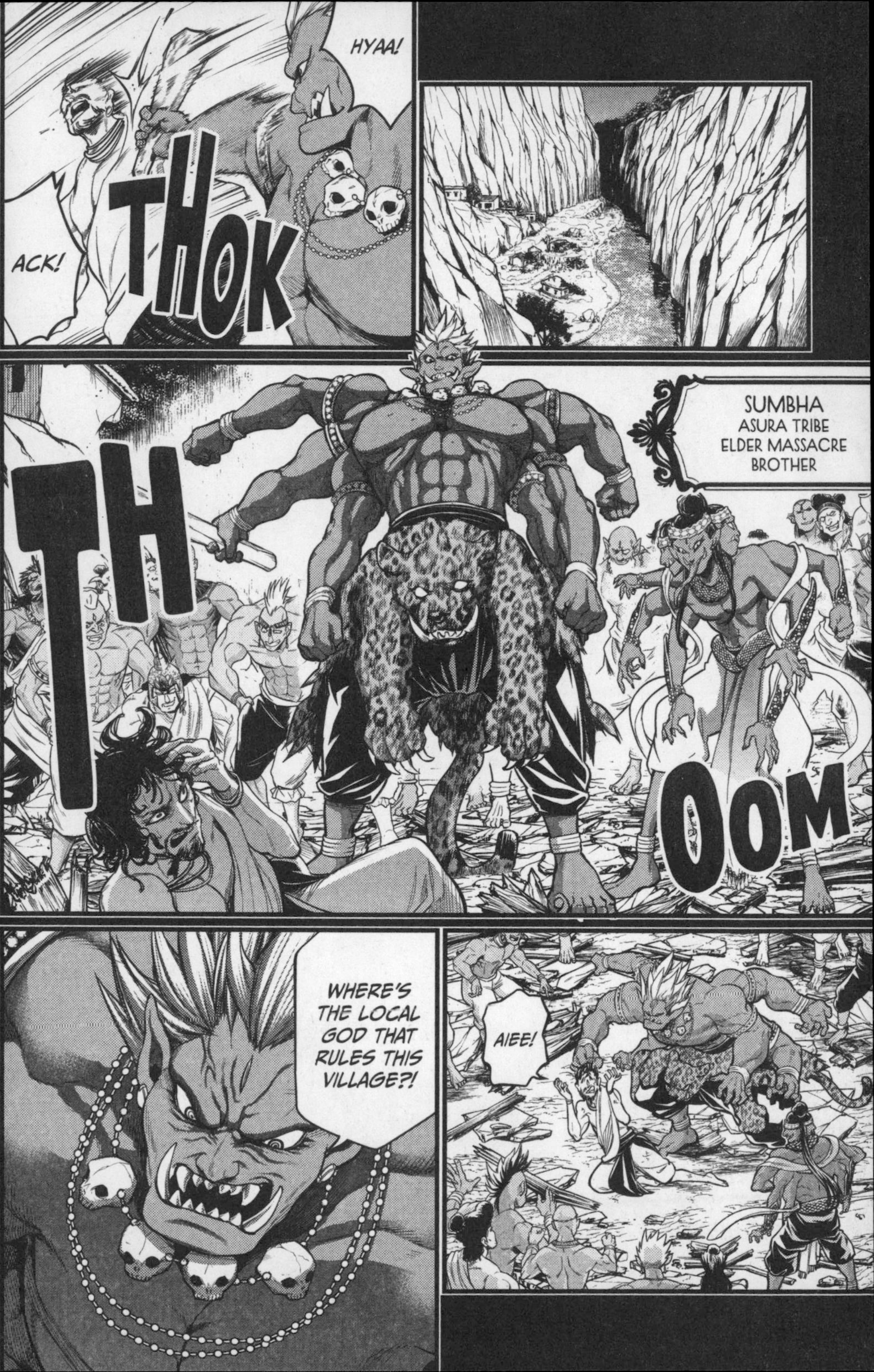
HYAA!
THOK
ACK!
SUMBHA
ASURA TRIBE
ELDER MASSACRE
BROTHER
THOOM
AIEE!
WHERE'S THE LOCAL GOD THAT RULES THIS VILLAGE?!

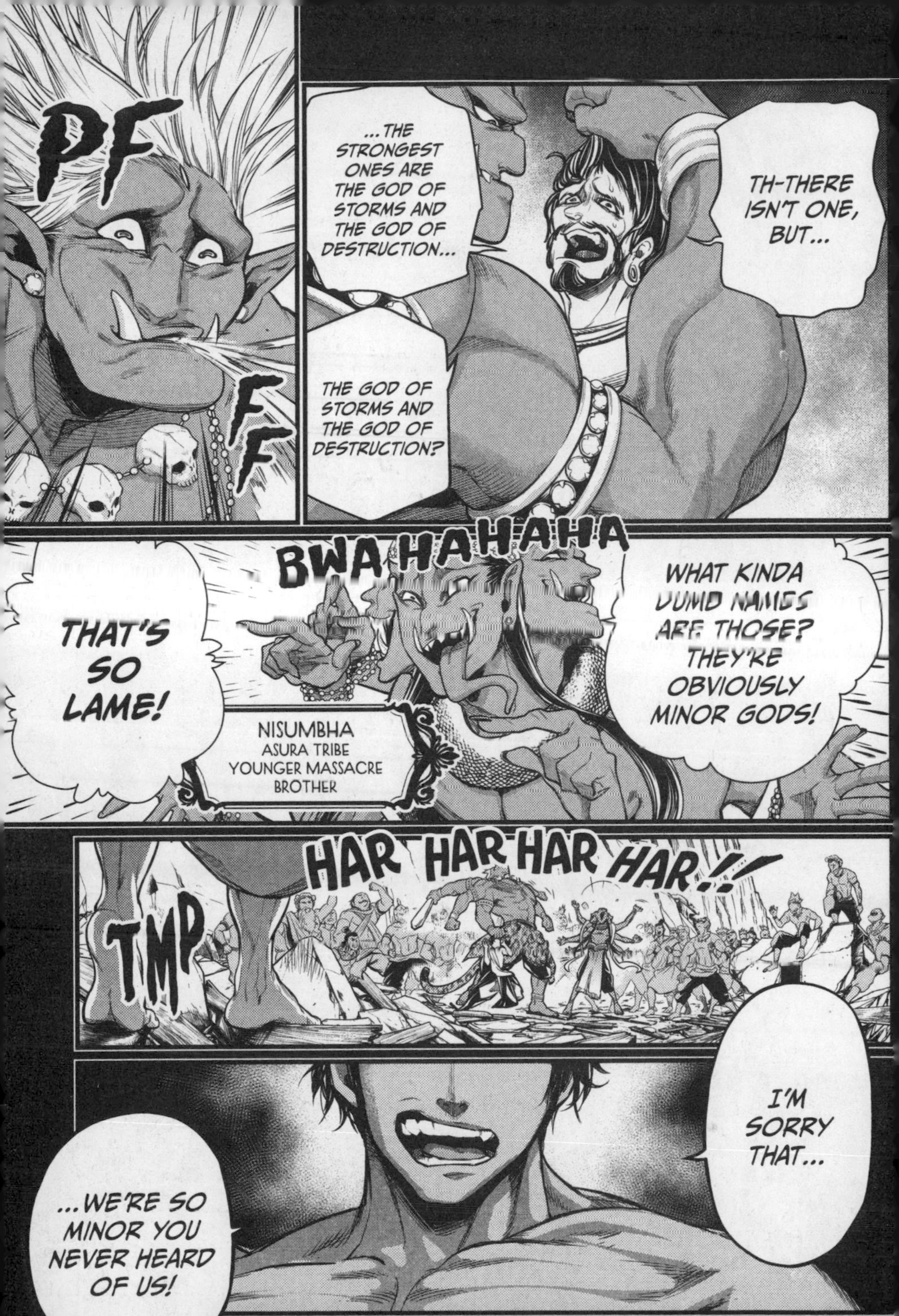
TH-THERE ISN'T ONE, BUT...
...THE STRONGEST ONES ARE THE GOD OF STORMS AND THE GOD OF DESTRUCTION...
THE GOD OF STORMS AND THE GOD OF DESTRUCTION?
PF
FF
BWA HAHAHA
WHAT KINDA DUMB NAMES ARE THOSE? THEY'RE OBVIOUSLY MINOR GODS!
THAT'S SO LAME!
NISUMBHA
ASURA TRIBE
YOUNGER MASSACRE BROTHER
HAR HAR HAR HAR!!
TMP
I'M SORRY THAT...
...WE'RE SO MINOR YOU NEVER HEARD OF US!

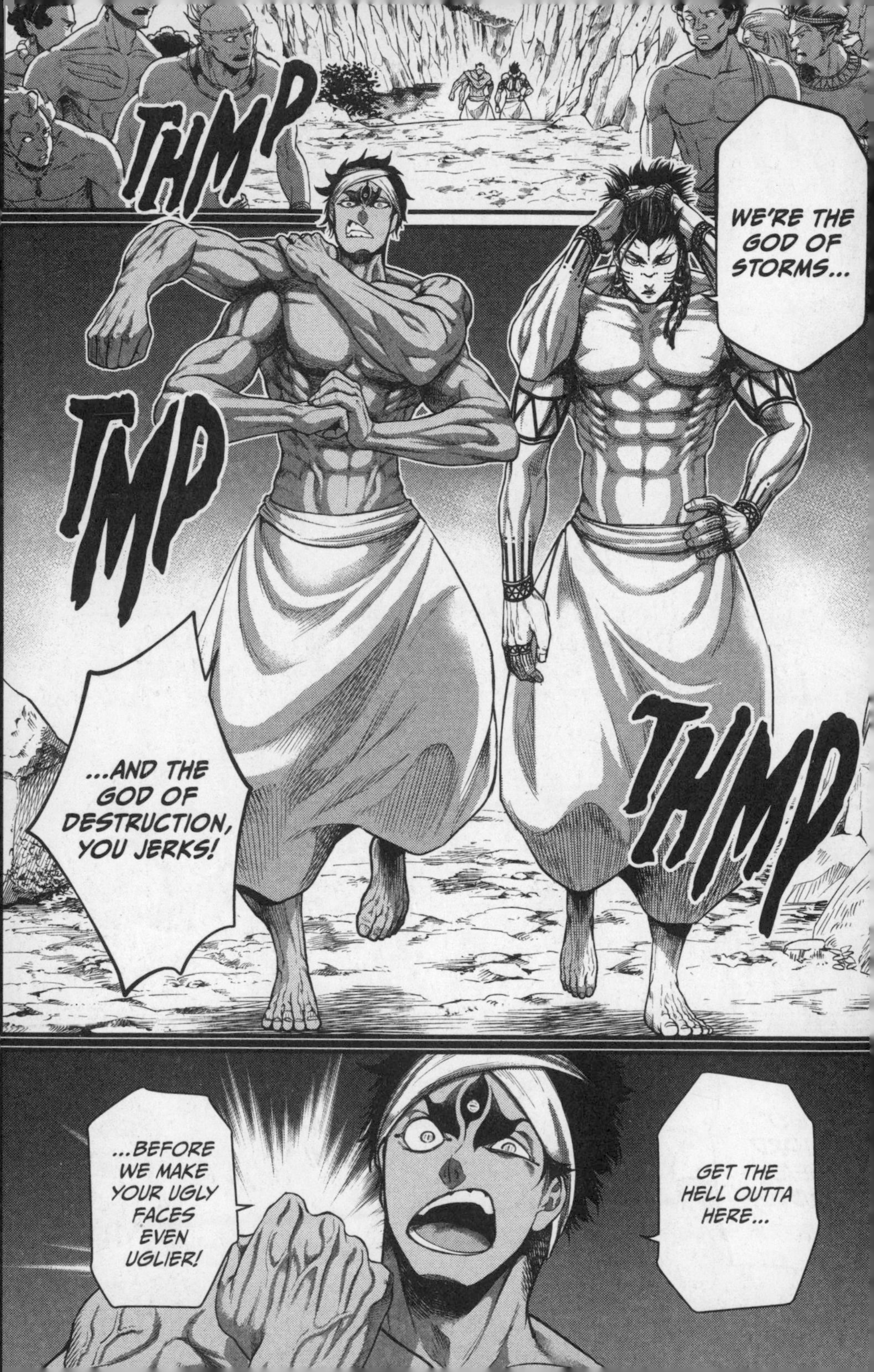
THMP
WE'RE THE GOD OF STORMS...
THMP
TMP
...AND THE GOD OF DESTRUCTION, YOU JERKS!
GET THE HELL OUTTA HERE...
...BEFORE WE MAKE YOUR UGLY FACES EVEN UGLIER!

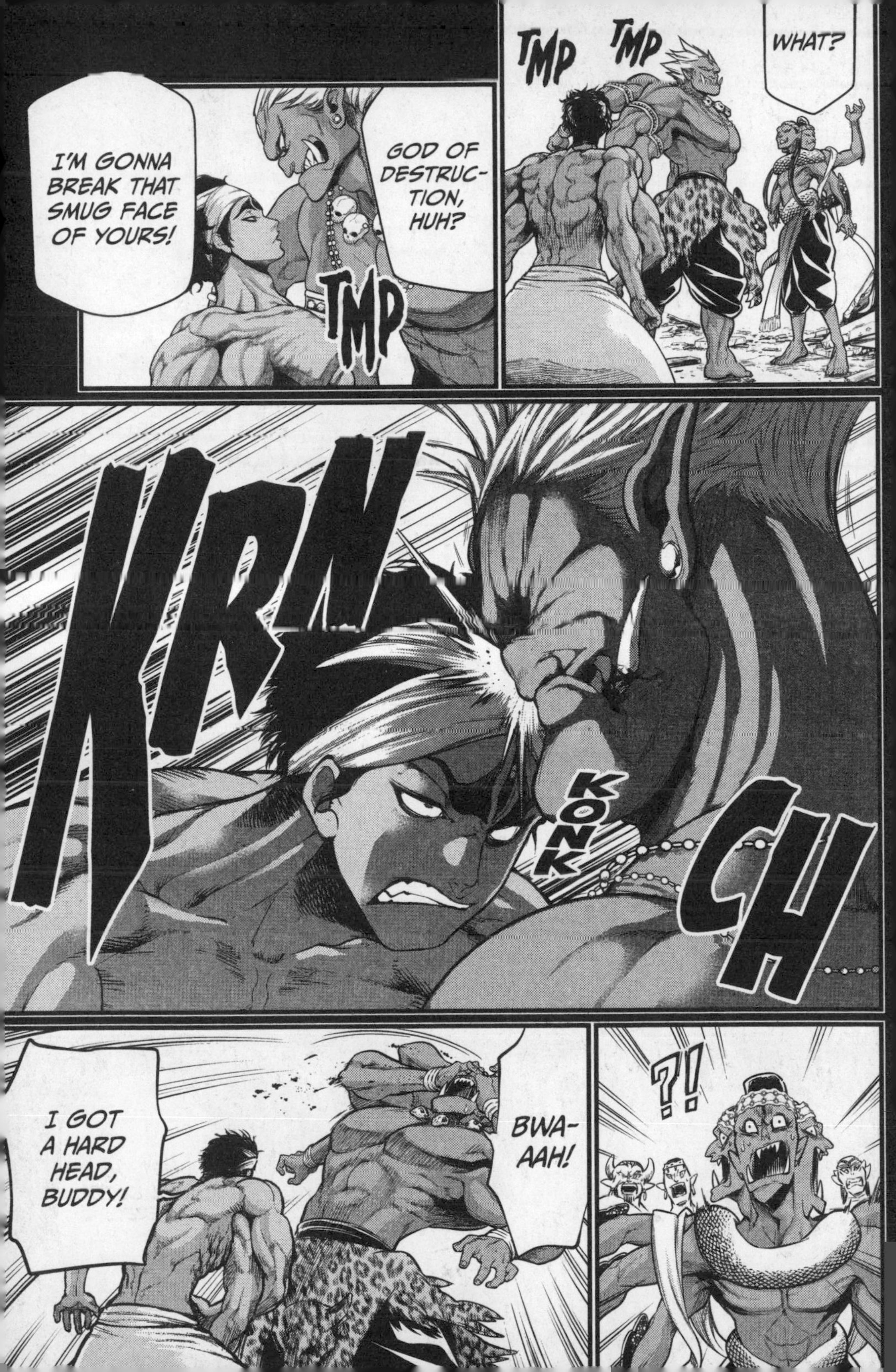
WHAT?
TMP
TMP
GOD OF DESTRUCTION, HUH?
I'M GONNA BREAK THAT SMUG FACE OF YOURS!
TMP
KRN
CH
KONK
?!
BWAAAH!
I GOT A HARD HEAD, BUDDY!

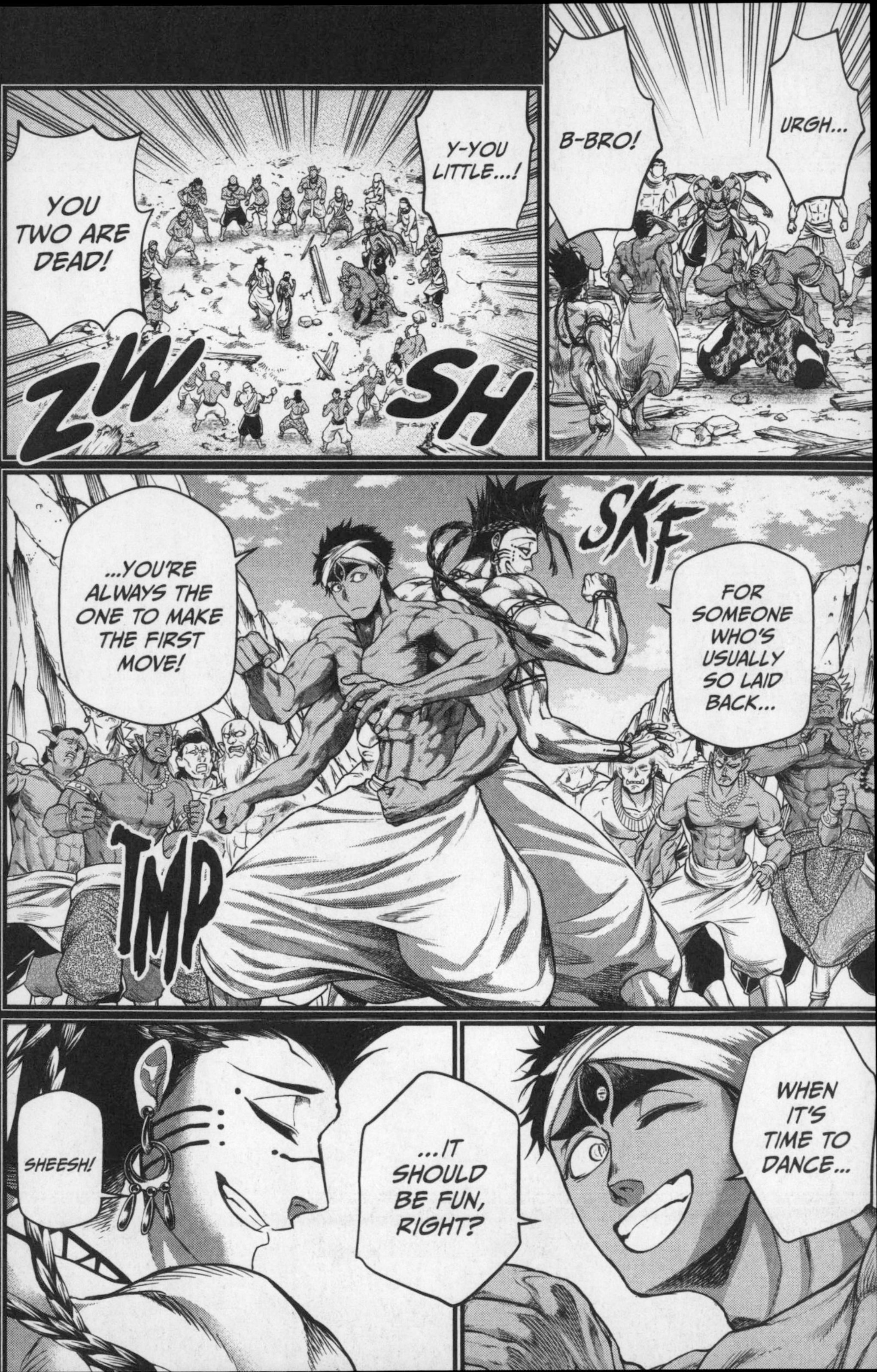
URGH...
B-BRO!
Y-YOU LITTLE...!
YOU TWO ARE DEAD!
ZW SH
SKF
FOR SOMEONE WHO'S USUALLY SO LAID BACK...
...YOU'RE ALWAYS THE ONE TO MAKE THE FIRST MOVE!
TMP
WHEN IT'S TIME TO DANCE...
...IT SHOULD BE FUN, RIGHT?
SHEESH!

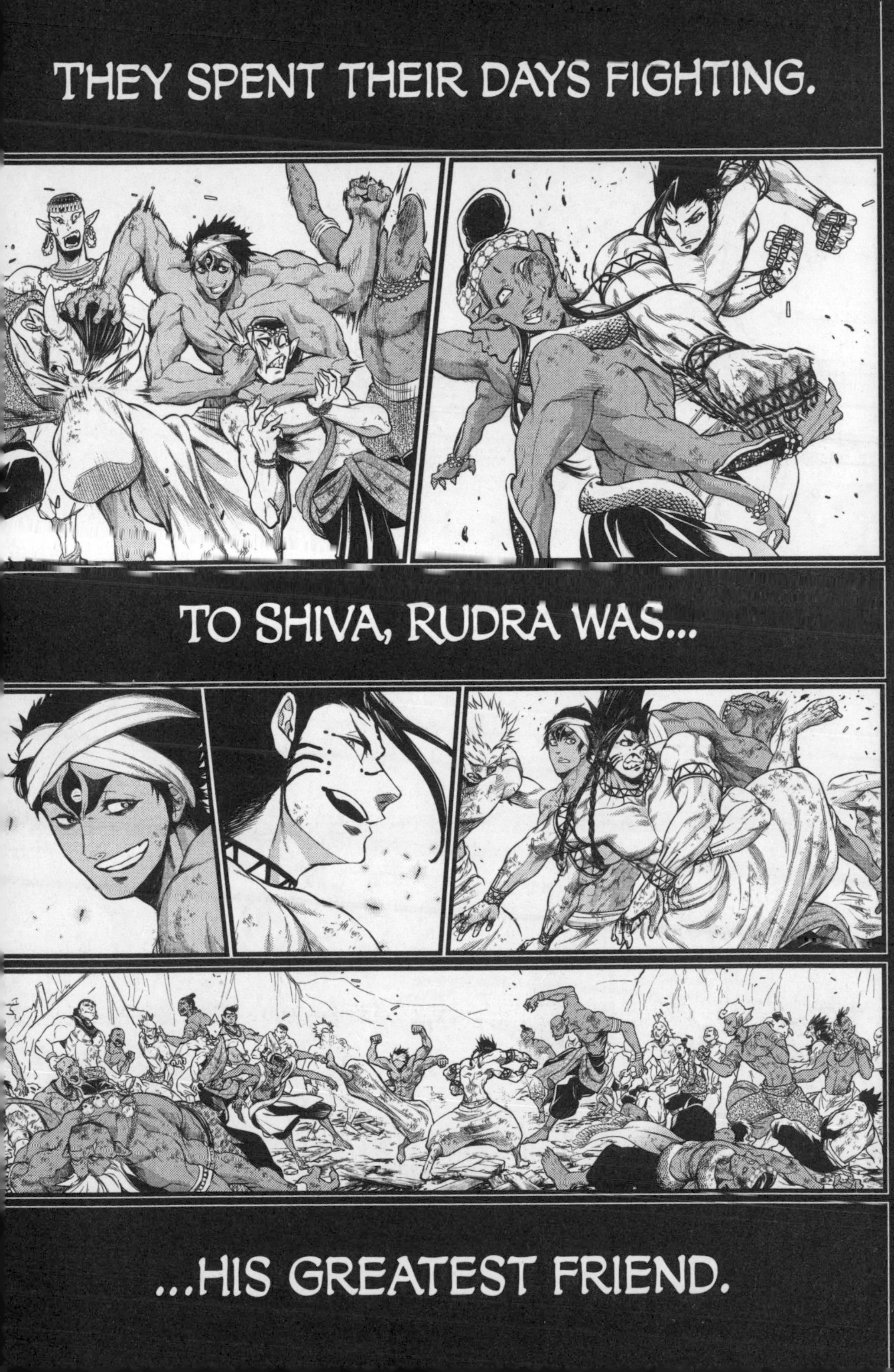
THEY SPENT THEIR DAYS FIGHTING.
TO SHIVA, RUDRA WAS...
...HIS GREATEST FRIEND.

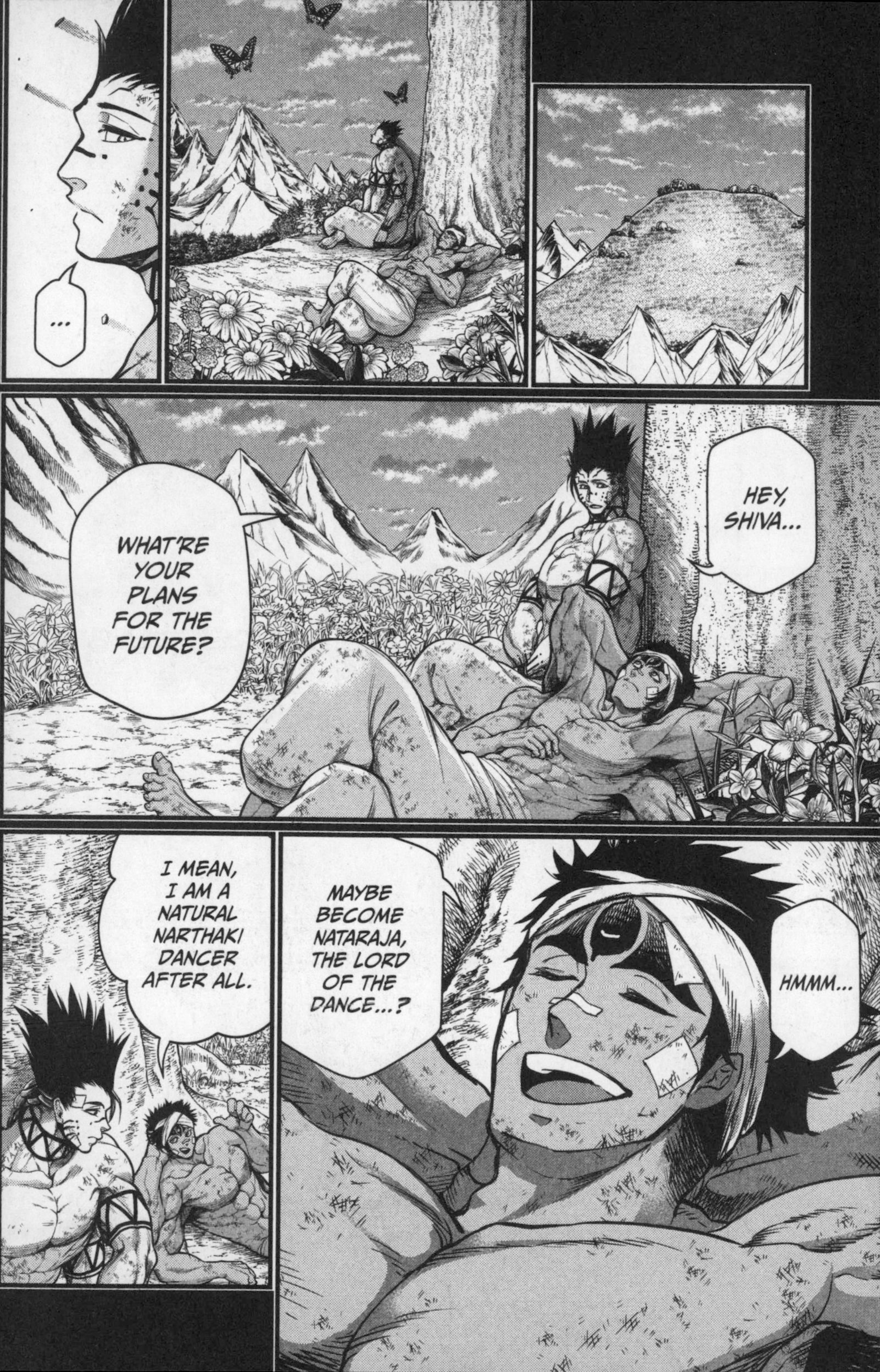
...
HEY, SHIVA...
WHAT'RE YOUR PLANS FOR THE FUTURE?
HMMM...
MAYBE BECOME NATARAJA, THE LORD OF THE DANCE...?
I MEAN, I AM A NATURAL NARTHAKI DANCER AFTER ALL.

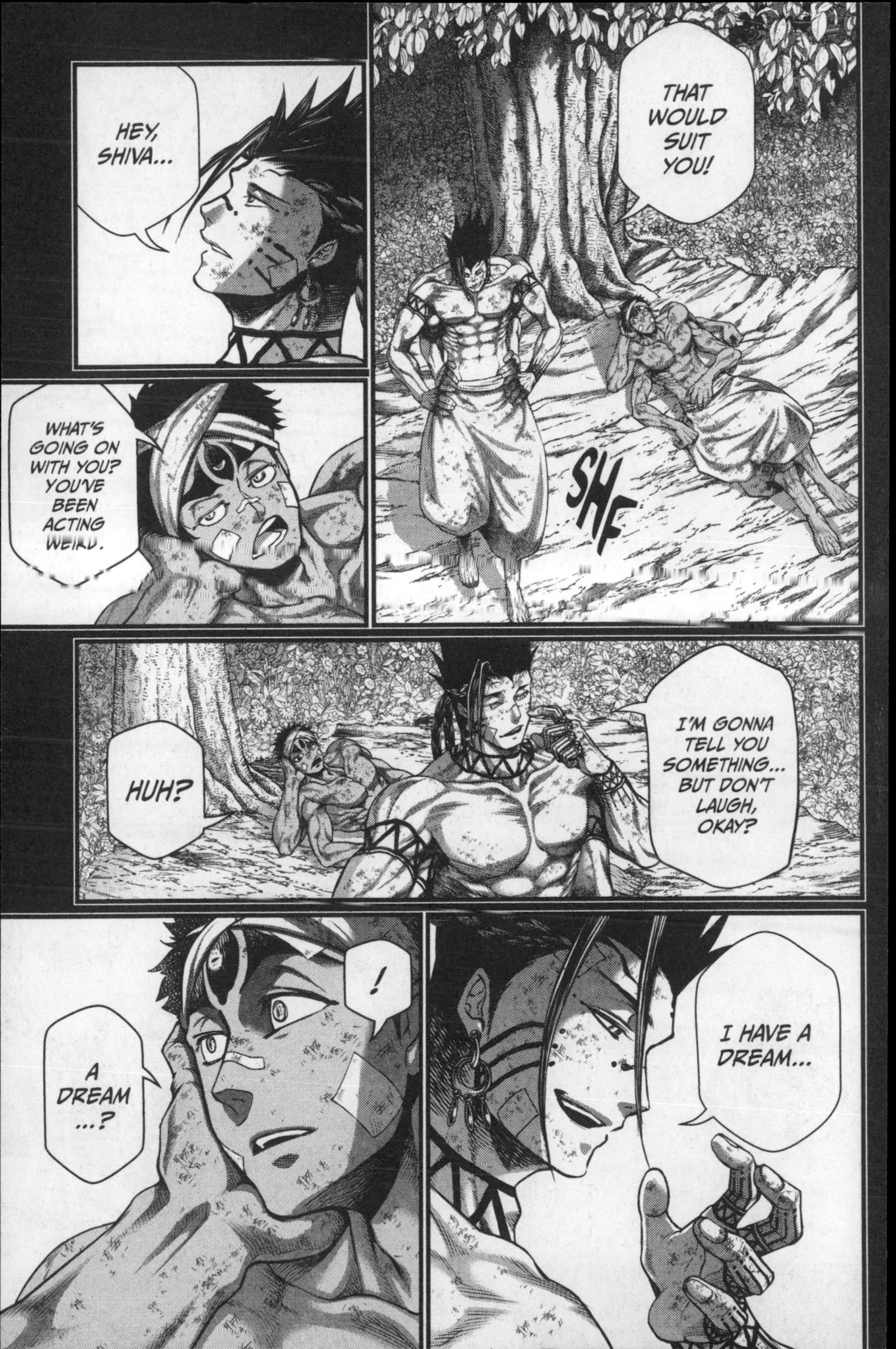
THAT WOULD SUIT YOU!
SHF
HEY, SHIVA...
WHAT'S GOING ON WITH YOU? YOU'VE BEEN ACTING WEIRD.
I'M GONNA TELL YOU SOMETHING... BUT DON'T LAUGH, OKAY?
HUH?
I HAVE A DREAM...
!
A DREAM ...?

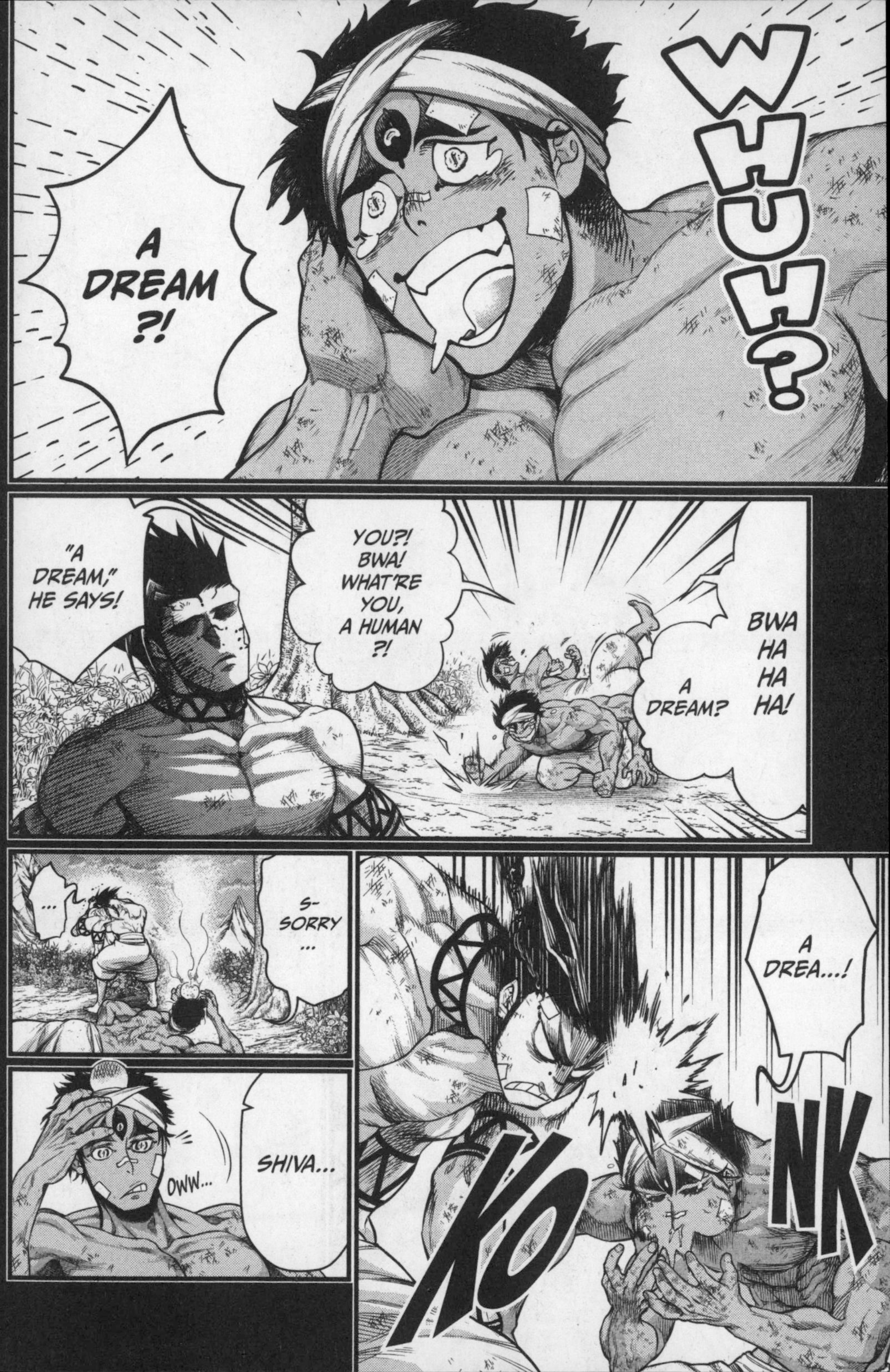
WHUH?!
A DREAM ?!
BWA HA HA HA!
A DREAM?
YOU?! BWA! WHAT'RE YOU, A HUMAN ?!
"A DREAM," HE SAYS!
A DREA...!
KONK
S-SORRY ...
...
SHIVA...
OWW...

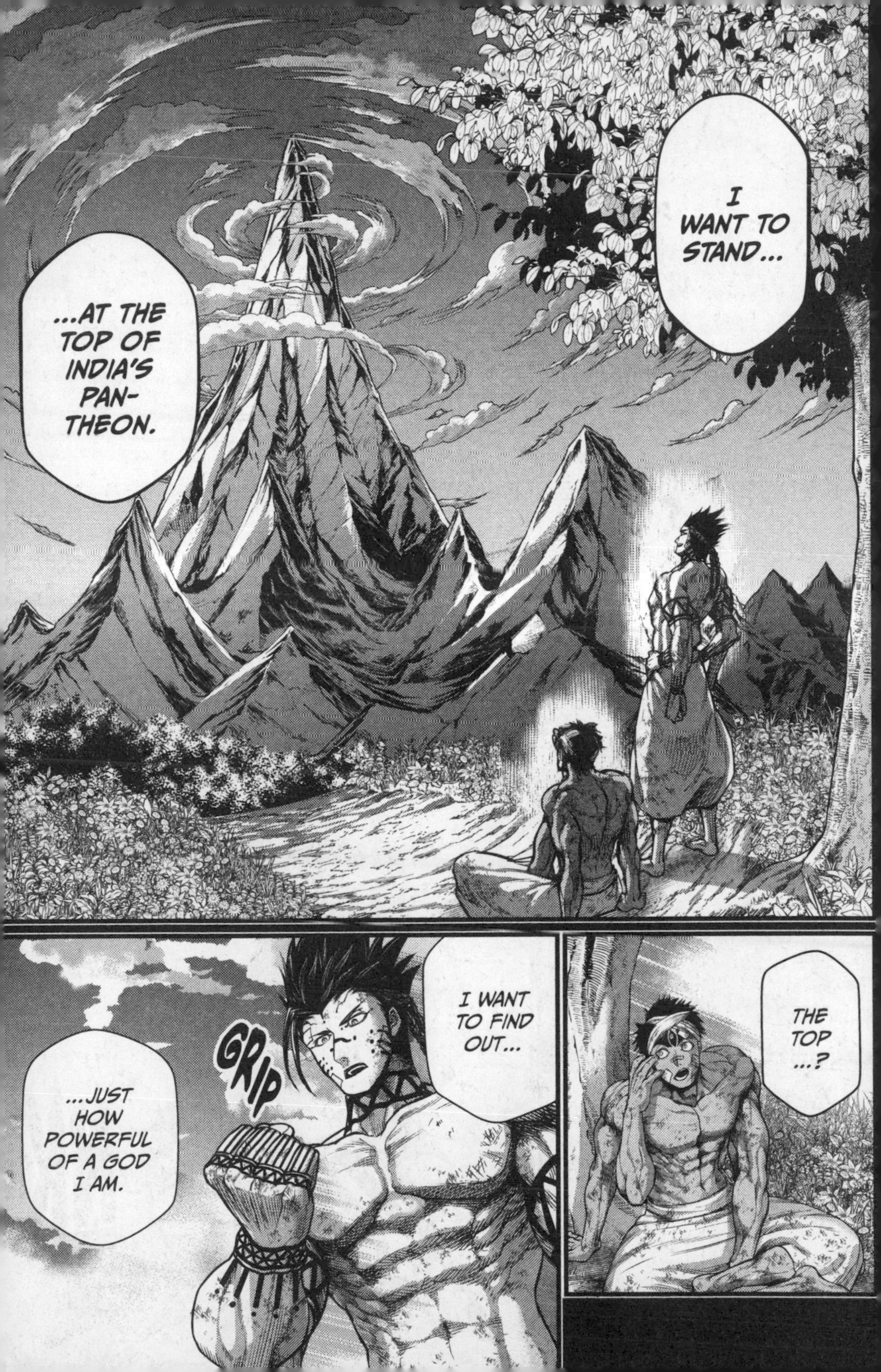
I WANT TO STAND...
...AT THE TOP OF INDIA'S PAN-THEON.
THE TOP ...?
I WANT TO FIND OUT...
GRIP
...JUST HOW POWERFUL OF A GOD I AM.

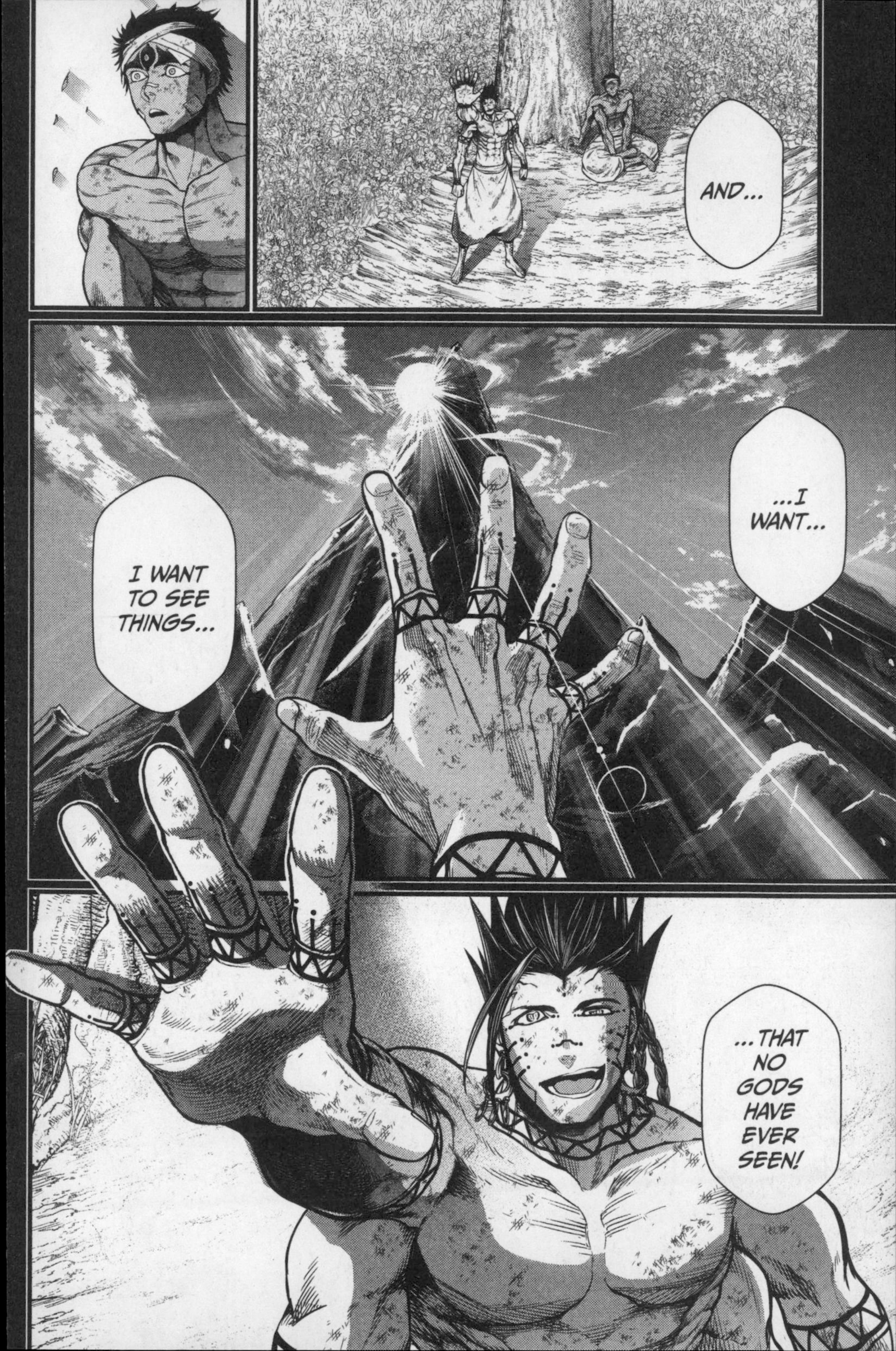
AND...
...I WANT...
I WANT TO SEE THINGS...
...THAT NO GODS HAVE EVER SEEN!

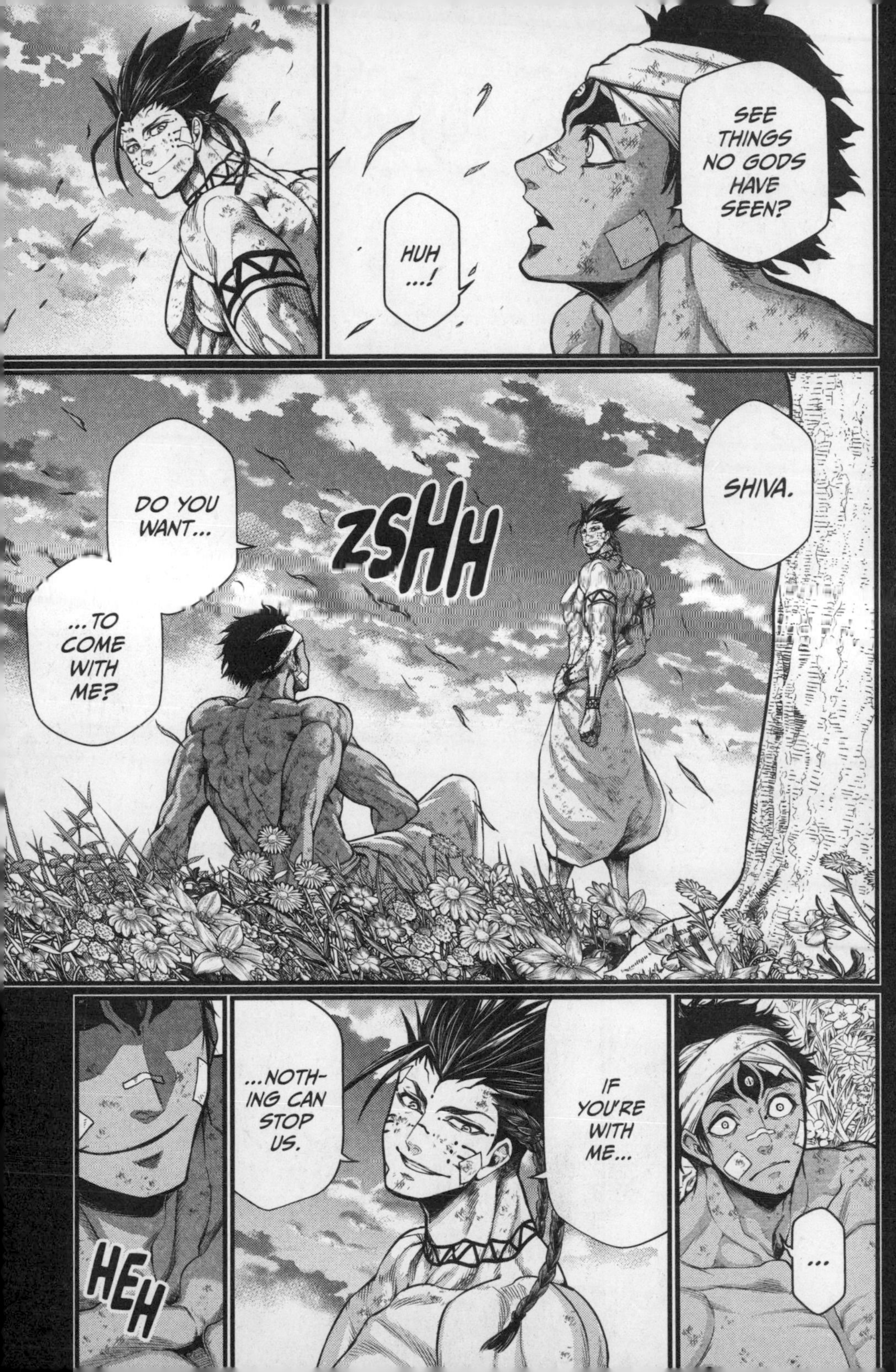

SEE THINGS NO GODS HAVE SEEN?
HUH ...!
SHIVA.
ZSHH
DO YOU WANT...
...TO COME WITH ME?
...
IF YOU'RE WITH ME...
...NOTH-ING CAN STOP US.
HEH

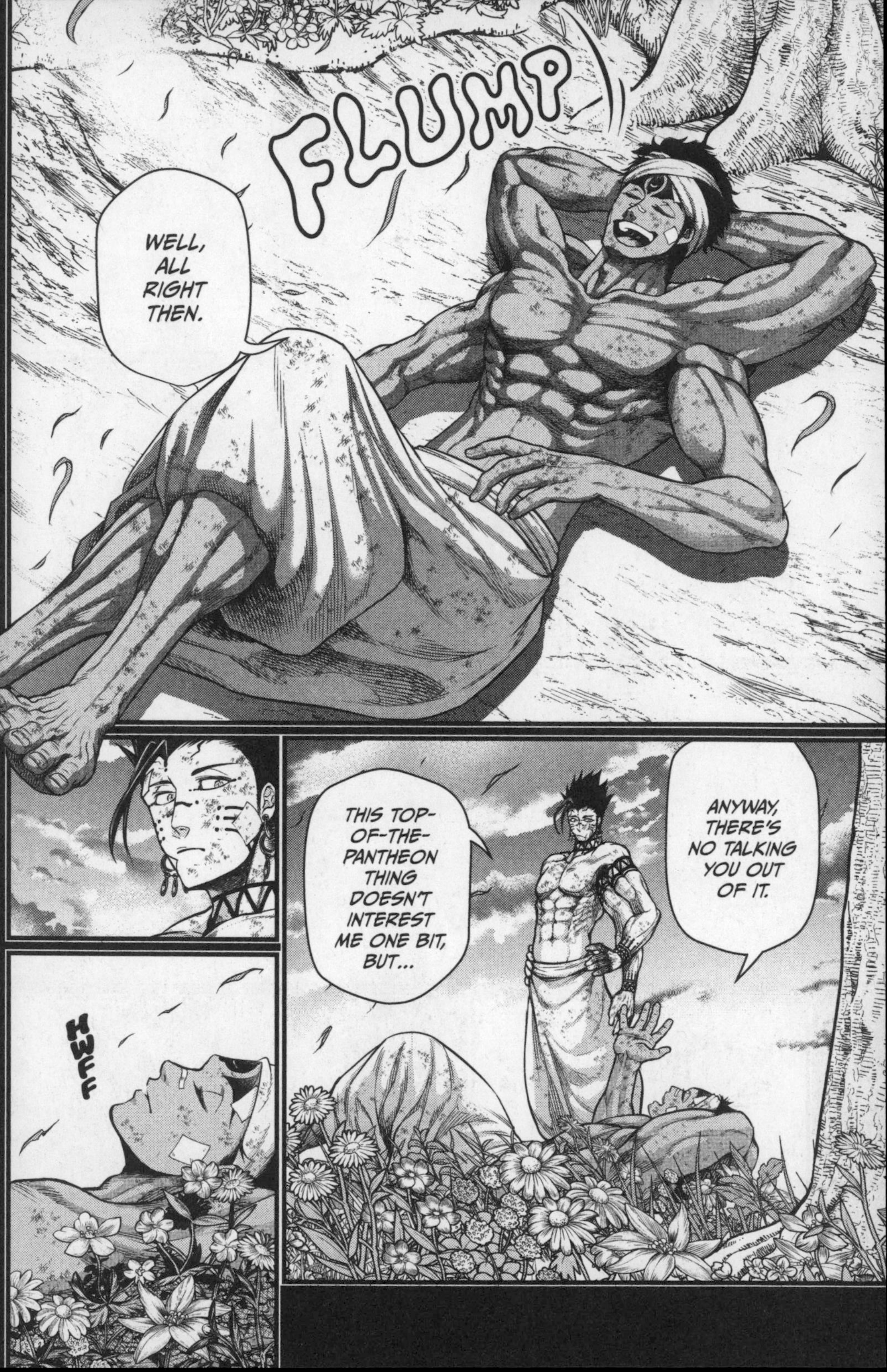
FLUMP
WELL, ALL RIGHT THEN.
ANYWAY, THERE'S NO TALKING YOU OUT OF IT.
THIS TOP-OF-THE-PANTHEON THING DOESN'T INTEREST ME ONE BIT, BUT...
HWFF

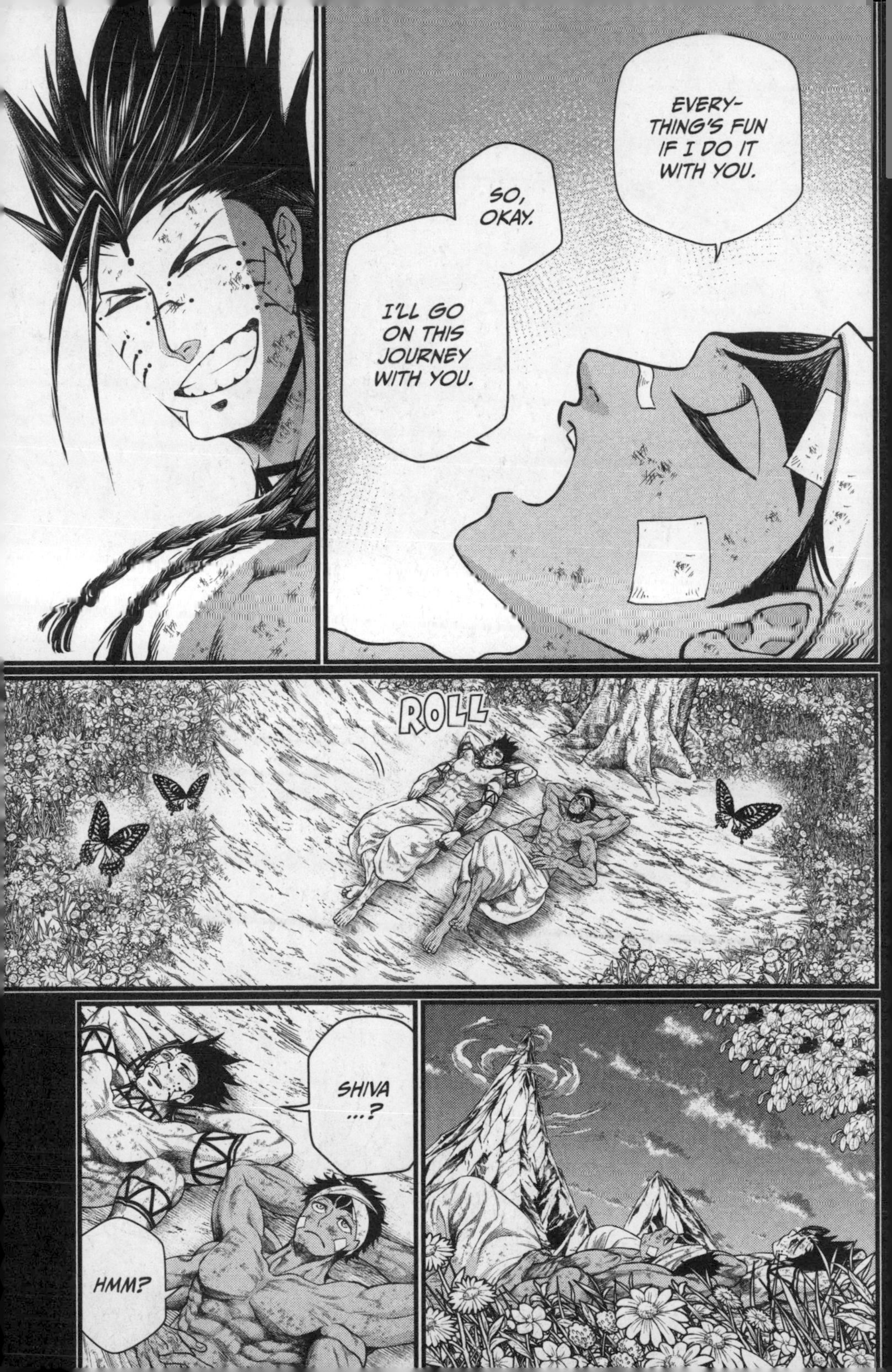
EVERY-THING'S FUN IF I DO IT WITH YOU.
SO, OKAY. I'LL GO ON THIS JOURNEY WITH YOU.
ROLL
SHIVA ...?
HMM?

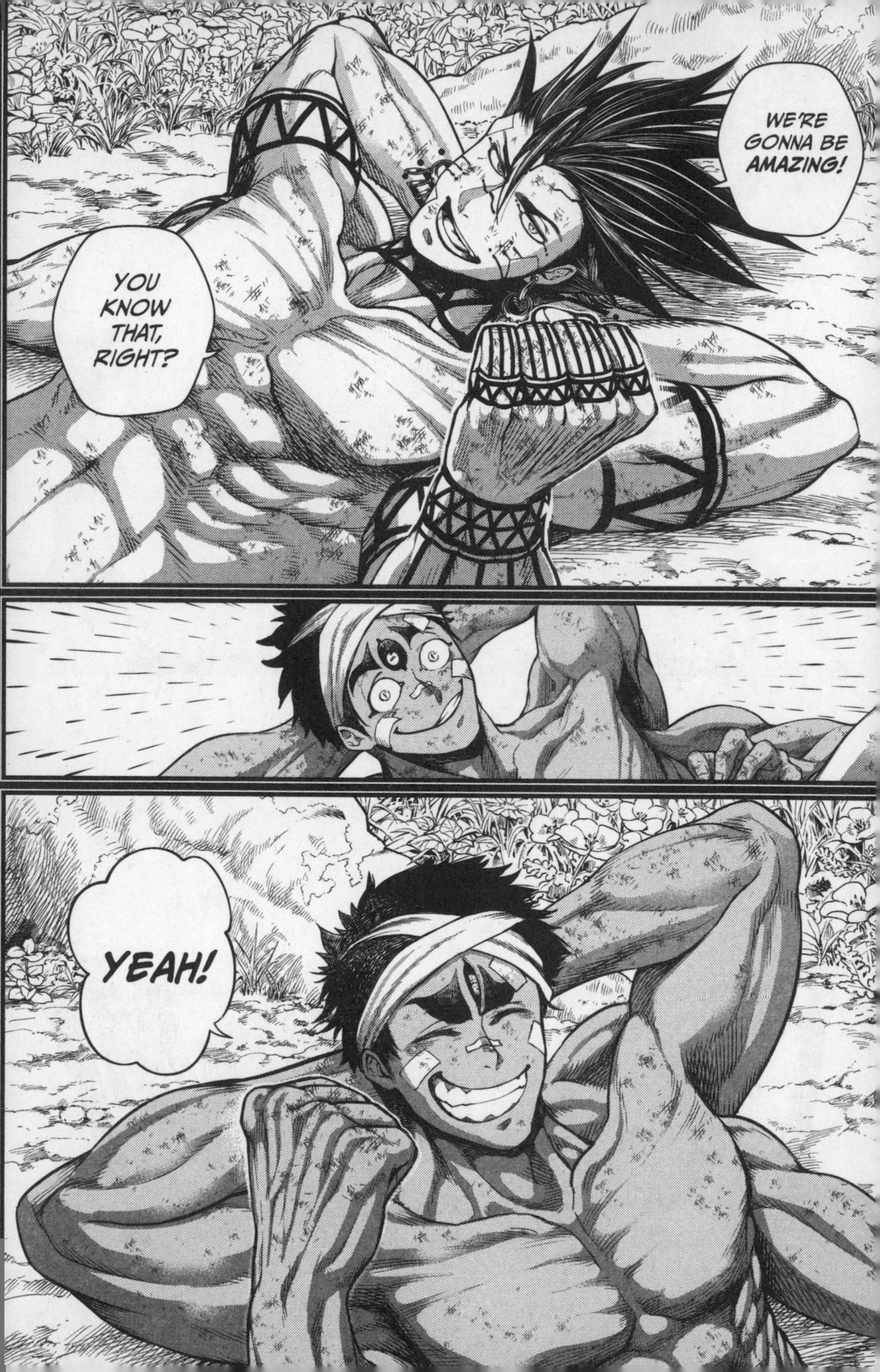
WE'RE GONNA BE AMAZING!
YOU KNOW THAT, RIGHT?
YEAH!

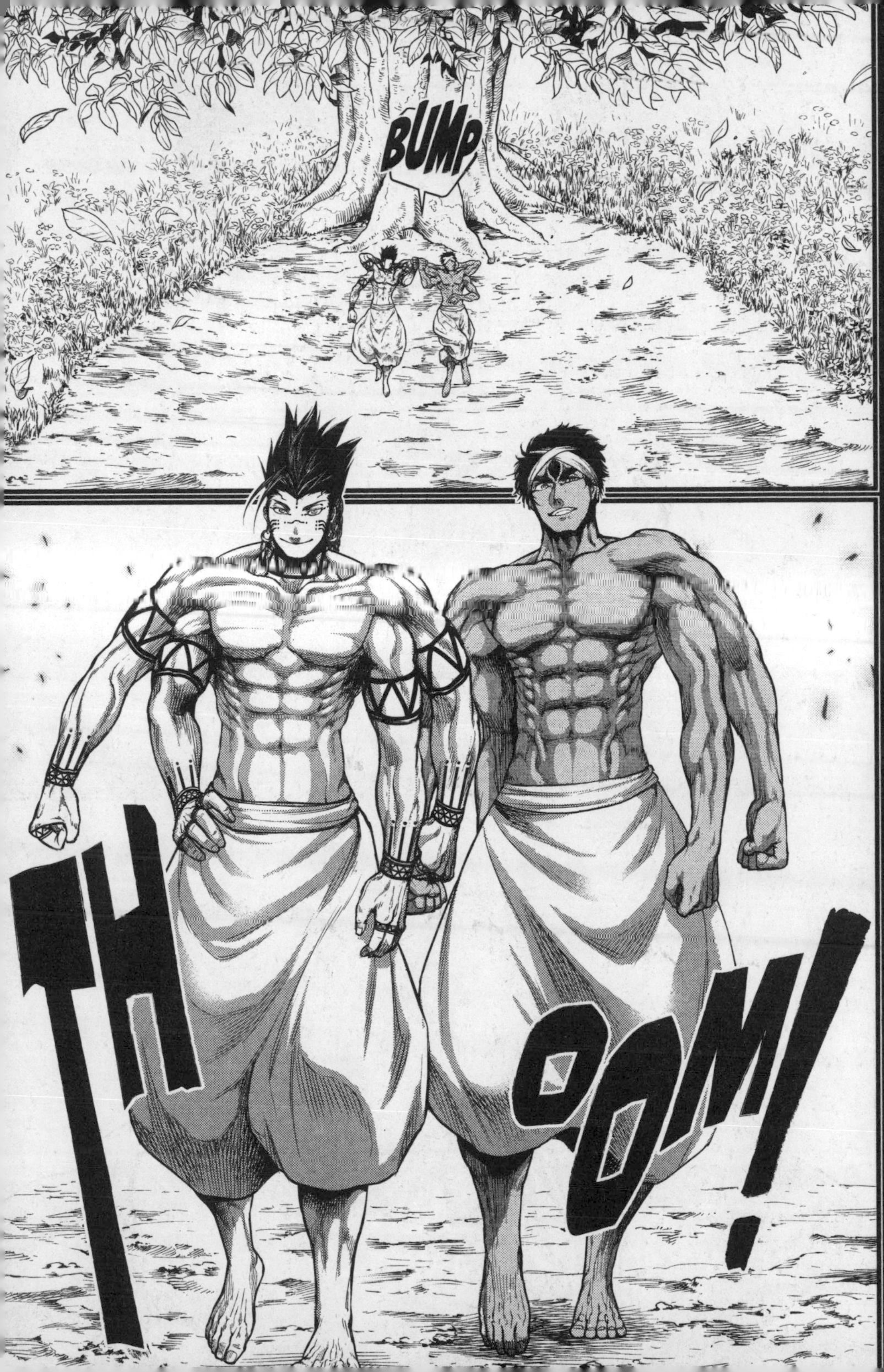
BUMP
THOOM!

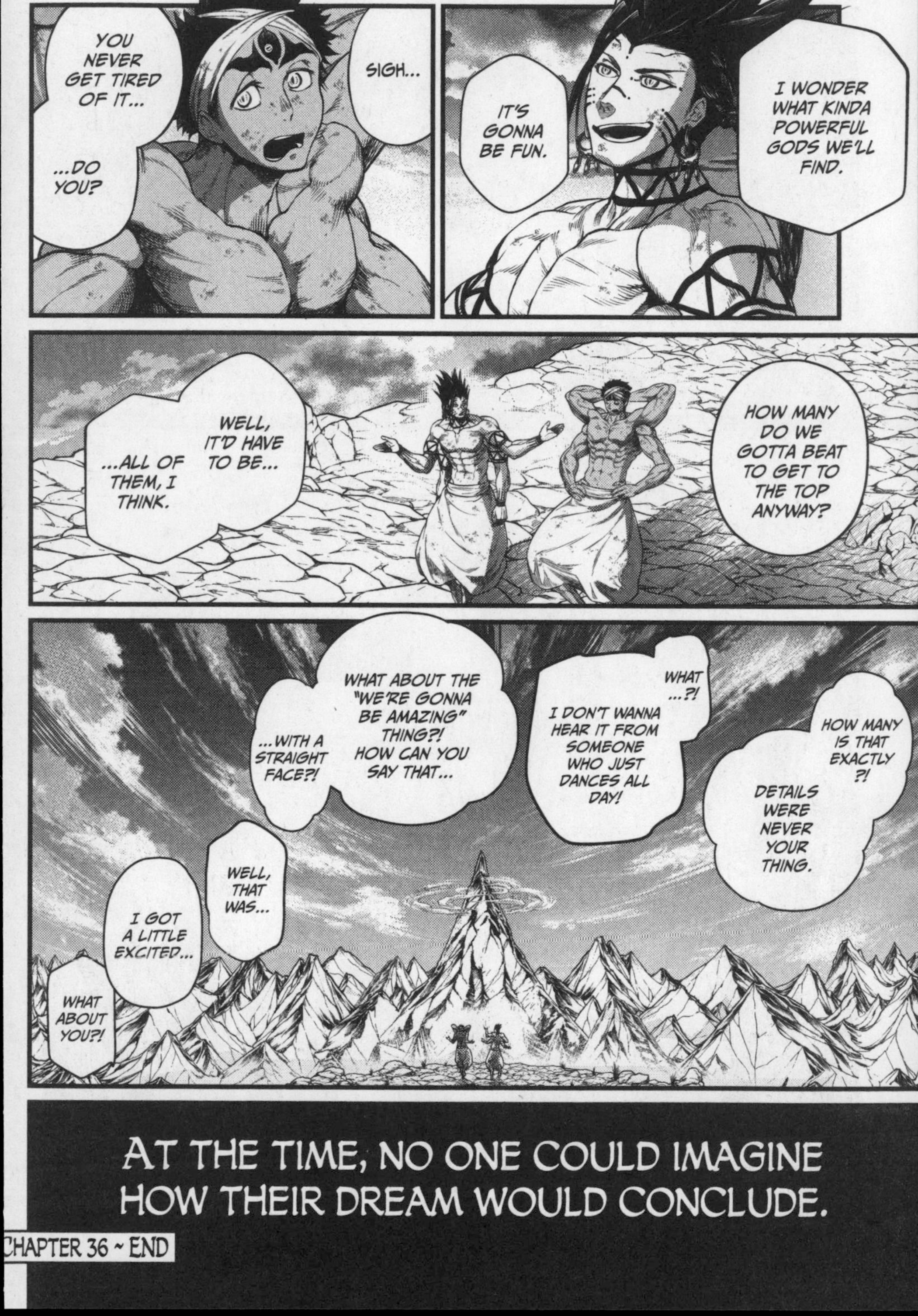
I WONDER WHAT KINDA POWERFUL GODS WE'LL FIND.
IT'S GONNA BE FUN.
SIGH...
YOU NEVER GET TIRED OF IT...
...DO YOU?
HOW MANY DO WE GOTTA BEAT TO GET TO THE TOP ANYWAY?
WELL, IT'D HAVE TO BE...
...ALL OF THEM, I THINK.
HOW MANY IS THAT EXACTLY ?!
DETAILS WERE NEVER YOUR THING.
WHAT ...?!
I DON'T WANNA HEAR IT FROM SOMEONE WHO JUST DANCES ALL DAY!
WHAT ABOUT THE "WE'RE GONNA BE AMAZING" THING?! HOW CAN YOU SAY THAT...
...WITH A STRAIGHT FACE?!
WELL, THAT WAS...
I GOT A LITTLE EXCITED...
WHAT ABOUT YOU?!

AT THE TIME, NO ONE COULD IMAGINE HOW THEIR DREAM WOULD CONCLUDE.

CHAPTER 36 ~ END

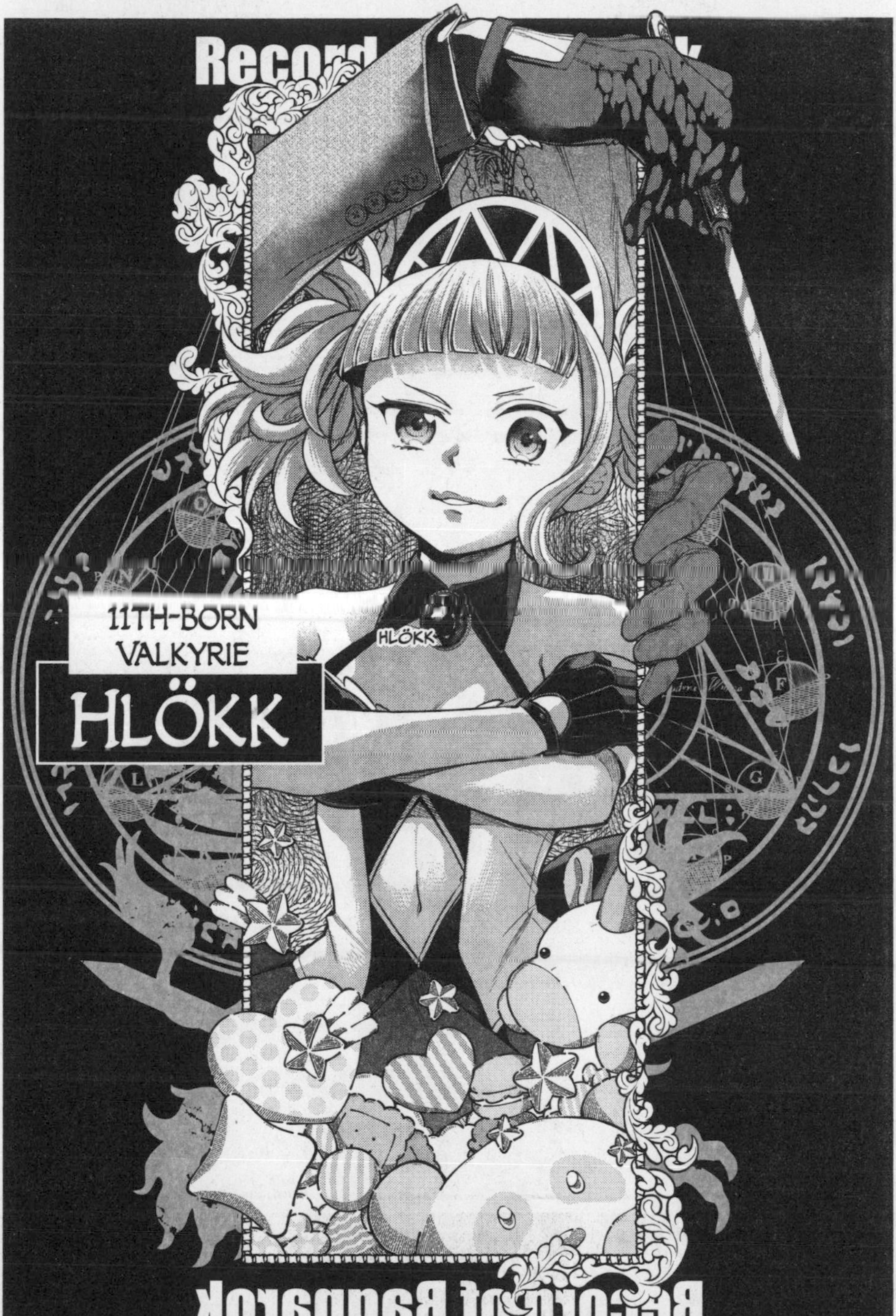
Record of Ragnarok
11TH-BORN VALKYRIE
HLÖKK
HLÖKK

RECORD OF

RAGNAROK

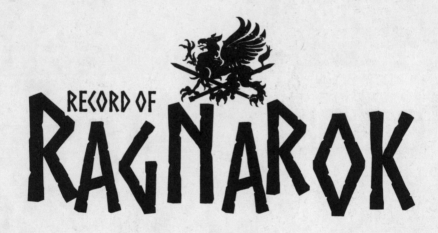

CHAPTER 37: THE TOP OF INDIA

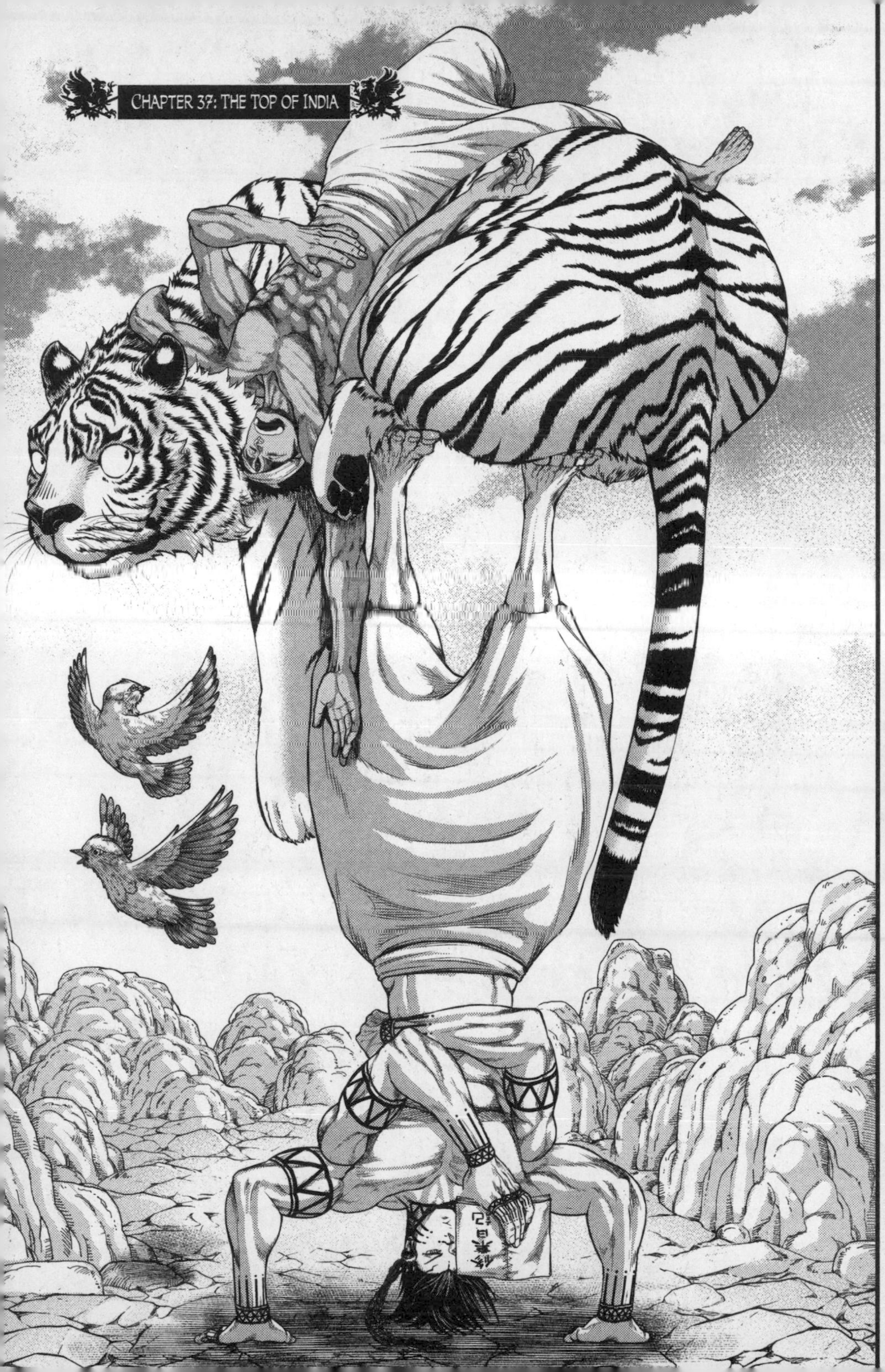

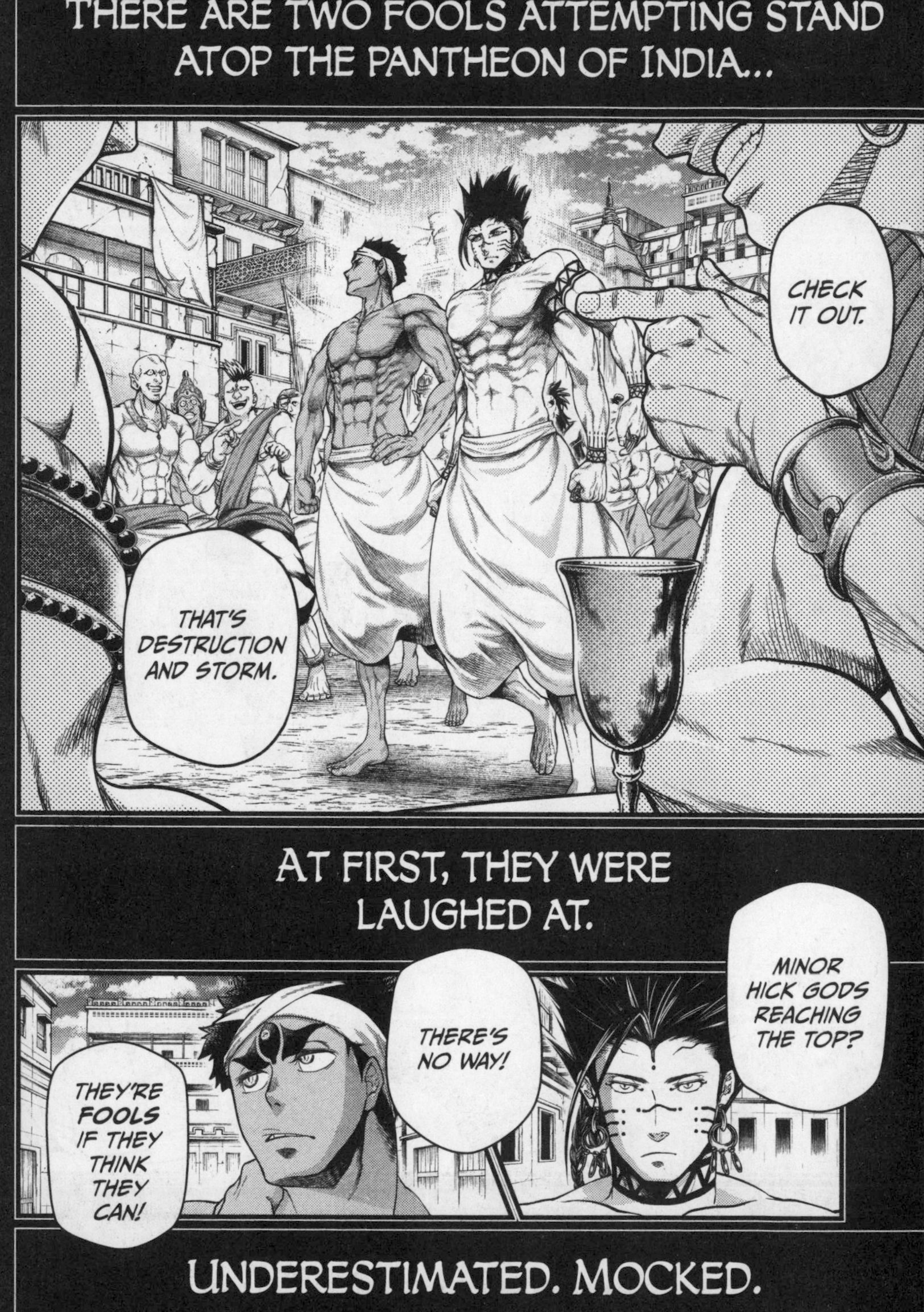
THERE ARE TWO FOOLS ATTEMPTING STAND ATOP THE PANTHEON OF INDIA...
CHECK IT OUT.
THAT'S DESTRUCTION AND STORM.
AT FIRST, THEY WERE LAUGHED AT.
MINOR HICK GODS REACHING THE TOP?
THERE'S NO WAY!
THEY'RE FOOLS IF THEY THINK THEY CAN!
UNDERESTIMATED. MOCKED.

HOWEVER...

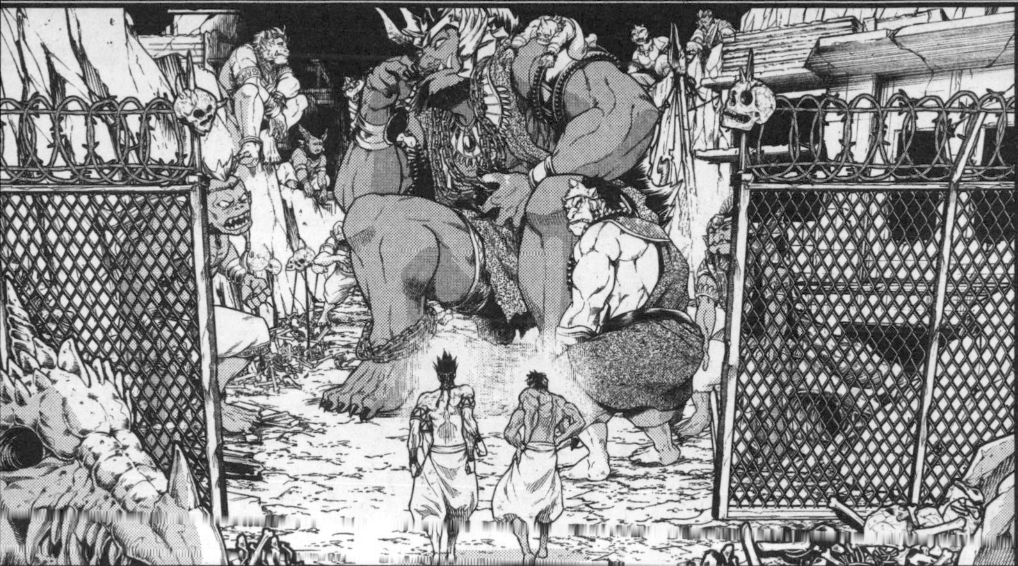

HOWEVER...

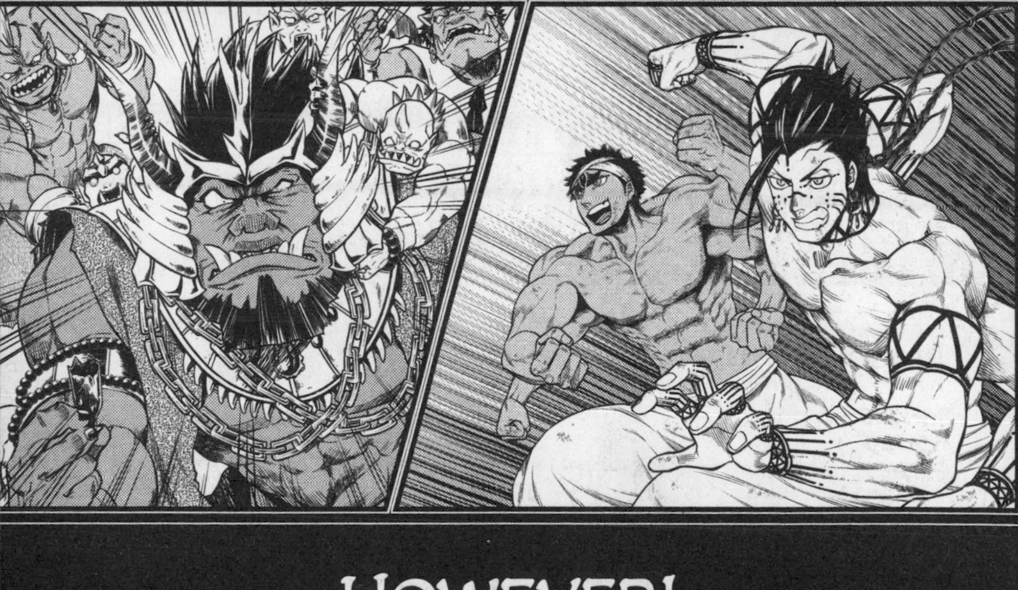

HOWEVER!

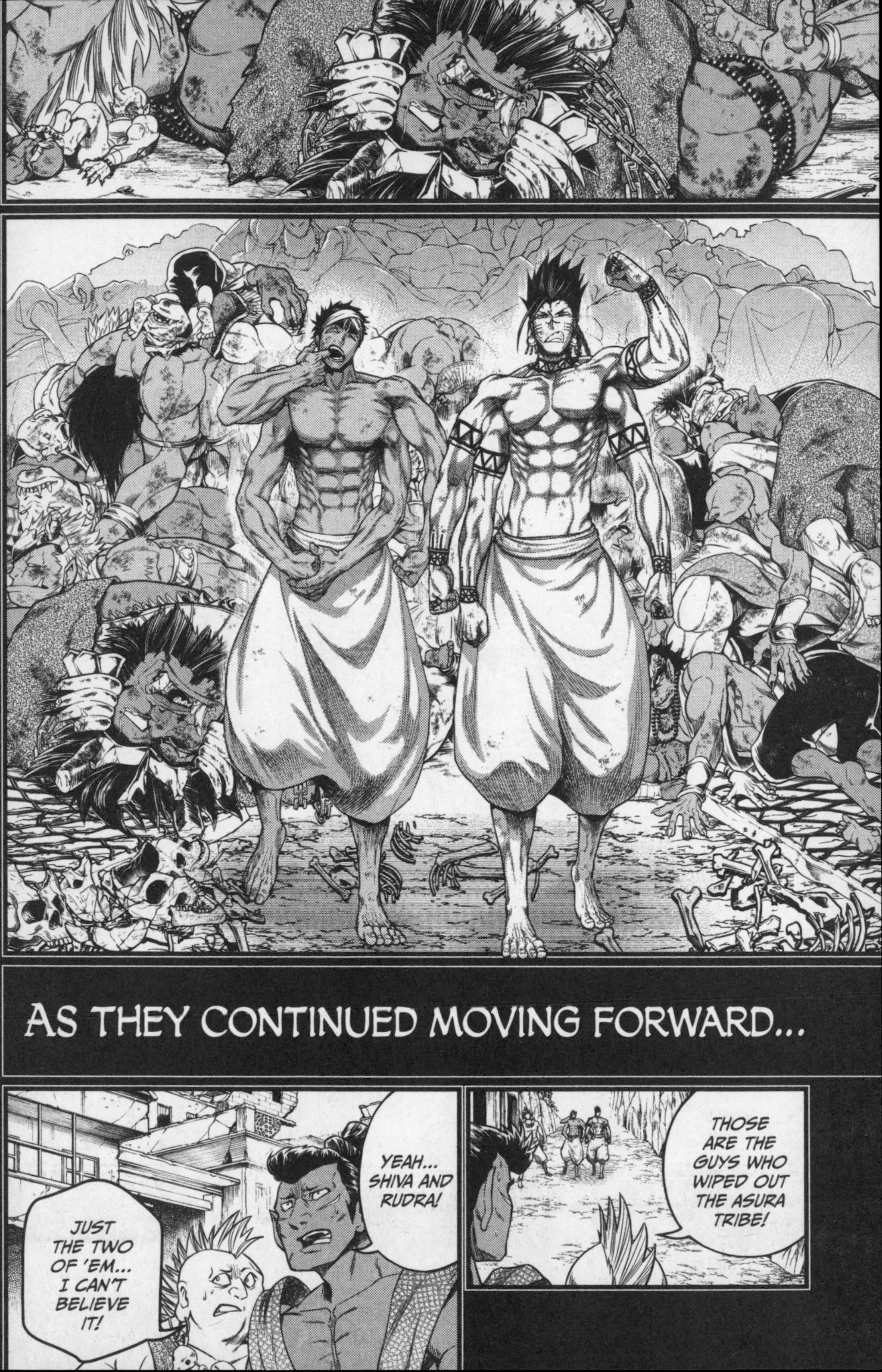
AS THEY CONTINUED MOVING FORWARD...
THOSE ARE THE GUYS WHO WIPED OUT THE ASURA TRIBE!
YEAH... SHIVA AND RUDRA!
JUST THE TWO OF 'EM... I CAN'T BELIEVE IT!

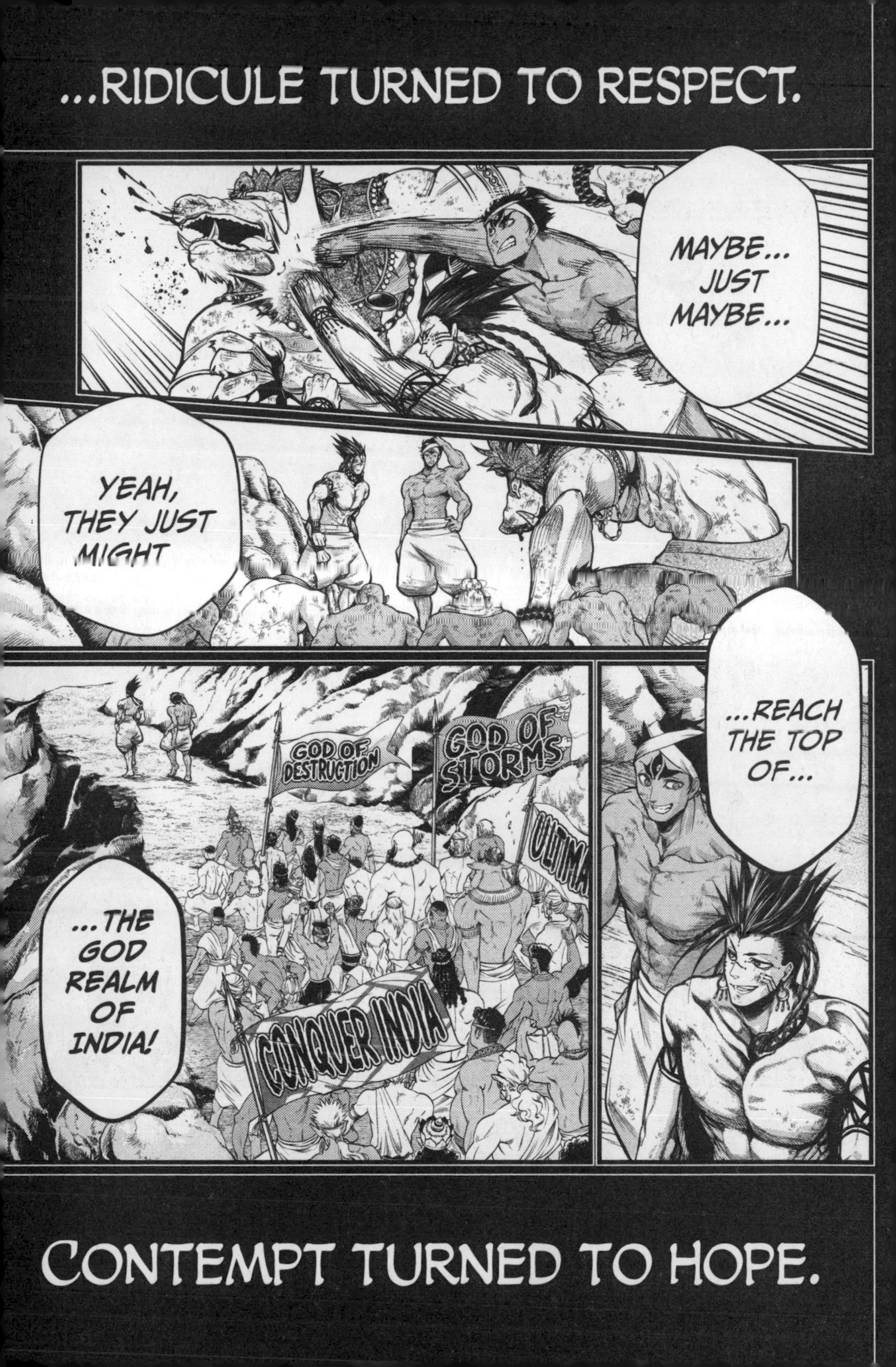
...RIDICULE TURNED TO RESPECT.
MAYBE... JUST MAYBE...
YEAH, THEY JUST MIGHT
...REACH THE TOP OF...
GOD OF STORMS
GOD OF DESTRUCTION
ULTIMA
...THE GOD REALM OF INDIA!
CONQUER INDIA
CONTEMPT TURNED TO HOPE.

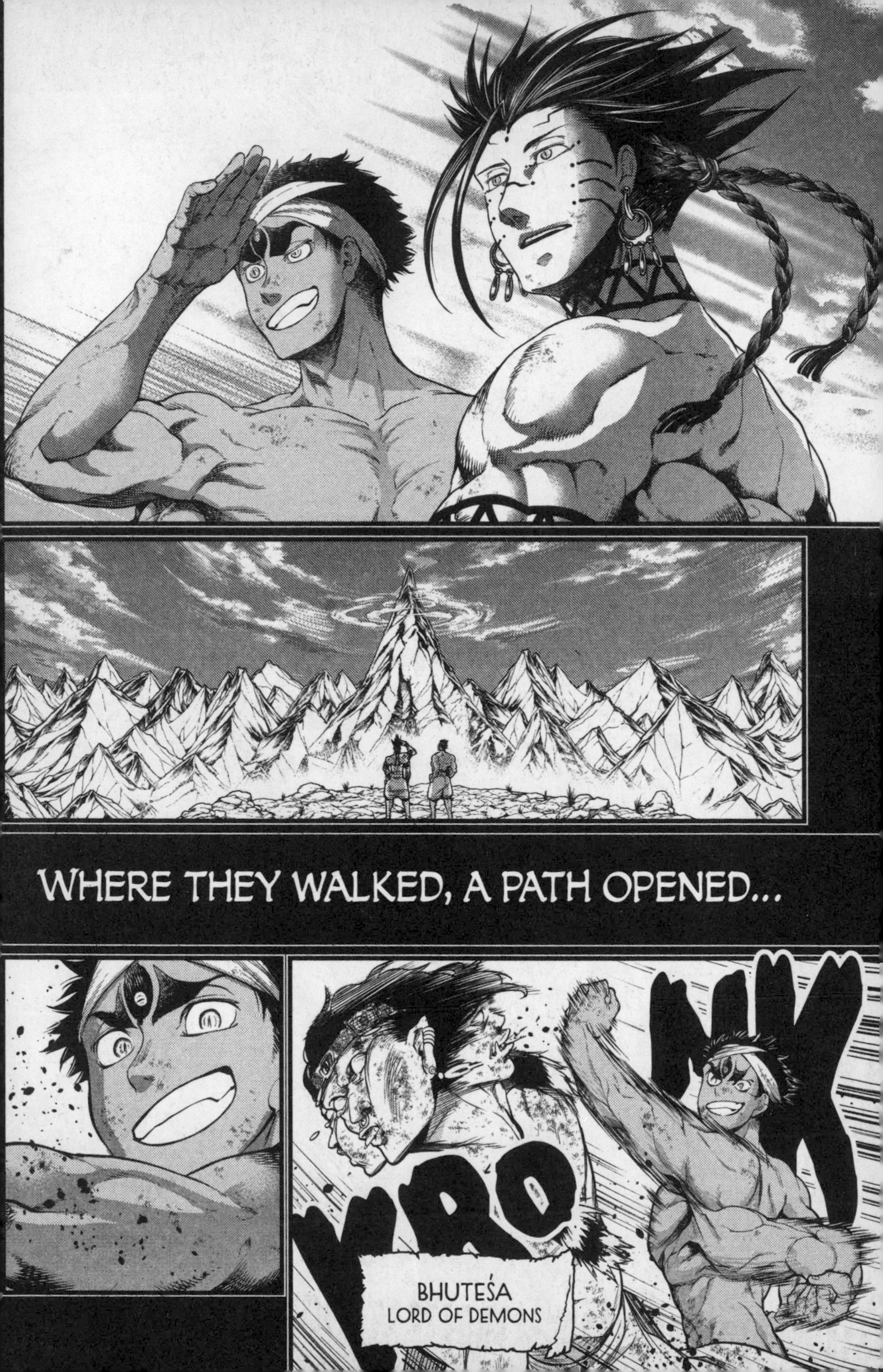
WHERE THEY WALKED, A PATH OPENED...
BHUTEŚA
LORD OF DEMONS

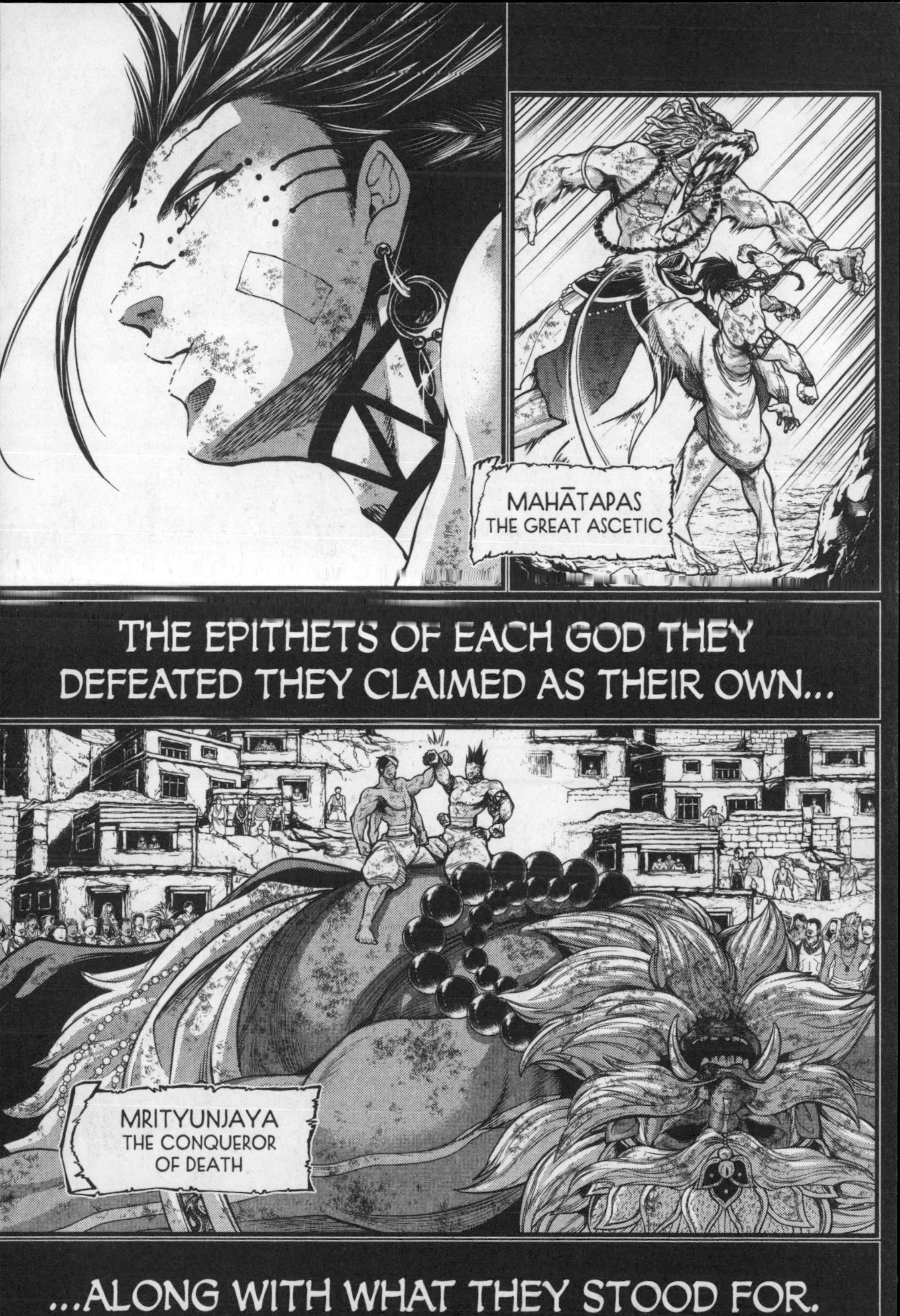
MAHĀTAPAS
THE GREAT ASCETIC
THE EPITHETS OF EACH GOD THEY DEFEATED THEY CLAIMED AS THEIR OWN...
MRITYUNJAYA
THE CONQUEROR OF DEATH
...ALONG WITH WHAT THEY STOOD FOR.

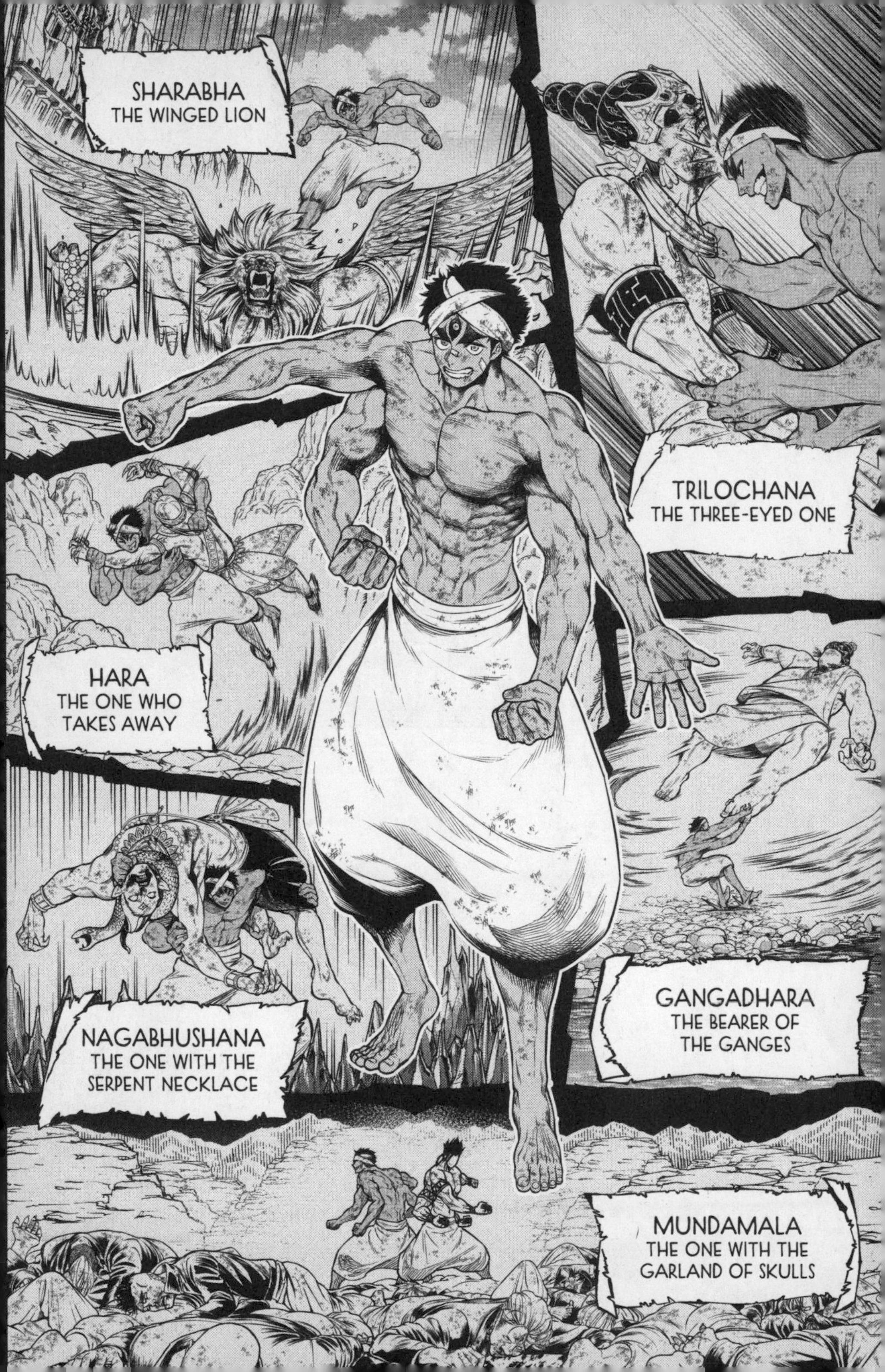

TRILOCHANA
THE THREE-EYED ONE
SHARABHA
THE WINGED LION
GANGADHARA
THE BEARER OF
THE GANGES
HARA
THE ONE WHO
TAKES AWAY
NAGABHUSHANA
THE ONE WITH THE
SERPENT NECKLACE
MUNDAMALA
THE ONE WITH THE
GARLAND OF SKULLS

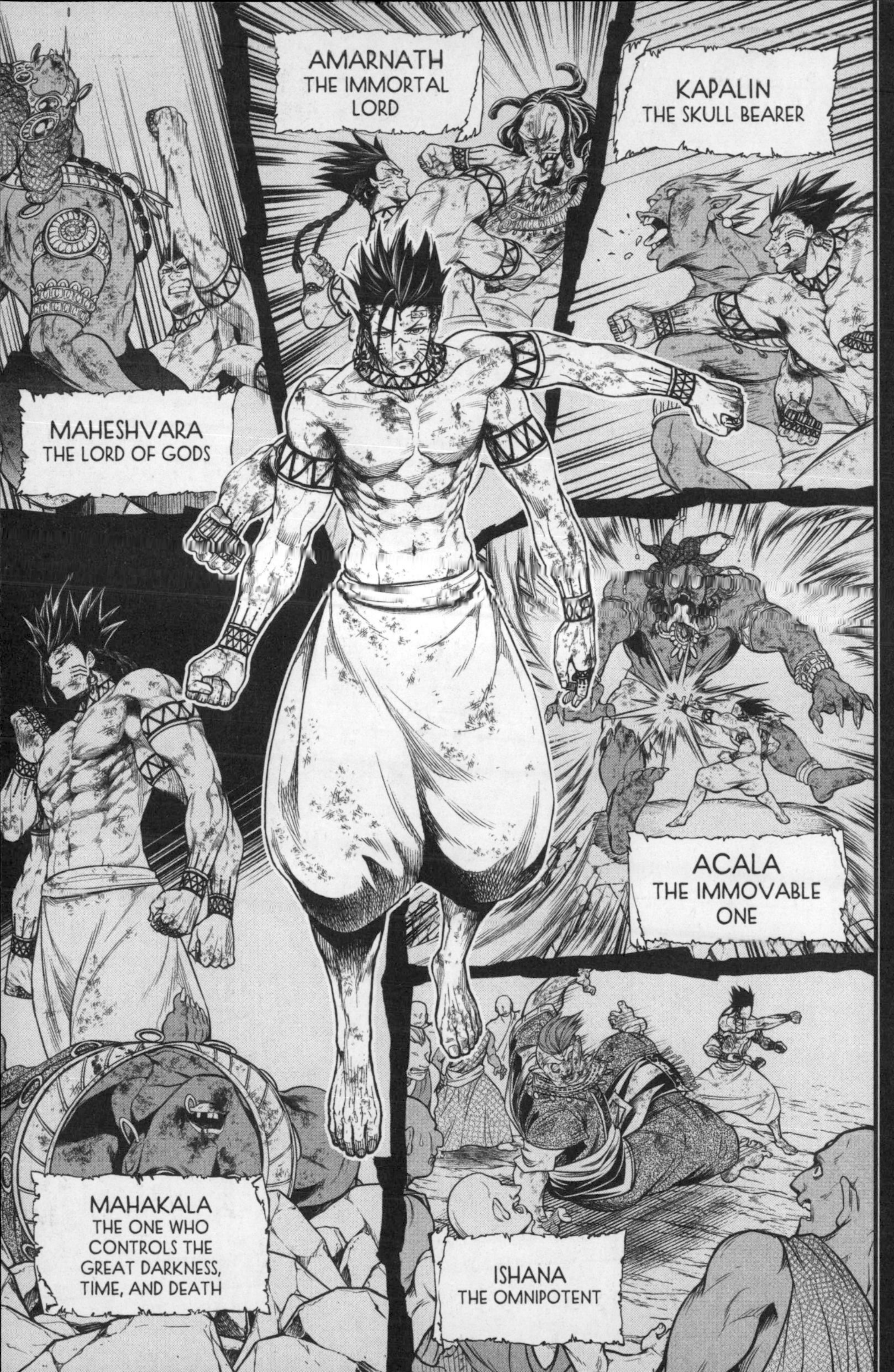
KAPALIN
THE SKULL BEARER
AMARNATH
THE IMMORTAL
LORD
MAHESHVARA
THE LORD OF GODS
ACALA
THE IMMOVABLE
ONE
ISHANA
THE OMNIPOTENT
MAHAKALA
THE ONE WHO
CONTROLS THE
GREAT DARKNESS,
TIME, AND DEATH

AND THEN...

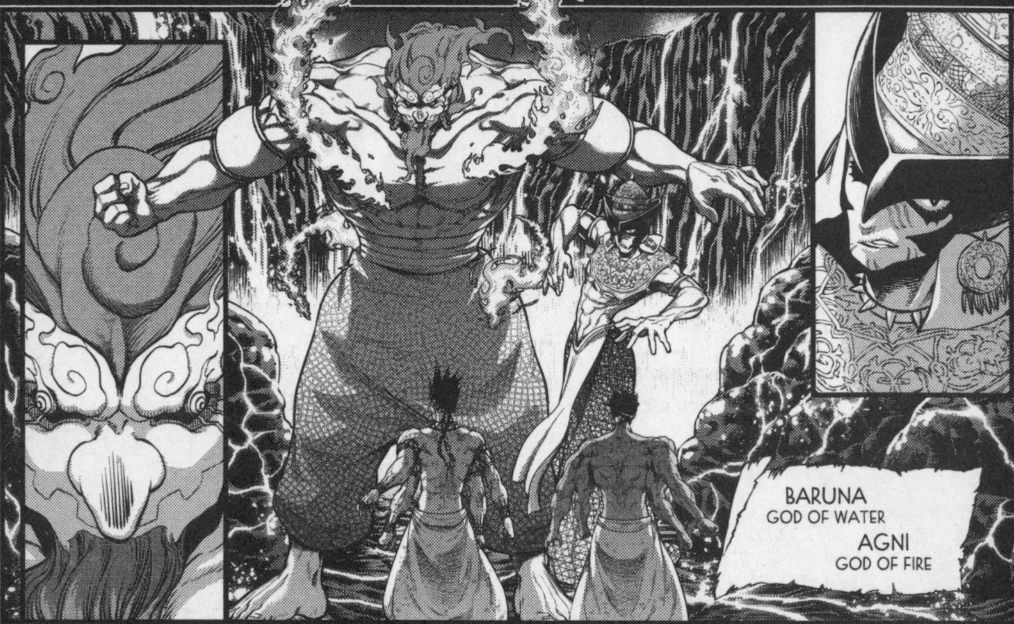
BARUNA
GOD OF WATER
AGNI
GOD OF FIRE

...AFTER COUNTLESS FIERCE BATTLES...

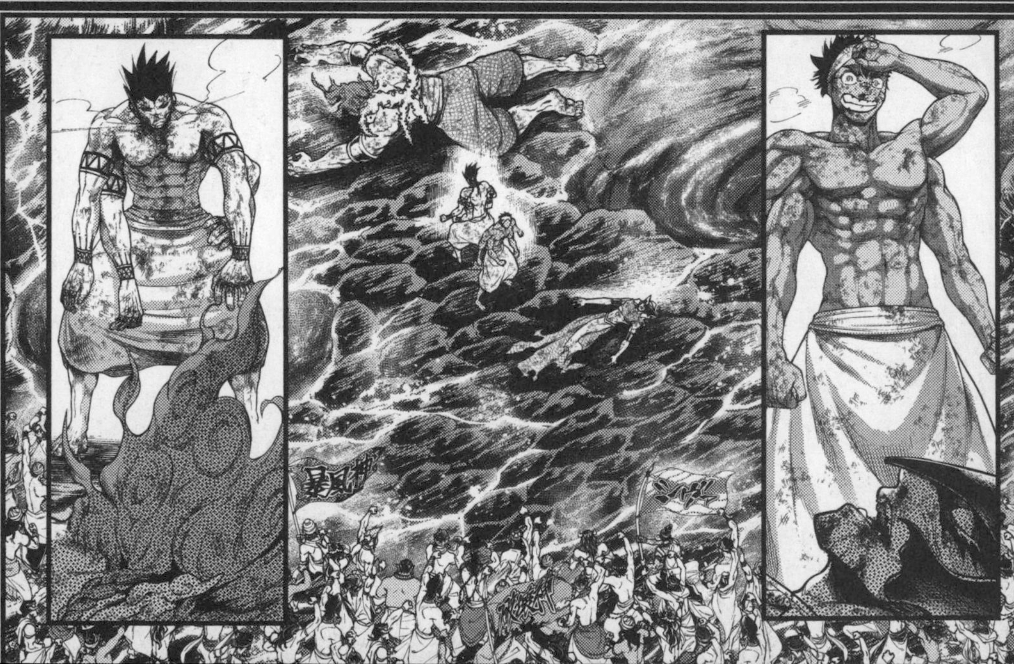

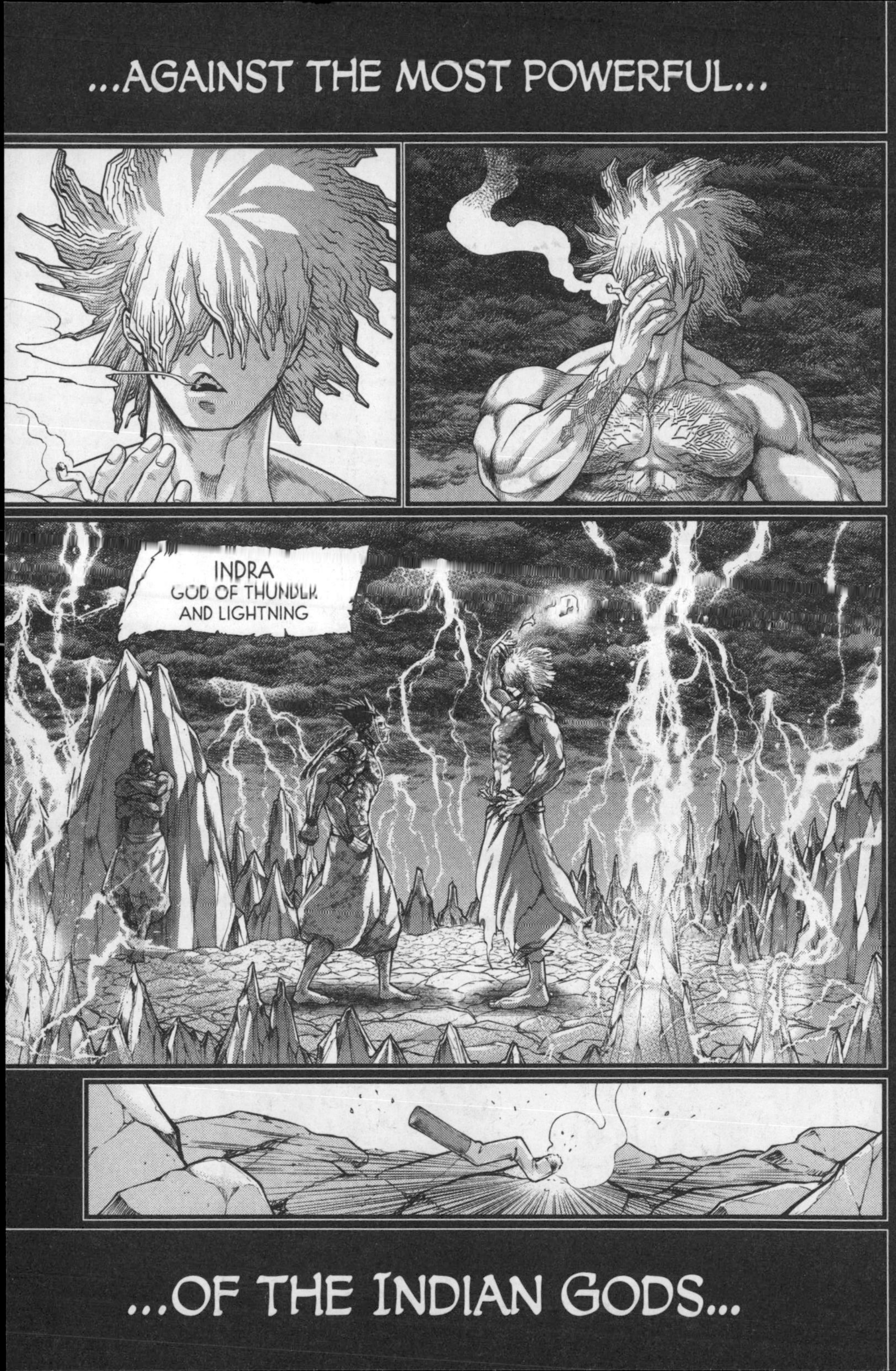
...AGAINST THE MOST POWERFUL...
INDRA
GOD OF THUNDER
AND LIGHTNING
...OF THE INDIAN GODS...

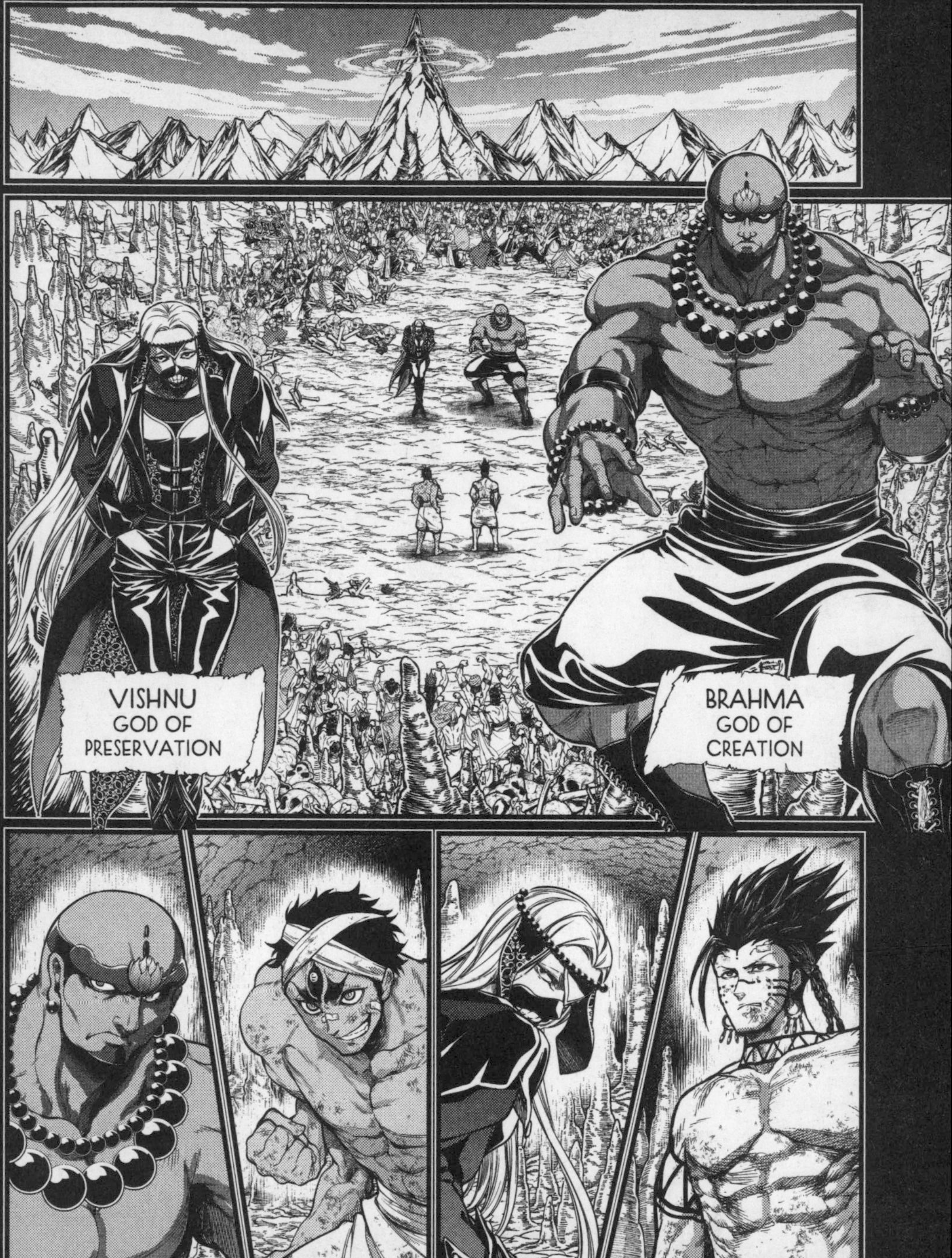
BRAHMA
GOD OF
CREATION
VISHNU
GOD OF
PRESERVATION

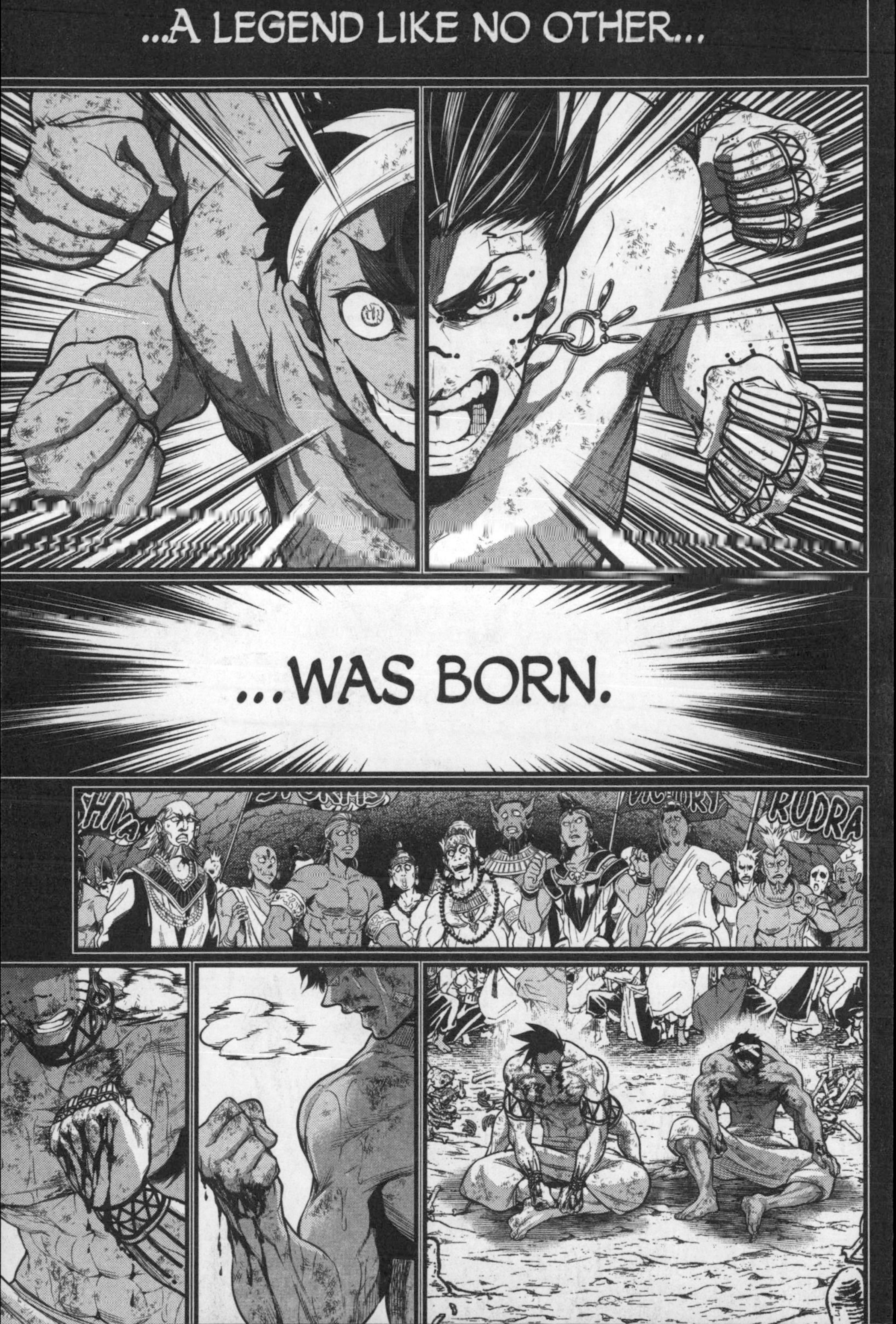
...A LEGEND LIKE NO OTHER...
...WAS BORN.
RUDRA

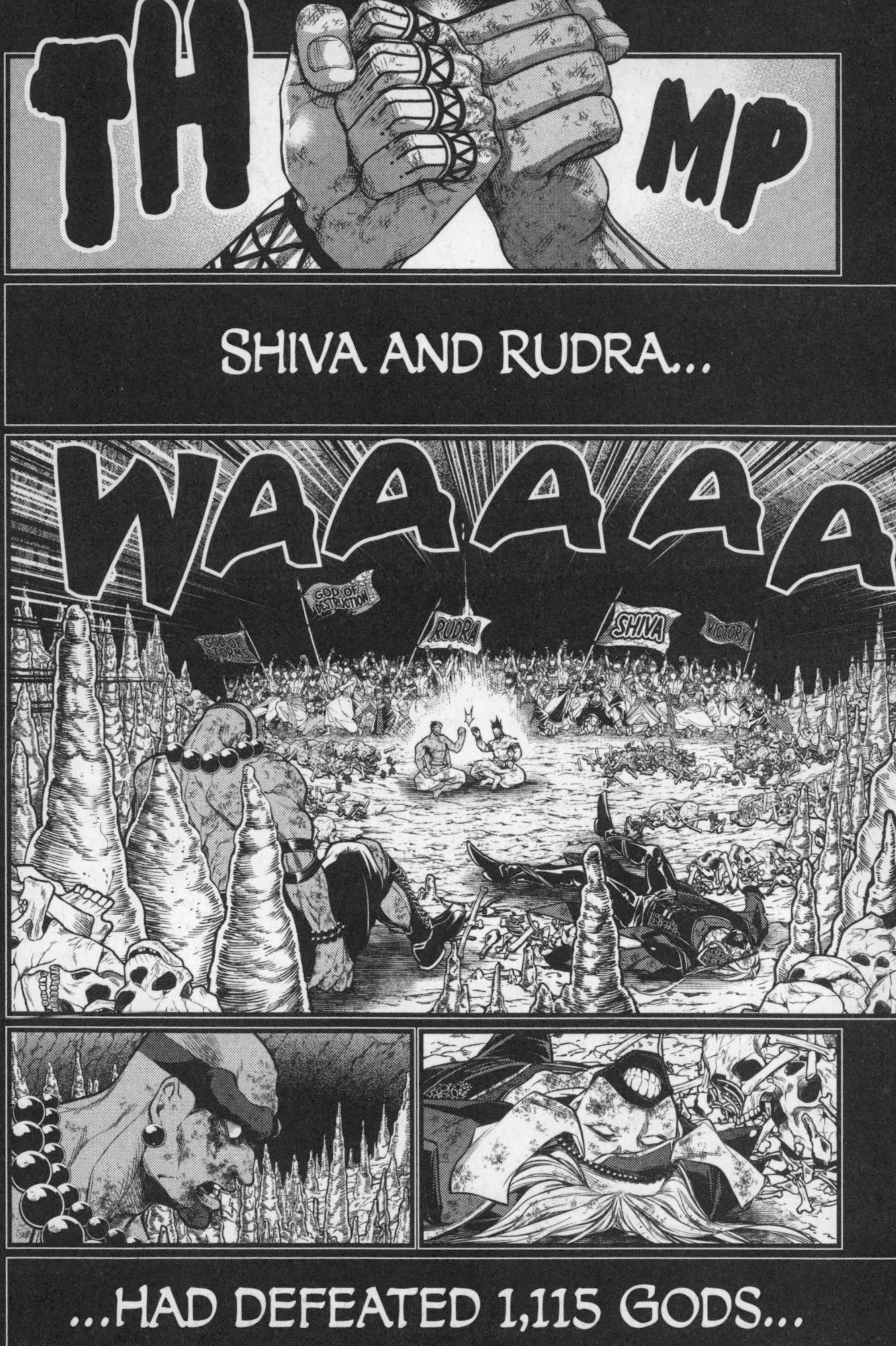
TH MP
SHIVA AND RUDRA...
WAAAAA
VICTORY
SHIVA
RUDRA
GOD OF DESTRUCTION
GOD OF STORMS
...HAD DEFEATED 1,115 GODS...

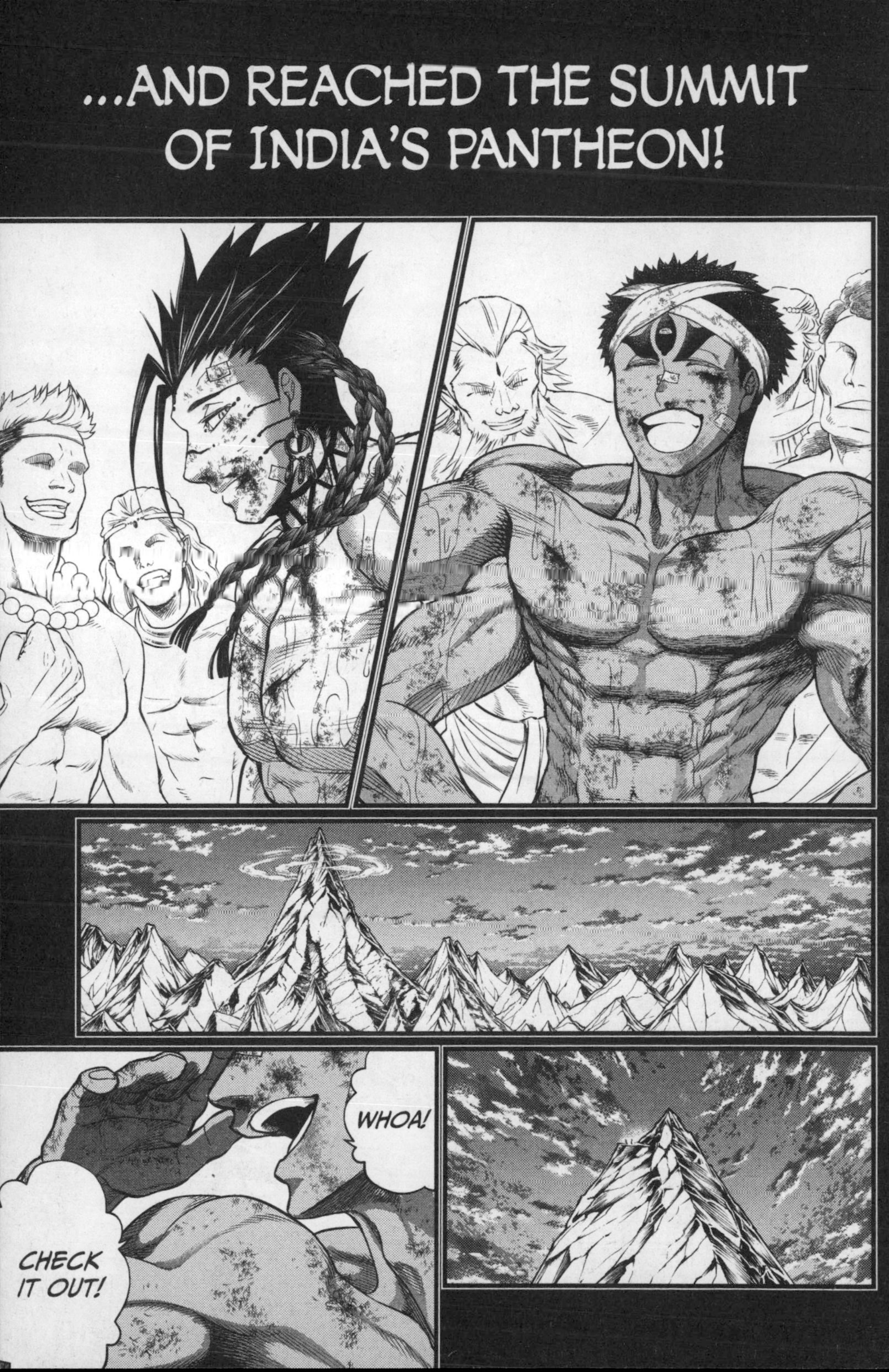
...AND REACHED THE SUMMIT OF INDIA'S PANTHEON!
WHOA!
CHECK IT OUT!

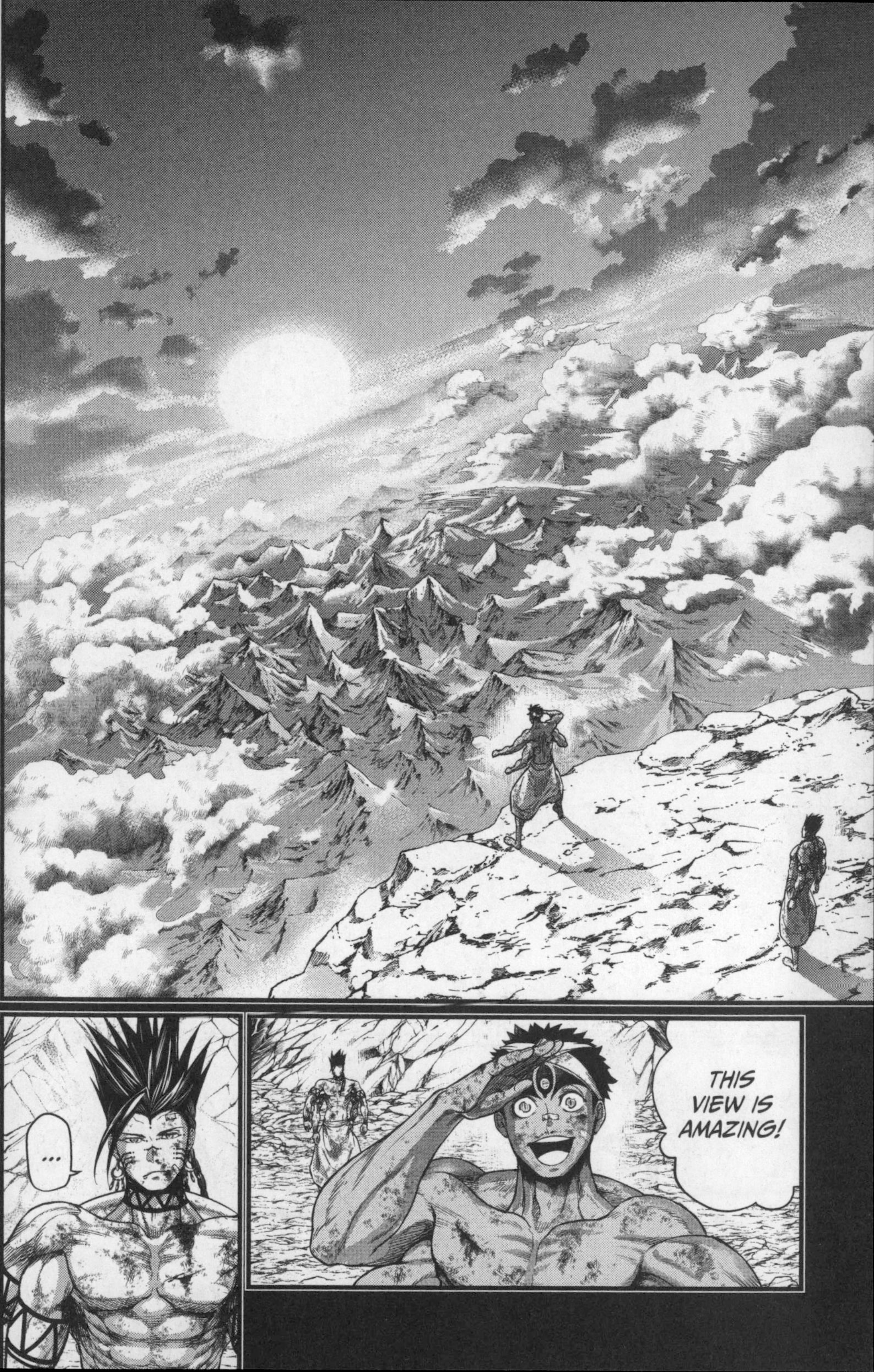
THIS VIEW IS AMAZING!
...

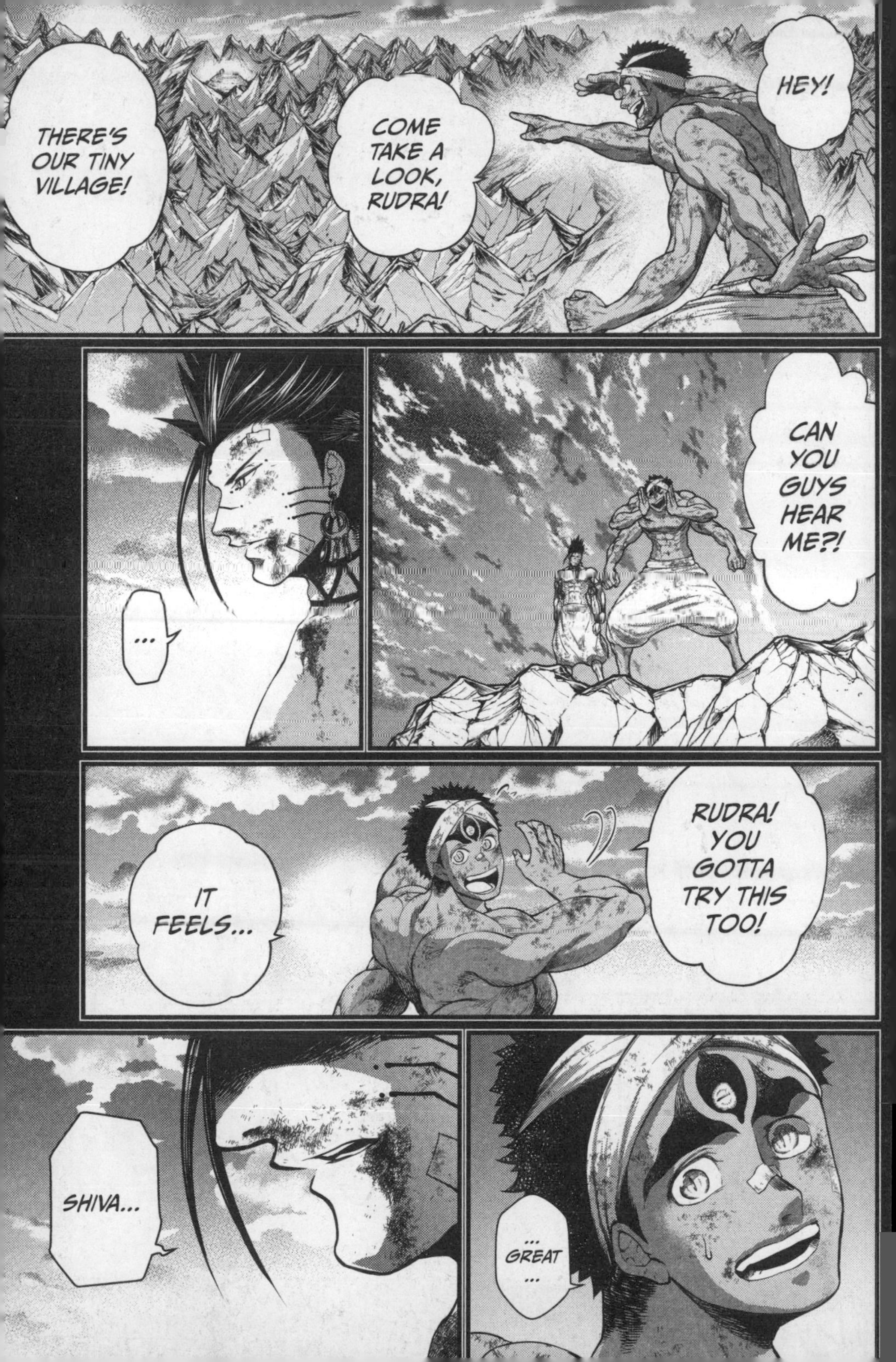
HEY!
COME TAKE A LOOK, RUDRA!
THERE'S OUR TINY VILLAGE!
CAN YOU GUYS HEAR ME?!
...
RUDRA! YOU GOTTA TRY THIS TOO!
IT FEELS...
... GREAT ...
SHIVA...

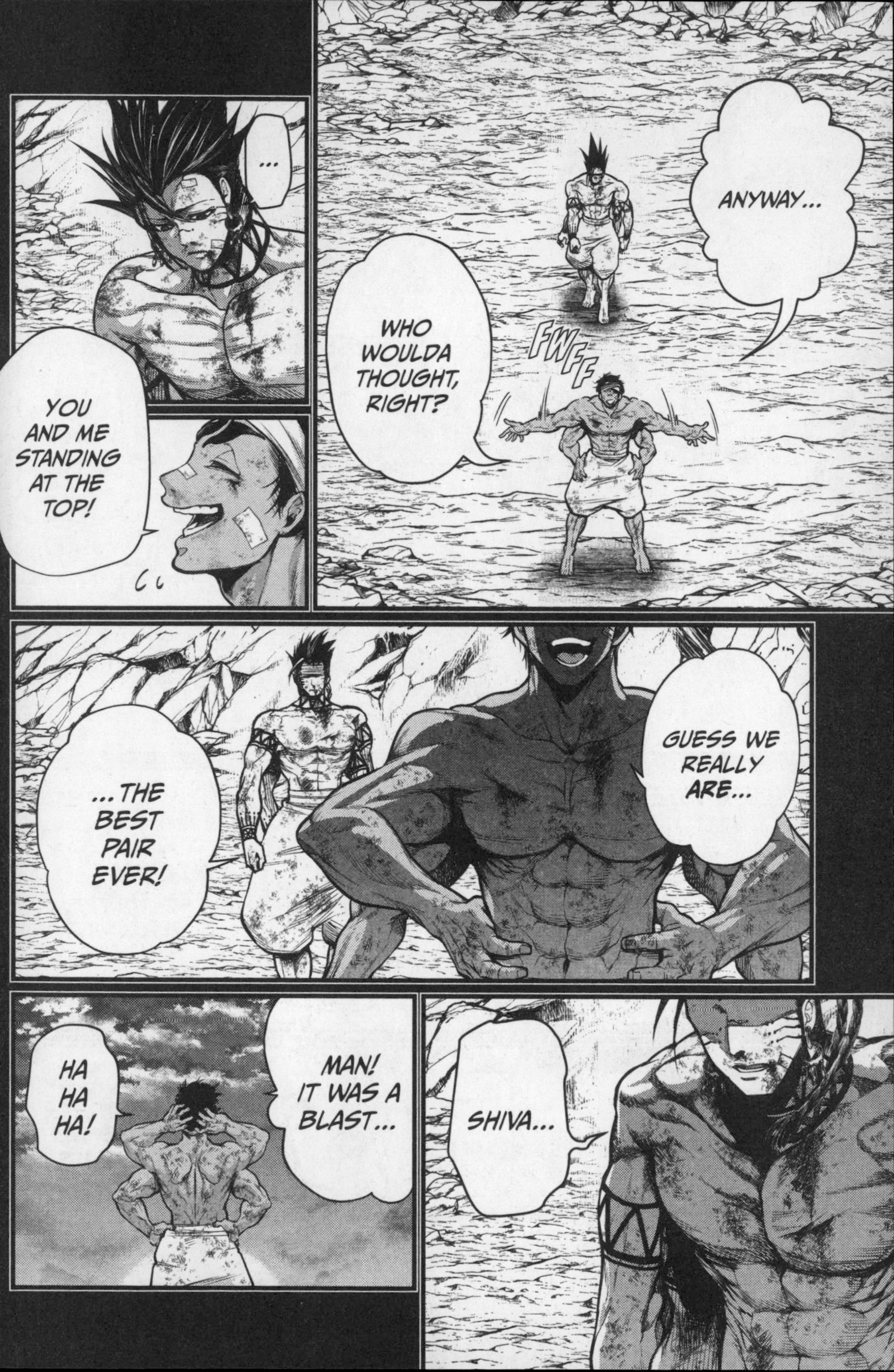
ANYWAY...
WHO WOULDA THOUGHT, RIGHT?
FWFF
...
YOU AND ME STANDING AT THE TOP!
GUESS WE REALLY ARE...
...THE BEST PAIR EVER!
SHIVA...
MAN! IT WAS A BLAST...
HA HA HA!

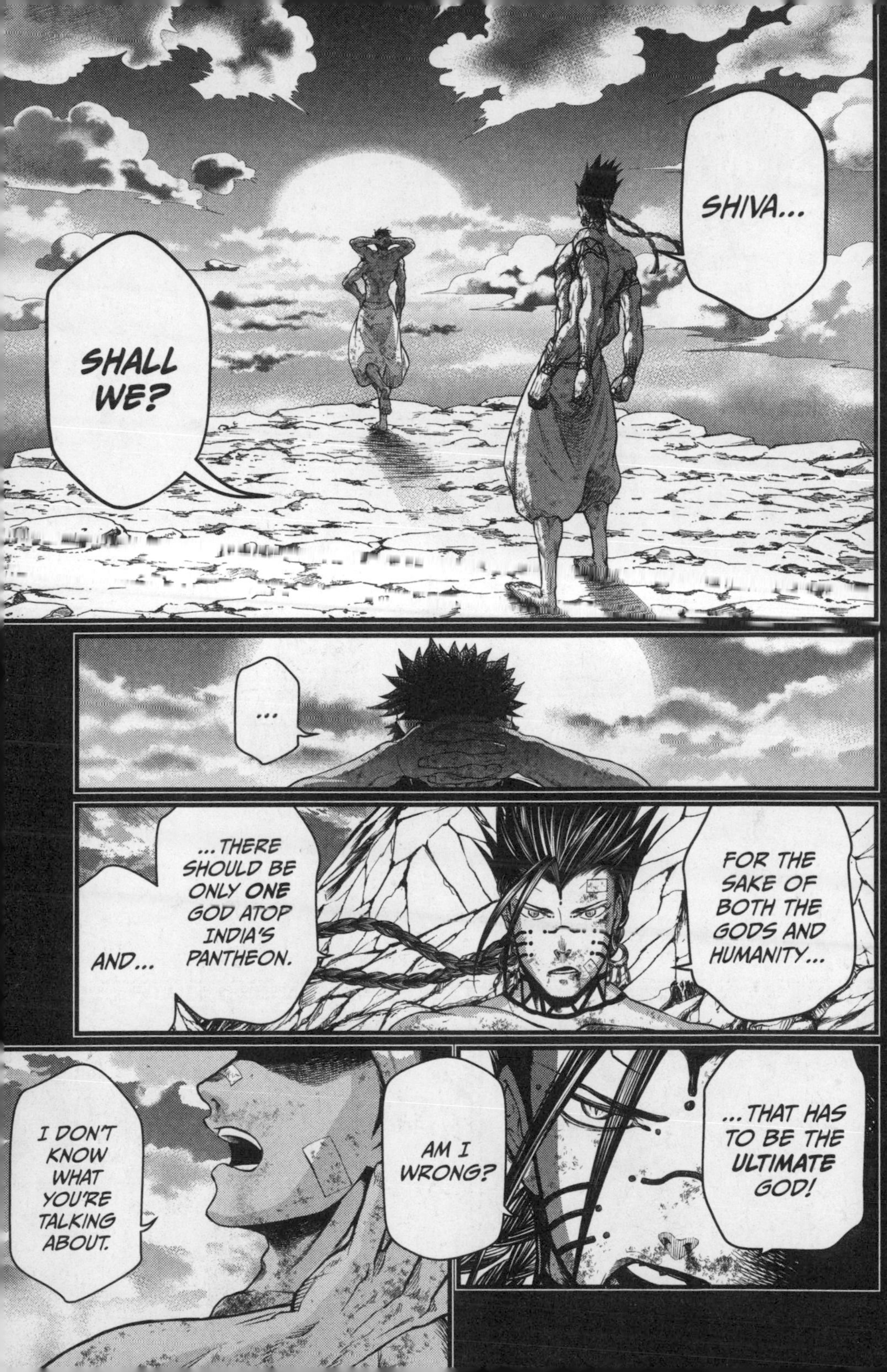
SHIVA...
SHALL WE?
...
FOR THE SAKE OF BOTH THE GODS AND HUMANITY...
...THERE SHOULD BE ONLY ONE GOD ATOP INDIA'S PANTHEON.
AND...
...THAT HAS TO BE THE ULTIMATE GOD!
AM I WRONG?
I DON'T KNOW WHAT YOU'RE TALKING ABOUT.

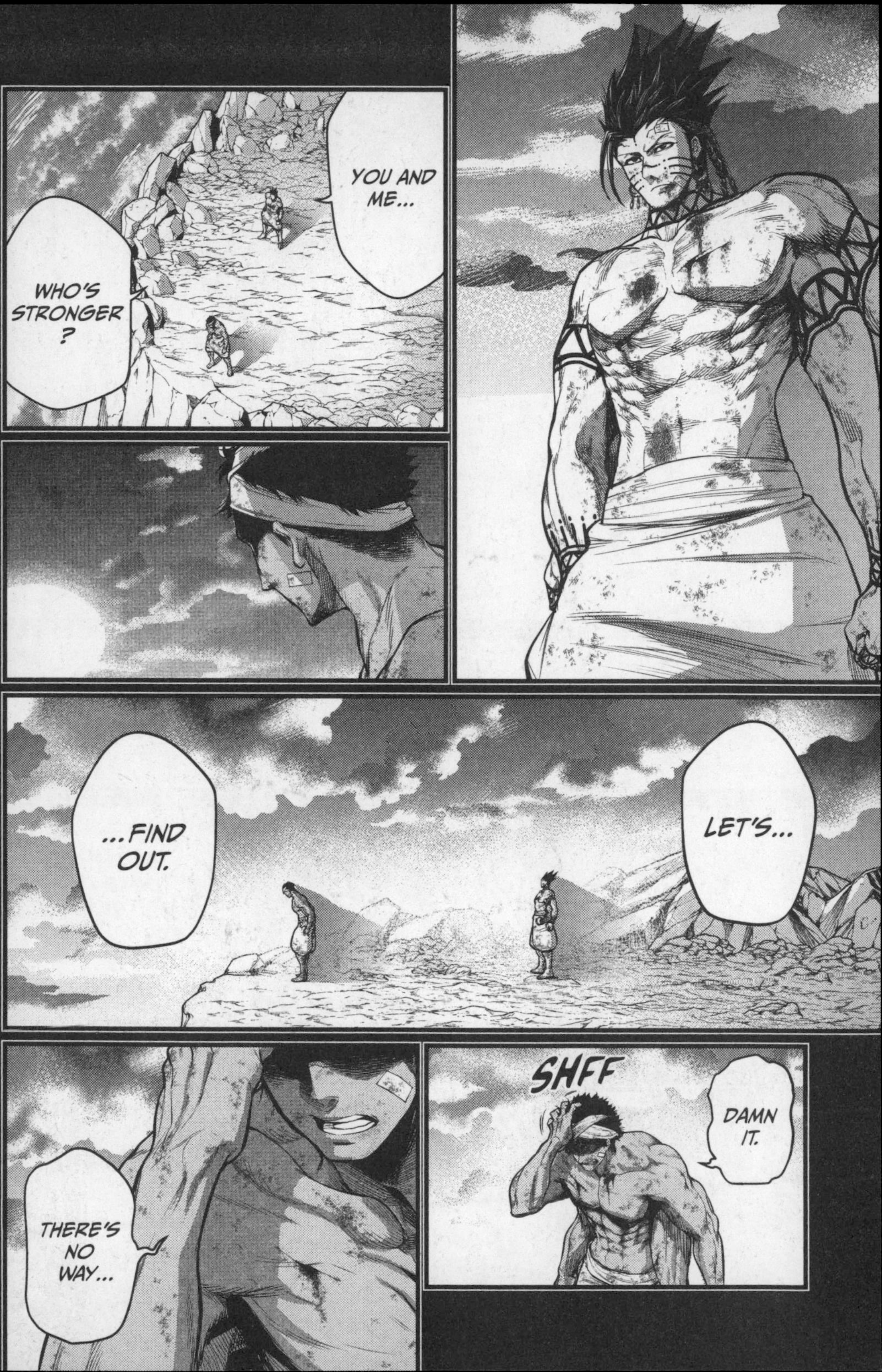
YOU AND ME...
WHO'S STRONGER?
LET'S...
...FIND OUT.
SHFF
DAMN IT.
THERE'S NO WAY...

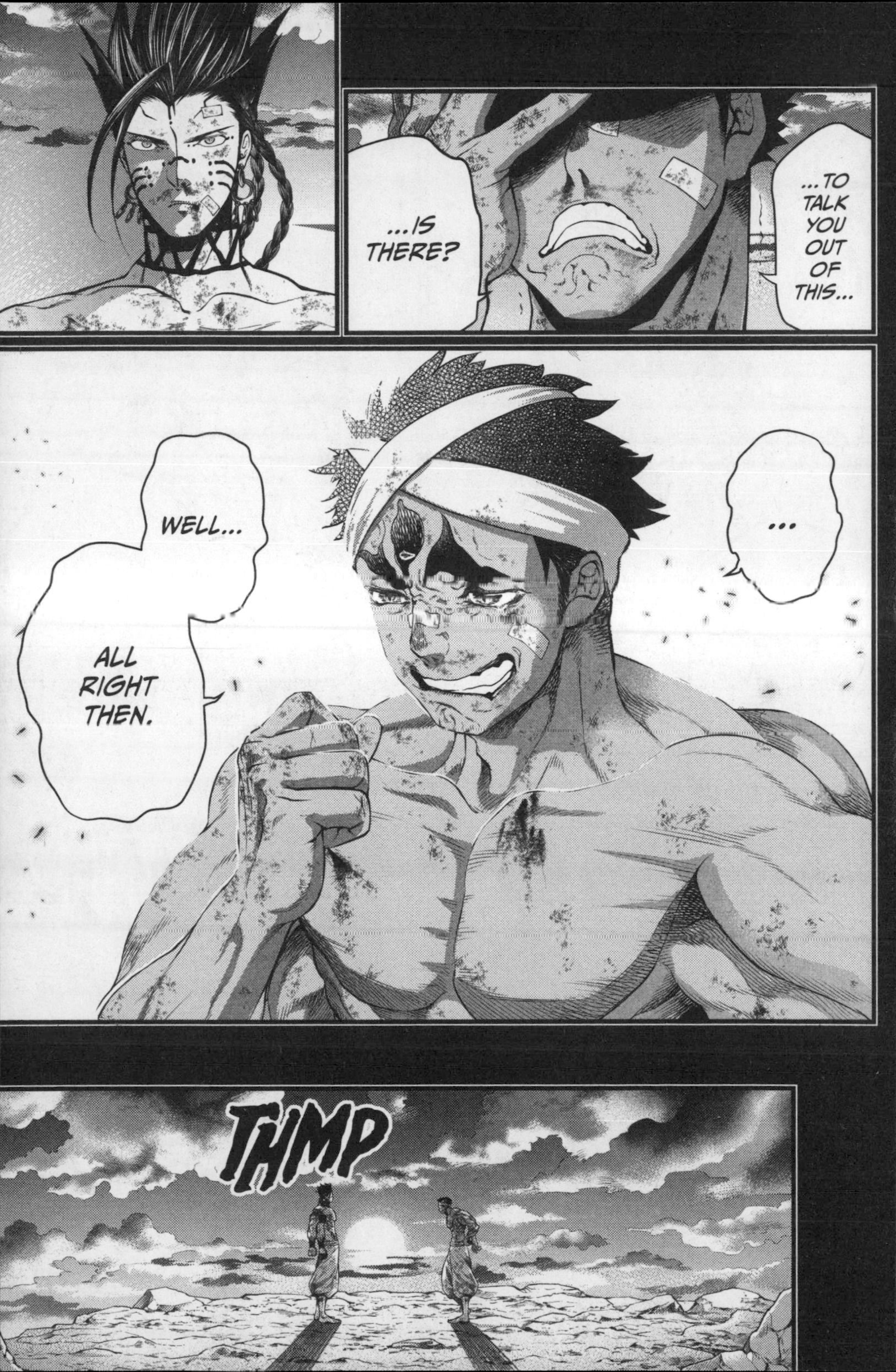
...TO TALK YOU OUT OF THIS...
...IS THERE?
...
WELL...
ALL RIGHT THEN.
THMP

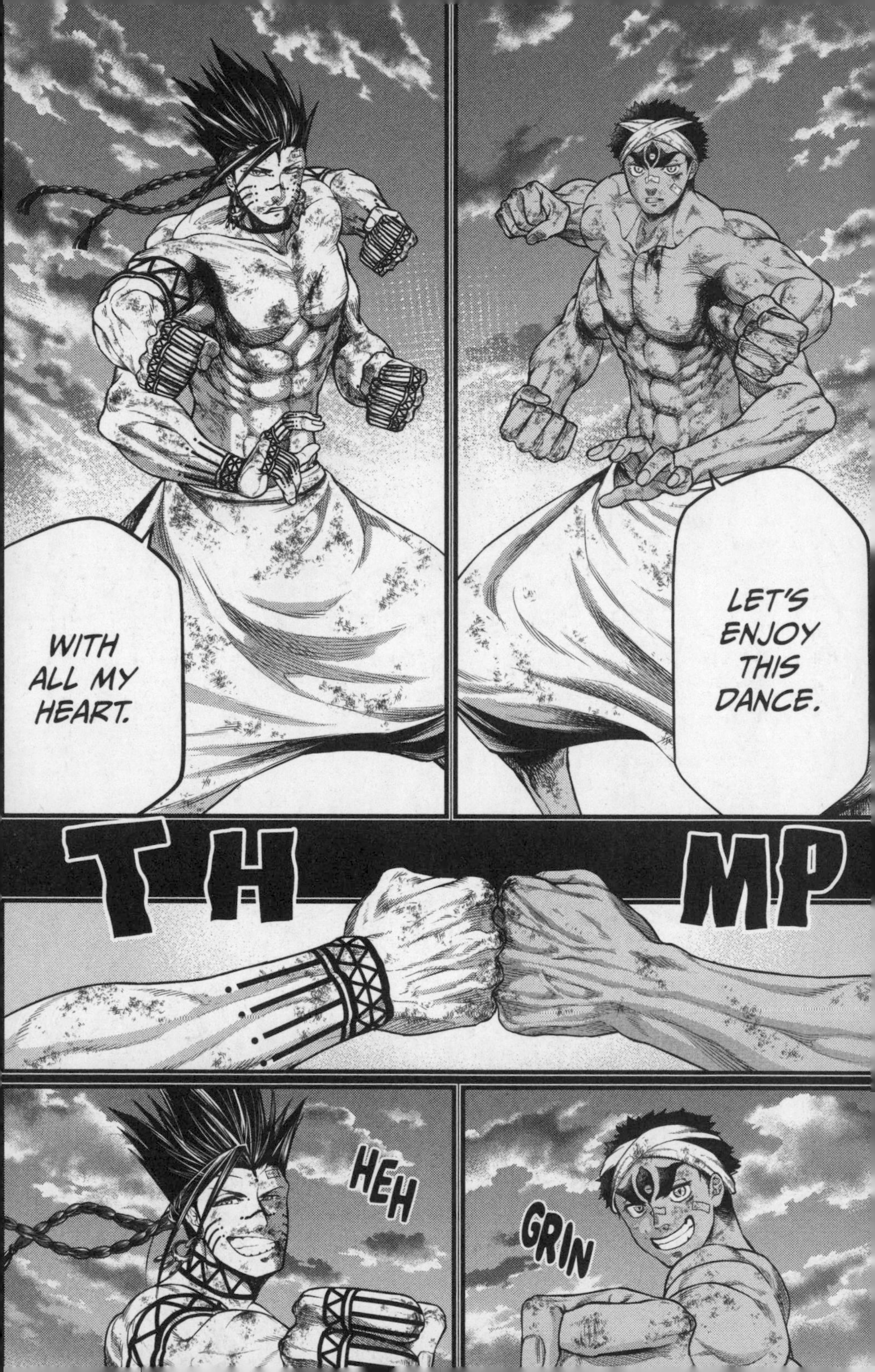
LET'S ENJOY THIS DANCE.
WITH ALL MY HEART.
TH MP
GRIN
HEH

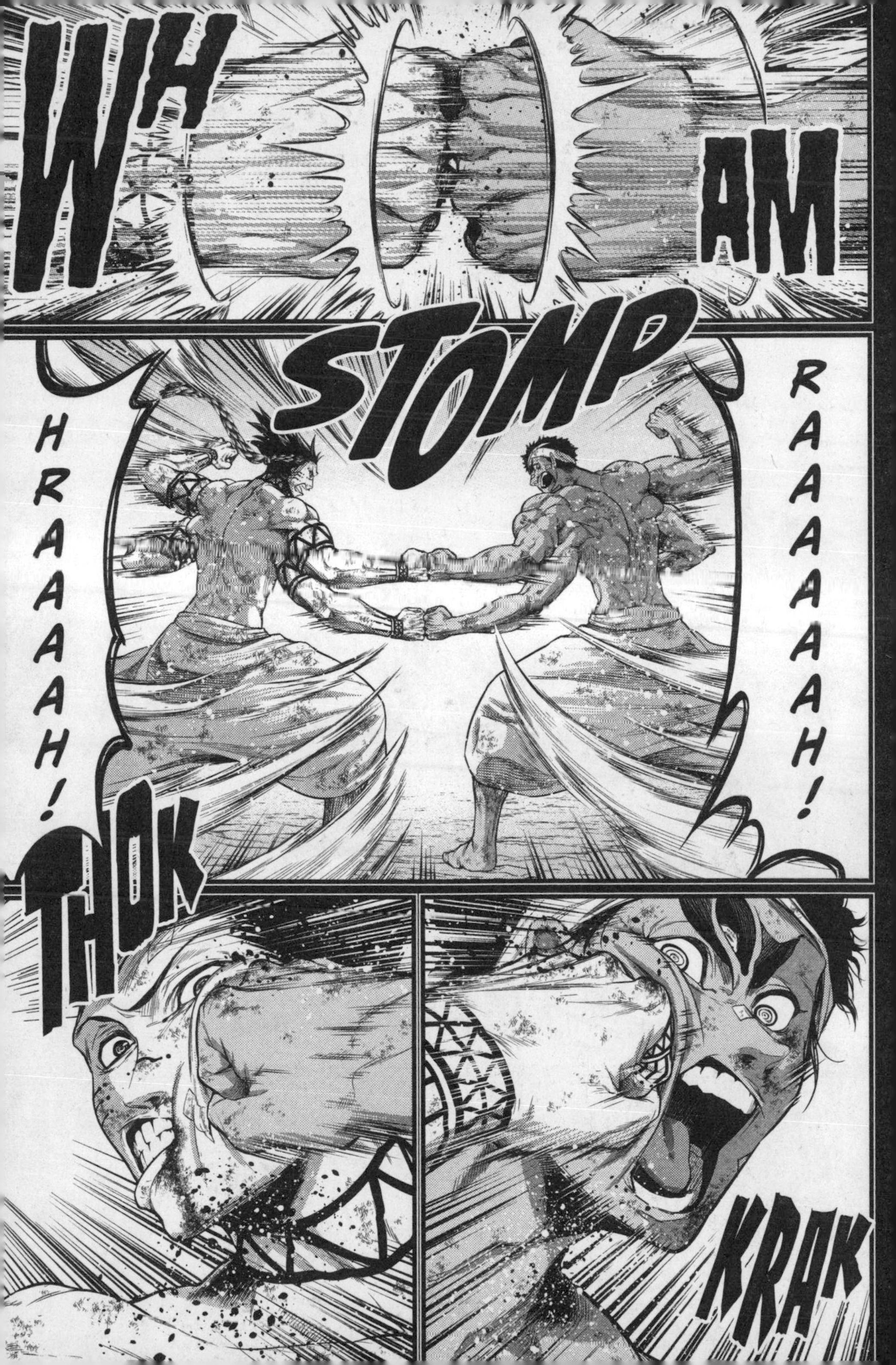
WH
AM
STOMP
RAAAAAAAH!
HRAAAAAH!
KRAK
THOK

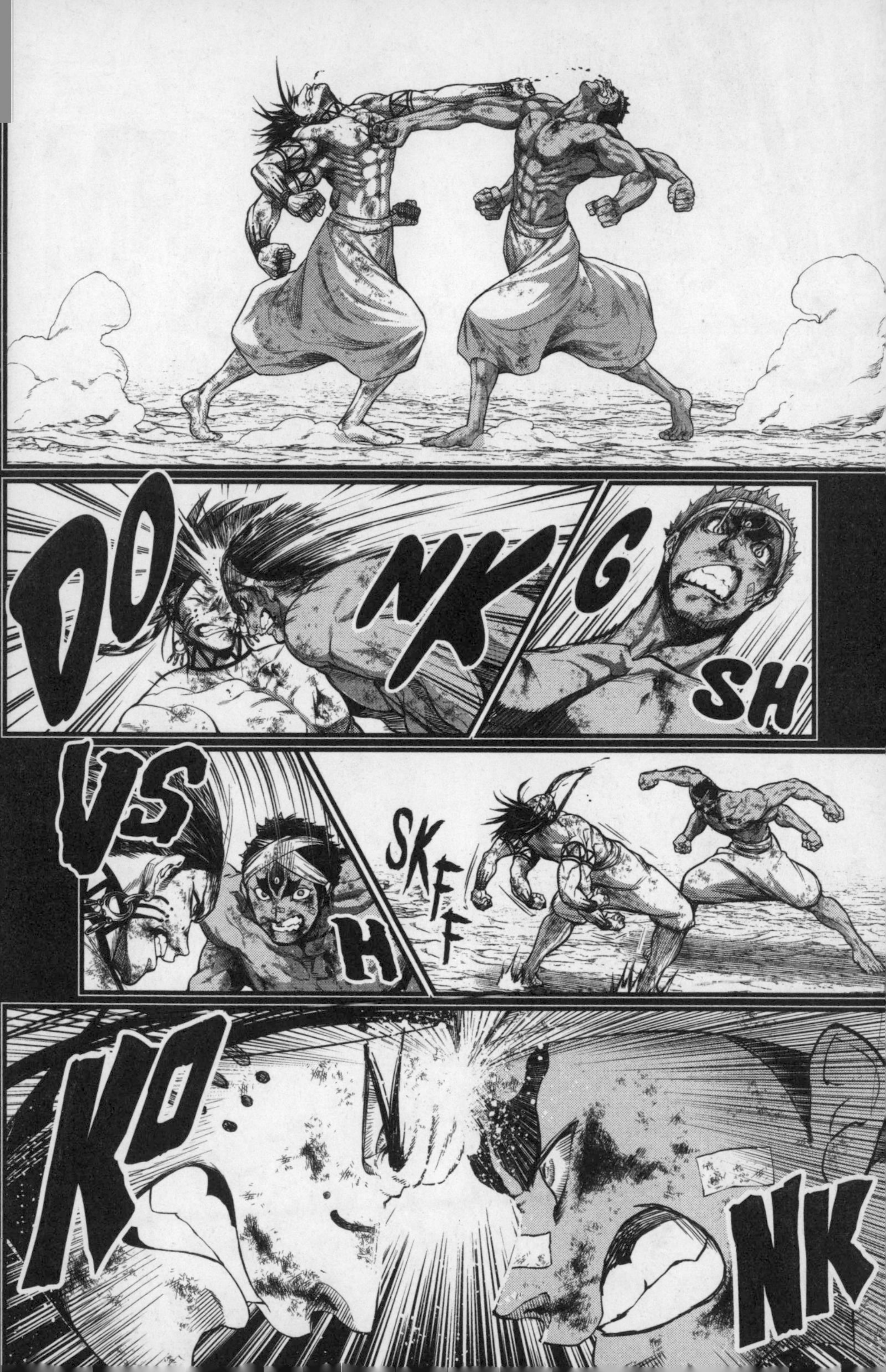
G
SH
DO
NK
SK
F
F
VS
H
KO
NK

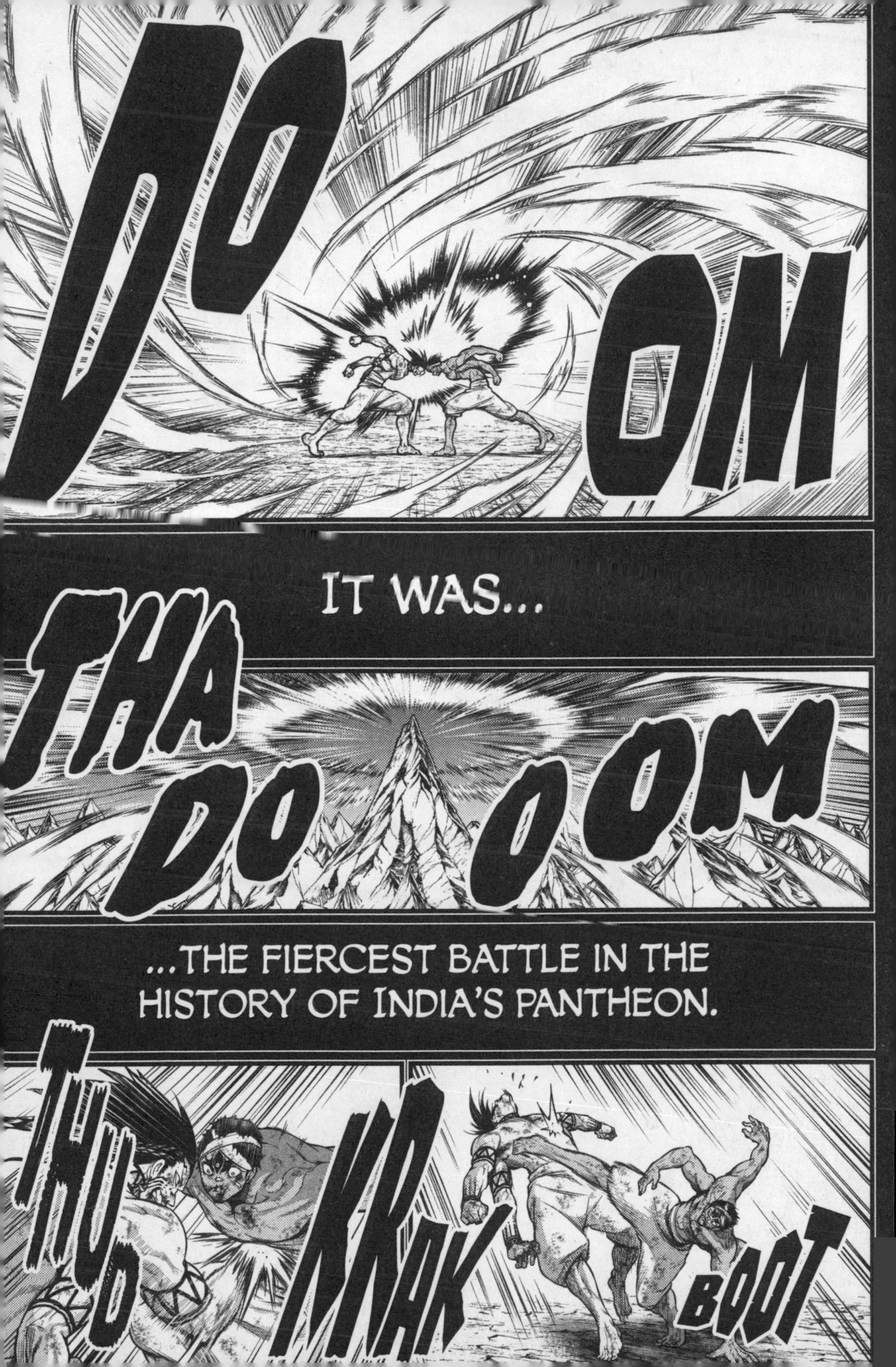
DO
OM
IT WAS...
THA
DO
O
OM
...THE FIERCEST BATTLE IN THE HISTORY OF INDIA'S PANTHEON.
BOOT
WHAK
THUD

THE SOUND OF THESE TWO GODS FIGHTING ECHOED ACROSS ALL OF INDIA.

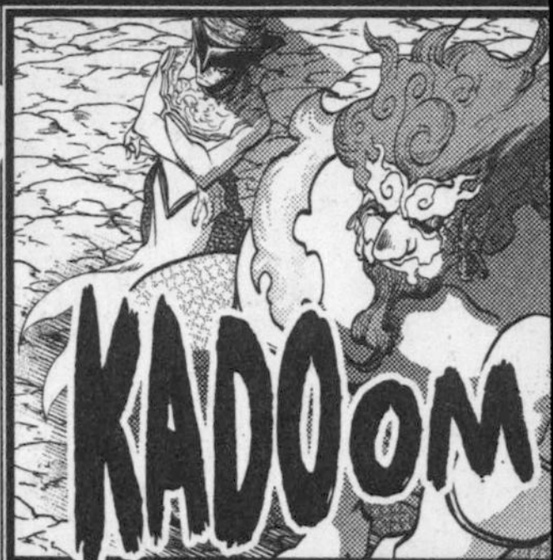
KADOOM

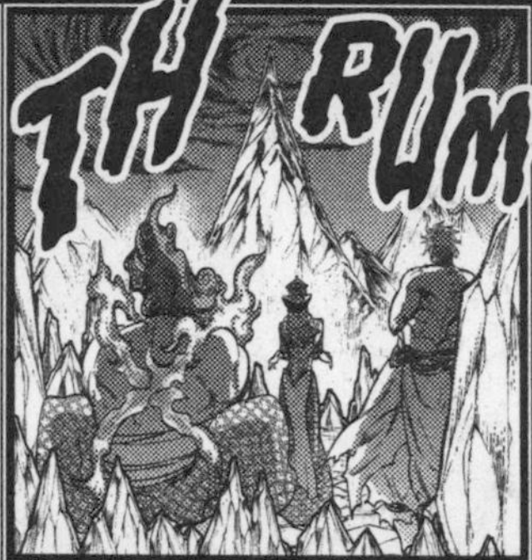
TH RUM

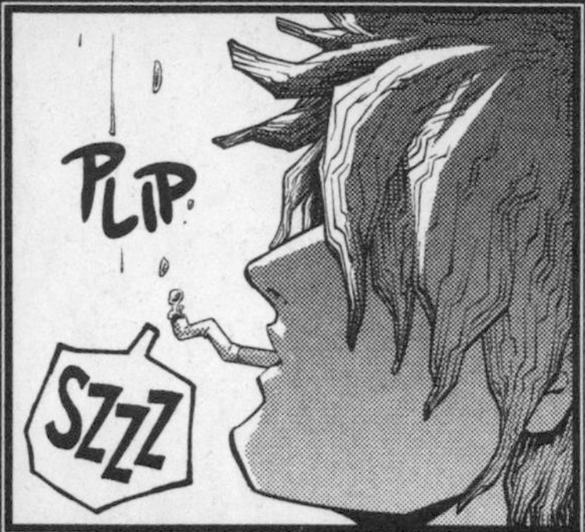
PLIP
SZZZ

THEIR SWEAT POURED DOWN AS HEAVY RAIN.

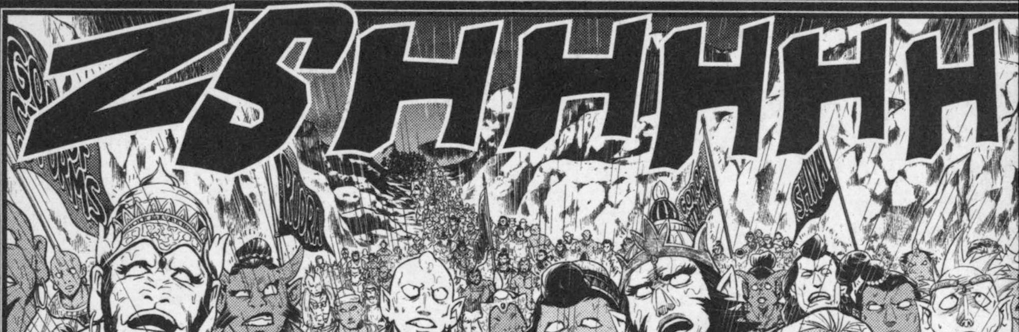
ZSHHHHH
SHIVA
RUDRA
GOD OF STORMS

FOR SHIVA...

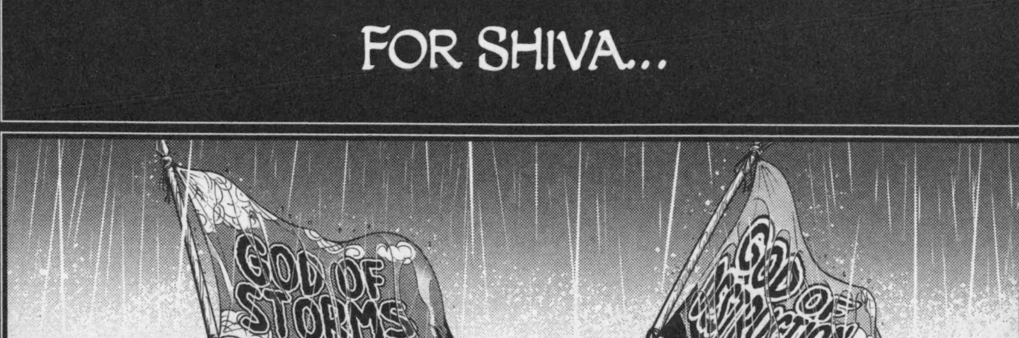
GOD OF STORMS

FOR RUDRA...

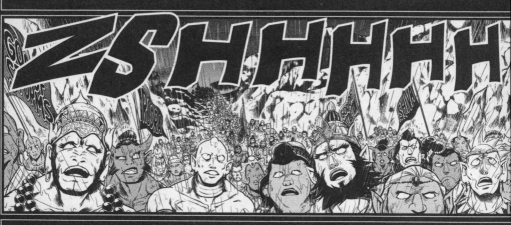

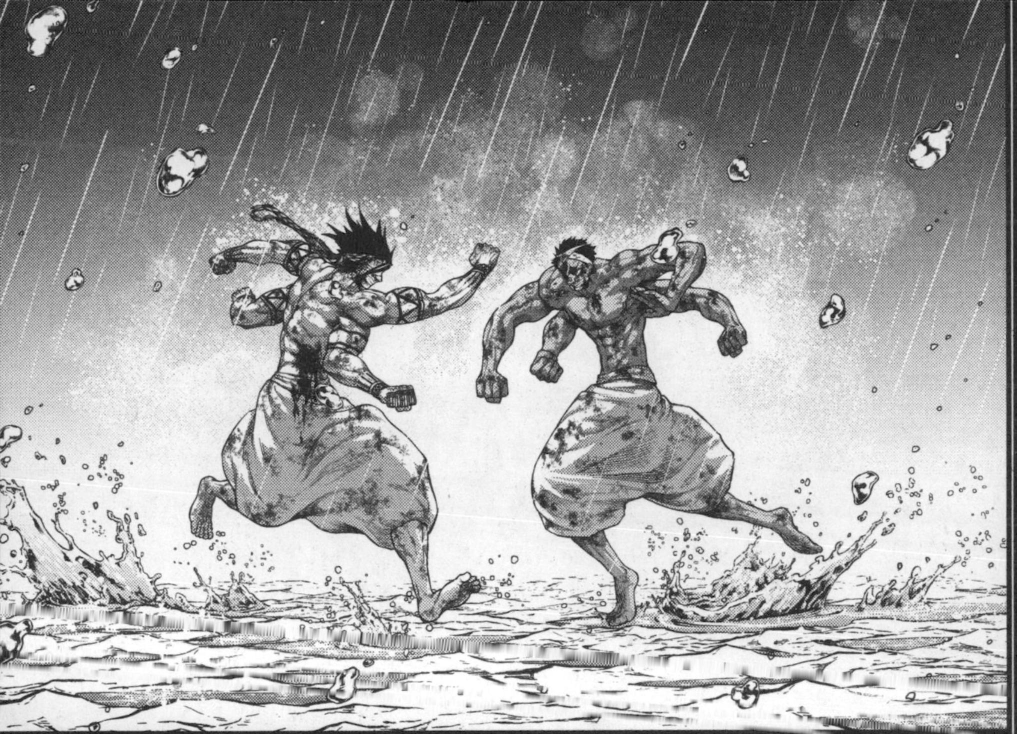

...IT IT WAS THE MOST EXHILARATING...

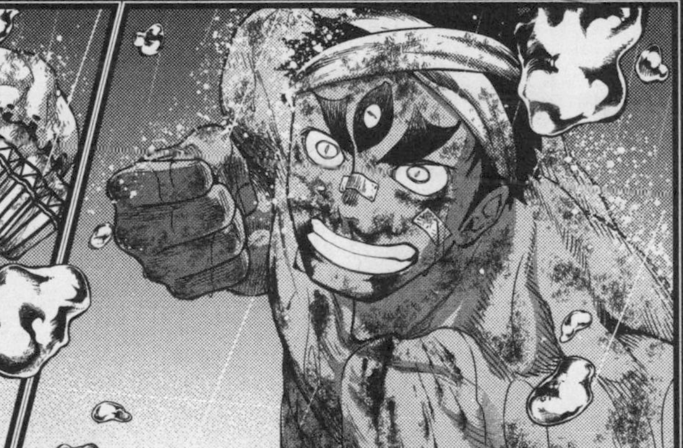

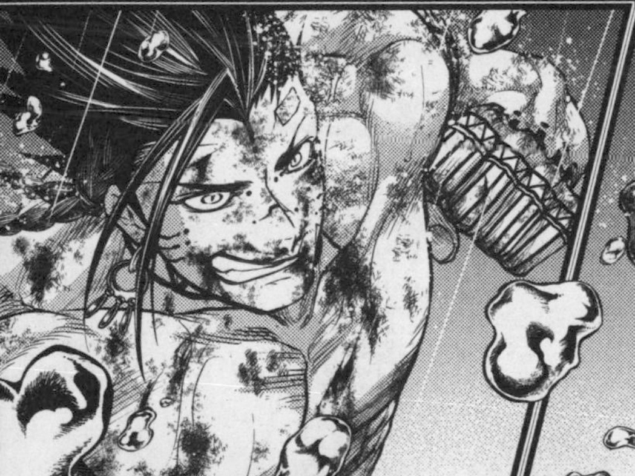

...AND MOST SORROWFUL MOMENT.

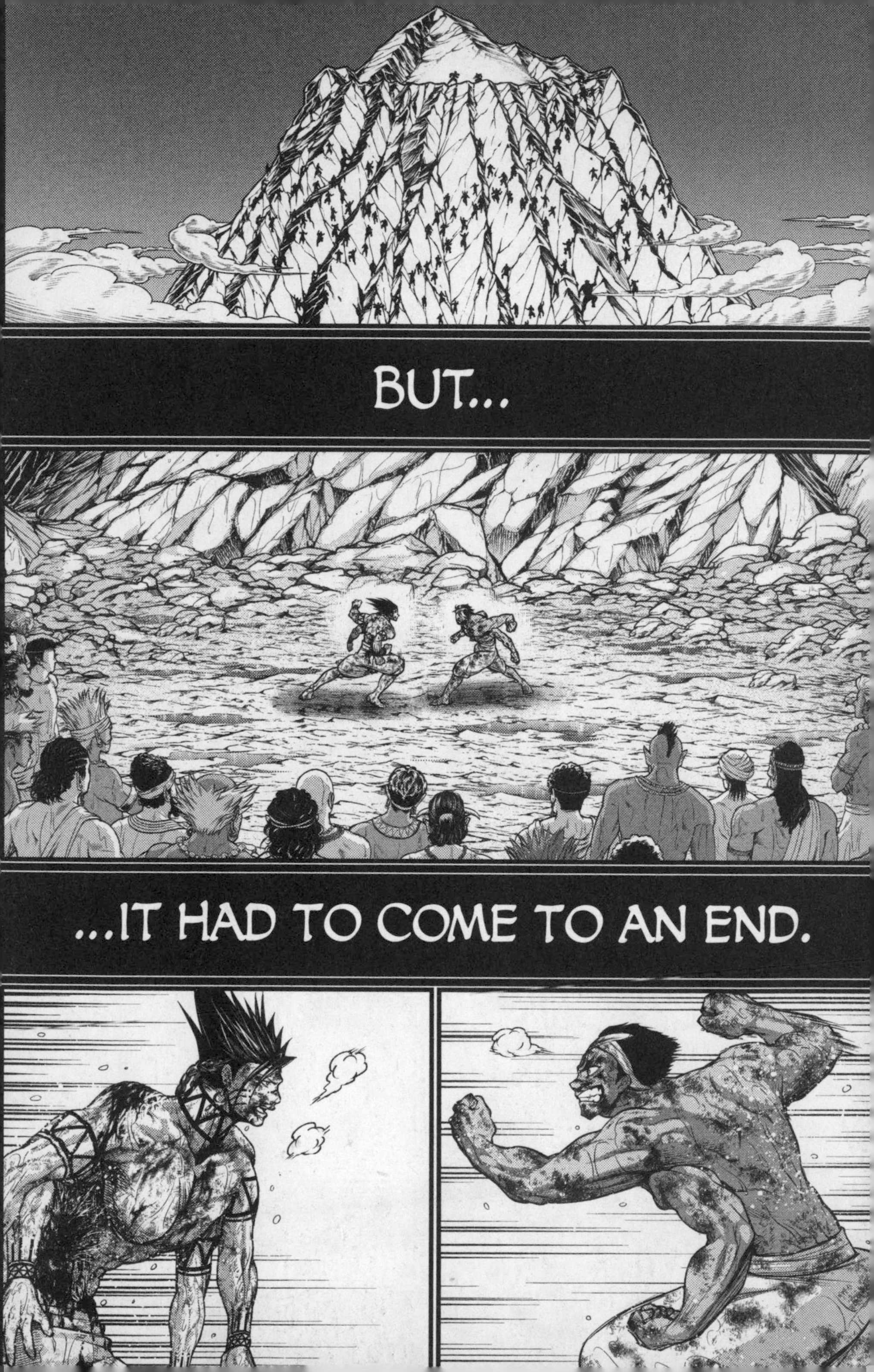
BUT...
...IT HAD TO COME TO AN END.

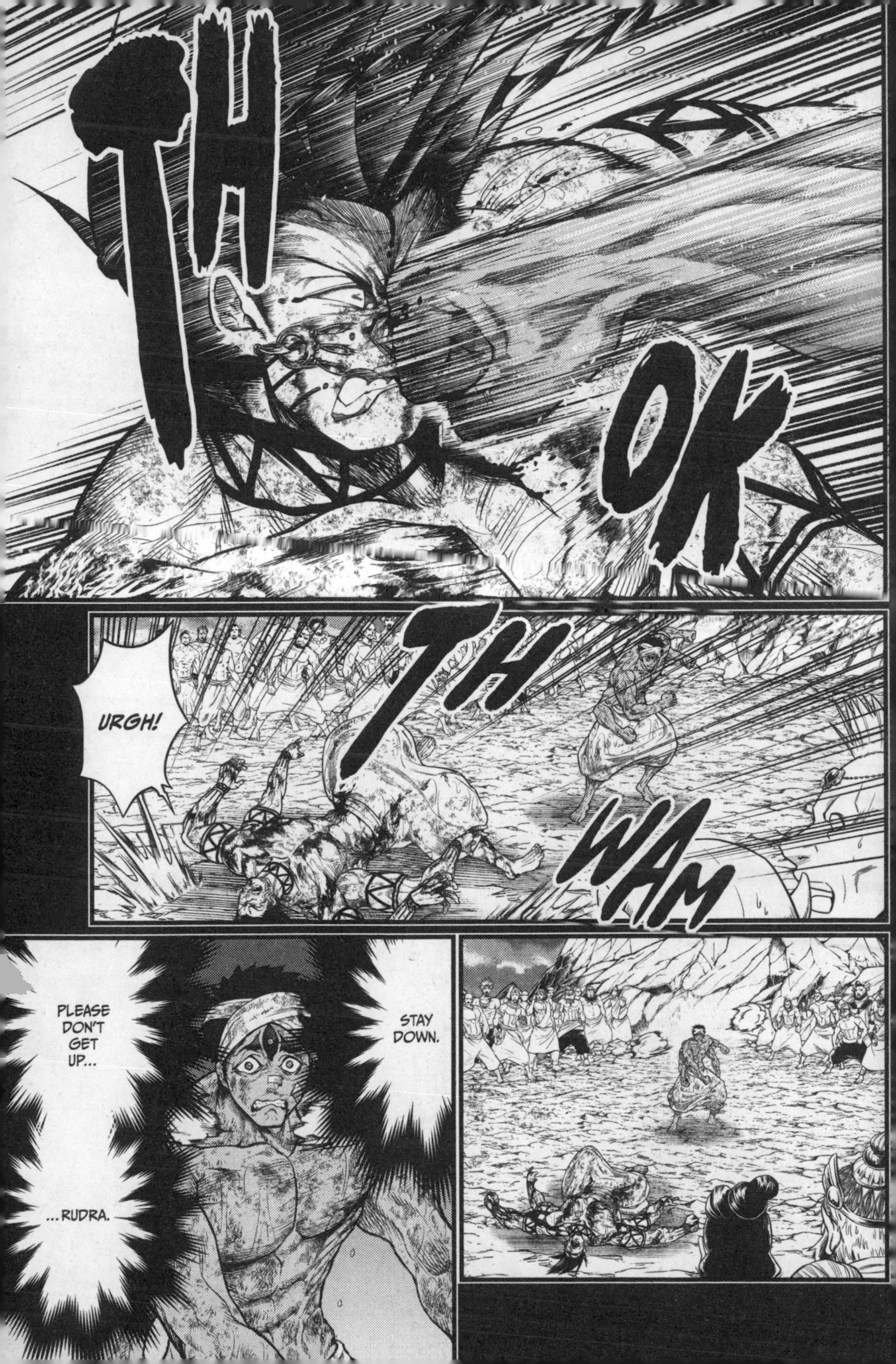
THOK
THWAM
URGH!
STAY DOWN.
PLEASE DON'T GET UP...
...RUDRA.

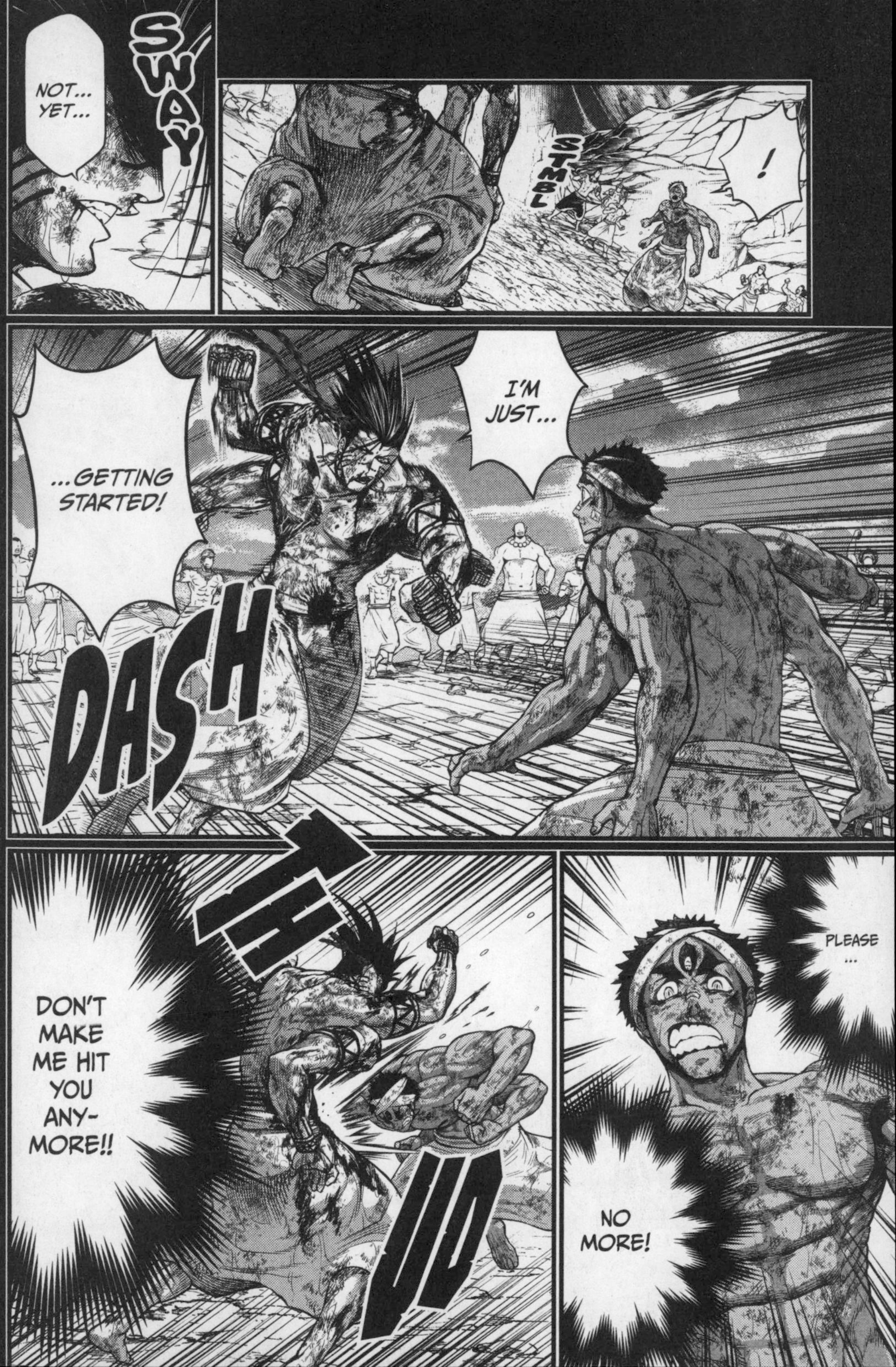
STMBL
!
NOT... YET...
SWAY
I'M JUST...
...GETTING STARTED!
DASH
PLEASE...
NO MORE!
DON'T MAKE ME HIT YOU ANY-MORE!!
THUD

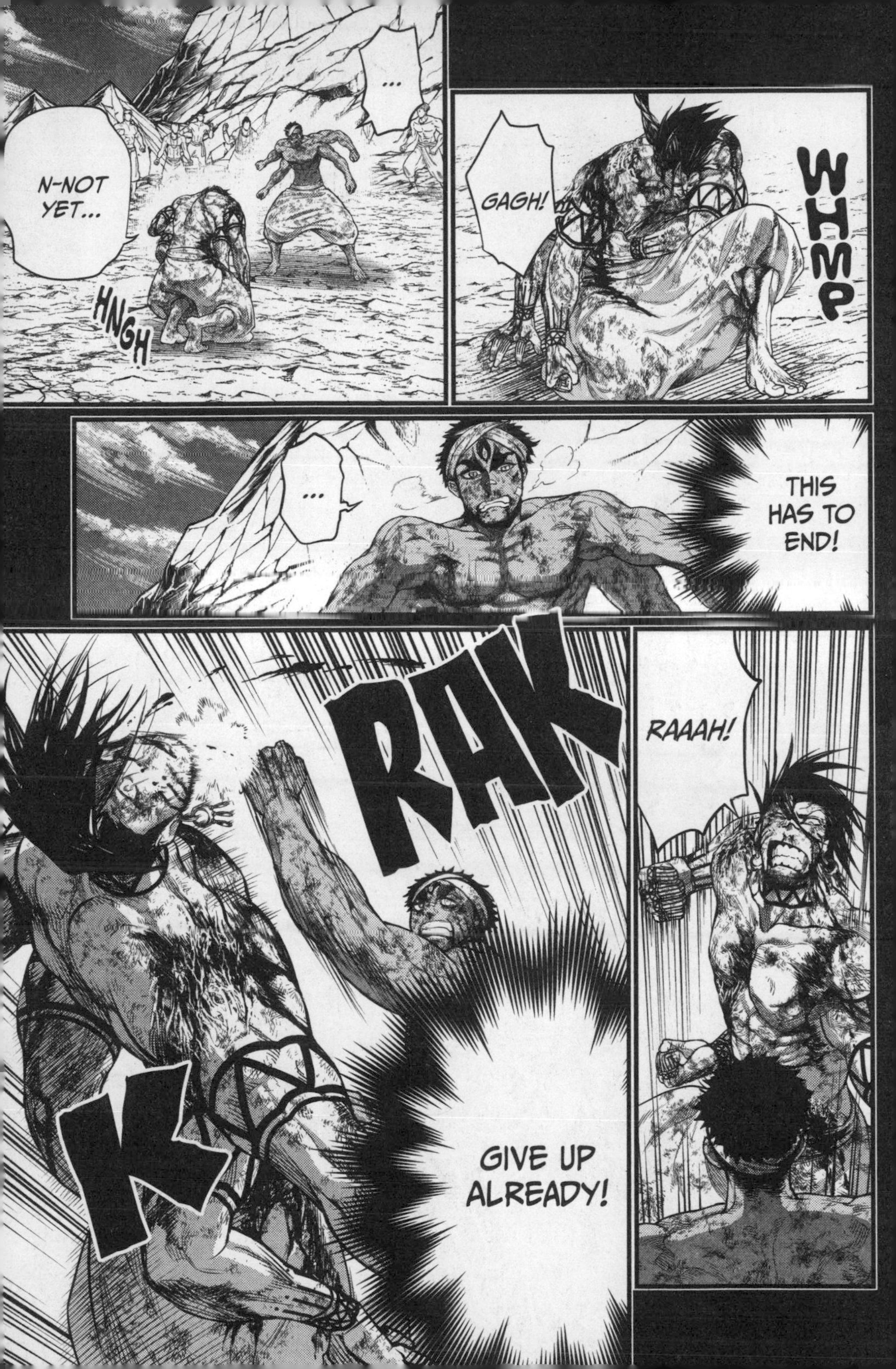
WHMP
GAGH!
...
N-NOT YET...
HNGH
THIS HAS TO END!
...
RAAAH!
RAK
GIVE UP ALREADY!
K

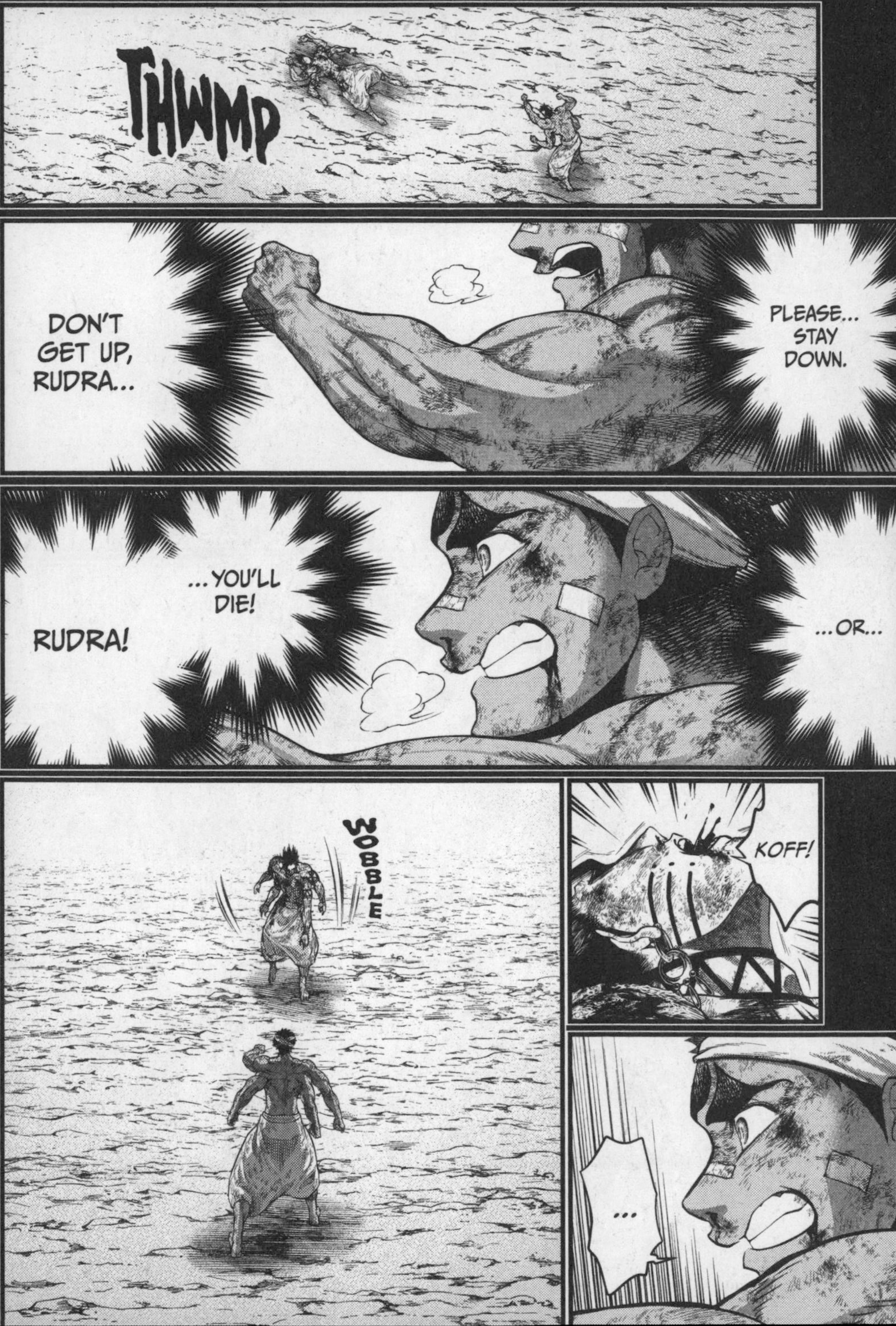
THWMP
PLEASE... STAY DOWN.
DON'T GET UP, RUDRA...
...OR...
...YOU'LL DIE!
RUDRA!
KOFF!
...
WOBBLE

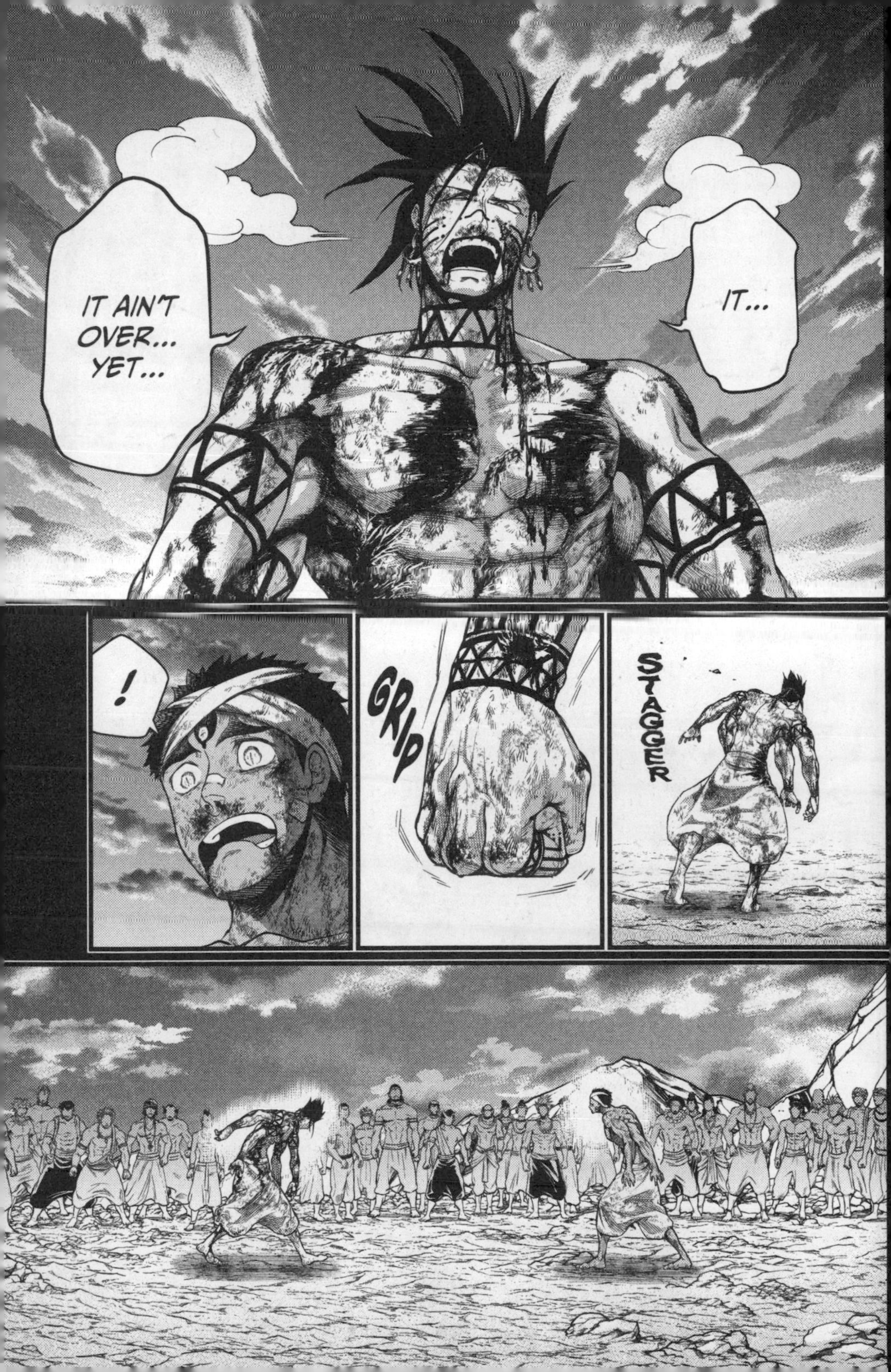
IT...
IT AIN'T OVER... YET...
STAGGER
GRIP
!

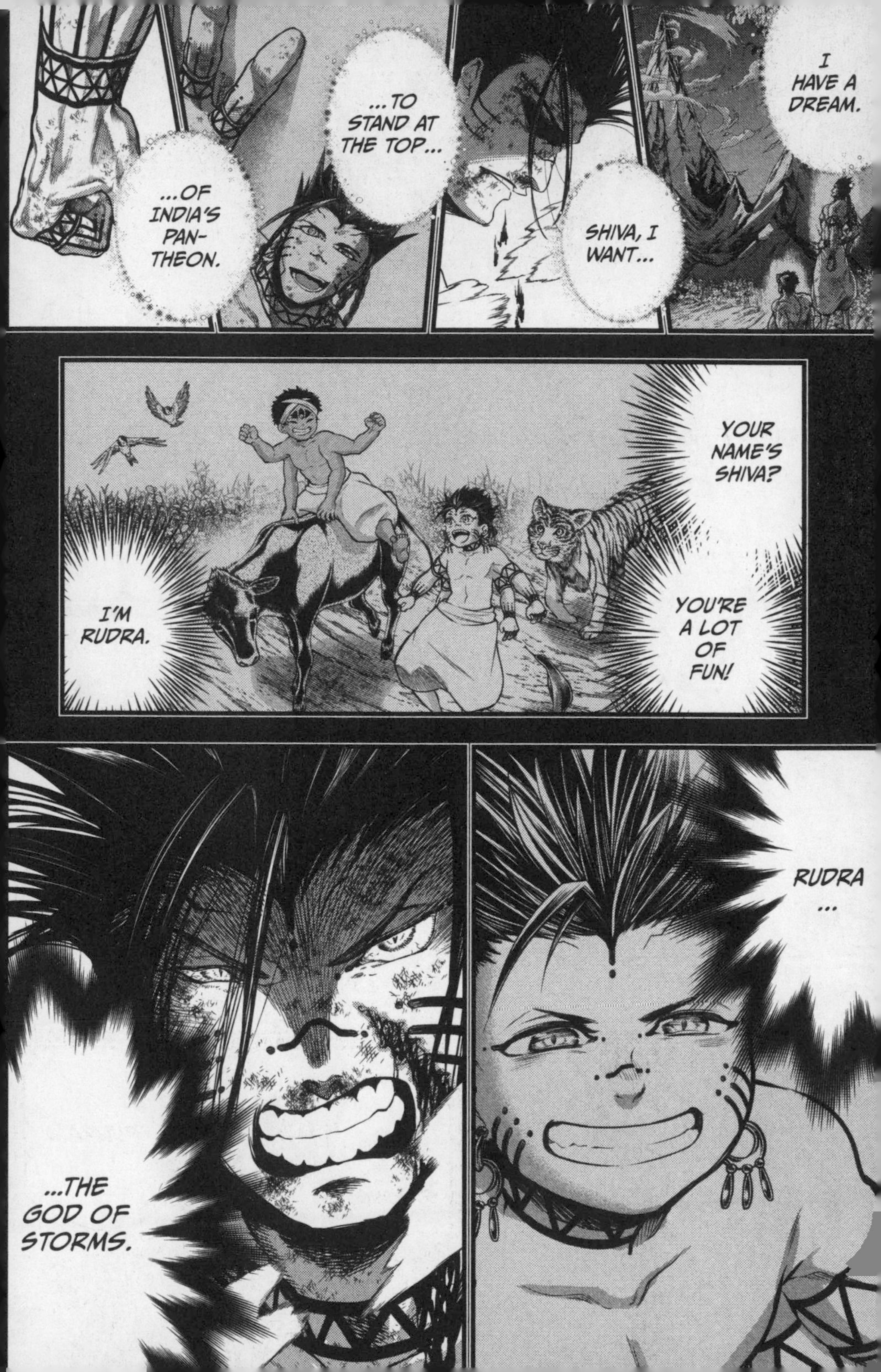
I HAVE A DREAM.
SHIVA, I WANT...
...TO STAND AT THE TOP...
...OF INDIA'S PAN-THEON.
YOUR NAME'S SHIVA?
YOU'RE A LOT OF FUN!
I'M RUDRA.
RUDRA ...
...THE GOD OF STORMS.

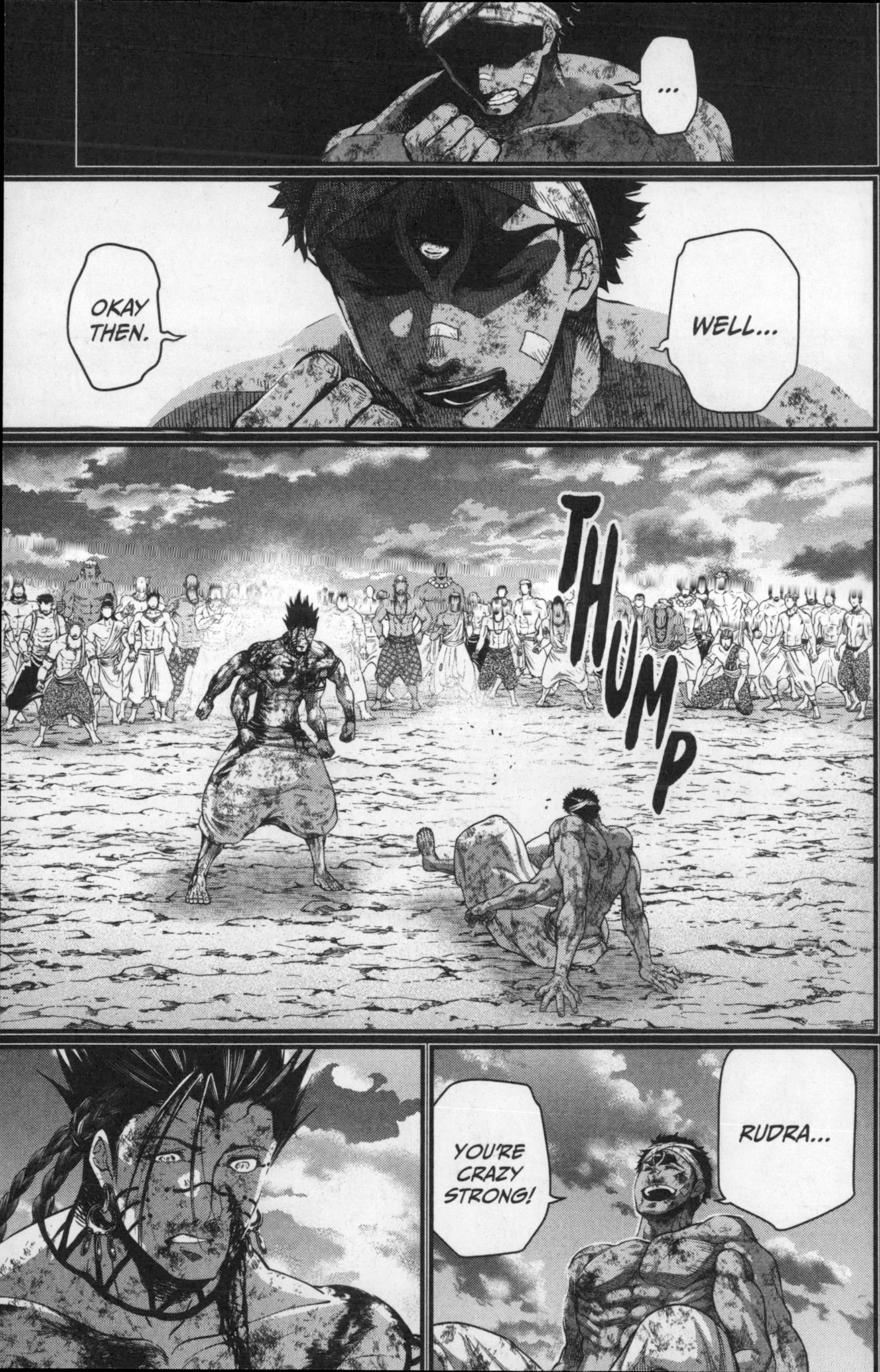
...
WELL...
OKAY THEN.
THUMP
RUDRA...
YOU'RE CRAZY STRONG!

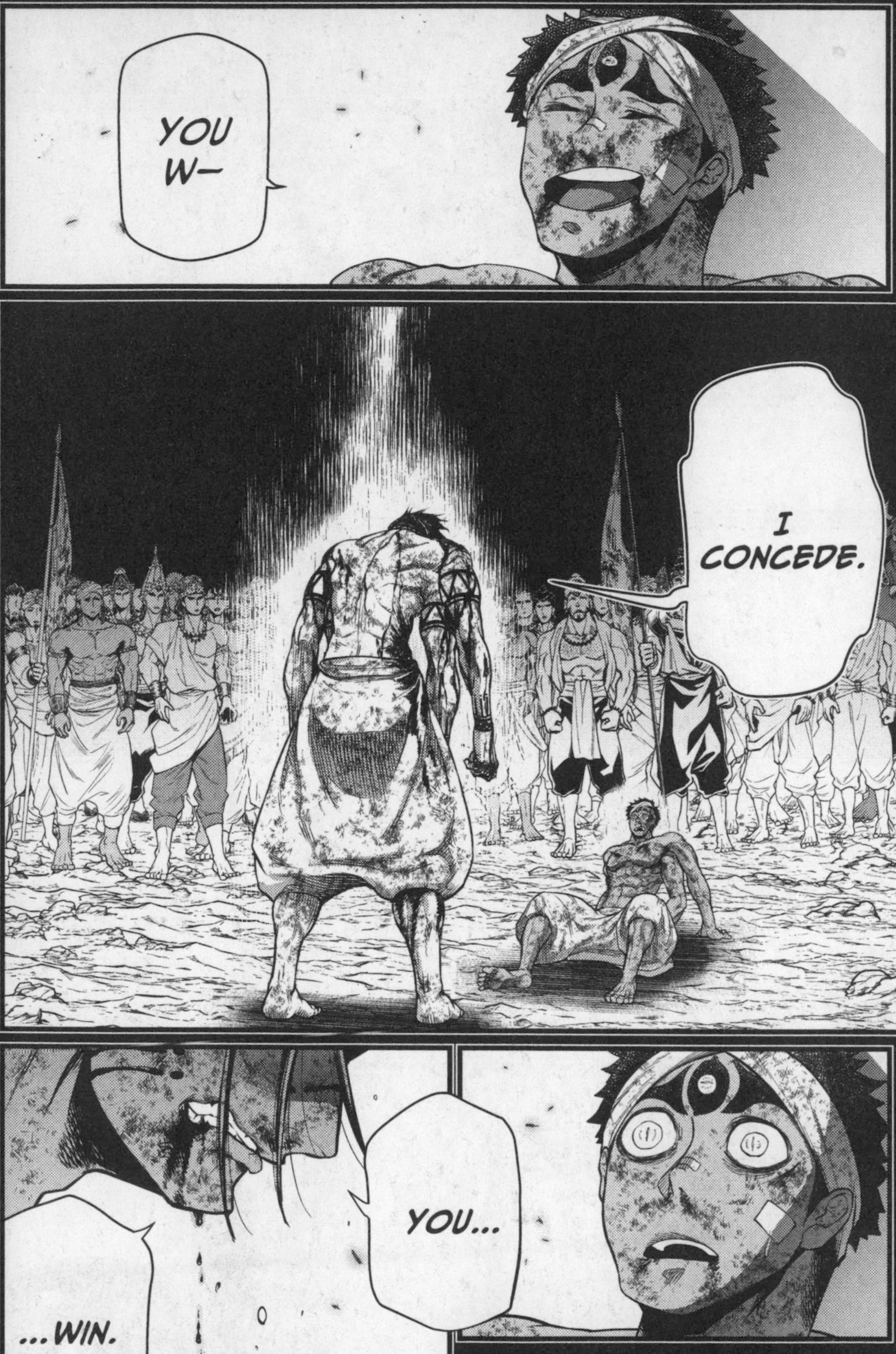
YOU W—
I CONCEDE.
YOU...
...WIN.

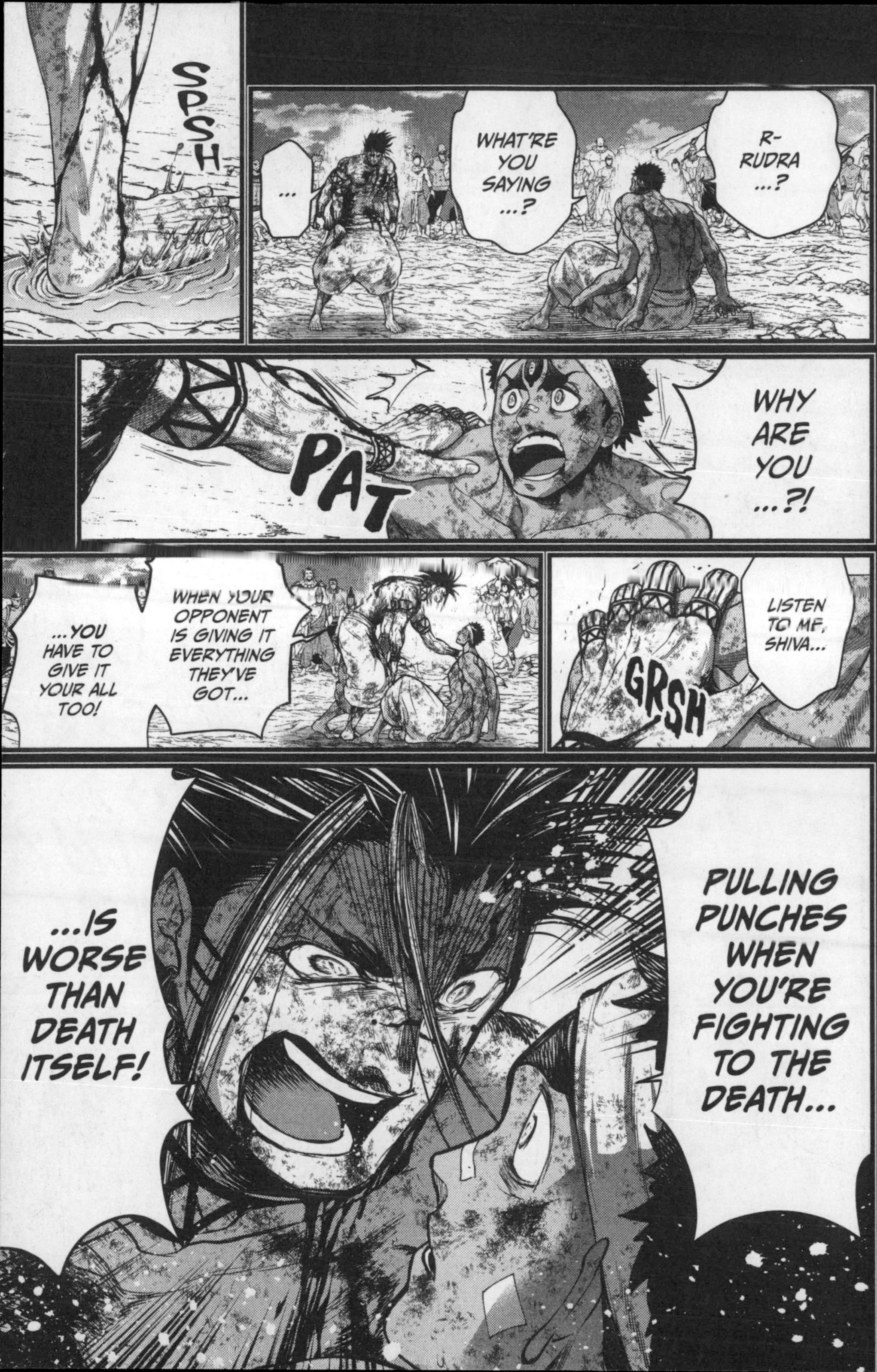
R-RUDRA...?
WHAT'RE YOU SAYING...?
...
SPSH
WHY ARE YOU...?!
PAT
LISTEN TO ME, SHIVA...
GRSH
WHEN YOUR OPPONENT IS GIVING IT EVERYTHING THEY'VE GOT...
...YOU HAVE TO GIVE IT YOUR ALL TOO!
PULLING PUNCHES WHEN YOU'RE FIGHTING TO THE DEATH...
...IS WORSE THAN DEATH ITSELF!

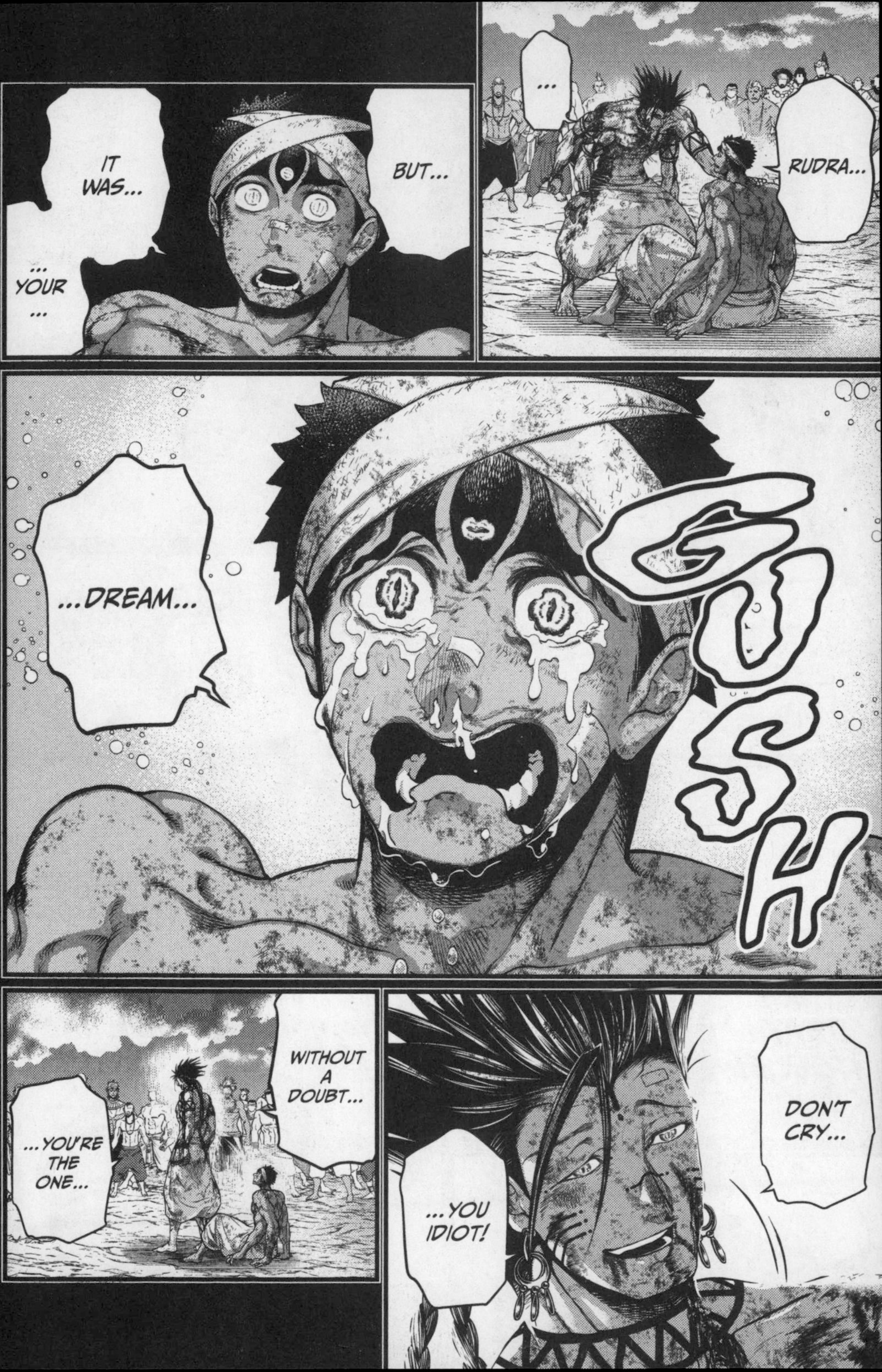
RUDRA...
...
BUT...
IT WAS...
... YOUR ...
...DREAM...
GUSH
DON'T CRY...
...YOU IDIOT!
WITHOUT A DOUBT...
...YOU'RE THE ONE...

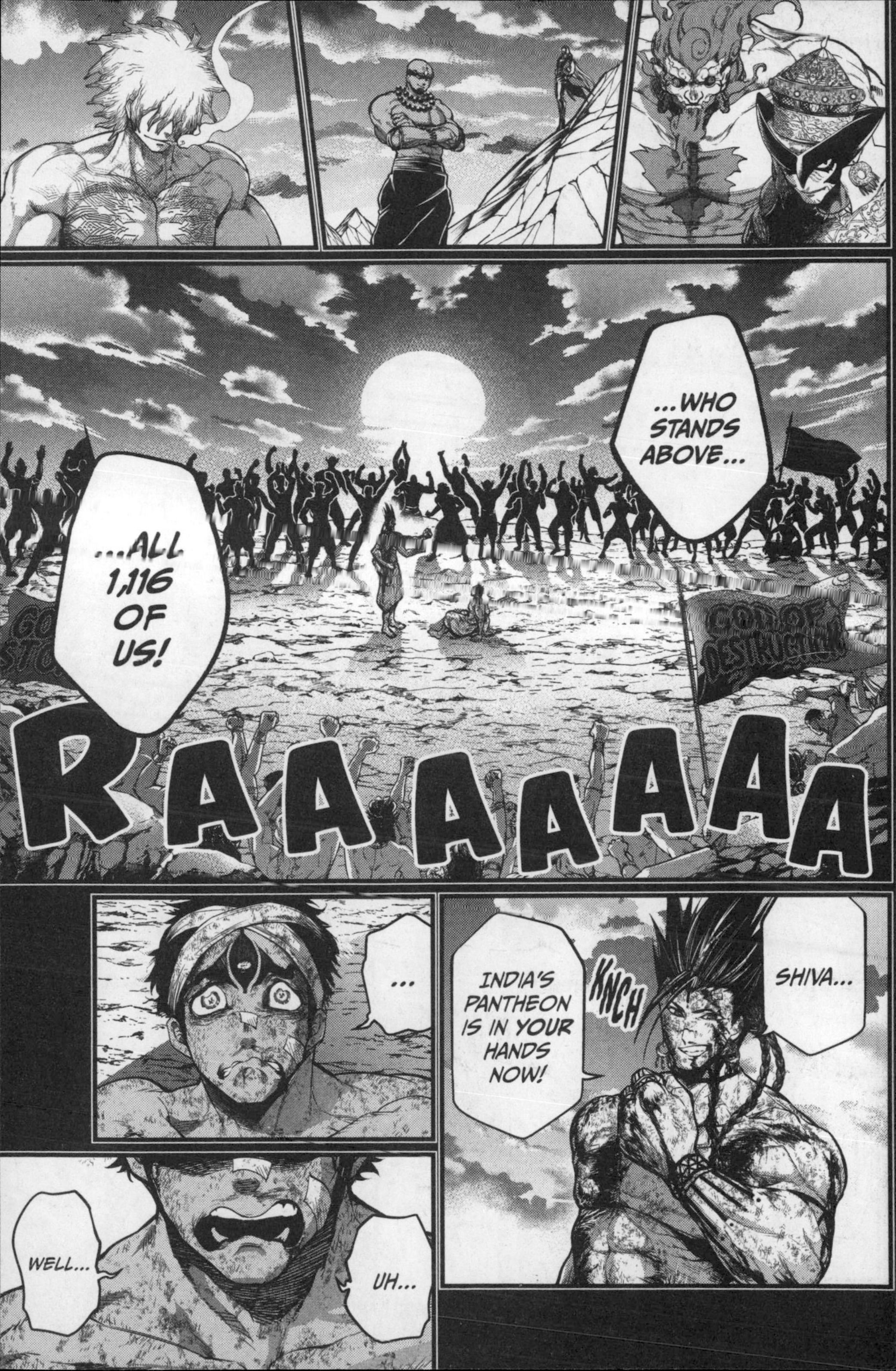
...WHO STANDS ABOVE...
...ALL 1,116 OF US!
RAAAAAAA
SHIVA...
KNCH
INDIA'S PANTHEON IS IN YOUR HANDS NOW!
...
UH...
WELL...

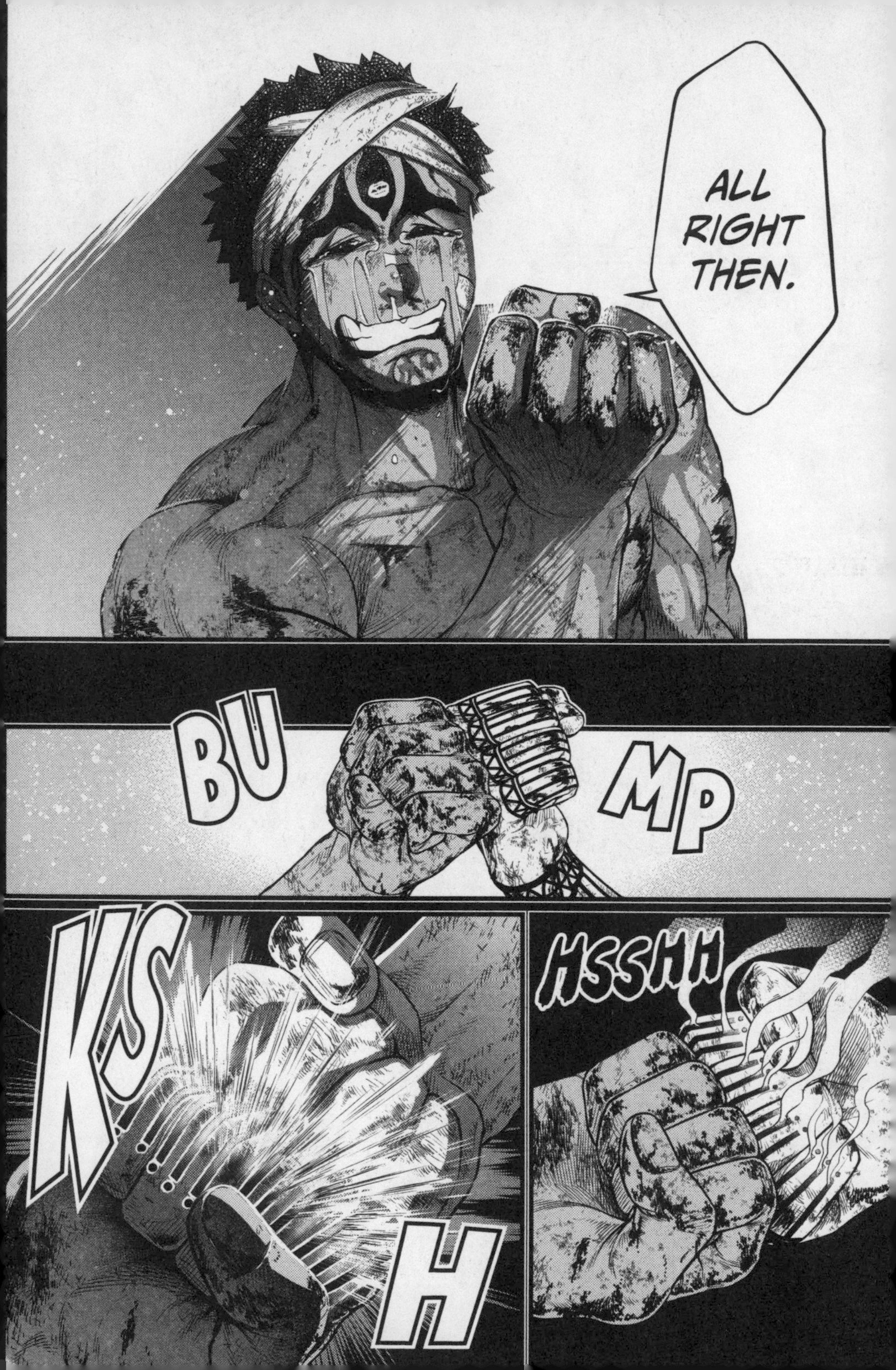
ALL RIGHT THEN.
BUMP
HSSHH
KSH

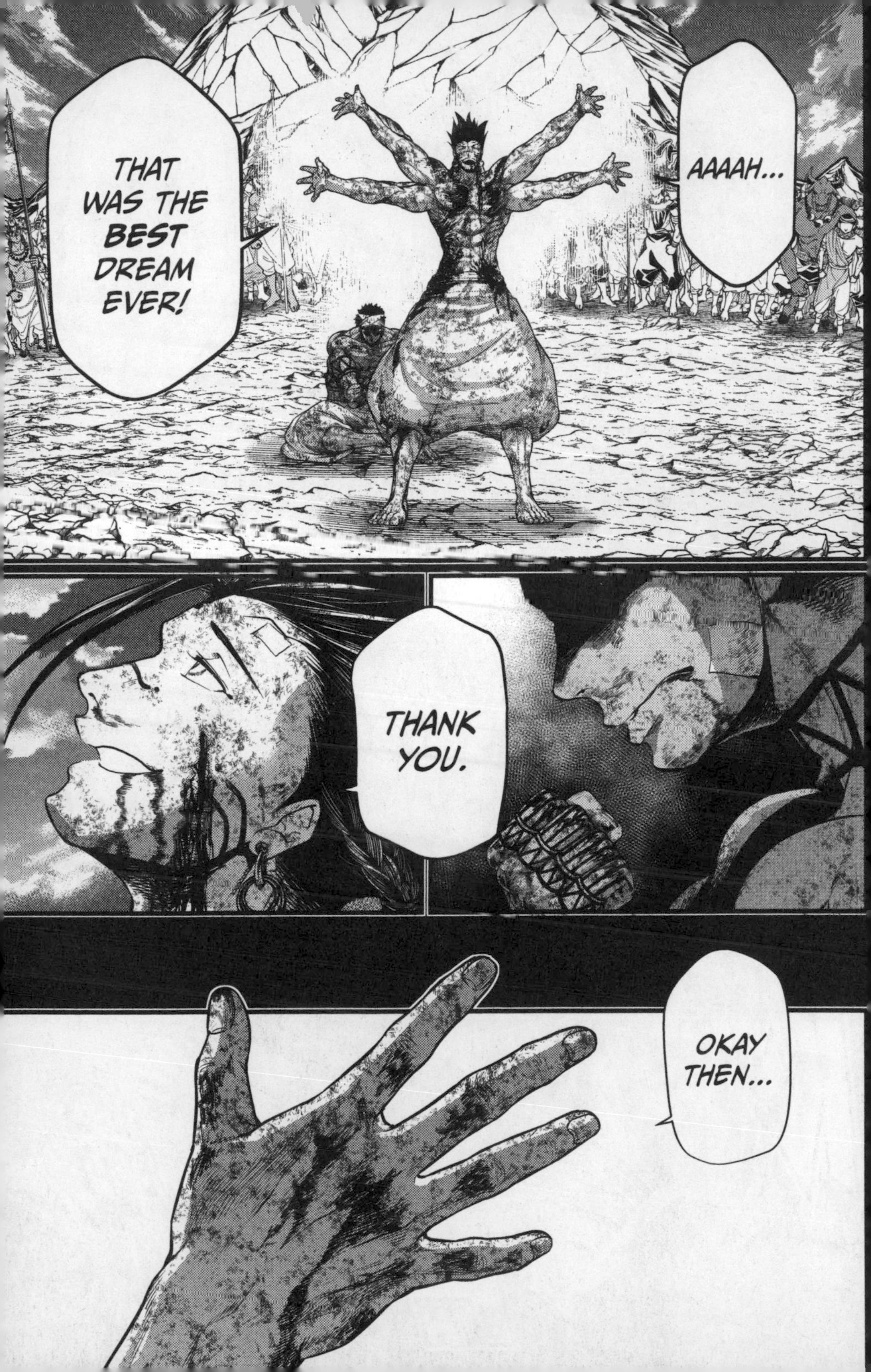
AAAAH...
THAT WAS THE BEST DREAM EVER!
THANK YOU.
OKAY THEN...

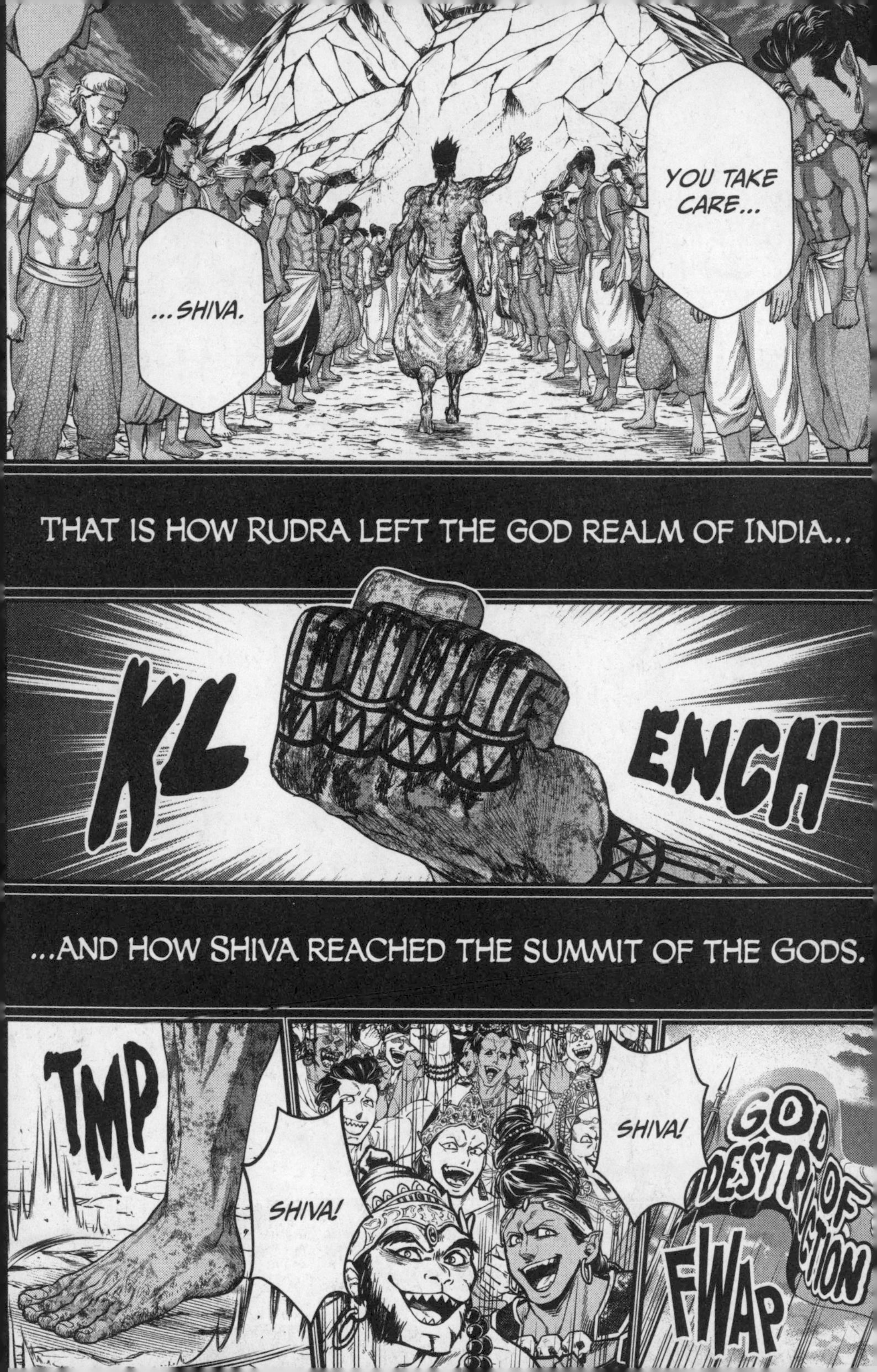
YOU TAKE CARE...
...SHIVA.
THAT IS HOW RUDRA LEFT THE GOD REALM OF INDIA...
KL ENCH
...AND HOW SHIVA REACHED THE SUMMIT OF THE GODS.
GOD OF DESTRUCTION
FWAP
SHIVA!
SHIVA!
TMP

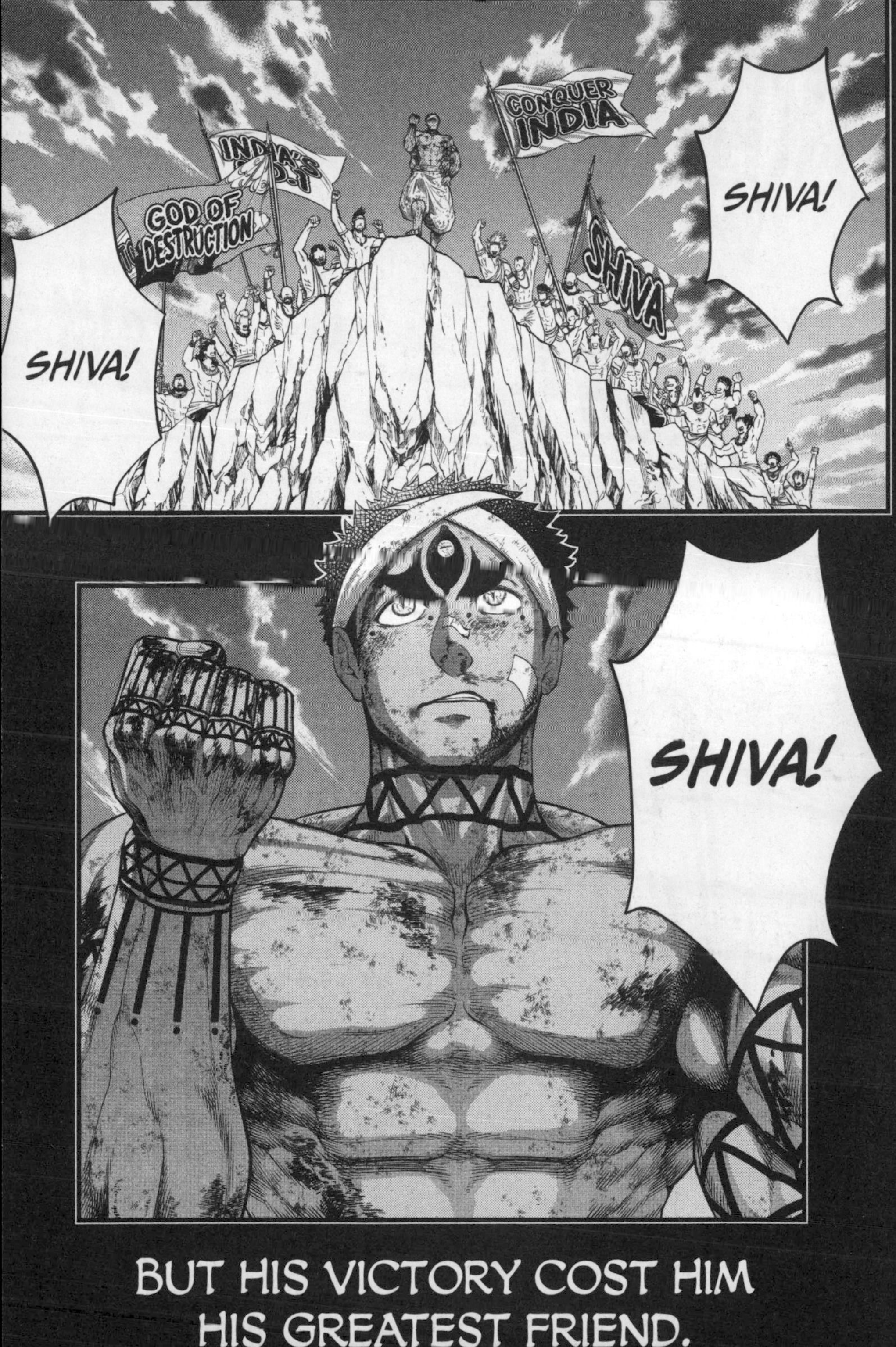
SHIVA!
CONQUER INDIA
SHIVA
INDIA'S
GOD OF DESTRUCTION
SHIVA!
SHIVA!
BUT HIS VICTORY COST HIM HIS GREATEST FRIEND.

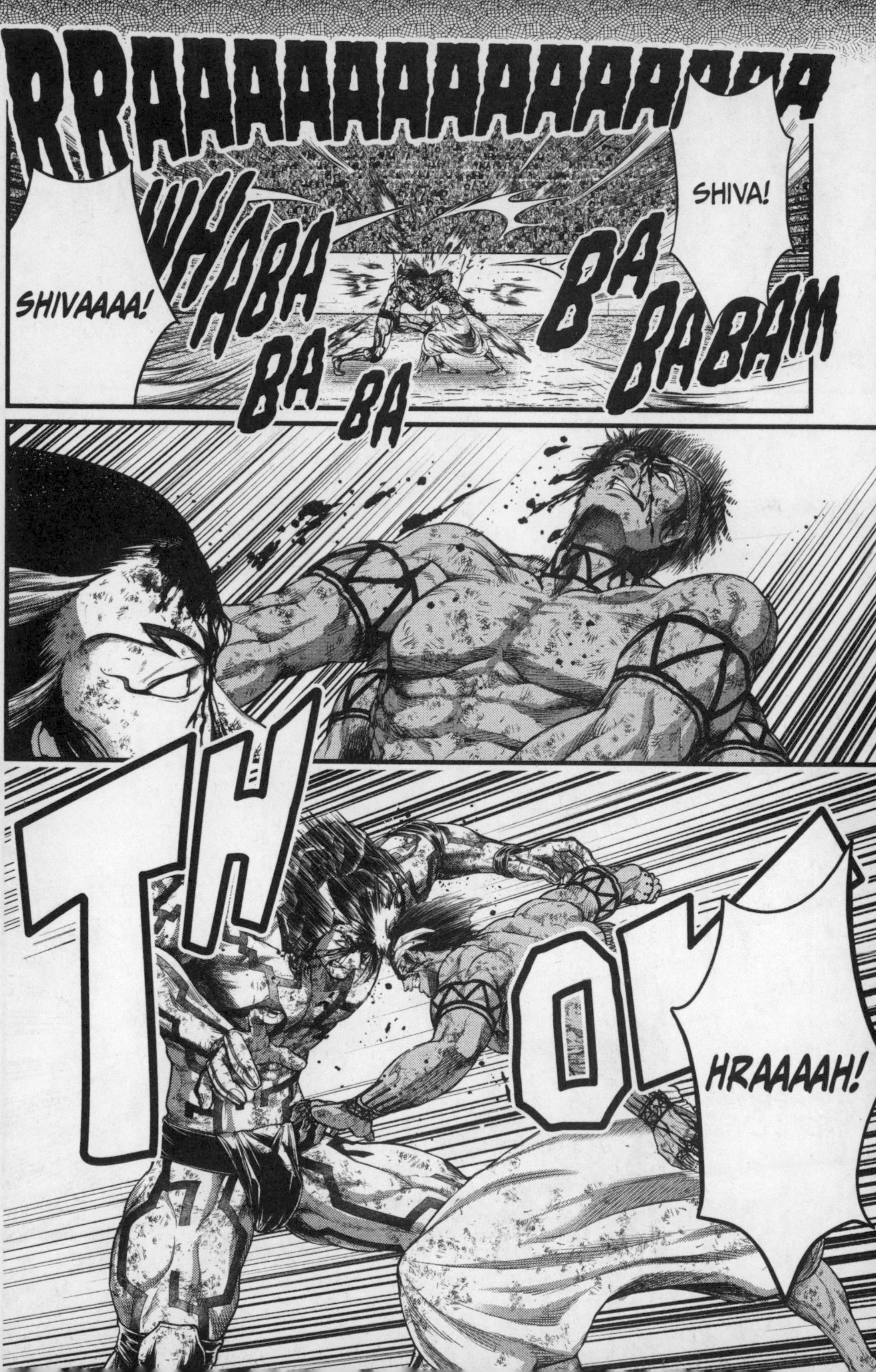
RRAAAAAAAAAAAAAA
SHIVA!
BA BA BABAM
WHABA BA BA
SHIVAAAA!
HRAAAAH!
THO

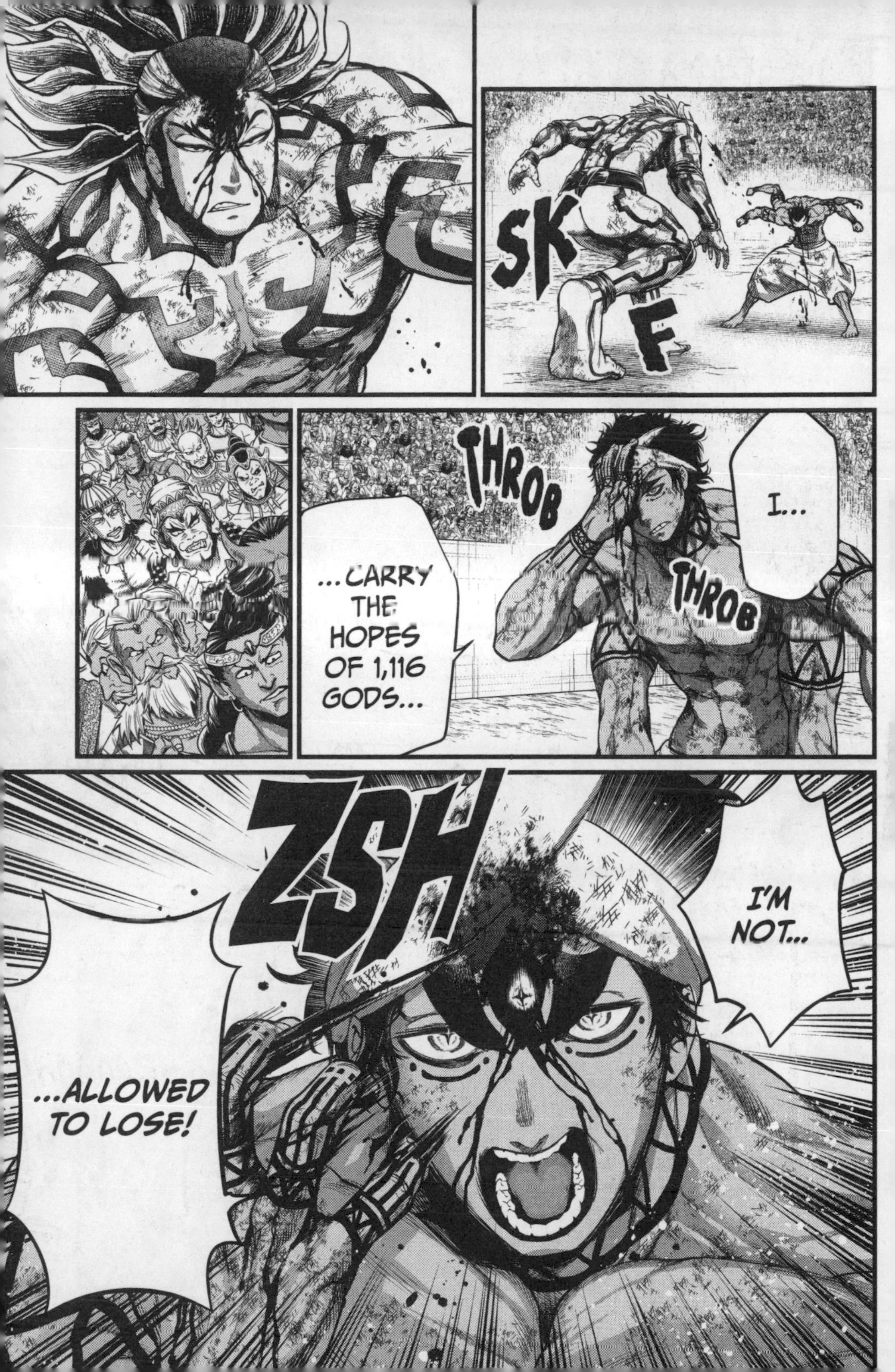
SK
F
THROB
I...
THROB
...CARRY THE HOPES OF 1,116 GODS...
ZSH
I'M NOT...
...ALLOWED TO LOSE!

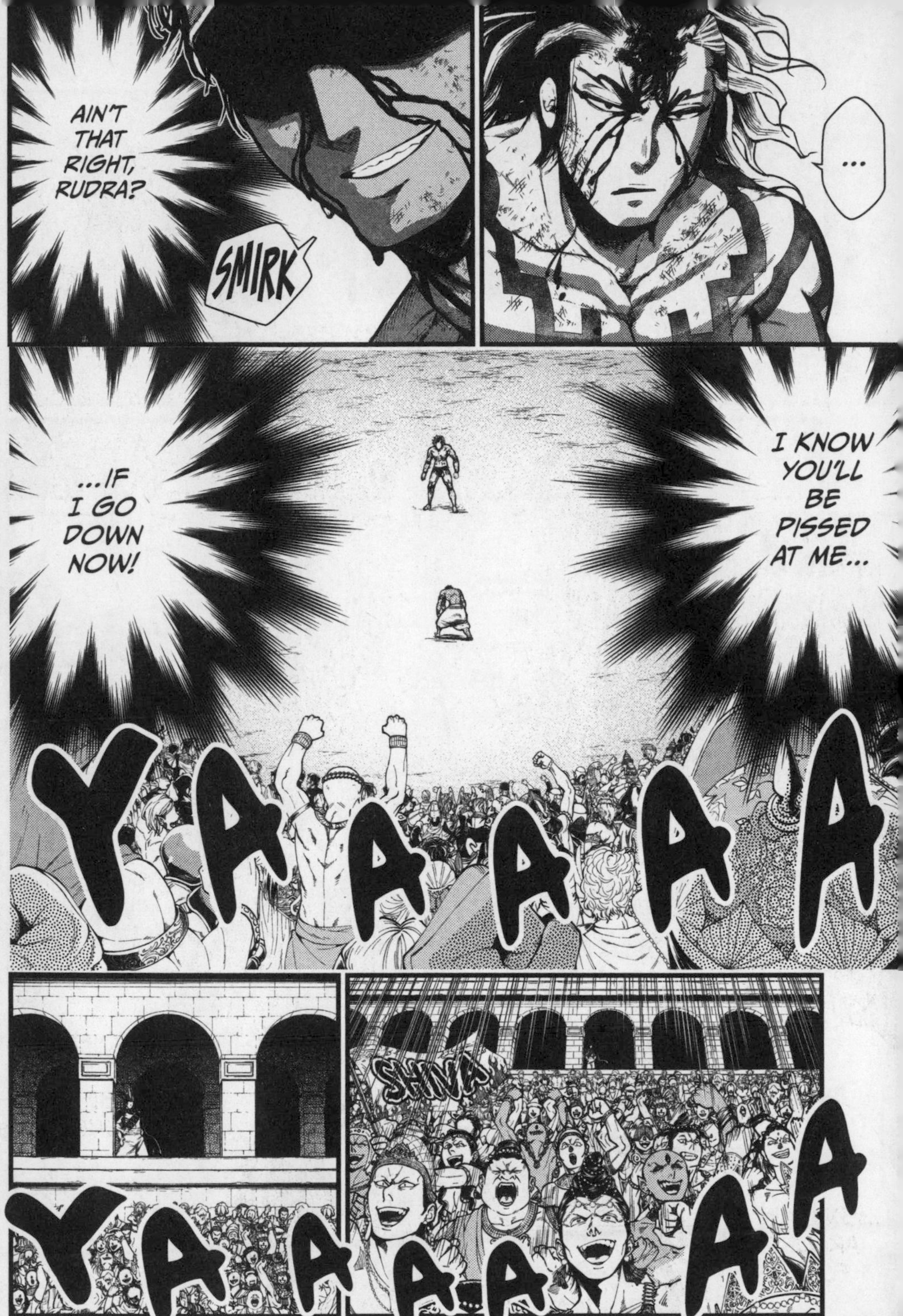
...
AIN'T THAT RIGHT, RUDRA?
SMIRK
I KNOW YOU'LL BE PISSED AT ME...
...IF I GO DOWN NOW!
YAAAAA
SHWA
YAAAAAAA

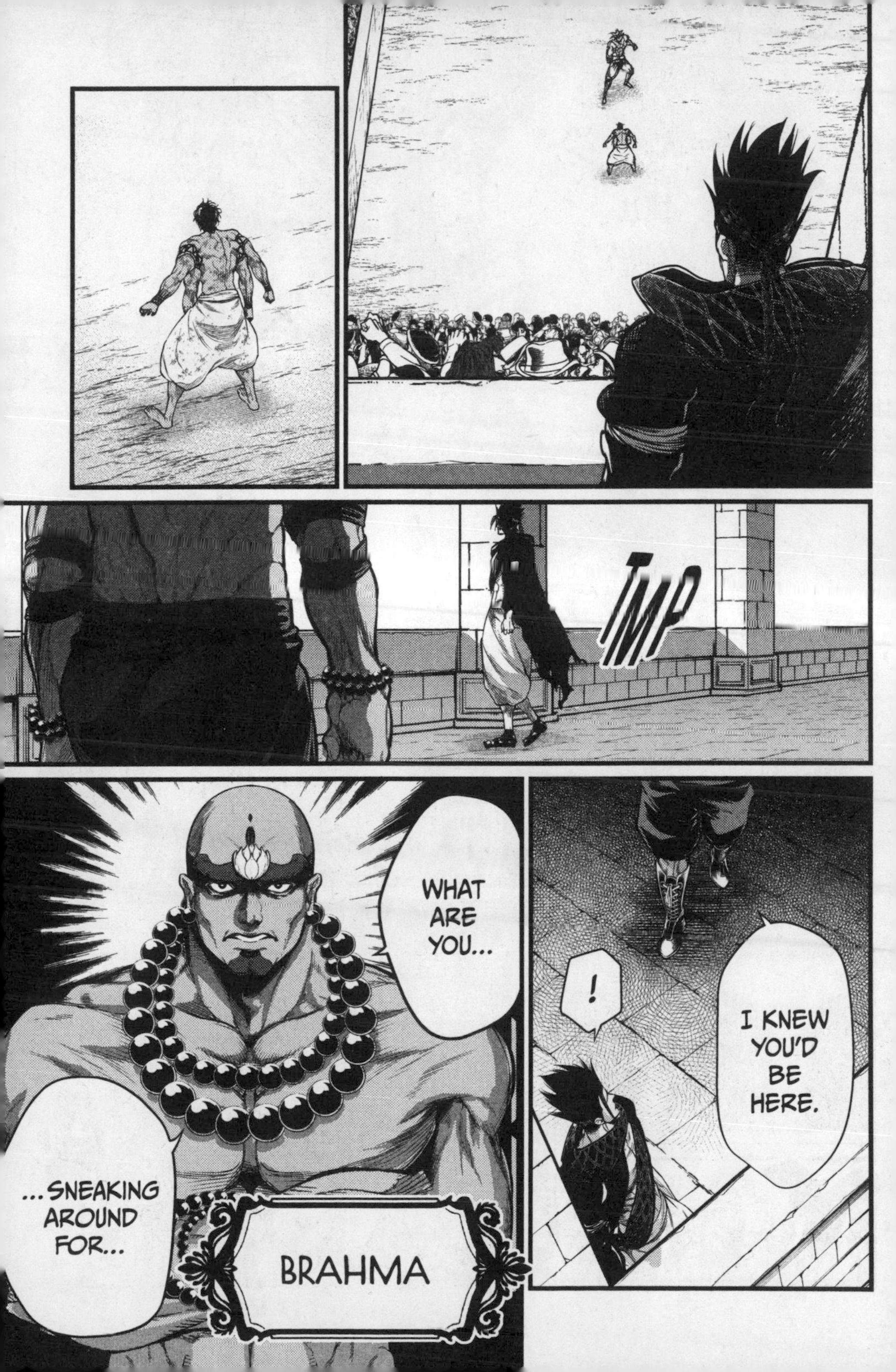
TMP
!
I KNEW YOU'D BE HERE.
WHAT ARE YOU...
...SNEAKING AROUND FOR...
BRAHMA

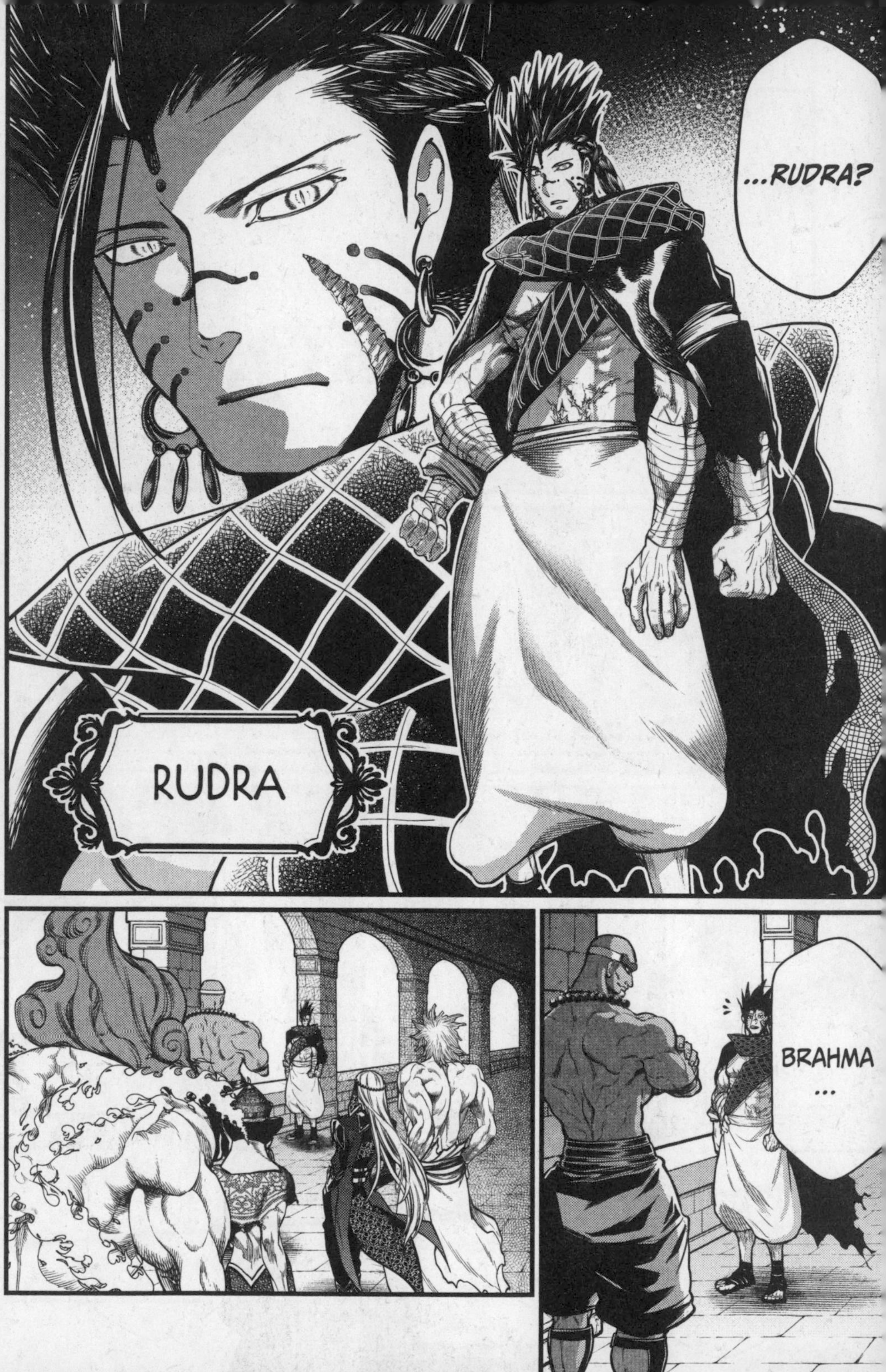
...RUDRA?
RUDRA
BRAHMA ...

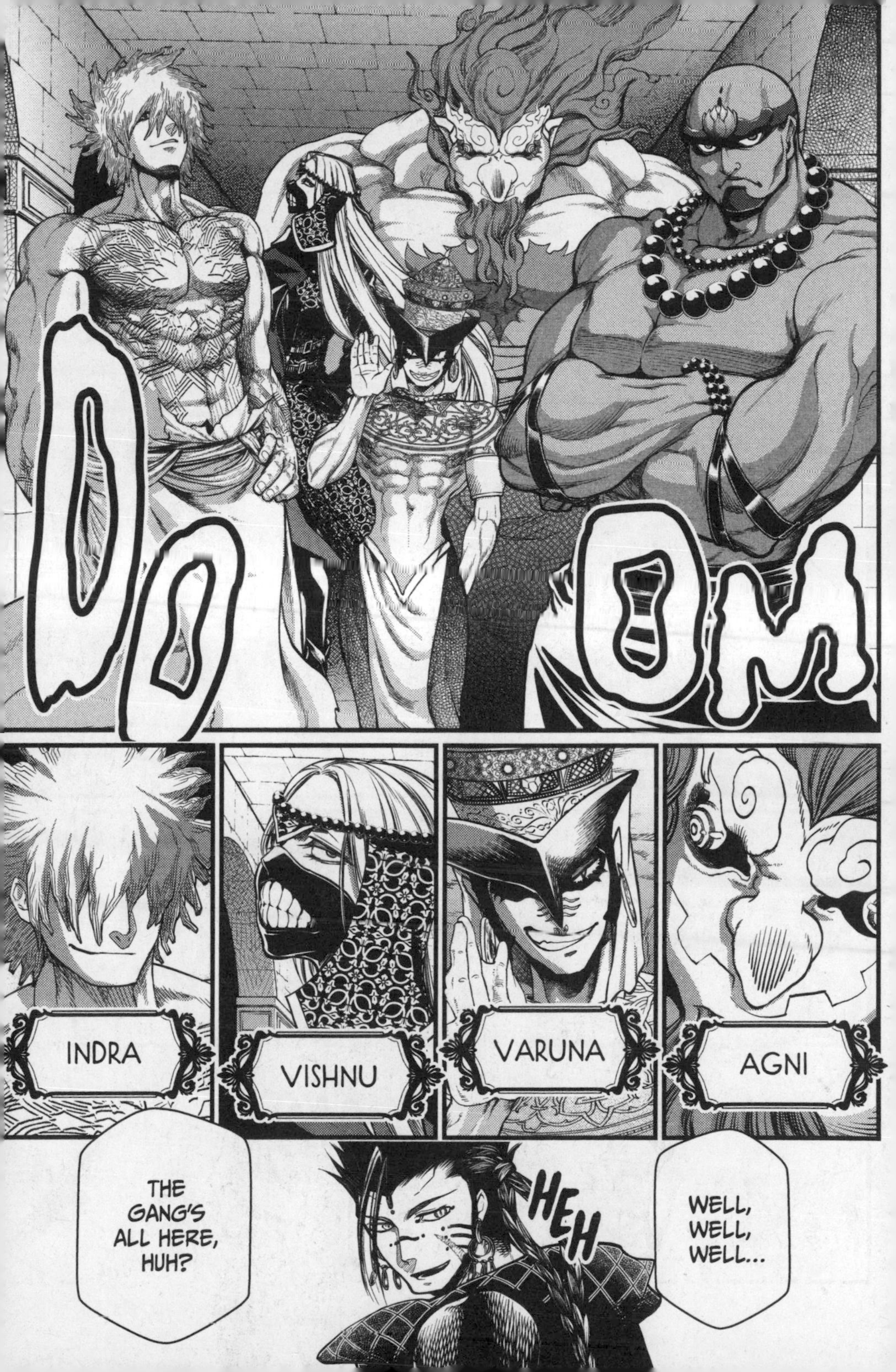
DOOM
AGNI
VARUNA
VISHNU
INDRA
WELL, WELL, WELL...
HEH
THE GANG'S ALL HERE, HUH?

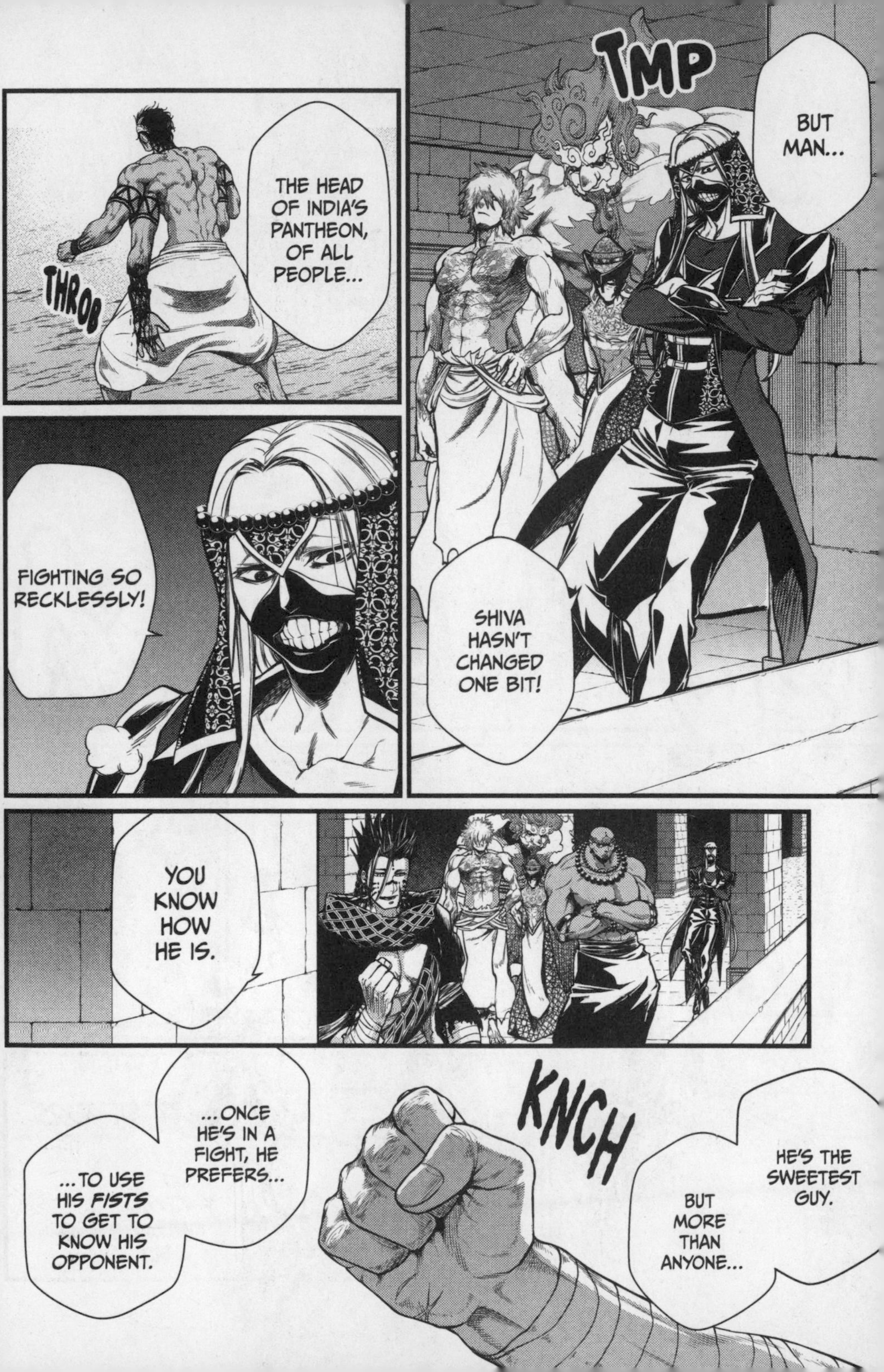
TMP
BUT MAN...
SHIVA HASN'T CHANGED ONE BIT!
THROB
THE HEAD OF INDIA'S PANTHEON, OF ALL PEOPLE...
FIGHTING SO RECKLESSLY!
YOU KNOW HOW HE IS.
KNCH
HE'S THE SWEETEST GUY.
BUT MORE THAN ANYONE...
...ONCE HE'S IN A FIGHT, HE PREFERS...
...TO USE HIS *FISTS* TO GET TO KNOW HIS OPPONENT.

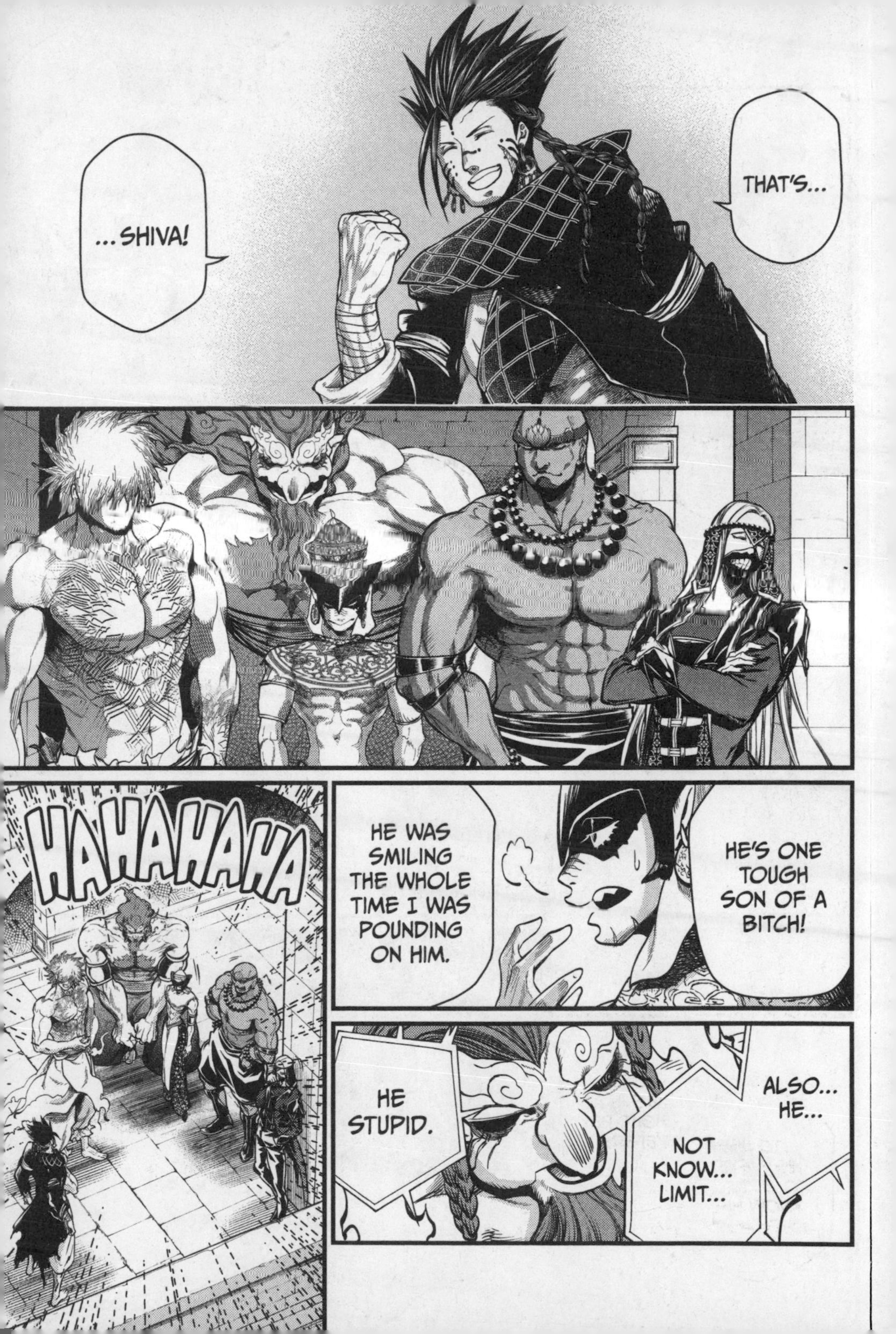
THAT'S...
...SHIVA!
HE'S ONE TOUGH SON OF A BITCH!
HE WAS SMILING THE WHOLE TIME I WAS POUNDING ON HIM.
ALSO... HE...
NOT KNOW... LIMIT...
HE STUPID.
HAHAHAHA

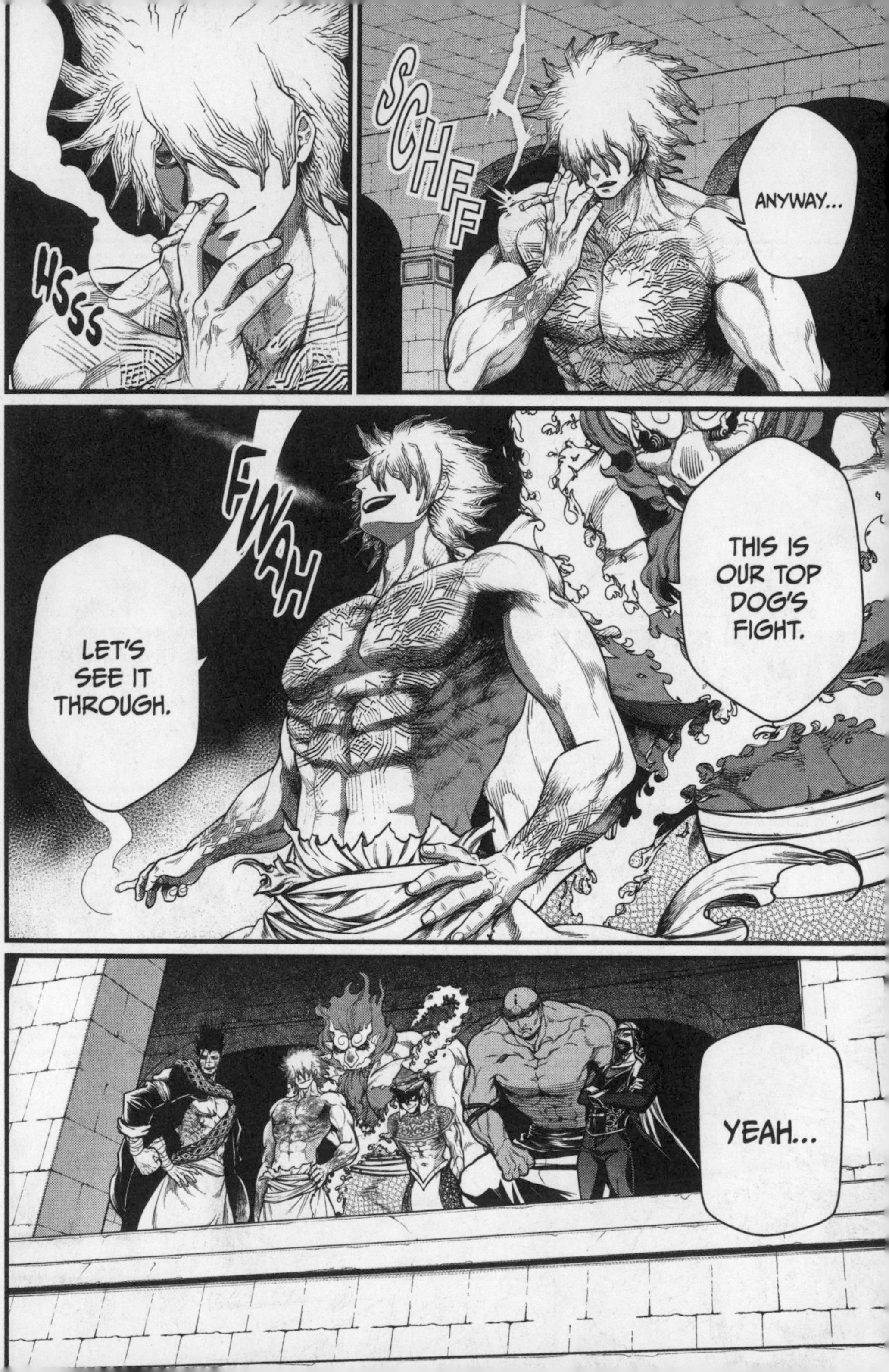
SCHFF
ANYWAY...
HSSS
THIS IS OUR TOP DOG'S FIGHT.
FWAH
LET'S SEE IT THROUGH.
YEAH...

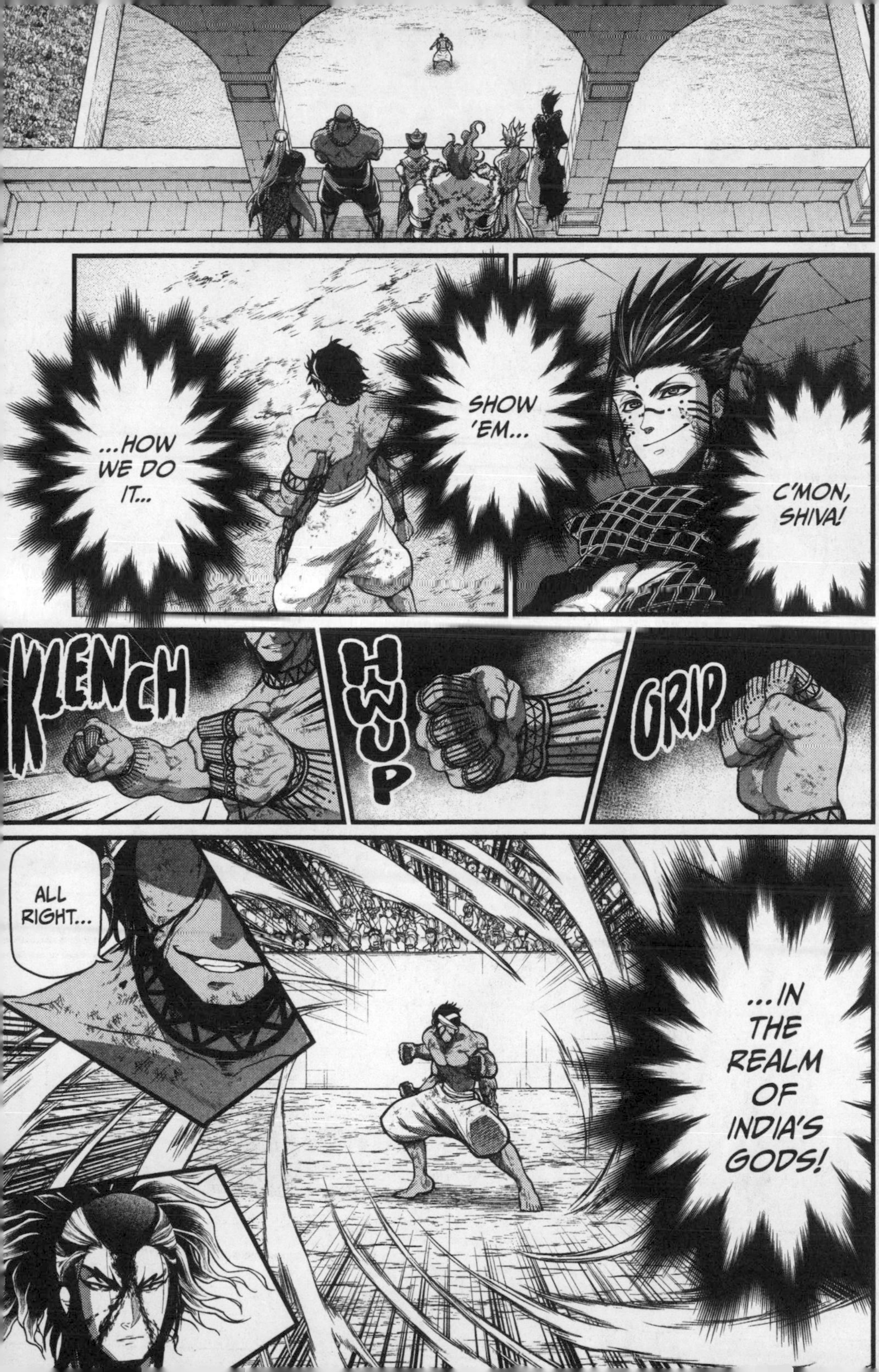

C'MON, SHIVA!
SHOW 'EM...
...HOW WE DO IT...
GRIP
HWUP
KLENCH
...IN THE REALM OF INDIA'S GODS!
ALL RIGHT...

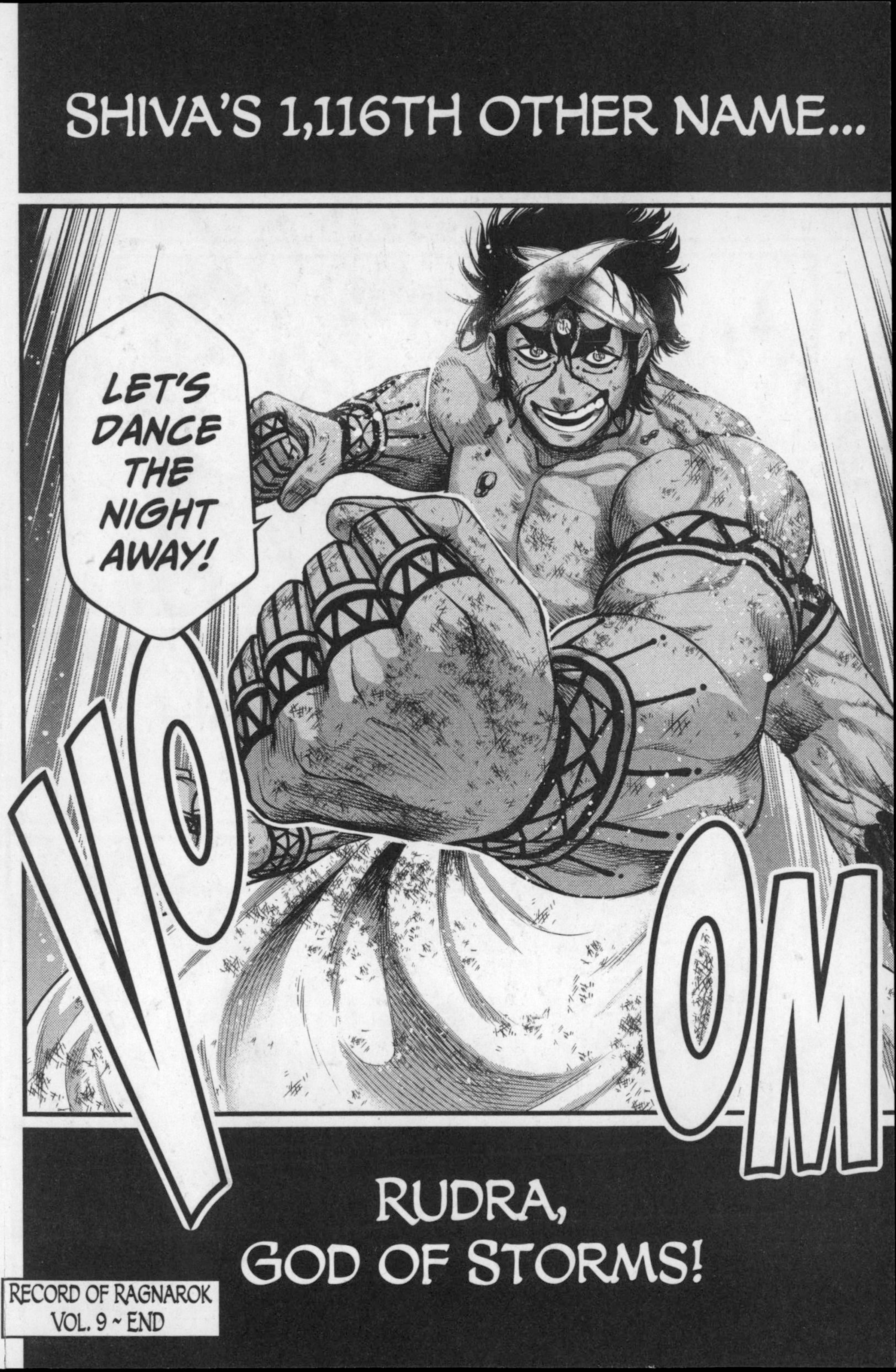
SHIVA'S 1,116TH OTHER NAME...
LET'S DANCE THE NIGHT AWAY!
VOOM
RUDRA, GOD OF STORMS!
RECORD OF RAGNAROK VOL. 9 ~ END

RECORD OF RAGNAROK

VOLUME 9
VIZ Signature Edition

Art by **Azychika**

Story by **Shinya Umemura**

Script by **Takumi Fukui**

Translation / Joe Yamazaki
English Adaptation / Stan!
Touch-Up Art & Lettering / Mark McMurray
Design / Julian (JR) Robinson
Editor / Mike Montesa

Shumatsu no Walkure
©2017 by AZYCHIKA AND SHINYA UMEMURA AND TAKUMI FUKUI/COAMIX
Approved No. ZCW-123W
First Published in Japan in Monthly Comic ZENON by COAMIX, Inc.
English translation rights arranged with COAMIX Inc., Tokyo
through Tuttle-Mori Agency, Inc., Tokyo

Printed in Canada

Published by VIZ Media, LLC
P.O. Box 77010
San Francisco, CA 94107

10 9 8 7 6 5 4 3 2 1
First printing, January 2024

PARENTAL ADVISORY
RECORD OF RAGNAROK is rated T+ for
Older Teen and is recommended for ages
16 and up. Contains graphic violence.

VIZ MEDIA
viz.com

VIZ SIGNATURE
vizsignature.com

'RE READING IT
WRONG!

RECORD OF
RAGNAROK

reads right to left starting in the upper-right corner. Japanese is read from right to left, meaning that action, sound effects, and word-balloon order are completely reversed from English order.

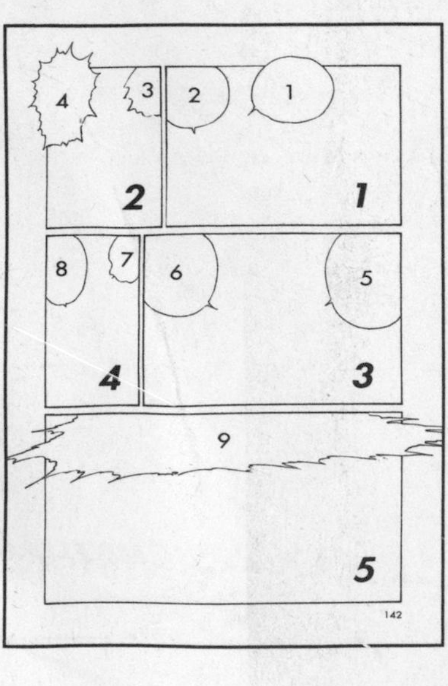

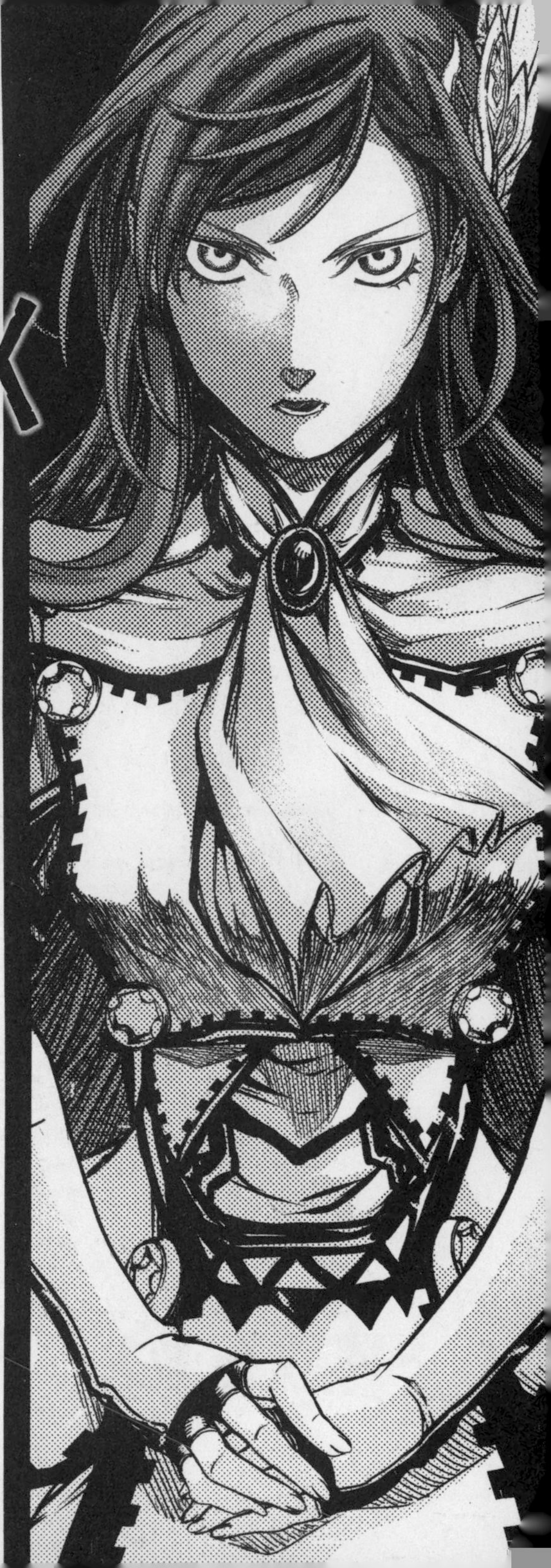